W9-CZJ-648

THE OFFICIAL FAN'S GUIDE

Frank Lovece
with Jules Franco

A CITADEL PRESS BOOK

Published by Carol Publishing Group

To my second son, Erik Morgan Lovece—different from the first, but just as great.

—Frank Lovece

To the memory of my parents, Delmira and Julio Sr., and to Beth, always.

—Jules Franco

Copyright © 1988, 1996 Frank Lovece, Jules Franco, and Paramount Pictures Corporation.

All rights reserved. No part of this book may be reproduced in any form,
except by a newspaper or magazine reviewer who wishes to quote brief
passages in connection with a review.

A Citadel Press Book
Published by Carol Publishing Group
Citadel Press is a registered trademark of Carol Communications, Inc.

Editorial Offices: 600 Madison Avenue, New York, N.Y. 10022
Sales and Distribution Offices: 120 Enterprise Avenue, Secaucus, N.J. 07094
In Canada: Canadian Manda Group, One Atlantic Avenue, Suite 105,
    Toronto, Ontario M6K 3E7
Queries regarding rights and permissions should be addressed to
Carol Publishing Group, 600 Madison Avenue, New York, N.Y. 10022

Carol Publishing Group books are available at special discounts for bulk
purchases, sales promotions, fund raising, or educational purposes.
Special editions can be created to specifications. For details contact:
Special Sales Department, Carol Publishing Group,
120 Enterprise Avenue, Secaucus, N.J. 07094

First published in 1988 as *Taxi: A Fare to Remember*

Manufactured in the United States of America

12 11 10 9 8 7 6 5 4 3 2 1

Library of Congress Cataloging-in-Publication Data

Lovece, Frank.
    Taxi : the official fan's guide / Frank Lovece with Jules Franco.
        p.   cm.
    "A Citadel Press book."
    ISBN (invalid) 0-8065-1801-4
    1. Taxi (Television program)   I. Franco, Jules.   II. Title.
PN1992.77.T38L68   1996
791.45'72—dc20   95-26387
                                                              CIP

We wish to thank the following people and organizations for the use of their photographs:

pps. 2, 51, 56, 64, 73, 102, 104, 108, 189: Copyright © 1978 Paramount Pictures Corporation. All Rights Reserved • p. 6, *top*: Photo by Frank Lovece • p. 6, *bottom*: Photo by Jules Franco • p. 7: Copyright © 1976 CBS • p. 11: Copyright © 1979 ABC • p. 12: Copyright © 1988 Paramount Pictures Corporation. All Rights Reserved • p. 14: Courtesy Bob James; photo by David Gahr • p. 20: Courtesy Frank Lovece • pps. 24, 40, 61, 114, 152, 153, 161: Copyright © 1980 Paramount Pictures Corporation. All Rights Reserved © p. 29: Courtesy Sam Simon • p. 36: Courtesy Randall Carver • pps. 38, 41, 49, 53, 59, 62, 68, 72, 77, 164, 168, 170, 173, 182: Copyright © 1981 Paramount Pictures Corporation. All Rights Reserved • p. 43, *right*: Photo by David Gahr, Copyright © 1979 CBS Records, Inc. • 43, *left*: Copyright © 1983 CBS Records, Inc. • p. 44: Courtesy Frank H. Lieberman • p. 58: Courtesy Peter Haas • p. 66: Courtesy Carol Kane • pps. 69, 78, 200, 204, 211, 214, 217, 218, 290-91: Copyright © 1982 Paramount Pictures Corporation. All Rights Reserved • p. 70: Copyright © 1982 NBC • p. 76: Courtesy John Murphy and PBS • p. 79: Copyright © 1988 NBC • pps. 123, 124, 127, 129, 130, 131, 133, 138, 139: Copyright © 1979 Paramount Pictures Corporation. All Rights Reserved • p. 228: Copyright © 1983 Paramount Pictures Corporation. All Rights Reserved.

ACKNOWLEDGMENTS

Television historians, like others who chronicle the living, follow in the footsteps of Blanche DuBois—we depend on the kindness of strangers. In an era of fashionable media-bashing and checkbook journalism, the authors are grateful to all those who spoke to us freely, and to all those who spoke for them.

Special thanks go as well to the talented people both on and off the screen who made *Taxi* a reality. In nearly every case, they made time for us when there was no time to make—often for multiple interviews. Their generosity for a project in which they have no financial stake reflects the essential human nobility of *Taxi* at its best. For their time and their interviews, we thank *Taxi* stars Randall Carver, Jeff Conaway, Tony Danza, Danny De-Vito, the miraculous Marilu Henner, Carol Kane, Christopher Lloyd, and, to a lesser extent, Judd Hirsch; *Taxi* writers, directors, producers, and creators James L. Brooks, James Burrows, Stan Daniels, Dave Davis, Ken Estin, Will Mackenzie, Earl Pomerantz, Richard Sakai, Sam Simon, and Ed Weinberger; producer Gary Nardino, the former head of Paramount Television; Joel Thurm, original casting director of *Taxi* and now an NBC vice-president; *Taxi* guest stars Ernie Hudson, Peter Jurasik, Penny Marshall, Rhea Perlman, Brian Robbins, Martin Short, Dee Wallace Stone, and Susan Sullivan; fellow TV and film professionals John Badham, James Bridges, William Converse-Roberts, Hector Elizondo, Christine Lahti, Garry Marshall, Peter Weller, and Wim Wenders; and Mark Jacobson, author of the magazine article on which *Taxi* was based. Thanks, too, to those who confided in us off the record.

We're extremely grateful to Barbara Duncan and Patty MacDonald at Gracie Films, who opened invaluable doors for us both literally and figuratively. As Jim Brooks's successive right-hand persons, they gave us, with his blessing and invaluable support, access to scripts and background materials, and helped us to nail down countless last-minute de-

tails. Additional scripts and photos were generously supplied by Sam Simon, Ken Estin, and Nancy Koppang.

Access to most of these people came through the help and support of their managers, agents, and publicity persons. In particular we thank Peter Haas of PMK and Sean Mahoney of Mahoney/Wasserman, who were there for us at the beginning and continued to be there throughout a long and daunting process. Also helping us immeasurably were Pat Baum; Jeff Berg of International Creative Management; Connie Frieberg of Management Company Entertainment; Michael Gersey of the Larry Thompson Organization; Robert Gersh; Vic Ghidalia of ABC; Alison Hanau of MCA; Gail Joseph; Judy Katz and Kim Gavin of Richard Grant & Associates; Jeff Kaufman of Carson Productions; Christine Kounelias; Tracy Ladd of Nancy Seltzer & Associates; Morton Levy; Frank Lieberman; Jeff Mackler of Fox Broadcasting; Calie Maitland of Tinsley Advertising, Paramount's Miami rep; Brian Robinette and Bob Meyer of NBC; Rachel Rosen; Stan Rosenfeld; George Shapiro; and all their support staff.

At Paramount, we wish to thank Linda Archibeque, Michael Camp, Tom Conner, Joel Dreskin, Shaylee Dunn, Loretta Milana, Howard Rayfiel, Susan Zilber, and Sally Zwiers. Shaylee in particular came through for us when we needed equipment and a room to screen more than 100 half hours of *Taxi*.

Frank's editors at United Feature—Diana Loevy, Evan Levine, and Paul Elie—showed wonderful patience when his weekly syndicated column kept sliding in just under the wire. Our good friends Hector Osorio and Kim Delgado put us up and put up with us in Los Angeles. Hilda Fernandez and Yolanda Suarez, travel agents *extraordinaire,* got us to Los Angeles and back again to Miami (Jules) and New York City (Frank), all at the last minute and somehow inexpensively. Toni Cohen did considerable research and helped to transcribe hours of taped interviews. Computer consultant Michael Isbell demonstrated surgical skill in saving chapter 1 from electronic oblivion, and his patient modification of our computer wordware saved us more man-hours than it took to build the Sphinx.

For help in finding unfindable data, getting us material overnight, and generally helping out, we thank Lisa Bell; Gwen E. Benson-Walker; Maureen Dunn and Ron Wilcox of CBS Records; Andy Edelstein; Deputy Commissioner Emma Elizondo of the New York State Athletic Commission; Harry Forbes; Wynston Gearhart; Tom Gillian; Jill Gorham; Vicki Greenleaf of International Video Enterprises; Sharon Harlos; Lynn Hoogenboom; Jeri Jenkins; Cindy Johnson; Joe Lovece; Jack Mendorff; John Murphy; Tony Perrotti; Alan Petrucelli; Howard Polskin of *TV Guide;* Anthony Sigel; Jim Sirmans; and Wendy Wallace. We thank the staffs of New York City's Lincoln Center library and the National Association of Broadcasters' Television Information Office. And we're indebted to the sometimes contradictory but always helpful works of authors Tim Brooks, Alvin H. Marill, Earle Marsh, Alex McNeil, Vincent Terrace, Vince Waldron, and John Willis. Jules Franco additionally wants to thank Larry Z., Javier Restrepo, and the gang at the Bel-Aire, who kept his spirits up.

In the battle trenches of publishing, Prentice Hall Press has some extraordinary soldiers. Deepest thanks go to our two editors: Gareth Esersky, who championed this book from the start, and her successor, Paul Aron, whose enthusiasm, charm, and openness to ideas were beyond our fondest hopes. With his assistants, Lyn Hogan and David Dunton, senior managing editor Laurie S. Barnett, and managing editor Leanne Coupe he expertly carved what we hope wasn't too rough a diamond.

Most of all, we wish to thank our agent, Lori Perkins, whose excellent advice, good humor, and relentless energy are a joy to behold; and our families and friends, whose dinner invitations and phone calls often went unanswered as we flew cross-country four times in six months and worked twelve-hour days throughout.

To the people who gave us *Taxi,* we hope we've given a scrapbook of those halcyon years. To the people who continue to watch it, we hope this book justly reflects the humor and the humanity of this exceptional piece of television.

—Frank Lovece
Jules Franco

CONTENTS

FOREWORD

I was so unbelievably flattered when Frank and Jules asked me to write the foreword to *Hailing Taxi*. Of course I said yes immediately, without realizing how difficult the assignment was going to be. How could I sit down and write in a few words what *Taxi* has meant to me when my head is so filled with so many thoughts and memories that I could fill an entire book just talking about a single episode, let alone five years' worth? Five years in the lives of very special people I feel so privileged to have known.

When I read the manuscript, it was as though I had entered a time warp and had been taken back to a moment in my life when I couldn't wait to wake up and go to work, where I would learn more about acting than any workshop could teach me, and where I would experience the true meaning of a collaborative effort. And that's what *Taxi* was—a group of artists who got together for the common purpose of "let's put on a show," where no opinion or suggestion was vetoed without consideration. In our business, that's very rare.

The births, the deaths, the marriages, the divorces, the unbelievable life changes we all went through together and separately—we were never afraid to bring any of it into our characters. And thank God our wonderful writers and producers would let us. Together, we made Alex, Louie, Elaine, Tony, Bobby, Jim, John, Latka, Simka, and Jeff real people that so many other real people have grown to know and love as friends.

Week after week, we would start with an original script on Monday, and by Friday night, after finally honing and crafting some misses, but mostly hits, we'd arrive at a place that somehow said what we wanted to say to the world on that particular week. That's what made it so special. We all loved each other and loved what we did with such a passion, and it showed. Today, when any of us get together and reminisce, there isn't a time when we don't talk about this experience as a golden period in our lives. As Jim Brooks always says, thank God we knew it then, and celebrated it then, so that there are no regrets.

Now, reading this book, I find myself stopping and going back and saying, oh, remember this episode, and remember this story. Every piece I read opened up a file cabinet of memories. And I can tell that we continue to be connected, because this book, too, was a collaborative effort. Everyone is represented; and virtually everyone was willing and eager to talk about the incredible *Taxi* experience. It's something that's still very much a part of us. It continues on in our hearts and minds, and it's obvious from this effort.

I know you enjoyed *Taxi*. I know you'll enjoy this book.

—Marilu Henner
June 27, 1988

PREFACE

"If you've been watching *Taxi* for the past five years, you're in for some great memories. And if you haven't . . . you dirty, miserable . . . !''

That's not us talking; that's Danny DeVito slipping into character as Louie De Palma, introducing the best-of *Taxi* retrospective that plays in syndication. He didn't know it at the time, but he was speaking for this book as well.

As millions of viewers in more than 40 countries know, *Taxi* is a mere TV "sitcom" like *You Can't Take It With You* is a mere comic play. At its best (a reasonable qualification when you're talking about 112 half-hour episodes), *Taxi* has all the heart, insight, tight plotting, and finely observed human details of any great one-act play, as well as some of the most natural dialogue ever uttered on film or stage. It was, in short, legitimate drama, and to condescend because it accomplished this within the strictures of television is the same as damning Elizabethan theater for requiring five acts. Even on TV terms, *Taxi* is special. In its poignant laughter, it recalls another comic-dramatic classic, *The Honeymooners*. In the virtuosity of its lighting, set design, editing, and direction, it is akin to television's earth mother, the pioneering *I Love Lucy*.

Taxi was blessed with some of the best comedy writers in the industry, as well as a rare milieu in which that talent could play and flourish with practically no adult supervision. The ensemble cast—an audacious mix of New York theater *actors*, talented young hopefuls, and a street-witty, untrained amateur—meshed and traded the spotlight with the grace of a British repertory company. Along with laughter, *Taxi* gave us more fleshed-out human drama than *The Mary Tyler Moore Show*, more sophisticated metaphor than *All in the Family*, and less self-conscious importance than *M*A*S*H*.

In these pages you'll find not only a complete guide to the 112 episodes of *Taxi*, packed with favorite bits, classic lines, and loads of plot details, but also behind-the-scenes stories and informed commentary. The authors spoke with every living *Taxi* cast member, several guest stars, the four producer-creators, and countless others to assemble both these backstage looks and the two opening chapters that detail the day-to-day creation, production, and untimely demise of *Taxi*. The authors screened every available *Taxi* videocassette in syndicator Paramount's library (taped off the air during the show's original network run), so the plot outlines may contain unfamiliar scenes that don't show up on your local station. Since local stations get only shorter, edited versions of *Taxi* to run, these tapes and those made at the time by collectors may be the only remaining uncut versions. We thought you'd like to know what you're missing. (We'd also like to recommend an excellent TV fan magazine, *The TV Collector* [P.O. Box 1088, Easton, MA 02334] for people interested in this sort of thing.)

You'll also find the most comprehensive filmography, *and* theaterography *and* discography of any TV book on the market. The authors spent literally months combining source materials and screening videocassettes to clear up conflicting credits, change titles, and erroneous information. (Contrary to *People* magazine, for instance, Danny DeVito did not appear in *Car Wash;* contrary to a couple of video catalogs, Judd Hirsch did not star in an obscure drag-racing picture called *Fury on Wheels*.)

Except in the rare instances where otherwise indicated, every direct quote here is factory fresh, gathered by the authors specifically for this book.

This holds true especially for our fancifully written biographical section (with the exception, of course, of the nonexistent Tony Clifton and gypsy lady in the late Andy Kaufman's bio).

We have also included an actual *Taxi* script ("Jim's Inheritance") as well as a never-used story outline and other behind-the-scenes goodies. You'll find lists of every major and several not-so-major awards won by the *Taxi* cast and crew; a 100-question trivia quiz; special notes on the real-life New York taxi industry; Latka's national anthem, and other nonsense; and several indexes. A final note: Sharp-eyed readers will find we did not adhere to what *Taxi* cocreator Ed Weinberger himself calls "an affectation"—spelling his first name with a period after it.

AUDITIONS
AND
AUDACITY

A writer's company. That's what Jim Brooks had found at MTM Productions, where he'd cocreated *The Mary Tyler Moore Show*. As big a star as Mary became, and as much power as her husband, producer Grant Tinker, wielded, the feeling around MTM was that the writers were just as important as the actors or the producers. This was astonishing. The joke around the TV and movie industry had always been, "Did you hear about the not-so-bright starlet who wanted to get to the top? She slept with the writer." At MTM, even if stars *still* didn't sleep with writers, they respected them in the morning.

Brooks knew he had something special. And he knew he *was* something special, though he's not the type to say so out loud. A college dropout who became a CBS News writer and then a documentary writer-producer for David Wolper Productions, Brooks had broken into TV comedy ignominiously—a script for *My Mother the Car,* followed by a couple for *That Girl* and other shows. Yet by 1969, a year before *The Mary Tyler Moore Show,* Brooks had concocted *Room 222.* That critical and commercial hit about an ideal and idealistic black high-school teacher won him a Best New Series Emmy Award right out of the gate and earned him a nomination for Best Comedy. Then, with the entire industry watching what would happen to *The Dick Van Dyke Show*'s beloved Mary Tyler Moore now that her movie career had fizzled, Brooks and *Room 222* producer Allan Burns fielded an all-star team of writers and took the World Series in straight shutout games: Not only did audiences stay home Saturday nights to watch this unconventional new show about

a "modern woman" but so did the critics. Along with the acclaim heaped on the talented cast, Brooks and Burns got Best Comedy and Best New Series Emmy nominations, and they walked off with the Comedy Writing award. The tall, bearded, thirty-one-year-old Brooks was suddenly a Jewish fair-haired boy.

But television is a factory. "You have a hit," explains Brooks's friend, producer-director Garry Marshall (*Happy Days, Nothing in Common*), "and now the network wants two hits. And so you do a *Laverne & Shirley,* and a *Mork and Mindy,* and a *Joannie Loves Chachi* and other things I don't even want to *tell* you about!" he spritzes. "And it's this wonderful logic they have that helps make television the great medium that it is—let's offer this guy lots of money and stretch him so thin that his shows become terrible and that he dies of ulcers!"

Brooks—an almost childlike yet quite unfragile visionary—didn't want to run around that particular track. After the first year of CBS's *The Mary Tyler Moore Show,* he found he had the clout to start pursuing feature films, the Holy Grail of most TV directors, producers, scriptwriters, and janitors. But Brooks's first effort as a movie writer-producer, the well-received *Thursday's Game,* stayed on the shelf for three years until being released as a TV movie in 1974. And even while he was picking up Emmys every time he sneezed, Brooks nonetheless blew it with the short-lived *Paul Sand in Friends and Lovers* and with *Rhoda, The Mary Tyler Moore Show* spinoff that spent four-and-a-half years getting progressively more unglued. By the time Brooks, Burns, and *M*A*S*H* cocreator Gene Reynolds had put

The first season cast: *(back row)* Tony Danza, Marilu Henner, Judd Hirsch, Randall Carver, Jeff Conaway; *(front row)* Danny DeVito, Andy Kaufman.

another spinoff, *Lou Grant,* on its feet, Brooks was looking to get out. And with fifty ways to leave your mentor, why not take a *Taxi,* Maxie?

"MTM was starting to burgeon," says Brooks. "It was just getting too big. The company started with everybody knowing everybody, but by now it was getting a little more impersonal. We wanted to be a small company again." "We" in this case refers to Dave Davis, Ed Weinberger, and Stan Daniels, the power trio of comedy-writing confederates who would form with Brooks the partnership that led to *Taxi.*

Initially, there were only two others, Davis and Jerry Belson. Belson and his partner, Garry Marshall, had written for *The Dick Van Dyke Show* and others and had cocreated the series *The Odd Couple* and *Hey Landlord* (which led to the joking suggestion of calling the new series, *Hey Taxi*). Davis, the son of TV comedy writer Phil Davis, had graduated from UCLA intending to be a movie editor and director and had wound up apprenticing on *The Many Loves of Dobie Gillis.* Through the sixties, he was a Dave-of-all-trades, everything from "script girl" to director to coscenarist of what became the Jerry Lewis movie *Hook, Line and Sinker.* ("They should've added a *t* to that last word and dropped the rest," Davis cracks.) While working as associate producer for the company that put out *Get Smart, The Good Guys,* and *The Governor and J. J.,* Davis started writing. He did well in that sideline, selling scripts to *Love American Style* and *The Glen Campbell Goodtime Hour.* He'd even cocreated a promising series pilot, *Shepherd's Flock.* Then Jim Brooks named him producer of *The Mary Tyler Moore Show,* and as Davis puts it, "After that, everything started to go incredible."

When Belson dropped out to successfully pursue movie writing, Brooks recruited the team of Weinberger and Daniels. The duo had worked together beginning with Dean Martin's variety show, and Weinberger had written for Bill Cosby specials, *The Tonight Show,* and elsewhere. When Davis left *The Mary Tyler Moore Show* to cocreate *The Bob Newhart Show,* Weinberger and Daniels took his place. Now the four MTM expatriates were ready to break out and start their own company. But where to begin?

The first and easiest place was with a name. For some reason they wanted it ultraWASPy. "We were looking around for ideas," Weinberger recalls, "and I happened to see a sign in an antique store in Los Angeles. It was from an English pub, and it said 'Charles Walters.' I liked the look of it, so I said to the other guys, 'Why don't we buy it? It'll be our logo, and we can call ourselves the Charles Walters Co.' Then we found there already was a Charles Walters [the MGM choreographer-cum-director of *Easter Parade, The Belle of New York, High Society,* and *The Unsinkable Molly Brown,* among other movies], who understandably resented the use of his name." They added a first name, and thus became The John Charles Walters Company. Like Monty Python, there's no real John Charles Walters to speak of.

Now that they had a name, they needed a deal. At that, Gary Nardino was an expert. Nardino had been an agent for eighteen years; Jim Brooks was a client of his firm's, and Nardino also had known Ed Weinberger since Ed's *The Tonight Show* days. Nardino had already been attempting to lure a couple of the MTM heavyweights from CBS to ABC, where his friend Michael Eisner reigned as head of programming. When Eisner became president of the venerable Paramount Pictures, Nardino agreed to serve as president of Paramount Television. "Michael said the first thing we're going to do is to get these four guys from MTM," Nardino remembers. "Because face it: There's television," the heavyset, get-it-done-now Nardino believes, "and there's Jim Brooks. It's like when Ben Hogan first saw Jack Nicklaus play golf—he said, 'He plays a game with which I am not familiar.' "

The first joint venture by producer John Charles Walters (JCW) and financer-distributor Paramount wasn't, however, *Taxi.* It was a TV movie musical called *Cindy,* written and produced by Brooks and the rest, with music by Stan Daniels. Airing on ABC on March 24, 1978, *Cindy* was an ambitious updating of the Cinderella fable, set in Harlem during World War II, and starring Charlaine Woodard, Clifton Davis, Scoey Mitchlll, and Nell Carter. It met with mixed response, and enough production problems to feed a year of I-told-you-sos whenever JCW and Paramount disagreed. But mitigating this was the extraordinary deal they pulled for *Taxi*—the kind of deal that only the likes of Steven Spielberg have pulled off since.

ABC, in an incredible show of faith, gave Brooks and company a sight-unseen, *on-air commitment* for thirteen episodes of virtually any show they wanted to do. Putting the apple*carte blanche* before the horse, ABC didn't even require a pilot episode—not even an initial script! As Nardino describes JCW's meeting with ABC Entertainment Division President Tony Thomopolous and other execs, "The boys pitched this *Taxi* concept, and that was a meeting, and that was a show, and that was that."

"Before the first *Taxi* script was even written," remembers Stan Daniels, "we'd made a deal with ABC for three series. One was *Taxi,* another turned out to be *The Associates,* and then Dave Davis retired and Jim Brooks was off into movies, and so I guess the last one was *Best of the West,*" a short-lived comedy-western he and Weinberger oversaw. "So there was no *Taxi* pilot per se; we had that commitment from ABC even before we sat down. It was simply a question of what that first series was going to be, and it turned out to be *Taxi.* That was the series we wanted to do."

Jim Brooks recalls that about a year earlier, "Jerry Belson had called my attention to a *New York Magazine* article about a cab company that at the time was sort of the 'actors' cab company. The key thing about the piece was its discussion of disparate groups of people whose occupations were working at this cab company when their preoccupations were something else. Jerry and I were going to pursue it with Dave Davis, and MTM actually went ahead and bought an option on this article. Then Jerry dropped out, we formed our own company, and we still wanted to do this taxi show. So [MTM head] Grant Tinker, being Grant Tinker, was terrific about it and supported our decision. He let us buy the option from him at the original price." Tinker himself doesn't quite remember it that way; he good-humoredly told Tom Shales of *The Washington Post* that "by the time they went to Paramount, our option was over and they just used the damn thing, and Jim has never paid me a nickel!"

The article, "Night-Shifting for the Hip Fleet" by Mark Jacobson, came out in the September 22,

1975, issue of *New York Magazine*. It spun a lively, winding tale of Dover Taxi Garage #2, at the corner of Hudson and Charles streets in Greenwich Village. Jacobson had driven a taxi there himself a year before, and now he'd returned to check out his old cabbie compatriots. As the article's subhead proclaimed, "It's Hooverville, honey, so anyone outside the military-industrial complex is likely to turn up driving for Dover." There were college professors, priests, Eastern European disc jockeys (shades of Latka!), musicians, sculptors, actors, and writers. There were women drivers even then; not unlike Elaine Nardo, one twenty-nine-year-old with three art degrees had come to New York to be part of the SoHo art scene.

The article described "shape-up time" at the garage, a daily ritual from about two to six in the afternoon when, just as in *Taxi,* the night shift waits around on a first-come-first-served basis for the day-liners to bring the cabs back in. The night shifters hang out, play cards, in good weather go outside to get a tan, and tell lots of stories about survival and getting out.

Over coffee in the East Village, Jacobson today smiles and shakes his head and says he hadn't even wanted to write that article. He was talked into it. "I was 'the beatnik reporter' for *New York,*" he remembers wryly, "and [editor] Clay Felker said, 'This is great! This is you! Who better to write about cabdrivers!?' Because I had *been* a cabdriver at Dover until I sold my first piece to *New York Magazine.* The day that piece was published, I went down to the garage and turned in my card."

Jacobson, now a columnist for *Esquire,* remembers the original MTM option "paid me something like five hundred dollars. Even Brooks told me later that was a 'pre-TV' price. After he and the others left MTM, they called me again." The upfront deal never got substantially better, but Jacobson, dealing with Weinberger, was able to wrangle $350 for each time a new episode aired, as well as a script-writing arrangement. (See episode #41, "Shut It Down, Part I," in the episode guide.)

"All my screenwriting friends tell me what a rotten deal I made, and from time to time I would mention it to Weinberger and them. One day Brooks called me up and said, 'Look, we could've ripped you off completely and just taken the idea, but we didn't, so don't complain.' It's not that big

At and inside the real-life Sunshine Cab Company—
the Dover Taxi Garage #2, at the corner of Hudson
and Charles streets in Greenwich Village.

hanging around a cab company is to wear a corduroy suit. The rest of us tried to dress so that we wouldn't look like Hollywood writers.''

''There were thirty seconds that happened that just made the series,'' Brooks remembers. ''During one fifteen-second period, I saw a guy come over to the dispatcher and ask for a certain cab and start to give the dispatcher a bribe for it. And the dispatcher saw me watching and started waving it away. That's how Louie De Palma was born. The other thing turned out to be the solution to a problem we were having, which was, how do you make a taxi driver a hero, how do you give it any grandeur? Now, we'd been told there was one guy all the cabbies liked, and they waited for him for hours because he came in at, like, six in the morning. And he was a genuinely charismatic, young, good-looking guy that four or five people all wanted to have breakfast with. And at breakfast, there was this conversation, everybody talking about what they really wanted to do, and this person says, 'Me, I'm a cabdriver.' That became the cornerstone of Judd's character.

''I don't think the series could have happened without either of those events happening,'' Brooks insists. ''I'm not exaggerating.''

Now that they had some idea where they were headed, the four writer-producers started coming up with characters and situations. The central role would be a career cabbie. There also would be a conniving dispatcher to serve as a foil. The rest would be aspiring something-or-others: aspiring actor—that was New York, that was realistic, you could do a lot with that—an aspiring boxer—that could be colorful. You needed a woman. Andy Kaufman was a given from the get-go, if they could just figure out what to do with him. Let's see, what else? Before they had a presentable script, they had characters. Now they literally had to flesh them out.

In their minds, the only person to play the career cabbie was Judd Hirsch, a downbeat middle-aged actor with a face like a retired hawk. Hirsch was finally getting a foothold on stardom with *Chapter Two,* a four-character Neil Simon play that had

a deal to me, especially now. As it was, I made some seven thousand extra bucks a year for five years without lifting a finger.''

MTM's original idea for *Taxi* would have been much different from the way it eventually turned out. ''MTM had wanted to do it as a one-camera, videotaped show rather than four-camera, filmed [as it turned out],'' says Weinberger. ''It just never materialized.'' This new version would, brilliantly, beginning with a three-day research trip to New York City.

In early 1978, Brooks and the rest flew in to meet Jacobson and to scout both Dover and another cab company, Ding-a-ling (at the time on 57th Street and 11th Avenue in Manhattan, and now located in Queens). They dutifully set their alarms for 2 A.M. and trooped off to watch the night shift straggle in. ''Ed is very impeccable,'' Davis recalls with a chuckle, ''and so his way of looking like a guy

CBS's *Delvecchio*: **Judd Hirsch as LAPD detective Dominick Delvecchio. The crime drama, Hirsch's second attempt at a series, aired during the 1976–77 season.**

even dragged *People* magazine down to Broadway to report on it. A respected journeyman stage actor for well over a decade, he'd recently attracted attention as a fast-talking DJ in a Listerine commercial; ironically, his performance there helped him snare the lead in the TV movie *The Law*. Directed by John Badham (*Saturday Night Fever, WarGames, Stakeout*), it won an Emmy and spun off a mediocre series in which Hirsch also starred. But after it and another so-so series, *Delvecchio,* Hirsch got disgusted with television. Later, before agreeing to do *Taxi,* Hirsch would get disgusted with Broadway. Hirsch gets disgusted about everything sooner or later. Who better to play the quintessential New York cabbie!

But there were problems. Joel Thurm, the original casting director of *Taxi* and presently NBC's vice-president for talent, remembers, "[Hirsch] is who the producers wanted, who everybody wanted—everybody except the network." As it had objected to Hal Linden, star of *Barney Miller,* ABC apparently felt Hirsch was "too ethnic" and wanted the Tony Award–winning stage and film actor Cliff Gorman instead. Talk about sticky situations—

Gorman was just then starring alongside Hirsch in *Chapter Two*! But Gorman himself helped resolve the matter by turning down *Taxi.* "Why he said no, I'll never know," marvels Thurm. "The man could've had an entirely different life today."

With the network still opposed to Hirsch, the producers and Thurm had to round up not only the usual suspects but also a cross-section of newcomers and character actors. Barry Newman, Jeffrey Tambor, Carmine Caridi, and Hector Elizondo were among those who auditioned for the role of Alex. "A lot of good people," Thurm remembers. "But nobody worked as Alex. They were talented actors, but when they read, they weren't funny. There was something in the way that role was written that nobody besides Judd could've made it work." Eventually, even ABC grudgingly agreed.

Hirsch, however, was playing hard-to-get. "I told them it was too early for me to go into another series," Hirsch claimed to Vernon Scott of UPI. But then, all three of his *Chapter Two* costars and the play itself were nominated for Tony Awards, leaving Hirsch with not so much as a home version of the game and a gift certificate from *The Speigel Catalog*. A resentful Hirsch decided to switch channels. The Tonys were suddenly nothing more than empty awards to fill up a TV special. "If Broadway is about television," he told Scott, "then it doesn't matter where you act. So I thought, why not do the next best thing, work in a television situation comedy?" The "next best thing"?

Now money became an issue. Hirsch told his agent, "Give them a figure they can't accept." He did so. But JCW had only begun to fight. "There was no way at first to pay Judd enough money for him to do the series; we couldn't make up the difference between what we had budgeted and what he wanted," Brooks recalls. "I remember getting out of a sickbed and making the rounds with Ed Weinberger, begging money for Judd because we thought he was crucial to the series. There finally came one day where ABC contributed some money and Paramount gave some, and we were able to come up with the minimum amount he wanted."

While all this was going on, Thurm and JCW had already cast some important slots. The first member of the *Taxi* acting troupe was a tough, bald, little bowling ball of a guy named Danny DeVito. Thurm had first encountered the diminutive actor while casting *Starsky and Hutch*. "I remember this well, because I didn't *want* Danny [for that 1975–1979 ABC cop show]!" he laughs. "The director was someone whose taste in casting generally was not that terrific, and now he suggested Danny, whom I didn't know. I wanted someone else. And what happened was, I got my way on everything else, so I said, fine, go with Danny DeVito for this part. Then when I saw the film on the first day of dailies, I said to myself, 'Wow, this guy is wonderful!' " He stayed wonderful, too. "Danny came in," remembers Brooks, "and the minute he came in, he was cast."

DeVito himself still gets a kick out of that audition. "Basically, I came in, took a couple of steps, threw the script on the table, and said, 'One thing I wanna know before we start is, Who wrote this shit?!' Then there was dead silence and then they laughed like crazy, and that was my audition."

More or less. Thurm assures that there were proper introductions before DeVito went into character. "When anybody does that, you know it's not

real. Very often that kind of joking around doesn't work, because the person who's doing it can't do it. It's sort of a dangerous thing for actors to try. But in Danny's case it was brilliant. He didn't even need it, because when he did his reading—well, he was Louie! It was *the* best moment in my life of casting up to that point. He read, we *all* were hysterical, he left, and everybody just turned to each other and said, 'I guess that's Louie!' "

The next role to be cast was that of Elaine Nardo, the cabbie who wants to be an art dealer. As originally conceived, Elaine was a tough-talking, thirty-three-year-old Italian single mother with a twelve-year-old daughter. (The writers took her last name from show assistant Patricia Nardo. Similarly, "Bobby Wheeler" and "Tony Banta" derived from two MTM assistants and sometime-screenwriters, Donna Wheeler and Gloria Banta. And "Latka" is Yiddish for potato pancake.) As usually happens, however, the right performer can redefine the role. Thurm, for one, wasn't limiting his choices. Among the nearly three dozen actresses who auditioned for Elaine Nardo was a slender blonde who went on to a bit of success afterward: Shelley Long. (Thurm's notes read, "Jane Curtin-ish, very nice, wholesome, and bland.")

Marilu Henner also didn't fit the mold, though she did fit her clothes well enough to demand attention from all males, straight or otherwise, within a fifty-yard radius. A busy Broadway and TV actress already at twenty-five, she also was as intelligent as she was outrageously sexy, with a memory that stands to make the *Guinness Book of Records*—literally, she can recite dates and times for almost every day of her adult life, off the top of her head, and they always check out. Most important for the role, however, Marilu had a knack for being just one of the guys.

On top of that, she swears she's psychic. "It's funny," Marilu recalls, "but when first I saw the word *Taxi* in one of the trade papers, the word just jumped out at me. I didn't know what it was, or that there'd be a part I'd be sent up for or anything, but there was something so powerful about that word for me. Then three months later, my first interview for it came up.

"The scene was just a telephone conversation between my daughter and me, and I was telling her

I was going to pick her up at the airport after she'd visited her father and his girlfriend—who was twenty-five, with red hair and a big chest!" She laughs. "Maybe I should've tried out for *that* part! Anyway, they really liked me, and I went back three more times until finally I said, 'Hey, you better cast this part already, because I'm running out of outfits!'"

Thurm also kept pushing Marilu to the producers, who just weren't sure. "Finally," he says, "I told them, 'If you don't make a decision today, we're gonna lose her.' My exact words were, 'I don't want to be here six weeks from now saying, Where's Marilu?'" It helped that she'd just appeared in the pilot for *The Paper Chase,* which looked as if it'd be picked up (which it was, by CBS and later Showtime). Nervously, the producers made the right decision. Elaine Nardo, née O'Connor, became Irish.

One Irishman in, one Irishman out. Similar to Henner's situation, the casting of Tony Danza rewrote the initial character of Phil Ryan, described in an early press release (rather graphically) as "Middleweight Bleeding Champion of the World. Phil is so inept he bleeds as he climbs into the ring." Lovely thought. Charles Haid—the future Officer Renko of *Hill Street Blues*—was among those who read for it.

Danza at this point had had almost as much experience in acting as he had had in professional boxing. He'd been a middling middleweight for only about a year when Stuart Sheslow, an independent producer, spotted him at the famed Gramercy Gym in Manhattan. Sheslow was looking for boxers he could use in a fight picture—this being on the heels of *Rocky*—and something about Danza proved magnetic. "He looked like he was lit up," Sheslow told Arnold Hano of *TV Guide.* "He sparkled."

The boxing movie never got made, and Danza returned to the ring. Not long afterward, Sheslow became an ABC executive. Remembering Danza's charisma, he got the young boxer signed to a pilot called *Fast Lane Blues.* The show didn't sell, but Tony did.

At ABC's suggestion, says Thurm, Jim Brooks went to New York to videotape a Tony Danza screen test. Danza left them impressed. "The qual-

ity we loved about Tony was he was like a puppy dog," Thurm remembers.

The puppy dog, meanwhile, was up for a part in the Paramount youth gang picture *The Warriors.* He remembers that the office of casting director Juliet Taylor tracked him down to say that Jim Brooks wanted to see him. "So when I want up there," Danza relates in his cheerful Brooklyn patois, "there were a whole buncha blond guys— y'know, 200-pound blond guys. So I read for Jim Brooks, and Mandy Patinkin read with me." Danza clicked, and so Irish heavyweight Phil Ryan became Italian middleweight Tony Banta. "First it was Phil Banta," Danza recalls, "then they changed it to Tony Banta. And I thought, 'What a nice thing, they changed it to Tony for me.' And then I realized," he half jokes, "that it was 'cause they thought I wouldn't answer to Phil!"

Much more problematic than the boxer role were those of lost soul John Burns and actor Bobby Taylor/Bobby Wheeler. (The producers kept going back and forth. Taylor was also Alex Reiger's last name at the start.) Brian Kerwin, who later played Sally Field's ex in *Murphy's Romance,* was one of the actors who auditioned for the part of John Burns. So was Jeff Conaway, who instead snagged the role of Bobby. John fell to a busy, fresh-faced actor named Randall Carver, who, with Norman Lear's *Forever Fernwood* under his belt, was the only *Taxi* star besides Judd Hirsch to have been a regular on a TV series.

Like a lot of other working actors in Hollywood, Carver had been taking classes to stay busy and to stay in touch. One of them was in improvisational comedy, taught by Harvey Lembeck, the immortal Corporal Rocco Barbella to Phil Silvers's Sergeant Bilko. Robin Williams was in the same class. So was Marilu Henner. "We were friends even then," Randy remembers. "Neither one of us knew we were both going up for roles in *Taxi.* But Marilu has these psychic feelings, and she told me she felt we were going to be working together."

Jeff Conaway doesn't recall if Marilu had ever had any psychic flashes about him, but they, too, had worked together. After having been a child actor and model, Conaway had gone on to play one of the leads in the long-running Broadway musical

Grease. He also had a big secondary role in the 1977 movie version. Now, it seemed, his *Taxi* auditions were running for more weeks than the Broadway show.

"It took us *forever* casting Bobby," Brooks sighs. "I mean, we read *everybody* for it." Conaway, recalls Thurm, "was the very last person to be cast on the very last day. I think we went into a production the next day, it was that close.'

"I'd done a *Mary Tyler Moore Show*," Conaway recalls, "and these guys struck me as really brilliant. So I asked about *Taxi*, because it looked interesting and told my agents to set up a meeting. So there I sat waiting . . . and waiting . . . and waiting! Hours went by, and doors kept opening, and people kept going in and out. Finally, Jim Brooks stuck his head out and said, 'Jeff, this is probably the first time you've ever been to read for an audition where while you're waiting, they're still writing it!'

"And now I'm thinking, 'What does he mean, read?' I thought I didn't have to do this anymore, that I had a reputation by now. But they were so nice and easy, none of this tense stuff, that you felt it was OK. They were at ease with themselves 'cause they *knew*—they knew they were hot stuff and they enjoyed it. It was like, 'Hey, man, we got a great deal here, let's have a ball!' " Conaway had originally tried out for the role of John Burns, but later, after getting a copy of a complete first-episode script, he decided to switch to Bobby—a move, he says, the producers were also thinking about.

And then there was Andy Kaufman.

The late Kaufman, was a given from the beginning, one of the strangest, most original performers ever. His theatrical heroes were professional play-wrestlers like Blond Buddy Rogers and Fred Blassie—showmen, really, with a wrestling mat for a stage. "Rogers *never* broke character," Kaufman admiringly told Jack Hicks of *TV Guide*. "These guys are real purists in show business. They have hair vs. hair grudge matches, spit on old ladies, taunt people outside on the street after the match." As socially questionable as their tactics were, their theatricality was indeed pure. To Kaufman, they were real-life examples of what Julian Beck and others called "living theater"—life as theater, theater as life.

Kaufman's version of "living theater" was wrapped in the traditional cloth of stand-up comedy. But he wasn't a stand-up comic—he was a performance artist masquerading as one. That's the tricky part. Kaufman was every bit as talented as his old friend Laurie Anderson and other avatars of the avant-garde, but rather than perform for Manhattan's chic elite, he went the comedy-club route. It was a double-edged tactic. On the one hand, it got him on "Merv," where his act would be seen by many more millions than would attend the latest Next Wave Festival at the Brooklyn Academy of Music. On the other, it made audiences incensed. They might accept Kaufman's intellectual tricks at some SoHo performance space, but in Peoria? Forget it.

One incredible routine, which metamorphosed into *Taxi*'s Latka Gravas, was "Foreign Man." An unwary audience would grow more and more embarrassed as an innocently inept comedian with a foreign accent would make an ass of himself on stage. He was obviously an amateur, and you watched and watched, and kept wondering why somebody didn't get him off the stage. Then the little guy would begin to realize he was bombing and start apologizing to the crowd. Then he began sniffling, and you just wanted to get up and leave. Everybody in the audience would be shifting uncomfortably and mumbling to each other, "Geez, why doesn't somebody do something?" Then, just as you're looking to pay your check and escape into the fresh air, he starts banging on conga drums in beat with his sobs. He turns into a calypso king and the audience suddenly sighs in relief. "Geez, it's only an act! He fooled us!"

"Somebody told us we had to see this guy perform," says Brooks, "and so we went to The Comedy Store, and this creep named Tony Clifton was the opening act. And as we're watching Andy later, somebody came over and whispered to us that it was the same guy. And we'd thought of ourselves as pretty sophisticated and all, and when we heard that, we went crazy! What a routine! What an act! I think we appealed to Andy's artistry; I think the fact that we were willing to sign both characters is the reason he came to the series. We simply made room on *Taxi* and created the character of Latka specifically for him."

"All the stories you hear are true," confirms Nardino. "There were two contracts, there were two parking spaces. Clifton was signed separately to play in one or two episodes that first season." The producers' sense of humor wasn't shared, unfortunately, by anyone else. The charade didn't last long (see episode #10 in the episode guide for the climactic story), and it wasn't even fun while it lasted.

Did the producers really think Tony Clifton was another person when they signed both him and Kaufman? "Of course not!" thunders Thurm. "We *all* knew that, and we all went along with this farce. We all laughed and enjoyed it—why not? It didn't cost us anything! Ed and Jim are very bizarre people," he adds affectionately, "and this brought a little more interest to the project. And also, Andy was adamant that this was the only way he would do the show." Brooks and company even allowed him a special arrangement: He only had to appear in about thirteen episodes a season, and he only had to rehearse two days a week. A stand-in provided by Kaufman filled in for him other rehearsal days.

Taxi initially was to feature one other cabbie as well: The original character breakdown included Nell, "a beautician. She's overweight, black, and sassy." If something about this sounds familiar, *Gimme a Break!*—the part was conceived specifically for Nell Carter, who'd appeared in *Cindy*. "I hated *Cindy*," says Thurm, "but I loved Nell. But it turned out she had just signed a holding deal with 20th Century-Fox. I talked to her agent and said the minute this women is free to do a television show, let me know. He called me three years later. I was at NBC then, and I made a holding deal with her that led to *Gimme a Break!*"

One black actor did appear as a regular, sort of— not as a cabbie but in middle management. This was Jeff (J. Alan) Thomas, who played assistant dispatcher Jeff Bennett. A professional extra, he did the impossible and worked his way up to guest-star status.

Thomas had done plenty of extra work for MTM Productions, and so was already familiar with the *Taxi* group. "He was an extra who somehow worked his way into Louie's [dispatcher] cage, and when we needed someone to say a line from there,

The irrepressible Andy Kaufman in the 1979 ABC special, *Andy's Fun House.*

he did it and he was very funny and that character slowly evolved," recounts *Taxi* director Jim Burrows, who went on to cocreate *Cheers*. "Jeff was so cute," Marilu Henner says, smiling. "He's got this beautiful shade of skin and green eyes, and he has this sweet, gentle sort of energy. He made a great foil for Louie." Yet while everybody knows him, nobody knows him. "It's very, very difficult finding Jeff," asserts Danny DeVito, who cast him in his black comedy *Throw Momma from the Train*. "As a matter of fact, when I wanted him for a part in this film, it took me a long, long time to find him." Thomas's most recent visible TV work was on a Halloween episode of *Cheers* and in several sketches on *The Tracey Ullman Show*. He also appeared in Jim Brooks's movie *Broadcast News*.

Another semiregular, Tommy (T. J.) Castronova, who played bartender/waiter Tommy at Mario's, the cabbies' hangout, has since become a TV producer (*Tales from the Darkside*.) "A sweet man who

Taxi coproducers Glen and Les Charles, with primary director Jim Burrows (*center*) on the set of *Cheers*.

way the director can represent the cast in a non-abrasive way to the producer and can represent the producer in a nonabrasive way to the cast.'' He laughs. ''Which is good, because the way *we* work, we sort of gang tackle!''

I Love Lucy had pioneered the resident-director procedure, as it had pioneered nearly everything else in television. Coincidentally, an *I Love Lucy* assistant director named Jay Sandrich had gone on to be the regular director on *The Mary Tyler Moore Show*. Burrows had apprenticed under Sandrich at MTM and had made his mark directing every show in that production company's stable. He also was called on regularly to film pilots, those all-important sample episodes designed to sell a series, and for which you hire top guns. (Interestingly, one Burrows-directed pilot that aired on CBS as a one-shot was *Roosevelt and Truman,* a sitcom costarring the dour Philip Michael Thomas of *Miami Vice*.).

''*Taxi* came about,'' says the calm and casual Burrows in between bites of lunch, ''because the creators were all MTM alumni and knew me from there. They came to me and wanted to know if I would direct their new show. I said 'yes' quicker

really held his space,'' recalls Burrows. ''He was a bartender for me one series too early.''

Burrows didn't do a bad job himself of holding his space. As talented a cast as had been assembled, and as talented as were day-to-day producers Glen and Les Charles (scriptwriting brothers from the MTM days), *Taxi* needed a cohesive force to visualize the great scripts and make that vision clear to the cast. In one of Brooks and company's most important moves, Jim Burrows was brought in as resident director.

For reasons of workload and preparation time, virtually all prime-time TV shows use a different director each week. With hour-long dramas there's usually no other choice, but on half-hour, studio-contained comedies, a regular weekly director is actually practical—if you can find one to commit that long. ''It's best, really, if you can do it that way,'' says Brooks. ''You like to have continuity in that job. Everybody's more comfortable, because this

THE BOOK ON BROOKS

James L. Brooks was born in Brooklyn, New York, on May 9, 1940, the son of Edward M. and Dorothy Helen Sheinheit Brooks, and was raised in North Bergen, New Jersey. He was a student at New York University from 1958 to 1960 before leaving to become a page at CBS and eventually a writer for CBS News. (Years later, the college dropout would become a guest lecturer at the Stanford Graduate School of Communications.) From his first marriage (July 7, 1964, to Marianne Catherine Morrissey), he has a daughter, Amy Lorraine. On July 23, 1978, he married his present wife, Holly Beth Holmberg. Along with his many Oscars, Emmys and Golden Globe Awards (see Part IV), he is also recipient of the Peabody Award for *The Mary Tyler Moore Show* (1977), the Writers Guild of America Outstanding Script Award for his TV movie *Cindy* (1978) and the Humanitas Prize for producing the *Taxi* episode ''Blind Date.''

than they could finish the sentence. I knew it would get great writing, which is always a big concern. Glen and Les Charles and I had all worked on *Phyllis,* and so I knew them, too.'' He'd get to know them so much better that the three of them would cocreate *Cheers.*

Burrows is second-generation showbiz, a fact he's worked hard to overcome. It was difficult, since his father, Abe, had cowritten the books for the Tony-winning musicals *Guys and Dolls* and *How to Succeed in Business Without Really Trying*—and get this, had won yet another Tony as *How to Succeed*'s director, and a Pulitzer Prize for the book. ''I'll tell you a story,'' says Burrows wryly. ''When I was living in New York, I was always 'Abe Burrows's kid.' So when I moved to California to get my own identity it worked out fine, except now people call me Jim Brooks. I had a woman sit at a dinner with me, and she kept wanting to say something, and she finally came over and said, 'I really enjoyed *Terms of Endearment*'!'' (Burrows's sole foray into feature-film directing yielded the 1982 comedy *Partners.*)

The *Taxi* cast ''came to me with their skills in place,'' he insists. ''I didn't teach them how to do anything, really. I just feel like the guy who has the ability to keep them all together, all these multitalented people, to get them to perform in an ensemble situation. I think that helped make *Taxi* a success, this wonderful feeling you get when you turn the dial and see people who so enjoy working with one another.''

Twig by twig, like birds at a nest-making contest, the other particulars of production whirled along. Paramount assigned *Taxi* to Stage 25 on the studio's landmark Hollywood lot. They also assigned an old hand named Budd Cherry to serve as associate producer. (On most filmed TV comedies, this is a low-level management position mostly in charge of ''postproduction,'' or the editing, color correction, and other processes the actual film goes through once an episode is shot.) Brooks and the boys themselves insisted on having a newcomer named Ron Frazier as ''Executive in Charge of Production.'' It was an oddly grandiloquent title for essentially an extra bookkeeper assigned to make

sure economies were kept and that Paramount wasn't overcharging JCW. Though he had nothing to do with the show creatively, and was in fact subordinate to the producers, Frazier was given one of the largest end credits on the show. But he learned his craft and has since become a bona fide producer of *Our Family Honor* and other shows.

For film editor—the person who decides in postproduction exactly where each shot the director has chosen will begin and end, crucial to comedy timing—the producers picked a big, burly guy with the unlikely name of M. Pam Blumenthal. Though a veteran of MTM who'd been Emmy-nominated for his work on *The Bob Newhart Show,* nobody seemed to know his first name—if he wanted to be called Pam, hey, Johnny Cash hit big with ''A Boy Named Sue.'' And since Blumenthal wound up winning three Emmys in a row for *Taxi,* he could call himself anything he damn well pleased. The other major slot, director of photography, was filled by Edward E. Nugent for the first two seasons. Afterward, it was filled by Kenneth Peach, Sr., a well-respected old-timer who had developed special-effects cinematography techniques in the thirties and, among other accomplishments, had served as director of photography for most episodes of *The Outer Limits.* His son, Kenneth Peach, Jr., worked with him on both that show and *Taxi,* and is credited as director of photography on a few episodes.

Now the *Taxi* team had to devise a look and a sound for the show, and a first impression that would help draw in the viewers each week. The job of coming up with the right music and main-title sequence fell chiefly to Dave Davis.

Davis had designed the main-title sequence for *The Bob Newhart Show,* with its melancholy commuter trains and the wistful, jazzy main theme (''Home to Emily''); he'd also revamped the opening of *The Mary Tyler Moore Show* in its second season. For *Taxi,* Davis devised a low-key, classically simple main title: A backward-looking shot of an old Checker cab on a bridge, preceded and followed by the New York City skyline and underscored by a gentle, jazzy instrumental (''Angela''). The feelings it evokes are nostalgic and urban, of a New

Jazz great Bob James, composer/arranger of "Angela (Theme from *Taxi*)."

York City of myths and gentle breezes. It hadn't started out that way.

"The original concept," says Davis, "was to have bits and pieces of different cabdrivers saying a sentence or two of what it's like to be a cabdriver. So Jim Burrows shot all these pieces and I cut them together. And the idea was good, but it just came out too long. And when we cut it down to a minute, a minute-and-a-half, it got to be just a lot of rapid talking; it was also hard to work a song into it." In the meantime, another piece of film had to be used temporarily while the theme music and other particulars were being worked out.

There was plenty of film around to use. Earlier, Davis had gone to New York to shoot the "connectives" for *Taxi*—outdoor shots of cabs driving around and shots from the cabbies' points of view, which could be used as transitions to connect scenes. Tony Danza was elected to drive the yellow Checker cab used in these connectives—one of which turned out to be a shot of him driving away

from Manhattan on the Queensboro Bridge. Davis was riding ahead, shooting from the back of a station wagon.

"I kind of improvised that shot," Davis remembers, "panning from the skyline to the cab and back to the skyline. Tony was great, positioning the cab just right and doing everything we asked. He got a big kick out of that. We knew right away the guy was really into the show." Budd Cherry, the associate producer of *Taxi* in its first year, started using that shot as a temporary main title, and Davis, to his surprise and delight, found "it worked like a dream. The problem was that it was too short, because I hadn't designed it to be the main title. It was only about thirty seconds long. We had to extend it by repeating the middle part a couple of times. You can see it happening when a couple of the actors' names pop on and off. But the thing that really made it work was the music."

The music was also partly an accident. Davis wanted to use jazz rather than the big-band sound generally employed on TV shows. Jazz soundtracks had been used occasionally in movies and television, but they were rare. Davis, however, had used the jazz duo The Brecker Brothers on *Bumpers,* an unsold pilot he'd done with writer-producer Charlotte Brown. For *Taxi,* he now wanted to use the Grammy nominated pianist-composer Bob James.

Davis brought rough cuts of the first few shows to James's New York office. "At the time he was putting together an album called *Touchdown,* and he said the title song on it would be perfect for *Taxi*'s main theme. And he played it for me, and it was great. So Bob was brought in, and not long after he wrote this beautiful tune to go along with the Angela character in 'Blind Date' [episode #2]. But then when we put 'Touchdown' against this film [of the cab on the bridge], it was too brassy, too big. It's a great tune, but it just didn't knock anybody out as a main theme. So I thought I'd give this tune 'Angela' a try. And it was magic. I mean, it's beautiful standing alone, and then together with the visual . . . ! I played it for the guys, and it was a smash."

Taxi was shot in front of a live audience, meaning that a few yards from the actual sets and the tangle of cameras and crew members were bleachers of people. Desi Arnaz, in his role as *I Love Lucy* producer, had pioneered the concept of live-audience filming eons ago. It gave a natural, give-and-take feel to TV comedies that movies and closed-set comedies lack. Some performers, especially those trained on the stage, thrive on audience interaction. For the home viewer, the sound of a natural audience—with its unseemly snorts and guffaws and its own peculiar response rhythms—is more pleasant than the cut-and-dried, calculated, and utterly predictable recorded laughtracks often used. (And anyone watching *Taxi* or any other Jim Brooks show knows they're getting the real thing by listening for one trademark—Brooks's wonderfully rich, goose-like honk, a laugh from the soul.)

Like most TV comedies, *Taxi* played out on minimal sets—usually just the garage itself and the hangout, Mario's. Often these were supplemented by the cabbies' apartments or a fancy restaurant, or, more ambitiously, a gym or a boxing arena. A JCW year-end summary, prepared after the first season was complete, proudly noted, "[O]ur sets are considered 'the Cadillacs of the lot.'" They were indeed amazingly grungy and realistic and not standard-issue TV. One reason they were so good, the summary goes on, is that they were cost-efficient: "A battle was waged for over two months on why our sets were costing so much money." At a climactic meeting, the studio "quoted the high price of labor and length of time necessary to build our sets. [JCW] quoted prices given from outside firms to build the exact same sets. Miraculously, the costs came down in a steep slide and we were able to design and build sets at a reasonable price."

Along with all the normal considerations—wardrobe, makeup, sound, lighting, props, guest casting, and the budget that swirls overhead like a vulture—was one that by its nature is special: special effects. One wouldn't imagine special effects to be a special concern: *Taxi* was not *Battlestar Galactica*. Then again, there *was* the occasional spaceship (albeit in a daydream of Jim's).

The major special effects on *Taxi* involved scenes inside a moving cab. Since the cabbies worked the night shift, the illusion of movement was a lot easier to create than it would have been with daytime scenes, which would have required "matting-in" moving backgrounds. (Remember how it used to look in old movies? It hasn't improved much since.) The major prop for these scenes was a Checker cab shell with no windshield. Behind it on the stage were two not-quite-parallel rows of flickering lights, which simulated streetlights and the lights of cars whizzing past. Behind them were prop persons holding lights that simulated the headlamps of a car behind the cab; the prop persons would move in and out to create the illusion of a moving car. There also were flashing lights colored red and green to simulate traffic signals. The cab shell itself was on a springy platform that crew members would rock to indicate motion.

Like most TV comedies, *Taxi* was produced on your basic five-day week, Monday to Friday. (This doesn't count, of course, the weekend and late-night sweat of writers pursuing deadlines.) The week followed a general routine.

On Monday at 11 A.M., the actors, sitting at a long table, "read through" the script. Then they break for two hours while the writers, after listening to the first reading, get together and figure out what needs to be cut. After lunch, the first act is put "on its feet," meaning the actors, script in hand, follow stage directions. Memorizing specific lines doesn't help at this point, since the script changes so much during the week.

On Tuesday at 10 A.M., the second act is put on its feet. Around 4:30, after more rewriting, there's a full, on-its-feet run-through with scripts in hand. The writers might stay up all night doing the week's major rewrite. By Wednesday morning there's usually a whole rewritten script, which is put on its feet and tweaked throughout the day. There might even be another big rewrite night.

Thursday is blocking day, meaning that the actors and the crew members who handle cameras, lights, microphones, etc., learn their "marks," or their places on and around the stage. It starts at 9 A.M. with an initial rehearsal with the cameras for blocking, and another rehearsal where the cameras fix their focus. More script changes follow. On Friday at noon, everybody plays through both acts twice with the cameras. At 4:30 is a final run-through with no film in the cameras. By now, on

Taxi anyway, Jim Burrows's eyes look so beat and beady that the cast starts calling him by his nickname, "Beads."

The actual filming for television is on Friday evening at 7:30. Afterward, the studio audience leaves, and the cast and crew shoot "pickups"—bits from that week's episode or earlier ones that needed to be redone because of technical foul-ups, rewriting, or an off night on the part of an actor. (*Taxi* additionally had the unusual and cleverly cost-effective habit of shooting two-part year-end shows almost completely in pickup, which was possible since they were done as short episodes featuring individual cast members; these "pickup shows" were "Memories of Cab 804," "Fantasy Borough," "On the Job," and "The Road Not Taken." See the episode guide.) Everything finally finishes up around 11 P.M. or midnight.

"Coming from movies," says Carol Kane, "I wasn't used to the way television works at first. I paced myself throughout the week, thinking that this is the script we'll be doing on Friday. So I'm thinking, OK, I'm not giving it the whole thing today, I'll be giving it out tomorrow. I didn't know that there *is* no tomorrow! You're going for performance level pretty much, maybe holding back a tiny bit, but basically going for performance level on Tuesday."

If the rewriting and the pace seem overzealous, they're not. The weekly crunch of producing a TV comedy demands that everybody on the writing staff—story editors, producers, script consultants—pitch in and pitch throughout the week, full steam. Much more so than the scripts of hour-long dramas, those of TV comedies are by necessity organic: We all cry at the same things, but since nobody really knows what's funny, smart producers listen everywhere for ideas. Actors and directors are free to fling them in if they come up with something; on *Taxi,* so were show assistants (to an extent). On some occasions, it was audience reaction that prompted rewrites after an episode actually completed filming.

Producers, writers, and consultants "would come to the run-throughs," recalls Henner, "and shout out suggestions from the audience. It was like a free-for-all! That's what was so great about it." There was a rail separating the stage from the front

row of studio seats, where the show's creators and other dignitaries sat. Changes are announced by the call, "Cast to the rail!" "You can always tell a show that's working," says Brooks proudly, "when you say, [that] and they rush. They were hungry for the stuff."

Unless a scriptwriter were on staff, he or she wasn't in on the rewrites; though a freelancer's name may be up on the screen after "written by," the script may have changed anywhere from a little bit to almost completely. There's no way to know, and it really doesn't matter; TV comedy is, to a greater degree than most types of filmmaking, collaborative. And the original story framework—the plot—is vitally important even though jokes may come and go. "Jim won't allow anyone to take their names off a script," observes Richard Sakai, who rose from *Taxi* gofer to a coproducer. "And in the same way, he believes in letting the guy who did the first draft keep the credit and in having the producers and rewrite guys all pitch in, himself included." Writers Guild rules do apply, of course, but Brooks's stance is admirable nonetheless. Often in television, it's not unusual for in-house writers to take credit away from freelancers.

One other unusual thing about *Taxi* happened every Friday after wrap-up: a party till dawn.

Different shows handle the Friday night wrap-up differently. With some, everybody says, "Good work" and goes home. With others, divided factions glare at each other and thank God they don't have to see these people again until Monday. In either case, there's often some sort of buffet and drinks laid out. With *Taxi,* that kind of spread turned into a full-blown festival.

"There were 112 shows and 112 parties," chirps Marilu. "The cast would pay for it. Four or six times a year we'd have a huge blowout that the producers would pay for, and *those* would go on till eleven the next morning! I was always in charge of the music," she bubbles. "I'd get in touch with the DJ that was coming and tell him everybody's favorite music. They were the most unbelievable parties!"

"It was like opening night every week," confirms Conaway. "It was like going to Mario's! It started the first week with ABC sending over champagne. And we liked it and said, 'Hey, let's do this every week!' '' The cast as a whole would put up two to four hundred dollars for each weekly blowout. Everybody on the lot used to show up for the *Taxi* party: friends, relatives, other Paramount players—wave your beer the wrong way and you might splash Robin Williams, Rhea Perlman, Tom Hanks, John Travolta.

The *Taxi* gang had a lot to celebrate. The early word of mouth was good. Hell, it was great! *Taxi,* wedged in between the hits *Three's Company* and *Starsky and Hutch,* and with *Happy Days* and *Laverne & Shirley* as lead-ins, was going to be another *The Mary Tyler Moore Show.* They could feel it. And as Shakespeare might have said (after a little too much mead), the fault would lie not only with the stars but with the producers, writers, and a director, all about the best in the business. *Taxi* was off, and the meter was running.

AWAKE,
A WAKE

Despite all the hoopla, *Taxi* didn't start out as the toast of the 1978 season. The premiere episode, "Like Father, Like Daughter,' seemed rushed: Characters are introduced and the milieu set, and then everybody hops a car to Miami where Alex has a brief reunion with his long-unseen grown daughter. Why Miami? Why create a microcosm and then leave it? The final scene could have been played at a New York airport, or, for that matter, in a rush at a New York hotel. The notion of pragmatic Alex being so moved that he'd drive to Miami could have been demonstrated without that strange change of locale. Other logic problems persist: Given the needle-thin margin of time he had to reach his daughter, why didn't Alex just hop a plane? Later episodes show he could afford it. The other characters wouldn't have joined him in that case, but then, they didn't do anything in Miami anyway.

Variety in its review accurately noted: "Both the script and the direction in this initial show had a hurried feeling about them, as though the producers were afraid that the audience would be bored if the show slowed down. . . . Hirsch is gruffly sentimental and appealing, but the others are such oddballs as to frustrate audience identification. . . . The show never goes for loud yocks or long dramatic yardage, and it's almost as though the producers knew from the beginning that it would have the safety net of ABC's Tuesday superseries. With a nice safe berth like that, *Taxi* should have time to develop some secondary characters." Kay Gardella of the New York *Daily News* cracked that *Taxi* ". . . will have to come up with better episodes than this week's before we'll leave any critical tips for the series. . . . Considering the creators of *Taxi,* much more was expected from this opening episode than what was delivered." Writing in *The Village Voice,* James Wolcott—normally one of our most astute commentators on pop culture—com-

plained after the first few shows that Judd Hirsch ". . . has a face the camera doesn't care for . . . [and] is so painfully self-conscious that he shies away from the lens and lets *Taxi* slide into a funk." He further notes left-handedly of the characters, "It's admirable that they haven't been turned into joke-machines, but they haven't yet bristled to life either."

"I don't think our first show fully realized its potential," Jim Brooks admits. "And maybe if it had been a pilot, *Taxi* wouldn't have gotten on the air. But in Alex's reunion with his daughter, the commitment to the kind of life we wanted the series to have was apparent. What we wanted, and what we were able to very often do, was *Taxi* as a morality play."

True. And the characters, to use Wolcott's phrase, did bristle to life. The early episode "Blind Date," for instance, was an emotionally honest and utterly nonsaccharine piece of work that won the well-regarded Humanitas Prize for its espousal of prosocial values. "Come As You Aren't" (episode #4) showed an ugly side of Elaine Nardo, and the great twist-ending of "Bobby's Acting Career" (episode #6) told us more about Bobby Wheeler than we learn about most TV comedy characters in years.

Already, *Taxi* was revealing itself as an almost-anthological series of social-realist morality plays. Wolcott himself called the series "laughtrack Eugene O'Neill" (a bit too glibly, since the live-audience *Taxi* refused to depend on a laughtrack). Soon, populist *TV Guide* reviewer Robert MacKenzie was citing *Taxi* as "one of my favorites of the season" and gleefully reciting one great bit after another. By year two, on the other end of the spectrum, John J. O'Connor of *The New York Times* was writing, ". . . the cast, headed by Judd Hirsch as the somewhat sour, deadpan Alex, happens to have coalesced rather rapidly into a first-rate repertory company. . . . For whatever reasons, by design or chance, *Taxi* connects frequently enough to lift the series out of the banal into the special niches accorded an *All in the Family* or, not surprisingly, *The Mary Tyler Moore Show.* Within its severely constricted borders, the show manages to be inventive and surprising.'' In the *Times*'s usual air of faint praise, he concluded, ''*Taxi* happens to be a superior example of its particular genre.'' It wasn't long before such critics as Tom Shales of *The Washington Post,* Ron Alridge of the *Chicago Tribune,* Eric Mink of the *St. Louis Post-Dispatch,* and even Kay Gardella of the New York *Daily News* had recognized the special qualities of *Taxi.*

''There's something about a good TV series that needs accidents to happen,'' says Brooks. ''It needs some casting accidents, it needs characters coming together with the script in a certain way. And if you can get a momentum going where the scripts inspire some actors to become these characters, and the characters in turn inspire scripts, and if you have your format right, then it's gold.'' But there is something else as well, something conscious. As *Taxi*'s later coproducer Sam Simon puts it, ''The problems you saw weren't these stupid sitcom problems.''

As its time slot and its gradually improving press predicted, *Taxi* began looming as a hit. The year-end Nielsen ratings put it in the top ten among weekly TV series, and most of the cast soon found themselves being interviewed by publications from *TV Guide* to *Tiger Beat.* Danza sighs. ''For me it was like a dream come true. I always thought I was gonna be somebody, but to have it really happen . . .! And I was talkin' it down!'' he says incredulously. ''My friends and family would call up all excited—*'Ya got a series!'* And I'd say, 'Yeah, yeah, I got a series.' '' DeVito, he remembers, started getting recognized on the street right away. ''But then little by little you start getting recognized yourself. And for me it was weird and nice because *Taxi* was this respected, critically acclaimed show. It was like, 'Where do I come in?' Like, I shoulda been on *Three's Company* or somethin' instead!''

Others, however, immediately saw a downside to sudden stardom. ''Sure, the popularity and everything was great,'' says Conaway. ''But then it dawns on you, that the people who say they love you were the same people who couldn't care less who you were a month before. Suddenly the business was becoming very transparent.''

At the same time, Conaway admits, ''In the beginning, the camaraderie was fun. We used to write graffiti all over the back of the set, stuff like 'Tony is gay.' '' He laughs. ''That used to drive him nuts. Tony and me would run around the lot and steal golf carts [from Paramount's security guards] and basically just have fun.'' Henner breaks out in smiles and says ''Yes! Yes!'' at the memory of that. She laughs. ''Tony was always terrorizing people on the lot! He'd 'borrow' one of those golf carts from this really sweet little security guy named Fritz. And he'd somehow hoodwink him into letting him take this golf cart all around the lot. I guess you can't take the Brooklyn out of the boy!'' Danza himself agrees, admitting with a huge grin, ''Generally, I tried to keep the place loose.'' Future *Taxi* cast member Carol Kane nods in recognition. ''If there ever were a dull moment,'' she intones, as serious as the Sphinx, ''Tony would hose down the backstage with a fire extinguisher.''

If Danza was still a Brooklyn bomber, Danny DeVito was still a Jersey hustler—but benign. In an excitable rap, he tells all about ''Louie's Rule'': ''See, they'd come to me all during the week, y'know—bozo after bozo would approach the cage and ask me to say their friends' names on TV whenever I had to call out the cab assignments. So Louie, see, wanted a buck for it. So if you wanted your friend's name called out—say 'Tadesco, cab 415!' or whatever—ya gotta pay for that. So ya gotta give me a dollar. See, that was the rule. And on some days, phew, did I make out!'' he chortles. ''Tony Danza's got relatives like forever, and the only way he could keep clean with them was if I say their name on television. And he was paying through the nose, this guy. Every day it was my aunt this, my uncle that. It was a good little side business Louie had.'' He chuckles. ''Good for me, too!''

Danza, to put it lightly, doesn't remember DeVito's comical extortion quite the same way. ''He says a *buck?!* His ass, a buck—it was a hun-

First baseman Judd Hirsch at one of the *Taxi* softball games.

everybody turned to to keep the refrigerator stocked with afterschool snacks. "It seemed like everybody was still trained from school," remembers Marilu. "We used to go in there around three o'clock in the afternoon and get a snack. I'd walk in, and Tony'd be eating a cheese sandwich and tell [macrobiotic vegetarian] me, 'Yeah, I know, this isn't good for me, but I want it anyway!' And Andy would have chocolates and Twinkies, anything with sugar."

Danza smiles. "Yeah, Marilu would always be watchin' what we ate. Cheese sandwiches she called mucus—'You're eating mucus!' As you're chewing, she'd be saying that!"

During the dinner breaks on Friday night, shoot night, the actors generally relaxed while the producers had their last-minute creative rushes. Andy and Marilu would send out for macrobiotic food, and Kaufman often got in some meditation. Tony might relax with a manicure, and the rest usually either studied lines in their dressing rooms or ate at the Paramount commissary. Later on, Chris Lloyd had the guts to actually leave the studio and eat at a nearby favorite restaurant.

On Sundays, they fielded the *Taxi* softball team. Danza usually pitched and Hirsch played first base, occasionally switching off. Randy Carver started out in right field, moved to center, and played second base on occasion. Other cast and crew members and writers joined in, though Marilu, despite the potential pleasures of seeing her run the bases, served only as scorekeeper. Save for Kaufman, the eternal outsider, the cast would get together as a bunch for rollerskating, concerts, dinners out—more like members of a small, regional theater ensemble than highly paid stars of a hit network show.

On *Taxi* there were no "comic misunderstandings." That's what a lot of sitcoms build stories around. You watch and watch and get so damn infuriated that Jack Tripper on *Three's Company* doesn't just tell Mr. Roper he's not gay, and that if Roper wants to throw Jack out of the apartment, he'll see him in landlord-tenant court and sue for sexual discrimination. Or that Laverne doesn't tell Shirley that no, she's not dating Shirl's boyfriend

dred bucks!'' He laughs ruefully. "That's just like Danny, he *would* say a buck! Danny DeVito would charge a hundred dollars to say a name. And not just me—I saw Jimmy Burrows pay him, too. A dollar? Naw," Danza says flatly, dead serious, "it was a hundred." A hundred does make more sense, if DeVito wanted to avoid every camera person and electrician asking. But Marilu Henner also remembers the fee as a buck. "Except he wanted more from me." More money? She laughs slyly. "No, not money!"

Backstage there was a combination prop room/kitchen where the actors would congregate: A poor, sweet prop person named Jack Mann became unofficial den mother. Even though the show after the first year had a "talent coordinator" whose job it was to keep the stars happy, Mann was the one behind her back and leaving hints around the apartment. People never sit down for five minutes to *talk*, for Chrissakes. Classics like *The Honeymooners* and *I Love Lucy* got away with comic misunderstandings on occasion, but they used them as minor devices in larger stories; they didn't dwell on them. *Taxi*'s first season, despite an inordinate number of clunkers, established the show as about human dignity and redemptive friendships in the real world.

On *Taxi*, the heroes occasionally lied and behaved selfishly and stupidly—and not just despotic Louie but all of them. John Burns lied to his wife about a crucial coin flip that decided who got to stay in school and who had to drop out to save money. Bobby betrayed Tony's trust, and rather than Bobby "learning his lesson" as on a typical sitcom, Tony grudgingly decided he has to accept his friends as they are—*he* ain't perfect, either. Neither is Alex, who likes to get on his moral high horse, nor Elaine, who has a big mouth and a nasty temper. Yet unlike the one-dimensional Frank Burns of *M*A*S*H*, for example, the *Taxi* characters weren't caricatures. They were imperfect people in an imperfect world, who cut corners sometimes but tried to do the best they could. Even Louie's belligerence grew understandable as the layers of his bitterness peeled away year by year, until his abusive (and let's face it, hilarious) comments became an acceptable and even funny personality trait within the family—all without him becoming goody-goody like so many TV antagonists after a few years.

"What you die for, first of all," says Brooks, "is that hopefully somebody in your organization can write a script! Believe it or not, a lot of funny writers can't write scripts, and [the executive producers] can't write everything. What you need then is stories. You die for stories, especially when you need twenty or twenty-two a year. *Taxi* stories were tough, but fortunately, it worked out as a true ensemble show. Instead of having to write twenty stories about this family, you do four Danny shows and three Andy shows and so on."

The Randall shows, however, just weren't happening, despite earnest, appropriate performances by Carver. "It wasn't the actor," says Stan Daniels. "It was a chemistry thing, and it was our fault in the way we created the role. It fell between the cracks of other characters. The kinds of jokes you could give that character sort of fell halfway between Tony and Bobby." Joel Thurm agrees. "That's absolutely right, and in fact they had the same problem between Bobby and Tony already. And that silly marriage subplot just never worked."

As the writers and producers were discovering the corner they'd written themselves into, a serendipitous savior appeared. It was one of the riskiest, most outrageous, and eventually most beloved characters to hit television in years: the burnt-out Reverend Jim, played by Christopher Lloyd. Or perhaps, as the character himself once announced in a voice like charred gravel, "Jim Ignatowski, as himself."

"We wanted to do a sixties drug casualty," says Brooks. "That was the whole thing. I remember Carole King or someone on a cable special was talking about sixties morality and stuff like that, and she said, 'I know, I know, but it wasn't all bad then, there was good stuff about it, wasn't there?' And I think Chris's character was about that. And it was an extraordinary bit of luck that the actor was available for that character and vice versa."

The character was an ex-hippie minister who performed the wedding ceremony between immigrant Latka and the call girl in episode #8, "Paper Marriage." Lloyd proved such a knockout he was invited back for another guest shot early the following season, and eventually became a regular—and later, perhaps *Taxi*'s most memorable character. All this from a small role by an unknown actor.

It was the kind of accident that Jim Brooks loves. "They were stuck," says Joel Thurm. "They had written a part no one could do. They also considered it a throwaway role, but I knew it wasn't: On *The Mary Tyler Moore Show*, when Georgette and Ted Baxter got married, the preacher was played by a then-unknown actor named John Ritter. So I'm thinking, this is a role that really can be terrific for Chris Lloyd."

Thurm had worked with Chris several years before in New York, on an Equity Library Theatre show. ELT was a showcase sponsored by Actors' Equity, the stage performers' union. Thurm was stage manager of a production of *Once Upon a Mattress*, which featured Chris as the wizard. "And years later, this agent calls and wants me to meet

Chris Lloyd. And I said, the same Chris Lloyd from New York? I almost couldn't believe it. Nobody knew him in L.A., no one knew he could be funny, but I knew how crazy he was. He'd be perfect.''

Perfect indeed. ''He'd come in clean-shaven and clean-cut on Monday,'' marvels Brooks, ''and by Friday, there would be Jim! The growth of beard would be just right, the hair would be crazy, everything!'' As director Burrows puts it with a grin, ''Chris was an actor who stayed in character a *lot*.''

Chris Lloyd reversed the biblical quotation about prophets not being without honor, save in their own country, their own house. Lloyd's country was New York theater, and he was known everywhere from Lincoln Center, where he did Shakespeare, to the cutting-edge Brooklyn Academy of Music, where he stunned the theater world with his horrifying clown-from-hell in Peter Handke's avant-garde German play *Kaspar,* a fact-based drama about a boy whose first sixteen years were spent locked in a closet. Lloyd had copped Obie and Drama Desk awards in the early seventies, and became a fixture of New York theater. What the hell was he doing in Los Angeles?

''I had a lot of apprehensions,'' Lloyd quietly, earnestly admits, sitting in a cozy neighborhood restaurant where he's at peace among pastel couches and wafting jazz. ''I resolved all those years in New York that if I ever came out here I'd never get involved in sitcoms. I thought my chances of getting into a decent one were . . .'' He searches for the right word and then just smiles conspiratorily. ''I guess I had a New York attitude problem, like, fuck Hollywood,'' he says. ''But then,'' he adds softly, ''this came up.''

Lloyd is an *actor,* a consummate, classically trained actor. Nonetheless, much like Jim, he has a wonderment about the world and marches to sounds no one else hears—a beautiful child. Carol Kane, who performed with Chris in New York, lovingly remembers that in those old theater days, ''We used to call him 'The Fog.' He had a rhythm unique unto himself.''

''I think more than anyone else on the show, we related to Chris as his character,'' says Brooks. ''You were gentler with him, easier with him, than with anybody else.'' Kane remembers ''touching him sometimes before a show, when he was in char-

acter as Jim. His whole body would shake. He always shook when he was Jim. That's how fully he was that person—so sensitive and vulnerable and fragile that his body shakes, just down to the physical being.'' He—or maybe ''they''—would return in the classic episode #27, ''Reverend Jim: A Space Odyssey'' and then, though officially still a guest star for a while, joined the troupe with episode #33.

Taxi wound up its first year as a top-ten series in a season where such silliness as *Three's Company, Laverne & Shirley,* and *Angie* beat out *M*A*S*H,* and the execrable *The Ropers* beat out *All in the Family.* The reviews were positive, and a few months later they would translate into a cache of Emmys—Outstanding Comedy Series, Comedy Film Editing, and Comedy Lead Actress (guest star Ruth Gordon). ''Blind Date'' was nominated for Outstanding Comedy Writing, Hirsch for Comedy Lead Actor, and DeVito for Comedy Supporting Actor. And theme composer Bob James even won a Grammy Award for ''Angela.''

On top of everything else, *Taxi* made money. JCW reported an average production cost for the twenty-two episodes of $260,000 per episode; about $8,000 of that went to the director, $15,000 to the writer(s), $50,000 to the producers, and $45,000 to the regular cast. (These figures would go up considerably in subsequent seasons.) ABC, which had contracted to pay $275,000 per show, actually got a refund of almost $340,000 at the end of the year. With Canadian licensing fees of $418,000, *Taxi* was $413,000 in the black—a neat trick in an industry that lives on ''deficit financing,'' or staying in the red until making profits when a show is sold to syndication.

For season two, the show was moved from Stage 25 to Stage 23, which was closer to the producers' offices and alleviated an audio problem that had plagued the first season. The immense Stage 25 had suffered from unexplained, low-level feedback—a constant murmur that showed up on the soundtrack and had to be doctored. The sets were dismantled and rebuilt perfectly on Stage 23.

The other, more visible change was the elimination (unexplained within the show) of the John

Burns character. The producers threw up their hands and decided to eliminate the character that had contributed to some of the clunkier episodes. "I would do the John stories," remembers script-writer Earl Pomerantz. "The writers somehow just never wrote for him. One of the reasons the character was taken off the show was just that nobody knew how to write for him." Conaway, who'd gone up for the role himself and changed directions when he saw the full script, believes, "They just didn't know where to go with the character. Randall did a really good job. The second year began, and it was like, 'Where's Randall?'"

Randy Carver took the bad news with the stoicism of original Beatle Pete Best. An experienced working actor, he was familiar with the odds against stardom. To this day he remains understanding and philosophical about the change in the show. "Success is a funny thing," he muses. "I didn't let it affect me too much—I kept the same apartment, the same car. On a hit show, you never know how it's going to go. They might change your time slot, or people's taste might change.

"When I left, I asked if there were anything I could have done as an actor that would have helped the character continue. And Ed Weinberger said it wasn't me, that there were just problems in the development of that particular role. I left the show with a warm feeling in my heart for those people and for that opportunity. I was very appreciative of that." John Burns was a lost soul; Randy Carver is a good one.

Departing around the same time was Dave Davis. He and Stan Daniels had begun to disagree on the direction of *Taxi,* and Ed Weinberger had sided with long-time partner Daniels. Brooks fell in the middle. Davis, who'd been in the business the longest and had had his share of successes, decided to retire; as the cocreator of *Rhoda,* of syndication hit *Bob Newhart* and future syndication hit *Taxi,* Davis wouldn't ever have to work again. Ironically, Daniels speaks well of him today, while Weinberger stiffens at a mention of the name.

Budd Cherry, the old Paramount hand who served as the first associate producer of *Taxi,* also exited. Elevated was a modest, personable production assistant named Richard Sakai. A UCLA film-school graduate whose classmates included Alex

Cox (*Repo Man, Sid and Nancy*), Sakai started out as a gofer who sometimes had to drive 250 miles in a day for JCW, using his own car; one of his jobs was driving Marilu Henner back and forth from the airport whenever she flew in to audition. He quickly rose to become one of the production assistants, an apprentice position. "Paramount had a terrific associate-producer training program for minorities," remembers Sakai, whose heritage is Japanese. "A lot of good people came out of that. And *Taxi* was set up like it was at MTM, where they only brought in assistants they thought would come along—they were always looking for fresh talent to help hold up the show. Either you make it or you don't." Sakai made it. He eventually ascended to *Taxi* coproducer, working in the production rather than writing end, then went on to produce a not-so-hot aerobics sitcom called *Shaping Up,* and Fox's *The Tracey Ullman Show.* He later became president of Brooks's company, Gracie Films.

In the make-believe world of *Taxi* itself came two important additions: Jim Ignatowski, who had debuted the previous season, and Zena Sherman. Zena, played by Danny DeVito's longtime mate Rhea Perlman, was that most improbable of creatures—a steady girl friend for Louie. She made five appearances throughout the show's run, two of them in the second season. Her work in *Taxi* led to her role in *Cheers,* for which she's won three consecutive Emmys.

"Rhea's addition, giving Louie a girl friend, was *enormously* important to the life of the character," says Brooks. "It led to all sorts of stuff with him and women, such as the episode where he's going to date Alex's ex-wife [episode #83], which I think is classic, and the Andrea Marcovicci shows [episodes #72 and #97], which are two more of my favorites."

Yet while Perlman looked the part and was indeed DeVito's girl friend in real life, she wasn't playing herself. To this day a giggly little girl despite three children of her own, Rhea never would have fallen for a crude, embittered man like Louie. Moreover, Perlman, who'd spent most of her modest career playing, as she puts it, "battered wives and social workers," had to audition for the role. Though DeVito's contract had been renegotiated after the first season (as is typical with a hit show),

The middle season cast: *(back row)* Andy Kaufman, Judd Hirsch, Jeff Conaway; *(front row)* Tony Danza, Danny DeVito, Marilu Henner, Christopher Lloyd.

getting his girl friend on *Taxi* apparently wasn't a contractual given. "I don't know if it was written with me in mind or not," Rhea contends. "They wrote an involvement for Danny, and I didn't know about it until they asked me to read for it."

"From the very beginning they knew Rhea was an actress," says DeVito. She had in fact done a voiceover for the premiere (see the episode guide) and had recorded a "*Taxi*-will-be-right-back-in-a-minute" tag. "Brooks and Weinberger had seen her in a couple of TV movies," DeVito elaborates. "She was a natural choice for the part, so they asked her to read for it. It was no shoo-in," he insists. "There was no giving anybody any roles. She auditioned along with other people. I'd like to think her getting it had something to do with the fact I liked her and everybody else in the cast liked her. But she was really right for the role." As subsequent events did prove.

Taxi again racked up Emmys. It won a second year in a row for both Comedy Series and Comedy Editing, and, in addition, Burrows won for Comedy Directing. The season opener, "Honor Thy Father" (episode #23), got a Comedy Writing nomination, and Hirsch once again was nominated as Comedy Lead Actor. As for the Nielsen ratings, the show slipped marginally in its second year, finishing thirteenth. *Taxi* and another ABC show, *Barney Miller,* were widely considered the best comedies on television, and *Taxi,* unlike its network mate, was also a commercial hit. Brooks and company were riding high. Nothing could hurt them now.

Something hurt them. With the show a hit two years in a row, the usual dance of salary demands grew frenzied. In the spring of 1980, right before production started for the third season of *Taxi,* Hirsch and DeVito both held out for more money. Hirsch, in fact, did so determinedly enough that Paramount filed a $1 million breach-of-contract suit against him. DeVito missed a day of rehearsal, but, as one top-level participant notes, "Paramount did the fair thing with him and adjusted his deal at that time." Hirsch and Paramount resolved their differences before the case could come to court. But then an even more potentially disastrous problem arose.

ABC removed *Taxi* from its relatively secure Tuesday-night spot following the popular *Three's Company.* The idiotic *Too Close for Comfort* took its place, shoving *Taxi* to a Wednesday ghetto amid three shows that would wind up being canceled that year: *Eight Is Enough, Soap,* and *Vega$.* By midseason, when the fates of that trio seemed evident, ABC reslotted *Taxi* to Thursdays following *Barney Miller,* in an effort to counter the hot new *Magnum, P.I.* Unfortunately, three preemptions in the six weeks just prior ruined virtually any hope of audience continuity.

These chess moves worked on the logic that *Taxi,* paired with another "adult comedy" such as *Barney Miller* or *Soap,* would draw an attractive slice of the audience—affluent, college-educated light viewers. It's a tactic that in other circumstances worked for the combination of *Cheers* with both the risqué *Night Court* and the quirky *The Days and Nights of Molly Dodd.* Yet two factors in 1980–81 threw logic into the cesspool.

First was a strike by the Screen Actors Guild, which lasted from July to October and delayed some shows' fall premieres (though not *Taxi*'s) until as late as January. Tied into this was a boom in cable television. Audiences faced with network reruns signed up in droves to see uncut movies (made before the strike) and music specials (unaffected by the strike). Worse for *Taxi,* the early majority of cable consumers were just the type of "affluent" people who watched "sophisticated" programs such as it and the fading *Barney Miller* and *Lou Grant* (both in their next-to-last season) and *Hill Street Blues* (which limped through the year with critical acclaim and a record number of Emmys but with a minuscule audience).

Second, the country was in the midst of the first Iran hostage crisis, and audiences now wanted the same type of escapist fantasy that movie musicals and screwball comedies provided during the Depression. As fantastic as some *Taxi* episodes were that year ("Latka's Cookies," "Latka the Playboy"), the third season also gave us Louie's confrontation with a bleak, lonely future ("Louie's Rival," "Louie's Mother"), a further career setback for Bobby ("Bobby and the Critic," compounding the previous season's "What Price Bobby?"), and such daring masterpieces as "Zen and the Art of Cab Driving'' and the Emmy-winning ''Elaine's Strange Triangle.'' Perhaps the special qualities of *Taxi* should have prompted ABC to showcase it nonetheless, as NBC did with *Hill Street Blues*. Perhaps then ABC would have attracted the same producers and creators who have given top-ranked NBC the rubric ''the quality network.''

Perhaps, perhaps, perhaps. Yet it's not hindsight to say now that *Taxi* was an exceptional, award-winning show with stable though not spectacular ratings, and that it deserved more support than it got. Despite the winds of a ratings war, *Taxi* flew along on a creative high during its third season. But another year of sea change was about to hit the calendar.

By the start of season four, *Taxi* had won its third consecutive Emmy as Best Comedy. Only three other shows have ever pulled that off in the forty-year history of the Emmys: *The Phil Silvers Show, The Dick Van Dyke Show* (with four straight wins), and *The Mary Tyler Moore Show*. If the critics and the word of mouth weren't enough to win ABC's faith in the ability of *Taxi* to draw an audience (as it certainly has in syndication), then the Emmys should have been. Nonetheless, this would be the show's last year on ABC—nearly its last year, period.

Creatively, *Taxi* was on a roll. One after another, episodes destined to be TV classics charged out: ''Mr. Personalities,'' with Andy Kaufman's multiple-role tour de force; ''Jim Joins the Network,'' a scathing bite on the hand that fed them, with guest star Martin Short's most precise and restrained performance to date; ''Louie's Fling'' and ''Louie's Mother Remarries,'' in which Louie bares what soul he has; and ''Of Mice and Tony'' and ''Tony's Comeback,'' two showcases for how good Tony Danza really was, the latter also containing Bubba Smith's best comedy performance yet. Moreover, the fourth season gave us two episodes universally considered among the best of *Taxi*: ''Elegant Iggy'' and ''Louie Goes Too Far.'' And it gave us ''Jim The Psychic'' and ''Simka Returns,'' a pair of episodes that—along with the ascending popularity of Reverend Jim—signaled a major shift in the show, as it moved further from social-realist drama to absurdist theater.

Jeff Conaway had left *Taxi* at the end of season three. He'd wanted to do it almost from the start. ''To tell you the truth, six weeks into the show, I already wanted to leave,'' he says. ''I was already unhappy. You see, the deal I had with Paramount was for star billing above the title. But the day before we're going to shoot the first episode, they called me up and said, 'We can't give you that billing!' Something about Judd's contract—very vague. So I say to myself, well, should I just walk now, say tough luck and split? Or should I say, who cares? I ended up staying because I was really into it, I really liked my character. So I opted to give up my billing, which would have read 'Judd Hirsch and Jeff Conaway' in *Taxi*. I ended up with the first costarring billing. The enthusiasm of the moment got me through, but I immediately saw I wasn't going to be able to do what I wanted to with that character.''

One big problem, as Conaway saw it, was the wealth of self-centered actor jokes. ''I wanted to get rid of the stigma that's put on actors,'' he maintains. ''Sure, there are egoists in acting, and users. But there are actors who really care about what they're doing, about their craft, their art, who want to say something about what they're doing and how much it means. I *did* get to convey that sometimes, but,'' he laughs ruefully, ''I had to do the other guy, too, and that got me upset at times. I just wanted Bobby to be a little more caring, a little more thoughtful, more of a person instead of this guy who only cares about himself and his needs. And that never really happened.''

''In a sense, having both Tony [Banta] and Bobby was a mistake,'' says Joel Thurm, ''because Tony [Danza] and Jeff always had the same things to play. Neither character was very bright, both were young and attractive, and so things began to overlap a little. Tony's character turned out to be easier to deal with—as did Tony.''

Both Thurm and Conaway are so close to the subject, it may have gotten away from them. Bobby Wheeler *was* a well realized character and very distinct from Tony Banta. Ego he had, the necessary ego for a public art like acting, but it was also Bobby who gave the young rival in ''Wherefore Art

Thou, Bobby?'' a place to stay and an introduction to an agent; his envy later in the episode simply shows he's no saint. Who is? It was also Bobby who convinced the others to help put Reverend Jim on his feet. It was Bobby who lent an ear to fired actress Joyce Rogers in "Alex's Romance," and Bobby who gave Elaine a place to stay in "Bobby's Roommate."

Bobby did have an ego, but he also had genuine artistic conviction. He wouldn't sleep with his manager to get ahead ("What Price Bobby?"); he helped out Louie in "High School Reunion" not because he liked him, but for the substantial acting challenge; and he performed all over the boroughs for no money. When Bobby returned to the garage in that one episode in the fourth season, having shot a successful TV pilot, it wasn't to play the big man but to share a small celebration with his closest friends. That reunion episode ("Bobby Doesn't Live Here Anymore") was funny and it was meaningful and it ended on a frighteningly cynical note—frightening because it rang so true. We knew Bobby wouldn't be coming back.

Through it all, Conaway still sees *Taxi* as "a real special time. For a while it was hard for me to look at the shows. Now I can, and they really crack me up. I mean, Danny totally blows me away!" (For Conaway's reminiscences on the events surrounding his departure, see his biography and the episode guide.)

Taxi kept changing, evolving. Carol Kane, who'd guested in the second season as Simka Dahblitz, the girl from Latka's homeland, now came back for two episodes: "Simka Returns" (episode #81), for which she won an Emmy, and "The Wedding of Latka and Simka" (episode #87; see the episode guide for Carol Kane's reminiscences). And behind the scenes, director Jim Burrows was around less and less as steam gathered on his first project as a creator-producer, *Cheers.*

Brooks left the show, too, for about a minute. As *Taxi,* good as it was, continued to struggle in the ratings, the usual network second-guessing began. Suddenly, after having accepted the Emmy-winning "Elaine's Strange Triangle," with its bisexual protagonist and a hilarious and tasteful scene inside a gay bar, ABC objected to a story featuring a gay hairstylist ("The Unkindest Cut," episode #84). The story wasn't even yet in script form, but the network demanded it be aborted. "They had never discussed a story with Jim or anybody before," remembers Gary Nardino. "Now, of course, networks have the right of story approval, and they don't have to give a reason. But when you're dealing with some of the most creative people in television, and you *insist* on *not* giving a valid reason, well, that's crazy. So I'm having these meetings and good-naturedly saying, 'Whaddya mean, question the story? This is *Taxi,* and how can you know what an episode will be like from just the story?' And they said, 'We've been in the business blah-blah years, and anyway, we can read.' But you honestly can't tell what an episode will be like from the story. I mean, who knows what it's going to be like until it's scripted? The *producers* don't even know what it's gonna be like till it's scripted!" He sighs. "It just got to be a pissing fight."

"Jim hears about all this," Nardino continues. "He sees me in front of the Paramount commissary, and he says, 'Gary, it's very simple: I guess ABC doesn't want me to do *Taxi* anymore.' Now I know how serious Jim is, so I went back and notified ABC: 'Brooks has left *Taxi.'* 'What?!' 'He's not going to be censored by you.' And they backed off. But they would get even. Canceling it was their way of getting even."

Perhaps it was. The signs were in the air. On April 28, 1982, Nardino sent a stern telex to ABC president of entertainment Tony Thomopolous, with copies to Brooks and to Michael Eisner, and asked him: "Please do something about the rumors emanating from ABC re: *Taxi'*s potential cancellation. If we are canceled, let the world know it on Sunday [May 2, the day of a major scheduling meeting]. Ed Weinberger, Chris Lloyd, Danny DeVito, [and writer-producers] Sam Simon, Ken Estin, Ian Praiser, and Howard Gewirtz have all received calls from potential ABC series to hire them. This kind of rabid flesh-stripping happens only when insiders spread information. Please put a stop to it. It is very, very demoralizing and insulting to all concerned parties. *Taxi* has been a good experience for us all. . . . Let's do whatever can be done to prevent hard feelings.''

The ratings were indeed middling, but nothing that three consecutive Best Comedy Emmys couldn't fix. And it wasn't like ABC had any other prestige shows to build upon. The winded *Happy Days* was finishing up its ninth year, *Laverne & Shirley* its seventh, and *Three's Company* its sixth. With the demise of *Barney Miller,* ABC had decided to stick to formulaic audience-pleasers, which—the network didn't realize in its shortsightedness—weren't going to keep on pleasing audiences forever. Carol Kane remembers seeing Brooks and Weinberger emerge from a meeting with ABC executives in Century City, near Los Angeles. ''Some of us were waiting in the bar downstairs, and they came down and they did not look good. They said, 'Well, we're still alive—but that's all.' ''

To Brooks, some of these meetings resembled *Twilight Zone* episodes. Thomopolous, he remembers, kept saying he was strong enough to ''take the heat'' for canceling *Taxi,* somehow taking pride in executive machismo. ''I remember using the word 'quality' once,'' says Brooks, smiling and shaking his head, ''and one of the executives said, 'Well! How can you talk to somebody who uses words like *that?* ' ''

''There had been a dialogue of hostility between ABC and Paramount about *Taxi* for a while,'' says Nardino. ''What I did, as soon as I sensed that, I started seeding Brandon Tartikoff and NBC as to, 'There may come a moment when you can get *Taxi,* and don't look at it as a show that's coming from ABC, look at it as a landmark television show that'll be a jewel in your crown.' Another thing I told Brandon is that if he would buy *Taxi,* it would be a pied piper—it would lead other top creative people to NBC. And it did.''

The verdict came down on Tuesday, May 4, 1982: *Taxi* was canceled. Nardino got the word in New York, and he relayed it to Brooks and Weinberger. At the same time, Brooks's assistant, Barbara Duncan, fielded a call from Thomopolous. It may have been she who started calling the day ''Black Tuesday.'' Everyone else remembers it as the day of the wake.

''Ed Weinberger called and told me that ABC had canceled the show,'' says Danny DeVito. ''I was shocked. It was like your friend's gone away and you didn't even get a chance to say good-bye. I went to Jim Brooks's office, and pretty soon, the rest of the cast began showing up.''

''I just got in my car, numb, as if somebody had died,'' says Kane. ''I think most of the others did the same. Within an hour-and-a-half, wherever they were in the city, they ended up in Jim's office.''

Chris Lloyd and Judd Hirsch were out of town, and Andy Kaufman was who knows where, but Kane and DeVito and Rhea Perlman and Marilu Henner and Tony Danza and the producers and the writers and others straggled in at around 10:30 in the morning, as if following some ancient migratory pattern. They slipped a tape of *Taxi* highlights into a VCR, and immediately began getting bombed on tequila. ''Shows you how depressed I was,'' says DeVito. ''I never drank tequila in my life.'' Neither had Brooks. It just seemed like the thing.

Within twenty minutes of getting the fatal call, remembers Duncan, ''Jim was sitting at his desk and I had gotten six bottles of José Cuervo Gold. And everyone just proceeded to get roaring drunk because there was nothing else that we could do. So we had a wake.''

''It was right after we got word,'' says Sakai. ''Jim called everyone into his office, and we all drank enormous amounts of tequila and sat there and commiserated. He called up Tom Shales [of *The Washington Post*] and also Grant Tinker.'' Adds Simon, ''He was offering to call up the White House if anybody'd thought that would've done any good!''

''So we're drinking and drinking,'' remembers Brooks, ''and one of the people I called while we were drinking was Grant Tinker [his old boss, who'd become head of NBC], just to talk and have my rage with a sympathetic executive. And the first thing he said was, 'Jim, I can't do anything,' and I hadn't asked him for anything. I talked to Michael Fuchs of HBO. I tried in a very ineffectual way, to do a campaign. It turned out the thing that motivated people was that Shales liked the series and called me, and then wrote a very influential column.''

At the one-hundredth episode party: *(left to right)* Christopher Lloyd, cocreator Ed Weinberger, J. Alan Thomas *(at top)*, Marilu Henner, Danny DeVito, Judd Hirsch, Tony Danza *(at top)*, cocreator Jim Brooks *(with finger near cake)*, coproducer Sam Simon *(partially hidden)*, coproducer Ken Estin.

That column, in the May 13, 1982, *Washington Post,* asks plaintively, "Why did ABC cancel its best comedy?" Shales wrote, mincing no words but quite a few network executives:

Just when it seems impossible to get any more outraged about the idiocies of network television, a lunacy comes along to reawaken indignation. . . . With the concurrent demise of *Barney Miller* on ABC, the network is left without a single surviving comedy program of any measurable intelligence; *Mork and Mindy,* which was at least cute, has also been

canceled. But *9 to 5,* a miserably unfunny— but trendily psuedo-feminist—comedy series has been renewed and will be moved in the fall to a virtually failure-proof time slot, after *Three's Company* on Tuesday nights. "It's gotta get a rating in that slot," says Brooks, "and as opposed as I am to saying bad things about other shows, what you have there is an hour of women who have big breasts. It's that kind of continuity of programming that governs ABC."

Maybe Brooks shouldn't have thrown stones about big breasts attracting viewers—*Taxi*'s Elaine Nardo wasn't exactly flat-chested—but he was right about the network's low-road philosophy.

"It was *folly* on ABC's part," Brooks, now a multiple Oscar winner, still believes strongly today. "It was just one of the worst moves they made, because they would have had *Cheers,* they would have had Danny—*everyone* was offering Danny on-air commitments. And I think we proved the following year that the series was still vital."

The critics and the Emmy judges thought so: ABC generated more bad press for the cancellation of *Taxi* than any network had received for ousting virtually any show, including NBC's *Star Trek* (whose support was more in the form of letters than of articles in the mainstream press). The vehemence of editorial commentators was astonishing. "For some time, one of the great mysteries in television has been the continued presence of Tony Thomopolous as president of ABC Entertainment," wrote Ron Alridge of the *Chicago Tribune,* responding to the *Taxi* cancellation and ABC's sagging fortunes in general. *St. Louis Post-Dispatch* columnist Eric Mink blamed the show's cancellation on "small-minded and shortsighted network nervousness." The imperial *New York Times* pronounced, in damning understatement, "ABC's decision to cancel *Taxi* was especially surprising." Though many of the people involved point to the influence of Thomopolous's deputy, the controversial Lew Erlicht, it got so bad for Thomopolous that he had to spend most of an annual fall-season press conference trying, with little success, to rationalize ABC's decision. The ratings averaged in the middle range, just above the conventional cut-off point. Even according to ABC, which put *Taxi* 55th out of 110 shows, it was in the middle—and in the middle with more awards than Bear Bryant.

At the Emmy Awards later that year, *Taxi* was again nominated for Best Comedy Series and won for Comedy Writing ("Elegant Iggy," with another nomination for "Jim the Psychic"), Comedy Supporting Actor (Chris Lloyd, with another nomination for DeVito), and Comedy Lead Actress (guest Carol Kane). Director Burrows and star Hirsch were nominated as well. This is a flop?

The "Black Tuesday" wake continued at Tony Danza's house, after Duncan had secured a dozen limousines for the painfully drunken mourners. It

went on until 8:30 the following morning. Duncan sighs. "It was a good way to end it, in a way, but we still wanted to have that last show. We wanted to have the right to be able to say good-bye. And we didn't have that."

Now what? Everyone refused to believe *Taxi* was over. Though Brooks was getting involved with the feature film *Terms of Endearment* and everyone else had loads of opportunities, no one wanted the ride to end. Lots of other shows had switched from one network to another; that notion wasn't unique. What *was* unique was that *Taxi* was getting an offer to do something no network series had ever done— cross over to cable.

These days, with the proliferation of alternative venues, it's not unusual for network series to continue with new episodes on cable (*The Paper Chase*), first-run syndication (*Webster, Fame, It's a Living*), and post–prime time late-night (*T. J. Hooker*). But at the time, it was unheard of—the networks were sacrosanct, weren't they?

Michael Fuchs, HBO's vice-president in charge of program development, didn't think so. If NBC wasn't interested in renewing *Taxi,* the cable giant certainly was. Fuchs met with Brooks for several hours and promised unheard-of creative freedom. Even the show's length didn't have to fit a rigid formula. And though *Taxi* had suffered very little from network censorship at ABC, the producers could be even franker on HBO. Marilu laughs, remembering Brooks's comment. "[He] turned to me and said, 'If we do this show on HBO, the first shot is going to be of your bare breasts—to let them *know* we're on cable now!' " While the deal was being worked out, the *Taxi* cast and many of their behind-the-scenes people met in New York, where DeVito was hosting *Saturday Night Live.* As a spur-of-the-moment thing, they took their final bow on that show. Live from New York, DeVito's seventy-eight-year-old mother called the ABC executives "stupid jackasses"—in Italian.

The HBO offer presented complications, however. Money wasn't an issue; HBO's license fee was approximately equal to NBC's eventual offer of roughly $450,000 an episode. The problem involved syndication. TV stations that would be re-running *Taxi* late at night and in the afternoon had been contractually guaranteed a show that had run originally on a network. Would they pay the same syndication fee for episodes that had run on HBO? Would they want those episodes at all? Since most TV shows don't make money until they run in syndication, and since at the time a five-year run was considered minimal to supply the syndication market, these were questions that affected the last several years of the *Taxi* group's lives.

HBO, in any case, had scored a big point in public perception; cable, the offer announced, could have the prestige and clout of a network. "My opinion on the HBO venture is that it was done for a splash," Brandon Tartikoff, NBC Entertainment division president, told one reporter. "It was a very good move on their part to try to get that kind of recognition. They ended up getting it without spending a penny." Though NBC had been reluctant at first to pick up an ABC "leftover," Tinker and Tartikoff donned their lances at the sight of the cable dragon. On Friday, May 21, 1982, Paramount announced that *Taxi* had been picked up by NBC.

The cast and creators were ecstatic. So were the many fans of *Taxi*. This didn't prevent, however, a round of salary renegotiations by the actors that almost killed the show they had mourned and cried out for. Hirsch in particular held out not only for a higher salary but also for all sorts of expensive perks—this after having told a Paramount executive he'd pitch in however he could to help save the show. Now, Hirsch's demands were about to torpedo it. Brooks today calls the star's holdout "just negotiations, that's all." Nonetheless, it took a stern phone call from NBC Chairman Tinker himself to make Hirsch realize the precariousness of the show's fate. *Taxi* had been saved by people who cared about quality television, people willing to give a good program the chance to find its audience. Hadn't it?

At first, it seemed so. Coproducer Simon recalls how "Ken Estin and I met with NBC's Program Practices office [the network "censors"], and they said, 'You're *Taxi*, you're special, we consider you like *Hill Street Blues*. The one problem we have is Reverend Jim.' We explained that the guy was a

walking advertisement against drug use, that he'd gone to Harvard, and now look at him, he's a space case. When we put it that way, they said, 'Oh, OK.' "

Everything seemed golden in the beginning. NBC, though its fall schedule was already set, decided to put *Taxi* on right away and not hold it as a mid-season replacement. *Mama's Family,* a shrill recreation of a bitterly poignant *Carol Burnett Show* segment, was pushed back. *Taxi* was placed between the promising new comedy *Cheers* and the surging *Hill Street Blues*. DeVito, in character as Louie, sneered in promotional announcements, "Same time, better network." Opposite *Taxi* now were *The Greatest American Hero,* which vanished by the end of the season, and *Simon and Simon,* a dumb detective show that couldn't possibly attract the kinds of viewers that liked *Hill Street Blues* and *Taxi*. Unless, as it turned out, those viewers were couch-potatoing after *Simon and Simon*'s leadoff—the massive hit *Magnum, P.I.,* which was in the top twenty the previous year and in third place by the end of the 1982–83 season.

Taxi, nonetheless, continued to cook. The fifth and final season didn't know the meaning of average. There were a couple of clunkers, most notably, "Travels with My Dad" (episode #98), which took Tony and his seafaring father on the most fake-looking ship to the lamest Singapore set in the world, with dialogue to match, and "Jim's Mario's" (episode #108), whose plot didn't have a leg to stand on. Mostly, though, there were masterpieces.

"Jim's Inheritance," "Alex Goes Off the Wagon," "The Shloogel Show," "Scenskees from a Marriage," "Louie's Revenge," "Get Me Through the Holidays," "Arnie Meets the Kids," "A Grand Gesture" . . . not since the "classic 39" of *The Honeymooners* has a show's single season been so rich in both comedy and tragedy. The series took a turn for the dramatic, approaching maudlin at times; where first-season shows ended in hugs, fifth-season shows ended in tears. And yet the team pulled laughs that season from places nobody had thought to look before. Ask yourself: How many shows could do screamingly hilarious and at the same time intelligent, sensitive episodes about topics like PMS and gambling addiction?

The general excellence of *Taxi* that season came despite the loss of director Burrows to *Cheers*. "Burrows was like a father figure," Henner recalls fondly. "At the time of the actors' strike, all we'd shot was the one episode where Jim goes back home. So we got together and said, 'We have to do something.' We decided to form the Taxi Repertory Company. We all met at Danny DeVito's house [on which some construction was being done]. We're only there a few minutes when this big piece of plywood comes flying and hits 'Beads' [Burrows] in the head. Blood gushing everywhere. We had to rush him to the hospital. Needless to say, the Taxi Repertory Company never met again. But what we did was mount a piece of the plywood onto a plaque that said: 'Taxi Repertory Company, Aug. 21, 1980 to Aug. 21, 1980.' " The constant new faces coming in week by week during the last season wouldn't have been able to—couldn't have been expected to—be a member of the family as Burrows was.

"As with *Cheers*," says Burrows, "it was my job to train these people to function on their own, help them come up with their own personal identities—sort of to make the actors 'director-proof.' It's real similiar to when I came in to direct *The Mary Tyler Moore Show*—the actors all knew their characters cold. It's good for a show, but it does make it real hard to come in as an outside director."

"By the time I got there," says Carol Kane, "Jim Burrows was practically doing things without words. He was saying things like 'D' [meaning Danny], and he'd point at a vague spot on the floor, and Danny would know where Jimmy wanted him to go and why. They had it down to sign language practically."

With Burrows gone, the cast didn't know from one week to the next how experienced or autocratic a director they'd get. Novice directors Stan Daniels and Richard Sakai had their shots, as did the surprisingly talented DeVito (who'd directed a few shorts for arts-festival consumption). Among the others were frequent *Barney Miller* director Noam Pitlik, an Emmy-winner; Michael Zinberg, who's known as much as a producer (*The Bob Newhart Show*) as a director; and Harvey Miller, an *Odd Couple* veteran and movie scriptwriter/producer/gadfly.

"It was kind of disrupting," Chris Lloyd remembers, "having a new director every week. Danny was great—probably the best guest director on the show. And Noam Pitlik was really good. It's surprising how few directors there are who can handle that four-camera format. And it must have been a real trial for *them* because we as a company knew, each of us, what was right for our characters and what was wrong for our characters. So then directors would come in with their own ideas, and it was, like, forget it." He laughs. "Like, 'My character does not *do* that!' " he adds, mock-pompously. Compounding matters, says Marilu mischievously, is that the cast saw outside directors "like substitute-teacher time. Spitballs and everything!" Director Will Mackenzie, who'd helmed the third-season episode "Zen and the Art of Cab Driving" (episode #57), fondly confirms that, "Marilu was the ringleader. I think she gave me an apple-for-the-teacher afterward to make it up to me."

The cast did need to let off a little steam. NBC, despite its good intentions, had begun to mishandle *Taxi* disastrously. It doesn't take a programming genius (should such a creature exist) to realize that placing a show on hiatus from late December to late January, moving it to a Saturday slot for three weeks, placing it on hiatus again from early February to late March, and then preempting it *five times* in a seven-week stretch would kill anything that moved.

"That last year, if you asked around backstage what night we were on, we literally couldn't tell you," says Kane. "There was just no way the show could survive that. Nobody could find it!"

"We felt mishandled by NBC," Brooks agrees. "Our time slot was changed so much that last year. And here we were, such good PR for that network."

As in a recurring nightmare, *Taxi* was canceled again. Quality seemed to mean nothing—this, on the network that preached quality programming as a sound business policy, so long as you still had *Knight Rider* for the kiddies. To be fair, ratings were only one factor in NBC's decision—the show was going to get very expensive in a sixth year, as the cast and crew got more and more in demand with moviemakers. Brooks and DeVito were already

TAXI

32

filming *Terms of Endearment* in Nebraska when they got the word. Ironically, they were shooting the wake for Debra Winger's character.

Brooks sighs. "So we're in the middle of Nebraska, at a strange family hotel. I got the news on the phone, and I told Danny and we just went in, had a drink at the bar, and got drunk. Somebody said to Danny, 'Aren't you on *Taxi?* I love that show!' We just looked at each other. That was it—y'know?"

That was it. We know. Danny DeVito shot an introduction to a retrospective show (broadcast as two parts in syndication), and that was good-bye. The last day of shooting had been earlier—February 18, 1983. "All through the years, whenever Louie called out my cab number," says Marilu, "it was always 'Nardo, 218.' It was prophetic in a way. That became the date that we shot the final episode." And neither a final jackpot of Emmys—for Hirsch again, Lloyd again, Kane again—nor a reasonable diatribe by an embittered Hirsch on the Emmy telecast would change things.

"We were able to do *Taxi* as a morality play," Brooks reflects. "Not self-consciously, but that's where the characters took you. The one thing we always say is, you're giving yourself trouble if you try to use a television series to deliver your own message to people. I think it's a very dangerous thing to do. But to create characters with complex internal lives is very proper. We had that on *Taxi,* and so any of them could take you to that wonderful point of self-examination."

"It wasn't just jokes," believes Simon, "but great stories—and great actors just playing the hell out of them."

"There were many scenes where there weren't laughs or yucks, where there were things going on between people," says Lloyd. "There were some real moments. They weren't just written to get a yuck every second."

"*Taxi* was where I learned," says Ken Estin, "it's where I started. Now that I've been in the business longer, I can see how unusual it was to get a close group of people like that. It really was like an extended family. I know that's clichéd, but it was less of a business atmosphere than anyplace I've ever worked."

"It *was* like a big family," says Marilu Henner. "It was like a playground or something. There were no egos on the show—everyone was part of the same team, it was like a repertory company. We all supported each other—this week you're the lead, the next week you're not. It was never the feeling like, 'Better watch out for the other guy.' "

"The thing about *Taxi* that was truly, truly exciting," says Carol Kane, "is that the writers were *so* incredible that you absolutely knew with complete comfort that by Friday night, whatever was wrong would be fixed." She smiles. "And now that I'm out in the cold, cold world, I recognize that treasure even more than I did then. I had already done a lot of movies by the time I did *Taxi,* so I had an idea of how fortunate I was. Because movies often don't get fixed if they don't work. You put on some sleight of hand or attempt to disguise the fact that a certain moment hasn't been properly constructed for your character. But with *Taxi,* the [writing] teams would just keep writing till it was fixed."

Out in the cold, cold world she talks about, the *Taxi* alumni are mostly doing well. Christopher Lloyd broke through as a star character actor with the film *Back to the Future,* and Danny DeVito has become the movies' most unlikely looking leading man. Tony Danza, after a couple of down years that reached a nadir with a well-publicized brawl and conviction, has since become the star of a hit sitcom, *Who's the Boss?* Judd Hirsch finally won his Tony Award and took *I'm Not Rappaport* from Broadway to a national tour. Marilu Henner is all over the movies and cable; so is Carol Kane, after having co-starred in the well-received series *All Is Forgiven.* Jeff Conaway was in the cast of a couple of series and does TV guest spots and B-movies. Randy Carver performs with comedy groups in Los Angeles and in TV movies and pilots from time to time. Andy Kaufman passed away in 1984. Jim Brooks has become a major filmmaker; Ed Weinberger cocreated *The Cosby Show* and just about everything else on television; Dave Davis is retired; and Stan Daniels, at work on a musical, is semi-retired. Some stay in touch, some don't.

"I still see Tony and Danny some," says Lloyd. "I haven't spoken to Marilu or Judd in a while."

He smiles. "Marilu's great." Henner keeps in touch with Danza, DeVito, and Brooks, and Jim Burrows recently directed the pilot for her unsold series, *Channel 99.* "I have such a special love for all those guys on the show, and they for me, because we've all been through this." Carol Kane, in between globe-hopping from feature to feature, says she still sees Brooks and DeVito and Danza frequently, and went to the wedding of Ed Weinberger and Carlene Watkins one New Year's Eve.

Conaway says he and Danza "kept in touch for a long time, but lately we haven't. Things just happen that way. Last year [1986] he called me up and the first thing I heard was [doing a perfect Danza impression], 'Hey, ya gotta do me a favor, ya gotta do my show. But I gotta tell ya, it's not a very big part, it's only four or five lines. But if you can do it, I can get better guest stars on my show.' So I said sure, why not? I'm a friend, I don't care. I haven't actually seen Tony in about a year, though." Randy Carver still runs into Danza around town, "and we still say hello and give each other hugs. Still feels like he's in top shape. Chris Lloyd saw me perform with an improv group at a comedy club on Sunset [Blvd.], and he gave me a hug and was very supportive. I haven't seen anyone else much. It seems when you work that closely and intensely together on a show that you become like a family, and then you go off to do another project and have to start over and build new emotional bonds with other people. It's kind of the dippy part of the business. It leaves a void."

When *Taxi* first wrapped, Jim Brooks and Ken Estin talked about doing a *Taxi* movie. Ed Weinberger has since vetoed the idea, but in our interviews with the cast, nearly everyone wanted to know if we'd heard about a *Taxi* reunion. "Maybe it's just that people hear of the book and that stirs up the idea," suggests Chris Lloyd. He smiles. "I know *I'd* love to do one." Stan Rosenfeld, Danny DeVito's manager, calls *Taxi* "a perfect show for a reunion. You could build a story around any of them."

"We were gonna pick up their lives sometime in the future," says Estin. "Alex might still be a cabbie, maybe one of the others, probably Louie's still there, but the rest would have gotten out. We were seriously discussing it, but Jim was busy with *Terms of Endearment,* and ever since then, it's just been too hectic, and everyone's gone their own way. Still, you never know." It wouldn't be the first time a feature film spun-off from a TV show—witness something called *Star Trek.* And if Andy of Mayberry could return in one of the highest-rated TV movies ever . . . like the man said, you never know.

That was the great thing about *Taxi,* after all. Unlike its real-life namesake, it never took you where you expected.

A TAXI DRIVER'S BIOGRAPHIES

checkered pattern graphic

I'm a New York cabbie. I work long hours all over the mean streets of this rambunctious city. I'll take a fare anywhere to make a buck—uptown, downtown, crosstown, midtown, Chinatown, even Jersey. And I'll pick up anybody—doctors, lawyers, models, pimps, hookers, sleazeballs, dental hygienists. Don't matter to me.

Lately I haven't been able to sleep. So I've taken to writing a journal—taxi memoirs. A lot of them are sick, venal—someday a real writer will come along and type the graffiti off these pages.

But a lot of the memories have been special. Memories of regular people with a gift. A gift to make us laugh, cry, even reevaluate our own murky pathos. These are people who count on both hands and still leave big tips. They've made my hacking worth remembering. Especially in my memories of— *Taxi.*

RANDALL CARVER

I knew he was from the Panhandle region the moment I saw him trying to flag me down on 42nd Street and Eighth Avenue. His kind could fly around the world with stopovers in Katmandu and Brussels and *still* end up at Port Authority.

When he got in my cab and asked if I had change of a fifty, déjà vu set in like mold on a three-month-old loaf of bread. I bet myself a Sabrett's to a steak that this was John Burns—or rather, Randall Carver, the actor who played that lost soul on the first season of *Taxi.*

When I asked him if I'd won my own bet, his eyes lit up like an electric plant from a Godzilla movie.

"I get recognized on the street more so *now* than when I was actually *on* the show ten years ago," Randall explained in a voice deeper and fuller than I'd remembered. "I found that people in L.A. who are in the business don't watch TV as much as other people because of their schedules—they do most of their business at night. And actors don't have their TVs readily available like they would if they worked nine-to-five jobs. But people manage to catch the reruns, so most of the industry knows who I am. Those who aren't sure tend to look at me like they know me from *somewhere,* like we went to high school together, or we're related. At least they remember me in a warm, positive sense."

This was true. Randy Carver had that easygoing, everyman approach to life as well as to his work. The character of John Burns *was* lame compared to a flamboyant Louie or an out-there Latka, but he could have had his space to grow into a more definite role as the out-of-towner caught in his own *Twilight Zone* episode.

"I found that after the first six, seven episodes my character wasn't growing," he observed. "It was in the writing, like they didn't know what to do with him. They started fine, but that's as far as it went. He was just *there.* But John was the only character who [was new to] New York, and they should have played that up more. I mean, there are a lot of people from the Midwest who don't know what it's like to be in a big city. They should have explored John's newness to living in New York City. There are a lot of physical problems to it, you know. John fit in, but not really well."

Before I could ask him about his acting background, he remembered his audition for *Taxi.*

"Joel Thurm, the casting director back then, didn't think I was right for the role. But my agent persisted and contacted Ed Weinberger, who said

Randall Carver.

fine, send him in. So I read for the part about five times, and they liked me a lot but couldn't get network approval on me. So they had me come in and help with a videotape audition for another actor who was reading for the part of Alex. And it was because of my reading *there* that they went ahead and got network approval and signed me. By then, everyone else except Jeff [Conaway] and myself had already been cast.''

Despite myself, I found that Randy Carver had an interesting and varied background.

He was born May 25, 1948, in Fort Worth, Texas, and adopted by Russell and Virginia Carver of the town of Canadian. His father was a businessman who co-owned an International Harvester dealership and later became a banker. An only child, Randy's first experience on stage was at the age of seven in a local curtain-club presentation of *Rest Assured.* Since his mother was active in community theater, he volunteered to hold scripts for her while she memorized her lines, and he readily mugged for his grandfather's home movies. As he grew up, Randy was always into public speaking, church affairs, and summer workshops. He attended Missouri Military Academy and after graduating was signed for a small role in the Oscar-winning film *Midnight Cowboy.*

''I worked ten days and had one line in that movie,'' he recounted, ''when they filmed those early scenes in Texas. My scenes were mostly with Jon Voight and Jennifer Salt.''

Randy entered the U.S. Army, was stationed at Fort Knox, Kentucky, and Fort Hood, Texas, and served for two years as a tank platoon leader in the Demilitarized Zone in Korea. ''I was Second Platoon Leader with 'C' Company, Second Battalion, 72nd Armor, Second Infantry Division for one year and one day—and I was only twenty-three. We ran combat missions in the DMZ, as well as guarding strategic bridges,'' he told me proudly.

Upon returning from Korea, Randy was accepted for graduate studies at UCLA's Theatre Arts Program. Back in the field, he was cast in the feature *Time to Run* and amassed a huge list of TV guest credits. He was also signed on as a series regular on Norman Lear's *Forever Fernwood,* playing, ironically, a character named Jeffrey DeVito. After *Taxi,* Randy costarred as straight-arrow Lt. Vaughn

Beuhler in television's first-ever Vietnam War series, *Six O'Clock Follies,* as well as the TV movies *The Daughters of Joshua Cabe Return* and *The New Daughters of Joshua Cabe.* (What? Was he one of the daughters?) Nicely against type, he played a killer in the TV movie *Detour to Terror* with O. J. Simpson as a cross-country bus driver and Lorenzo Lamas as a fellow hijacker.

''I got to shoot a guy in the back in that film,'' he said, smiling devilishly, ''but I played the killer just like me, only with a gun. I didn't play it satanic or evil, I just played him like a John Burns who didn't feel anything about shooting people.''

Lately he's been doing L.A. clubs with an improv group and played in the Charles Bronson movie *Murphy's Law* and in a made-for-TV movie, *Flag.* He also starred in the independent series pilot *Those Days.*

''My career has been continuous, if not real strong,'' he admitted. Yet Randy reeked of determination. He was out there, honing his skills at L.A.'s Theatre East, where he'd been a member for sixteen years, and was teaching an acting class.

As we reached our destination, I asked Randy if he had fond or bitter recollections of *Taxi.*

''I look back, and I think I did some nice stuff in some really difficult situations and circumstances,'' he told me as I gave him change for one of his three fifties. ''If I could go back and do it differently, I don't think I would. How I played it was true to my own personal creativity at that time and space. That year on *Taxi* was a great time for me. I got to work with the best people in the business, and it was just a great learning experience.''

JEFF CONAWAY

Times Square was alive with the sound of music, if you wanna call it that, from boom-boxes, cheap speakers outside of souvenir holes-in-the-wall, and peep-show circuses promising live girls for the price of a shoeshine. It was a dull, hot, moist August day, and you couldn't keep your neck dry with a beach towel. Even in sunlight, Broadway looked like the set of *Blade Runner.*

Yet these white, shiny, sweaty streets were filled with a special breed of people; people carrying

Jeff Conaway.

oversized portfolios, people who were impeccably coiffed, people with a Fosse beat to their steps. These people were the actors and actresses of New York, on their way to or from that *one* audition that would change their lives.

I was cruising in my cab, looking for an air-conditioned phone booth, when a leather portfolio struck my windshield. Since I hadn't made enough money that week to buy a secondhand harmonica, I braked and let this anxious passenger in. He was tall, wiry, with long, shaggy-dog hair that blocked my rearview mirror. He was handsome, eternally young, with a golden tan and a three-day stubble. His white linen jacket, jeans, and sockless loafers gave him the look of a skid-row Sonny Crockett. He had a jittery manner, but a warm smile. He belonged on Broadway. After he spoke, telling me he was on his way back home to the Coast, I knew for sure my fare was Jeff Conaway, who played Bobby Wheeler on three seasons of *Taxi*.

Conaway's Wheeler was the consummate struggling actor, a textbook example of what a New York thespian has to go through to survive in that low-blow business called *show*. Wheeler, like Banta, was about the most true-to-life character on *Taxi*, and Conaway's rendition was maybe more honest than Dustin Hoffman's portrayal of a similar character in *Tootsie*.

Of course, Jeff, who was born in New York City, ate all these accolades up, and getting him to talk career was easier than buttering toast.

"I always thought I'd be forty years old before I had any real success. Right now I think I'm very close to accepting the potential that I have, to be able to deal with it and my personal life." Since it wouldn't be long until October 5, 1988 rolled around and he'd turn thirty-eight, I guessed that meant he believed in numbers. I did, too. I just hoped he could figure out a 15 or 20 percent tip. But it looked like he was gonna pay more attention to my questions than to the meter.

"I really felt embarrassed a lot of the time on *Taxi*, because of the jokes that were made about actors," he told me defensively. "I tried to sit in on the writing meetings, but they told me, 'You can't—we say things in there you might take the wrong way.' I'm not a writer, but I had ideas, and

maybe I could have learned what the real process was and used it.

"It was an ensemble show, and I appreciated that going in. I didn't mind having only five lines as long as those five lines meant something, did something for the character, show a side that maybe you didn't see before. I really believe that it wasn't so much an ego thing as it was that I wanted to feel as if I were doing something worthwhile. See, not being basically a happy person, acting was the only thing that made me feel like I was worth anything."

I wondered if I were treading on bald tires. Even though Jeff was an integral part of *Taxi*, he *did* leave the show to pursue other things, and everyone was happy about his decision. I decided to save the yang and asked about the ying—how he got the part of Bobby Wheeler.

It took Conaway four red lights, one Con Ed barricade, and two unfiltered cigarettes on my part for him to get to his involvement with *Taxi*. Conaway was a hot property after having played Kenickie in the hugely successful film, *Grease*. (He'd played the lead role of Danny Zuko for two-and-a-half years on broadway while John Travolta, a friend with whom he shared a manager, played

---

BOBBY WHEELER'S KNOWN ACTING JOBS

Commercials:
Athlete's foot medication
Suntan lotion
Brickhauser Beer
Two days on the soap opera *For Better For Worse*
In an unnamed, quick-closing experimental play
As Biff in the 88th Street Actors' Workshop production of *Death of a Salesman*
Stalled, an experimental play produced in Brooklyn
Under the Yum-Yum Tree: Month-long Florida tour, from which he was fired before opening night
Charles Darwin Tonight, a one-man play
Boise, a successful TV pilot, from which he was let go after it was picked up as a series

Jeff Conaway: "Acting was the only thing that made me feel I was worth anything."

Doody in the chorus.) Paramount, which distributed *Grease,* got interested in him. From the sound of things, I got the feeling that he felt it was about time, too.

"I was your usual broke actor, and I was tired of being broke," he said. Right. Tell me about broke. But damned if he wasn't on the level. "My managers didn't want me to work because they knew the movie was coming out and they didn't want me taking just anything. But I'd say, 'Hey, listen, I gotta eat! You guys wanna put me up or what?' " He laughed.

"So now [major TV producer] Aaron Spelling has a series he wants me to do—*Beach Patrol,* like a new *Mod Squad.* [It aired as an unsold TV-movie pilot in 1979.] My managers called Paramount and said, 'If you don't want him to do this series, then pay him some money not to do it.' So they offered me $25,000 not to work in TV for anyone else and to pick something I wanted at Paramount."

He took them up on it and spent the time looking at countless scripts and development projects, finally doing a TV movie. He was offered TV series,

naturally, including the *Saturday Night Fever* clone *Makin' It,* and then found Paramount's *Taxi.*

Turns out Jeff had done an episode of *The Mary Tyler Moore Show,* and *Taxi* was the product of the same guys. He went up at first for the part of John Burns, which eventually went to Randall Carver. "But then one day I got the whole script and became real interested in the actor character, then called Bobby Taylor. And [the producers] said they had been thinking along those same lines, so I read again.

"Later I got a call from [original casting director] Joel Thurm, who says, 'Well, it's not good news, but it's not bad news either.' He says I'm the only choice for a white actor, but that they'd had a meeting and thought that maybe Bobby should be black and that now they were looking at black actors. I couldn't believe it! It was like, 'God, why are you doing this to me!' " He laughed.

"So I went back to read, and it was me, Cleavon Little, and somebody else, both of whom *freaked* when I walked in. Anyway, I ended up reading with Judd and it went really well."

According to Conaway, the deal he had with Paramount was for him to share star billing above the title with Judd Hirsch. On the last day before they were going to shoot the first episode, he said, they called him and said they couldn't do it anymore because of a clause in Judd's contract. Instead of rocking the boat, Conaway diplomatically opted for the first co-star billing.

Without my having to ask the touchy question, Conaway selflessly went into the reasons behind his leaving *Taxi.*

"I wanted to do things with Bobby, but as the show went on, I could see I wasn't going to get that chance. For instance, Bobby and Tony were supposed to be best friends. So why couldn't they have had Bobby call up Tony when he had a problem or just to say, 'How ya' doin', man, you need anything?'

"Lemme tell you—I loved Bobby, I identified with Bobby. So yeah, I kind of took everything personally. I had a lot of meetings with [the producers] because I was unhappy. I asked if there were something I could do to make Bobby Wheeler a nicer person. And to be honest, it was also hard for me because ever since I was a kid, I'd been doing lead roles, so it was a little difficult all of a sudden to have just five lines. Sure, partially it was ego, but let me *do* what I *do* best. It was frustrating. I remember leaving the studio feeling really guilty and unhappy. I just couldn't appreciate it and use it just as a job, as a learning experience. Instead I saw it as, 'Hey, anybody could do this character.' Like nobody else could do Louie or Jim, they were such defined characters. But Bobby—anybody could walk in and say, 'Hi, Alex.' "

The heat didn't make the ride to the airport any easier. Traffic wasn't murder, it was genocide. The humidity was thick enough to build a condo on. I took off my cap and wiped my forehead. None of this *miseria* seemed to bother Conaway, who was as cool as a cucumber and twice as fresh.

His background was as varied as the Sunday *Times*'s classifieds. His father was an actor, producer, and publisher, and though his parents were divorced when he was three, he lived with a mother talented in both acting and music—at one point, she taught at New York's Brook Conservatory. At the age of ten, Jeff accompanied Mom to a call for Arthur Penn's Broadway production of *All the Way Home.* He ended up with a featured role as one of four young boys, in a company that included Colleen Dewhurst, Lillian Gish, and Arthur Hill. He stayed with it for its entire year-long run and then traveled with the national company of *Critic's Choice.*

When he returned to New York, he worked as a child model and enrolled in the Quintano School for Young Professionals, where he began to learn guitar. At fifteen, he and four friends formed a rock group called 3½, opening for the likes of Chuck Berry and Gladys Knight and the Pips. When the group disbanded, Conaway attended the North Carolina School for the Arts, later transferring to New York University, where he learned body movement from Martha Graham. While at NYU he appeared in numerous commercials and had the lead in a school production of *The Threepenny Opera.* Then came *Grease,* and by the time he was twenty, Conaway made his feature film debut in *Jennifer on My Mind* (1971), the cast of which included a bit player named Robert De Niro. At twenty-one, he had a short-lived marriage to a dancer he'd been seeing for two years, but it didn't work out and was annulled.

Jeff Conaway as Bobby Wheeler.

His career, on the other hand, was getting hotter than my hood. He had a run of movies, TV shows, and TV movies after that, breaking into the small screen in 1974, and he does TV and direct-to-video movies today. After *taxi,* he starred in the fantasy-adventure series *Wizards and Warriors* and played a womanizing heel in the cast of a prime-time soap called *Berrenger's.*

During his stint on *Taxi,* Conaway also kept getting TV and film offers. One particular movie deal was supposed to pay him, he says, almost *two years* of *Taxi* salary. "But they wouldn't let me out to do the movie," he told me. "Paramount had originally told me they'd find a way to let me out to do films, but when I finally got the chance I couldn't get out of the show." Somewhere, somehow, someday, his managers and Paramount couldn't work out a deal suitable to everybody. Before Conaway could say, "Hi, Alex," he was out of the show.

"Ed Weinberger called me and said he thought I was really making a mistake," Conaway told me in almost a whisper. "He pitched me on coming back and doing guest shots. I just started crying, I got so emotional. See, Bobby Wheeler *could* have left for weeks or months, as actors do—*that* was the essence of the character, and it paralleled my real life. It made sense to have Bobby come and go. But then you get into professional jealousy. Like, 'Well, if he can do it, why can't I do it?' They already had to deal with the fact that Andy had a special arrangement.

"I just wasn't together then," he admitted to me. "I should have phoned each person and talked to them and explained that this was what I had to do for myself, and I hope you understand.

"*Taxi* did give me a chance to diversify, to do things like the mime bit or the Shakespeare bit. I just didn't see it then. I'm glad I understand this now, 'cause life was hell. That experience on *Taxi*

THE RECORDS

Jeff Conaway
Producers: Mike Appel and Louis Lahav
Assistant Producers: Robert Martinot and Bob Brody
1979. Columbia JC 36111

Songs
City Boy
   (P. Floyd, C. J. Ellis, M. Appel)
Livin' on the Edge of Love
   (P. Floyd, M. Appel)
Oh It's So Easy to Fall in Love (But It's So Hard to Fall Out Once You're In)
   (P. Floyd, C. J. Ellis)
No Getting Over You
   (P. Floyd, C. J. Ellis)
She Must've Had Her Reasons
   (P. Floyd, C. J. Ellis)
Fever in the Blood
   (P. Floyd, C. J. Ellis, M. Appel)
Still in Love With You
   (R. Javors)
I Ain't Nobody's Fool
   (P. Floyd, M. Appel)
I'll Love You Again
   (P. Floyd, C. J. Ellis, M. Appel)
I Don't Want to Be Alone Tonight
   (P. Floyd, R. Deans, M. Appel)

The Musicians
Keyboards and synthesizers: Skip Anderson
Guitar: Stephen Cavaretta, Abdul Zuhri, Louis Lahav, Nick Moroch
Pedal Steel Guitar: Mark Horowitz
Bass: Ivan Elias, Andy Oleartchik
Drums: Omar Kahin, J. T. Lewis
Percussion: Sammy Figueroa, Jose Rossy
Sax: Andy Statman, David Luell
Background Vocals: AURA, Jim Haas, Jon Joyce, Stan Farber

Bob James: *The Genie: Themes and Variations from the TV Series TAXI*
Producer/Arranger: Bob James
Associate Producer: Joe Jorgensen
Special Thanks to Dave Davis, Diane Brooks, and Richard Sakai
May 1983. Tappan Zee/Columbia FC 38678

All songs composed and arranged by Bob James
Brooklyn Heights Boogie
The Genie
Last Chance
Ballade
Groove for Julie
Hello Nardo
The Marilu
New York Mellow
Night Moods
Angela (Theme from TAXI)*
*This short (2:30) version has the "Goodnight, Mr. Walters" voiceover at the end. The song originally appeared—without the voiceover—in a 5:42 version on Bob James's *Touchdown* album (1978). A 7:17 live version, recorded at The Bottom Line in New York, appears on James's double album *All Around the Town* (1981).

The Musicians
Keyboards and synthesizers: Bob James
Guitar: Eric Gale, Steve Khan
Bass: Gary King
Drums: Peter Erskine, Steve Gadd, Sticks McElhiney, Idris Muhammad, Alan Schwartzberg, Buddy Williams
Percussion: Leonard "Doc" Gibbs, Jimmy Maelen, Ralph MacDonald
Vibes: Dave Friedman
Trumpets: Randy Brecker, Mike Lawrence, Marvin Stamm
Reeds: Michael Brecker, Eddie Daniels, George Marge, Tom Scott

Bob James: *The Genie: Themes and Variations from the TV Series* Taxi (Columbia Records, 1983).

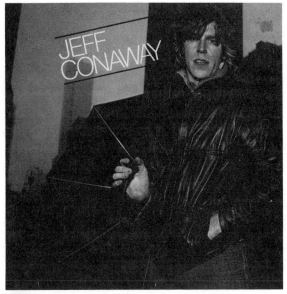

Jeff Conaway on his 1979 debut album, *Jeff Conaway* (Columbia Records, 1979).

helped me realize something about myself, that I could have a real life instead of constantly battling myself. I mean, I'll get up and run an obstacle course, but you've got to have yourself together to run that course." Part of that course involved stabilizing his relationship with his son and his one-time significant other, Rona John, older sister of Olivia Newton-John. He married his present wife, Kerri, in 1990, just before a drunk-driving accident that broke a bicyclist's leg and spurred Conaway to recover from longtime drug and alcohol abuse.

Besides slinging sausages in a hash house or mixing martinis in a gin mill, most actors support themselves between gigs by driving cabs. At least back then, anyway. That was one of the most believable things about Bobby Wheeler. Yet according to Conaway, Bobby Wheeler couldn't grow as a person because he *hated* being a cabdriver.

"I've never had to really drive a cab or do anything else but act," he told me as we neared the airport. "I mean, I wouldn't *do* anything else. I was lucky enough to always get sufficient work and go on and act and study."

Another side of Conaway was his rock'n'roll. Currently working on new material for an upcom-

ing album, he had had a seven-album deal with Columbia Records in 1978, about halfway through his first season of *Taxi*. But only one album, *Jeff Conaway,* came out of it.

"I got out of the contract because Columbia didn't do anything with the first album," he said. "Mike Appel, who was Bruce Springsteen's first manager, was one of my album's producers. I think Columbia's falling out with him [Appel had been involved in a lawsuit with Columbia and Springsteen for years, finally settling out of court] had a lot to do with it. I just got caught in the middle.

"It was a good album, it got great reviews— except for *People* magazine. But if the label wasn't going to promote me, I just didn't want to make the effort to do another LP. Again, the thought processes were wrong. It should've been: 'Go, use their money, do the next LP and the rest. Sooner or later, something's gonna happen.' "

As we reached the terminal, I rehashed my impressions of Jeff Conaway. The guy was alright. He'd bared his soul to me and been straight about his successes *and* his failures. In my racket, I hear from all kinds of Bobby Wheelers and Dealers, but Conaway was the real thing. And on a hot day like this, that was refreshing.

Tony Danza.

TONY DANZA

ROUND ONE

The guy in the back seat of my cab was as big as a baby grand. I felt like charging him for excess luggage. He was a retired pugilist, an Irish middleweight by the name of Phil Ryan. He'd fallen on hard times and was looking to make a comeback as a manager, and now, he wanted to go to the Gramercy Gym.

The Gramercy! Hidden in plain sight on East 14th Street. Anybody who had delusions of being a boxer knew it was there, three stories up, between what was once the great Lüchow's Restaurant and what is now The Palladium disco. May's Department Store was gone, as well as S. Klein's. Now rummies, yuppies, thrift shoppers, and shoplifters were all that adorned the area. The gym was the only impregnable survivor on the block, and Ryan had enough brains left to go back to where he belonged.

He got out of my hack, slipped me a pound, and shook my hand. I felt like I was in a Mixmaster.

As the old pug turned away, a lithe figure danced out the door of the building and into the street. He was shadowboxing to an invisible Walkman that played the rattle of a speedbag, the skip of a rope, and the ringing of a bell. Ryan looked a hundred years old next to this youthful contender. I didn't place the Italian-looking middleweight right away. I knew I'd seen him before on television, but was it on the ropes, or in the arms of a slender, classy broad?

He smiled, perfect teeth, and dodged and drifted into the back seat of my cab. He was tan, surprisingly tall and hefty, with wispy hair cut shorter than I'd remembered. He was wearing a gray New York Rangers T-shirt and baggy green sweat pants. It wasn't until he spoke, telling me he wanted to go to a Feast in Little Italy, that I placed him. Geez, I deserved a one-way ticket to Palookaville. This wasn't a fighter anymore—this was Tony Danza, "da actor." A mere ten years ago, Danza couldn't act his way out of a paper bag, but here he was, a Nielsen's champ.

ROUND TWO

In that respect, Danza has always been one lucky *paisan*—first as Tony Banta for five years on *Taxi*, and now trying to break that record as Tony Micelli on *Who's the Boss?*. It can safely be said that Danza is now a TV superstar. Yet the Brooklyn-born Italian wore his modesty on his cuff, at least with me. (From what I hear about the *Who's the Boss?* set, he mostly just cuffs.) In our ride together, Danza was cordial, funny, sentimental about his *Taxi* years, and way down to earth.

ROUND THREE

To make a short story long, let's get Danza's acting credentials out of the way. Besides his two hit TV shows, he's tag-teamed for a lot of ABC specials that weren't exactly world champs, to wit, *99 Ways to Attract the Right Man*. He started out in TV movies with the innocuous *Single Bars, Single Women* and *Murder Can Hurt You* (in which he did a hilariously accurate takeoff on Baretta), and then moved into dramatic roles with the well-regarded *Doing Life* (a fact-based story about the convict who studied law in prison to become the nation's first jailhouse lawyer) and *Freedom Fighter* (about a GI in 1961 Berlin, at the building of the Berlin Wall). His movie credits are undistinguished, however, and his theater credits are none. Shakespeare in the Park? He wouldn't know where to find it. Neither has he been in comedy troupes or improv groups, although he's naturally very quick and funny and did some great guest-hosting on *The Tonight Show*.

"Tony and I couldn't work more differently," I'd been told just the other day by Christine Lahti, the classically trained actress who glowed in the movie *Swing Shift* and costarred with Danza in *Single Bars, Single Women*. "I write journals about the character and her background, and I'm very preoccupied and concentrated. Tony is completely loose and joking with the crew and having a ball. But then when the scene starts, he's there—really there, moment to moment. He may not have been very experienced at acting, but he was very good at it."

That may explain why Tony Danza has become a household name without first having racked up earth-shaking credentials. He never went the acting-class route. His was the discovered-by-a-

TONY BANTA'S KNOWN BOUTS

After his final recorded fight, in episode #107 ("Tony's Baby"), Tony Banta's record stood at 9-25. Until his fight in episode #85 ("Tony's Comeback"), he'd been knocked out three times in his previous five fights, and fourteen times in his career.

This list is a compilation based on Tony Banta's references and bouts seen in the episodes. The win-loss statistics below are a running count of known decisions. Banta had several other fights in between these; the early fight with Manzo, for instance, was not his first.

Early Bouts
A boxer named Manzo, whom Tony beat on a TKO (1-0)
A boxer named Wilkes, whom Tony beat when his opponent took a dive (2-0)
Ron Thomas, to whom Tony lost (2-1)
Rocky Sinacori, who KO'd Tony in the second round (2-2)
A boxer named Rodriguez, to whom Tony lost (2-3)
A boxer named Jefferson, to whom Tony lost (2-4)
Two boxing brothers named Camilio, to whom Tony lost separately (2-6)

Bouts Occurring During the Run of the Series
An unnamed boxer to whom Tony lost on a TKO the night before episode #1 (2-7)
Frankie Wallace, to whom Tony lost (2-8)
The unnamed New Hampshire middleweight champ, to whom Tony lost (2-9)
Benny Foster, whom Tony KO'd (3-9)
An unnamed boxer whom Tony beat by default (4-9)
A boxer named Gomez, who KO'd Tony in the second round (4-10)
Rocky Sinacori: a rematch, no decision revealed
A boxer nicknamed Shotgun, who KO'd Tony in the first round (4-11)
Eddie "The Albany Assassin" Burke, whom Tony KO'd (5-11)
Dean "Big Bang" Gentry, to whom Tony lost on a decision (5-12)

Unaccounted for, including the Sinacori rematch, for which the decision isn't known, are seventeen fights comprising four wins and thirteen losses. It can be assumed that virtually all of these wins happened early in Banta's career, since (a) he otherwise could not have continued getting so many matches, (b) a mobster in "The Road Not Taken, Part I" (episode #89) speaks of Tony as a promising young boxer generally expected to win, and (c) by the time Tony was working at the Sunshine Cab Co., Louie could count on Banta's losing as a sure thing.

---

producer scenario, only without the soda fountain and the angora sweater.

ROUND FOUR

Tony Danza kids that his boyhood ambition was to stay out of jail. He was born April 21, 1951, in Brooklyn, and raised on Pitin Avenue in a tough Italian-Irish neighborhood by parents Ann and Matty Iadanza. (Tony dropped the "Ia" part when he was nicknamed "Tough Tony Danza" on boxing bills.) His father was a sanitation worker who was even tougher than Tony. The family—which included a younger brother, named Matty like his dad—eventually moved to suburban Lynbrook, Long Island, and from there to nearby Malverne. A born scrapper, Danza's early loves were sports, mostly wrestling, baseball, and football. To him, boxing wasn't a sport—it was a way of life on the streets.

He attended the University of Dubuque (Iowa) on a wrestling scholarship. There he met his future wife, Rhonda, whom he married when he was just eighteen and from whom he was separated after two years, he says. They have a son, Marc Anthony, who as a child appeared twice on *Taxi*. Danza married second wife Tracy Robinson on June 20, 1986; they have two daughters, the eldest of whom inspired the name of Danza's production company, Katie Face.

Tony came back from college with a degree in social studies and education. He tried such odd jobs as furniture-moving and bartending and helping to run a car wash his family pressured him into buying a piece of. He even thought of driving a cab, but his parents strenuously objected.

Around this time, some friends signed him up for boxing's amateur Golden Gloves competition, sponsored by the New York *Daily News*. "My pals told me, 'You're a tough guy, let's see how rough you *really* are.' " In two years, first as a light heavyweight and then as middleweight, Danza proudly claims he "had nine fights in the Golden Gloves and won seven. I was in the semifinals my first year, 1975. But I have no delusions," he amends. "I was a club fighter; I was nobody. It was only *after* that everybody got interested in me as a fighter."

That fact makes it difficult to get a clear handle on Tony's professional record. It's been given in some biographies as eight wins and three losses, yet Danza himself claims 12–3. The New York State Athletic Commission has him as 7–2, but that's only for fights in New York State (see "Tony Danza's Real-Life Boxing Record"). Calls to New Jersey and Pennsylvania didn't turn him up in those states, and—his having been one of hundreds of unknown club fighters—the authoritative but hardly exhaustive *Ring Encyclopedia* doesn't list him. Danza told me, "I fought all over—Jersey, Phoenix even. But I was mostly a New York guy. Never lost in Brooklyn, but I went to Dover and got my ass kicked!" His last fight was at the Madison Square Garden's Felt Forum in 1979, just six days after his twenty-eighth birthday, and a couple of months after the first season of *Taxi* had made him a star. As "the actor-boxer," he got paid $10,000 for the main event, and knocked out Max "Sonny" Hord in the first round.

He told me a story about the old days, now, about a sports promoter and old friend named Cha Cha, who presently runs a restaurant on Mulberry Street. "Cha Cha was a big help in my life," Danza remembered gratefully. "In fact, when I was broke, he bought me a seventy-dollar [sports] cup. Yeah, that sounds funny," he admitted when I broke into a little laugh, "but I couldn't afford it! It was expensive, seventy bucks to me back then." I asked him what he did before Cha Cha's largesse. "Whaddya think? I was fighting *without* a cup, or

TONY DANZA'S REAL-LIFE BOXING RECORD

The New York State Athletic Commission record of Middleweight Tony Danza: Given name, Anthony Iadanza; weight 160; license issued 9/7/76; managed by Joseph M. Gentile of Waterbury, Connecticut. This is a record of bouts in the state of New York (7–2). Danza had no recorded bouts in New Jersey or Pennsylvania.

DATE	PLACE	OPPONENT	DECISION		
			Won	Loss	Draw
8/13/76*	NYC (Queens)	Earl Harris	TKO1		
10/1/76**	NYC (Queens)	Johnny Locicero		KO1	
5/5/77	Comack, NY	Thomas E. Molloy	TKO3		
5/24/77	White Plains, NY	Joseph Mascetta	TKO1		
9/9/77	Nanuet, NY	Ricky Garcia	KO1		
11/9/77**	Westchester County, NY	Morris A. Watkins		TKO2	
12/21/77	NYC	Sugar Ray Bryant	KO1		
5/26/78	NYC	Billy Perez	KO1		
4/27/79	NYC (Felt Forum)	Max A. Hord	KO1		

Numbers following TKO and KO represent the number of the round in which the decision took place.
   TKO   Technical Knockout;   KO   Knockout
   *Before receiving his license, Danza fought legally on a temporary permit.
   **Temporarily suspended afterward due to injury; reinstated

a cheap one. Lemme tell ya, the first time ya get hit in the balls, you ask yourself, 'WHY did I buy that cheap cup?!' ''

It was while working out at the Gramercy Gym that an independent producer named Stuart Sheslow, checking out boxers for a *Rocky*-era movie, became impressed with Danza's look and charisma. He asked Tony to screen test. As Danza so eloquently put it, ''Stu at the time was just a guy that came into the gym; he couldn't rub two quarters together then anymore than I could, but he was looking to do this boxing thing.'' It was to have been called *Augie,* and as Danza described it, was ''sorta like *Chico and the Man* meets *Rocky.* It never got off the ground, but he always remembered me and kept pushing me and pushing me until [he became an ABC executive] and got me that [series] pilot,'' a sitcom called *Fast Lane Blues,* for which Danza reportedly was paid $5,000. ''The pilot didn't get picked up, but I got noticed a little bit. By then Stu had become a network bigwig, and he really believed in me.''

Danza laughed. He was always laughing while reminiscing. And why not? His was a Cinderella story with a left hook. A kid who made $40 on his first fight, Danza was suddenly being offered figures he couldn't count. ''They gave me three thousand dollars to move!'' He grinned, still not believing it. ''To come to L.A. ! Unbelievable!''

But wait—it gets better. After the pilot divebombed, Danza returned to New York and went back to the gym. Sheslow kept wheeling and dealing and arranged for Danza to meet with the New York producers of a now-cult film called *The Warriors.* I remembered the movie, one of director Walter Hill's best. It had a great ensemble cast of young unknowns such as Michael Beck, David Patrick Kelly, and James Remar, who now are all costars on schlock TV shows or guest stars who sneer a lot. That could have been Danza's fate, but something called *Taxi* steered him away.

''I went to an open call for *The Warriors* in New York,'' Danza remembered. ''I was supposed to play the part of 'Cowboy,' '' which went instead to an actor named Tom McKitterick. ''So I read for it. I wasn't too sure about my acting abilities, but I knew I could fight, so I brought this poster from my first main event, fightin' on Manhattan Cable.

And I told 'em, 'You really want to see a warrior, come down and see me fight.' So they did—Walter Hill, [producer] Larry Gordon, whole bunch of 'em. I knocked a guy out [Sugar Ray Bryant] in forty seconds. Larry Gordon said it was the greatest audition of his life.''

Taxi intervened, however. At the suggestion of casting director Joel Thurm, Jim Brooks had made a videotape of Danza in New York. Danza then went to Los Angeles for *The Warriors,* and while ''at Paramount, gettin' costumed for *The Warriors,* I'm called upstairs.'' Brooks had Tony read for the part of Irish boxer Phil Ryan—a part that eventually became Italian boxer Tony Banta (the last name taken from sometime-scriptwriter and show assistant Gloria Banta).

In essence, Danza was not just cast in *Taxi,* but typecast. Yet all those years at the Gramercy and the nearby Gleason's Gym gave Danza experience no acting class could teach.

''I trained with Chicky Ferrar at Gleason's, and then I went with Tony Canzi,'' he recounted sadly, saying their names in a proud whisper. ''Those were great years, man. Tony's dead, Chicky's dead, all the guys who were there when I was training have passed away. It was a great experience with all those old-timers. What was great was that to play a boxer after having been with all those old-timers, you get that much more depth. You really get to see things with the old guys that you don't see with the young guys.''

ROUND FIVE

Traffic on Mott Street was so thick you'd think the pope was blessing every car. We could smell the Feast from where we sat, and Danza would have gotten there quicker by walking. But he hung in and just stared out the window. After a few moments, he shook his head and said, ''God—*Taxi.*'' For once, I didn't have any witticism or gaudy patter. I felt the same way.

So did his costars, who warmly reminisced about the guy. ''On the set, Tony was always getting into trouble,'' Marilu Henner said with a giggle. ''His pranks were legend.'' Referring to Danza's conviction for assaulting a security guard in a brawl at New York's Mayflower Hotel on February 3, 1984,

Marilu had called him, "poor baby. At least he didn't have to go to jail." Accompanying Danza that night was his friend Albert Sinacori, whose name Tony used for an opponent on *Taxi*. Tony was sentenced to three years' probation and 250 hours of community service, which he completed at Bellevue Hospital in Manhattan and The Jewish Home and Hospital for the Aged up in a ritzy section of the Bronx.

Chris Lloyd had told me that when he started on *Taxi*, he naturally felt like an outsider. "Tony was great," said the normally very shy Chris. "He helped to make me feel like I belonged there. He put me at ease." Director Jim Burrows called Danza, "just a kid in a grown-up's body."

Jeff Conaway and Danza were buddies on and off the show. "Tony loved doing *Taxi*," Conaway had told me. "He was in heaven. He'd always say, 'You'll have to pick me up and drag me kicking and screaming outta here!' Tony and I were always goofing, writing graffiti all over the back of the set, running around the lot, having fun. Lotta women— though we basically didn't compete for them."

Danza's prodigious womanizing included dating shapely actress Teri Copley (*We Got It Made*) and even costar Marilu Henner briefly, and for a long time Danza lived with *Taxi* assistant Robin Chambers and her teenage daughter. In between relationships, he said, smiling wickedly, "Jeff and I chased everything that moved! I mean, five years in a series—you go to the bar and you could have *anybody*. I used to go home alone 'cause I couldn't make up my mind!"

ROUND SIX

On *Who's the Boss?*, Danza and his attractive co-star, Judith Light, have an on-going chemistry that has kept the show interestingly sexy. On *Taxi*, Tony Banta occasionally had girl friends, but it wasn't until the last season that anything serious developed. On two episodes, Banta had a more rugged than sexy relationship with Vicky DeStefano (Anne De Salvo), to whom he proposed in "Tony's Baby" (episode #107).

A boyish Tony Danza: "It was, like, where do *I* come in?"

"The way I saw it," said Danza, "was that if Tony got married to Vicky, they'd have done the same thing to him they did to [Randy] Carver"— write the married couple out of the show. Still, "I never really thought they were tryin' to get rid of me by marrying me off or shipping me to Singapore [episode #98]. First of all, they knew I'd haunt them," he said with a chuckle. "Secondly, they knew one of my uncles would be coming by to see them," he added, jokingly—I think. In any case, this was already toward the end of the fifth season. "There was some talk that we were getting canceled anyway.

"In a way, I think *Taxi* had run its course," he said philosophically. "A lotta people were surprised, thinkin' it'd go a lot longer. Don't get me wrong, I woulda loved for it to have gone another ten years, but I thought we'd started to get a little bizarre there, the fifth season."

Since we were talking about cancellations, I brought up the infamous *Taxi* wake, the second part of which was held at Danza's house.

"That's right, we had a wake party at my crib," he answered, talking about it as if it had happened last night and why wasn't I there? "Had a taxi in a little coffin, everybody had candles. Really ironic, that it ended up being the greatest party. Went on till, like, 5:30 in the morning. I had to practically throw them out; nobody wanted to leave. It was really weird that we were celebrating our own demise. Everybody really loved each other. Everybody pulled for each other . . ."

THE FINAL DECISION

Amid a boatlift of cannoli-starved people, Danza breezed out of my hack. He clapped his hands, rubbed them together, and grinned a big oh-boy! It was like watching Tony Banta on any episode. Only this guy was ten years older, rougher around the edges, gruffer around the vocal cords, and smarter than he let on. He did a little tap dance and I lost him within seconds. The crowd ate him up, as if he were Ali leaving the ring after one of his more spectacular dances. The final decision on Danza? The card on his life deems him a "winnah"! And they say tough guys don't dance.

DANNY DEVITO

I. DISPATCHER BLUES

Down at the garage, we've all seen *Apocalypse Now*. We also live it. Our dispatcher is like the Robert Duvall character, Lt. Col. Kilgore—only instead of napalm, he loves the smell of exhaust in the morning. This guy hates everybody except himself. He runs the cab company as if every day is the day after Pearl Harbor. When a cabbie isn't booking enough, he'll send him to a part of town where cannibalism is legal.

He treats cabbies as if they're buzzard bait. Our self-esteem is like change of a penny. He calls us all "screwheads" and says that if we'd been at the Bay of Pigs, everybody'd be eating rice and beans today. Sure, maybe we could fight back. Unfortu-

nately, ol' Kilgore is as big as a beer truck. He wears a barbell for a tie clasp and could fit a gorilla in his hip pocket. His sneer could warp time. I've seen him rip out urinals because they flushed too slowly.

The only thing we have in common with Kilgore is money. He wants to make enough dough to buy an island near Tahiti and become its dictator. We just want to make enough to survive.

II. JUST MY LUCK

I was feeling as rotten as cottage cheese on a beach. Some brave soul had swiped Kilgore's autographed picture of Richard Widmark as Tommy Udo in *Kiss of Death,* and all hell was to pay. We'd been given fare ultimatums, double-duty shifts, and more threats than a declaration of war. So I was cruising the hotels, the airports, anywhere that would bag me big fares.

I'd just dropped off a pair of jocks who were about as cute as a couple of lost tennis balls, when a familiar, diminutive figure jumped into my cab. He was wearing a yellow, '85 Lakers World Champion T-shirt, baggy blue slacks, and sneakers. He was thinner than I thought, with less hair on top and more coming out around his ears, and he needed a shave. I couldn't believe my luck. After having to put up with Kilgore's intolerable abuse, here sat Louie De Palma, another tyrannical, acid-tongued dispatcher.

With my sweaty fingers on the meter, I waited. Any second now I was going to get it: "Whaddya spray this cab with, kitty litter?" Or, "Even a loser with a single-digit IQ oughta be able to find Manhattan." Instead, a friendly, even gentle, voice greeted me and asked if I would please take him to Asbury Park in New Jersey.

III. BACK TO REALITY

Suddenly, my mush-mind came back to life. Louie De Palma was just a character on a TV show. Sitting in the back of my cab was Danny DeVito. Here was an actor who'd won a Golden Globe Award for the role, and who'd earned three Emmy nominations and won one award. He may have gone onto play similar lowlifes in such movies as

Danny DeVito.

Ruthless People, Romancing the Stone, The Jewel of the Nile, Wise Guys, and even *Tin Men,* but in real life, Danny DeVito was a regular guy.

On the long ride to the town where he was raised and that Bruce Springsteen made famous, he was so pleasant I wanted to give him a thank-you card for his company. As coincidence would have it, I'd already driven around enough of his *Taxi* co-workers to know that DeVito was someone special. We began reminiscing about those bygone days on *Taxi,* and Danny confided in me like a cellmate at Sing Sing.

He grinned mischievously, "I have in my possession the *very first* photograph ever taken of the complete *Taxi* cast—a Polaroid. We were all together for the first time, after two, three days— they only gave us ten days to do the first show. At the time, we were on ABC, and they sent a photographer down to do the *Taxi* poster—the first one, all of us, including Randy Carver. I'm sorta standin' on the cage door, and everybody's grouped around. Now, what [photographers] usually do, to set up, is to take a Polaroid first to get an idea of the lighting and everything. So the very first snapshot of the entire cast is at my house."

"You scarfed it!" I interjected.

He cackled. "Yeah, yeah, I scarfed it! 'Cause I *knew!* I got it now in a nice frame, behind glass, in my office at home. But I'm afraid I'm gonna have to get it protected soon—it's fading fast."

IV. ST. FRANCIS AIN'T NO SISSY

Whoever said you can't go home no more never heard of cabs. Sure, a ride from New York to the Jersey shore could dent anybody's piggy bank, but for DeVito it seemed well worth it. Memories of a happy childhood laced his mind like fine wine. Born to Chet and Julia DeVito on November 17, 1944, in Neptune, New Jersey, Danny was the only son in an Italian-American family that's stayed close. (His father passed away a few years ago, though, happily, after having seen Danny become a TV star.) Danny grew up across the swamp in Asbury Park, and his Wonder years were spent hanging loose, creating mischief, juking and jiving on street corners and at candy stores. He went to elementary school at Our Lady of Mount Carmel, did some

penance as an altar boy, did some time at Asbury Park High, and ended up at nearby Oratory Prep. Although he was a prankster and a little tough guy, Danny's values outweighed those of many of his friends, some of whom succumbed to drugs or delinquency.

It was at prep school that Danny first acted—the lead in a play supposedly called *The Billion-Dollar Saint.* In a far and possibly sacrilegious cry from his Tasmanian devil cab dispatcher, Danny's first role was St. Francis of Assisi. His reviews were a mixed bag of guffaws, complaints, and disinterest—and this from his family and friends.

They were a tough audience. His dad was a hustling entrepreneur from Brooklyn who ran everything from a luncheonette to a pool hall and did a little bookmaking on the side. Danny's friends hung out at Bacchi's, the candy store on the corner. It was a regular Jersey Disney World: chocolate cherries in red wrappers for a penny, three cigarettes for a nickel, egg creams, a pinball machine that paid out, and a jukebox filled with early Motown and rock'n'roll. His pals had names like Weeds and The Seed. They were ball-breakers, pulling stunts on the squares.

It was in this role-playing world of would-be tough guys that Danny discovered he wanted to be an actor. His friends didn't object—they were all actors, too, in their own ways. There was the time, for instance, they staged a mock shooting in front of an ice cream stand—Danny and Russell Moraglia screaming and shoving, Russell blowing away Danny with a starter's pistol loaded with blanks, their friend Sal screeching around the corner in his father's black Buick, throwing a "dying" Danny into the back seat and driving off. Danny always remembered the stiffs who dripped ice cream all over themselves watching this; in 1983, he recreated that scene (and then some) with such pals as Tony Danza, Vincent Schiavelli, and John Ratzenberger and George Wendt of *Cheers,* in a *Twilight Zone*-ish short called *A Lovely Way to Spend an Evening.*

V. IN COLD L.A.

It all sounded like a Muppet version of *Mean Streets.*

After high school, DeVito decided to pursue acting seriously. He says the greatest encouragement he ever received toward that goal was his father's response when Danny told him he was going to be an actor. "Why not?" his father replied.

The long road began with two years of training at the prestigious American Academy of Dramatic Arts in Manhattan. Then came hitting the bricks, and occasionally the toll booths: He got his first big break in Waterford, Connecticut, at the 1966 Playwrights Conference held at the town's Eugene O'Neill Theatre. There to act in a former teacher's play, Danny fortuitously met another unemployed young actor—Michael Douglas, son of Kirk, later to become not only a TV and Oscar-winning film star but a successful producer as well.

Right now, though, Douglas was working as an unpaid carpenter, waiting for a part to open up in the play. He and DeVito wound up bunking in the same farmhouse dormitory. Looking for all the world like Ratzo Rizzo and Joe Buck in *Midnight Cowboy,* they struck up a close friendship. Their love of goofing around, riding motorcycles, and swilling pizza, beer, and less savory substances was almost as great as their love of acting. After that summer, DeVito split for Los Angeles to try to win the role that Robert Blake eventually made his own in the film version of Truman Capote's *In Cold Blood.* Douglas remembers DeVito, looking every bit the psychopathic killer, showing up at a commune where Michael was staying.

Los Angeles and DeVito didn't take to each other. By early 1969, Danny was back in New York. There he shared a West 89th Street apartment with Michael Douglas and, later, Rhea Perlman. In 1976, Danny and Rhea moved to L.A. for good.

Rhea and Danny must have been partners even in past lives. They hit it off immediately— ka-bing!—when a mutual friend introduced the two backstage after a one-performance, off-Broadway bomb called *The Shrinking Bride.* In less than two weeks they'd moved in together, and during a *Taxi* lunch break in January 1982—eleven years to the day they met—they were married. Danny and Rhea have since had three children: Lucy Chet, born in March 1983; Gracie, born almost exactly two years later; and a son, Jake Daniel Sebastian, born in October 1987.

Danny DeVito as Louie De Palma.

By the time they'd met, Danny had launched a struggling off-Broadway career. DeVito romantically rearranges some details about his start: He tells of returning from his ill-fated L.A. sojourn to spend a long night in "Hotel Wheels"—riding the bus—and the next day, on a phone call made with his last dime, having his friend and former Academy instructor, Michael Simone, land him a gig performing Pirandello. I don't know about that last dime business, but I do know DeVito had returned some months before, and had made his off-Broadway debut in *Shoot Anything with Hair That Moves.*

In any case, he performed all over the off-Broadway circuit, even landing two Joseph Papp Shakespeare productions, *The Merry Wives of Windsor* and *The Comedy of Errors.* Doing regional theater, he trekked to Philadelphia for *The Line of Least Existence,* where he acted for the first time with future *Taxi* costar Judd Hirsch; DeVito played Hirsch's philosophical, cigar-smoking bulldog, Andy. But his breakthrough role, in 1971, was that of the eternally smiling psychotic, Anthony Martini, in off-Broadway's *One Flew Over the Cuckoo's Nest*.

As fate, friendship, talent, or whatever it was would have it, DeVito's old friend Michael Douglas happened to see him in *Cuckoo's Nest*. Not long afterward, when Michael was producing the movie version, he remembered Danny's performance. DeVito reportedly was the first actor cast for the film, which went on to sweep the 1975 Academy Awards.

Soon afterward, DeVito and Douglas went on to appear with Michael's dad, Kirk, in the pirate adventure *Scalawag*. (Danny had previously done the low-budget New York flick *Hurry Up, or I'll Be 30*, and a Sophia Loren vehicle, *Lady Liberty*.) During *Taxi's* run, DeVito and costar Tony Danza did a silly orangutan picture called *Going Ape!* After *Taxi*, DeVito gradually moved from supporting roles (in *Terms of Endearment*, the Jack Nicholson Western *Goin' South*, and Michael Douglas's *Romancing the Stone* and *The Jewel of the Nile*) to full-fledged stardom with *Ruthless People* and *Tin Men*.

VI. SHORT SOUP

The more I learned about DeVito, the more impressed I became. Along with being an actor, he's also a long-time filmmaker. Under the aegis of the American Film Institute, he starred in and coproduced with Rhea, a short film, *Minestrone*, which reputedly was presented twice at the Cannes Film Festival. Perlman describes it as about "a paranoid Italian film director who finds a frogman in his soup, spying on him with a film camera, trying to steal his ideas." She laughs. "It's a little fantastical. Danny directed it and also plays the director; I play the producer, a Lina Wertmuller type."

Even earlier, he and Rhea had made a 16mm black-and-white short called *The Sound Sleeper*. "I wasn't in that," remembers Rhea, "I just helped produce it. It's about a housewife in Baltimore who comes to New York one night while her family is asleep, changes into a hooker at the airport, goes out to Times Square, picks up some guy and murders him, and goes back home before her family awakes in the morning." One other short in which they both appeared was, *Vinyl Visits an FM Station*, a bizarre tale of a radio show.

Nowadays, Danny and Rhea have their own company, New Street Productions, under which DeVito directed two shorts for a comedy anthology series called *Likely Stories*. (Originally meant for cable, the series wound up on videocassette.) For The Movie Channel, Danny also directed and, with Rhea, costarred in the TV movie *The Ratings Game*, a satire about the TV business. (It was later rerun on Showtime.) DeVito also directed the first two episodes of *Mary*, Mary Tyler Moore's short-lived newspaper sitcom, and an episode of *Amazing Stories* that starred Rhea and himself. He scored a hit with his feature-film directorial debut, the black comedy *Throw Momma from the Train*, starring himself, Billy Crystal, and Anne Ramsey. And, of course, he directed three episodes of *Taxi*.

VII. GIVING *TAXI* DIRECTIONS

By now we were driving through Belmar on our way to Asbury Park. DeVito didn't mind my endless questions, and he even perked up when I asked about those fifth-season episodes, which I'm guessing he'd been promised as an enticement to return for that final season.

"I had a great time directing those episodes," he told me fondly. "Since the cast was so good, they made it easy—put themselves in the right spot all the time. I've always liked working with the camera, and it was a good opportunity to do it in a place as safe and comfortable as home. I never got any flack like, 'Oh, this actor, who does he think he is, directing?' I'd directed before, I wasn't a virgin." But to be on the safe side, he started out with an episode "where I didn't have a lot to do as Louie."

Turning to DeVito the actor, I wondered whether he and the rest of the cast had had much room for improvisation on the set.

"Right from the beginning, they allowed you the freedom to improvise," he recalled. " 'They' being who they are, Brooks and them—*very* talented people who were always on the lookout for anything they could incorporate and build upon. Certainly during rehearsals we'd add lines and bits. There were no egos like, 'Hey, I'm the writer and you have to say *these* words.' Same with the director, 'Beads' Burrows.''

I told him I'd *heard* they'd had a nickname for Jim Burrows, the primary director of *Taxi* and later the cocreator of *Cheers*. DeVito grinned impishly. "Yeah, I'm the one that gave Jim that nickname, Beads. 'Cause his eyes, after the first day [of rehearsals], they *looked* like beads. And you shoulda seen 'em by Friday!" He chortled.

"I think it was always in the minds of the creators," he went on, "that *Taxi* was an ensemble piece with Judd as the star. I'm sure Judd recognized that, and he never insisted upon every episode revolving around him or anything like that. That would have gone against the concept of the show."

DeVito himself, so I was told by his manager, once illustrated the ensemble cast's loyalty to each other in a very concrete way. During *Taxi*'s run, a reporter interviewing DeVito assumed that, like on many other TV shows, there were ego battles on the *Taxi* set. The reporter tried to ingratiate himself with DeVito by knocking the other cast members; DeVito, ever loyal, ground the interview to a halt.

DeVito isn't De Palma, obviously; they even handle the Italian *de* in their last names differently. I asked *de* one about *de* other.

VIII. DE PALMA AND DA FAMILY

As the Jersey countryside rolled by, I asked Danny about Louie's background, about his parents and siblings.

"There was his brother Nick [shown in episode #10]," he replied. "What a jerk. Louie's dad, he died some years before. I don't think Louie was a mama's boy, but he very much loved his mother [played twice on the show by DeVito's own mother, Julia]. No matter how much he bitched and moaned and gave her a bad time, he took care of her, which is the important thing.

"I don't think that after she got remarried [to a Japanese man in episode #74] that there was a major change in Louie. They always kept in touch, talked; she bitched and moaned about the Japanese food and so on. Lemme tell you a story about that," he said excitedly, launching into a reminiscence about his mother's first appearance on *Taxi* (episode #62). "After the show, we all went out together to a restaurant of a friend of [*Taxi* cocreator

Ed] Weinberger's. We took up the whole back room. The food was French-Oriental cuisine. Now my mother, she's Italian, and she won't eat anything that ain't Italian. Like, 'Who knows *what's* in there?' So Weinberger sent out! We're all eating French-Oriental, and he got her a delivery from a nice Italian restaurant! She had a nice big plate of beef and spaghetti and she was happy."

IX. *TAXI DRIVER* IN THE CAGE

I turned on the radio. A Muzak version of Springsteen's "Hungry Heart" was playing. We were getting near Asbury Park for sure. A sour chord struck a nerve, and reminded me that I'd read DeVito was a skilled musician, adept at piano and violin. Acting the part, he'd played a doo-wop sax player and two-stepper in Billy Ocean's video for "The Tough Get Going," from the soundtrack to *The Jewel of the Nile*.

What else, I asked myself as I lit a cigarette. Two puffs and I was hacking. I put it out before DeVito could say, "Good." He'd quit a long time ago and now was also a vegetarian.

In my mind I ran through everybody on the show, virtually all of whom, strangely enough, I'd had in my cab. Except for one: J. Alan Thomas, who played assistant dispatcher Jeff Bennett.

"I really enjoyed working with Jeff," DeVito said. "I used to really break his balls, though. Used to tease him a lot. See, when I first moved into the cage, I brought a lot of my own belongings with me. I managed to get a picture of Robert De Niro and Marty Scorsese standing by a taxi, and on it I forged, 'To Louie—Love, Bobby and Marty.' They never showed it on the show, but it was there in the cage the whole five years. I put it in a nice frame. Louie used to tell Jeff, 'This week for *sure* they're comin' down to the garage.' The idea, see, was that the [fictional] Sunshine Cab Co. was where they shot *Taxi Driver*. It was just Louie's scam to Jeff every week. It was part of the life we created.

"See, Jeff [the actor, not the character] didn't have a lot to do, but he was there every week. So I used to give him chores and tasks to do. He used to actually file papers, add up tallies, do all kinds of things in the cage while the show was going on. I'd give him accident reports to make out—he did,

Danny DeVito (with Judd Hirsch): "Those five years were just the greatest."

like, a million things in those five years!"

By now, Danny was laughing like Louie. It was remarkable how easily he'd gotten back into character.

X. A FARE WELL

We were in Asbury Park and I didn't even know it. He did. He could smell Bacchi's and his old man's pool hall and the streets he hung out on. It didn't matter if they were still there or not. He was home.

Before he got out, I asked about the possibility of a *Taxi* reunion. If such a thing could come to pass, it was obvious that Danny DeVito would be one of the most crucial actors, and probably the hardest to bring in. With such a successful and busy film career and such a blessed family life, timing would be everything.

"The whole experience was wonderful," he said in a sad, soft voice. "A great work atmosphere. Very healthy in that way, and I'm sad that it's gone. Not gone—sad that it's over. It'll always be with us, but it's over. Those five years were just the greatest."

He got out, took a deep breath, and gave me a tip I could fly to Pasadena with. It was going to be rough returning to my real garage. I'm glad I didn't sob my spleen out to Danny about *my* dispatcher— I didn't want him to know there actually *were* people like Louie De Palma, whose ethics were filthier than the rear floor of my cab after a holiday weekend.

As I drove away, I could still see DeVito in my rearview mirror. I'd probably always see him. He was a little giant.

MARILU HENNER

It was late at night, and I'd just dropped off a half-baked hooligan and his bleach-bottle bimbo at an all-night gin joint. Cruising Fifth Avenue, I spotted a vision of loveliness standing in front of one of those new "tower" hotels that are smaller than the Taj Mahal but probably have more windows than the Chrysler Building. I cut off an armada of city vehicles and screeched to a halt in front of her. She looked uncommonly familiar. She had long, wavy red hair, a warm mouth, aqua-green eyes that gave me a look I could feel in my hip pocket, and a full set of curves that could put Jack LaLanne out of business. She gave me a smile that hardened my arteries and got in the back seat.

It wasn't until she spoke and I saw her gorgeous dimples in my rearview mirror that I recognized Elaine Nardo. Or, I should say, Marilu Henner.

As we drove downtown, I struck up a conversation. My nosiness didn't bother her anymore than water bothers Hoover Dam. She told me she was born April 6, 1952, in Chicago to Joseph and Loretta Henner, the third of six children (four girls, two boys) in a close, warm, sentimental Polish-Greek family that to this day still gets together for holidays and plays charades.

She laughed. "We send people to the hospital during charades." I could picture the *You Can't Take It With You* madness. Henner's mother owned a dancing school, which was situated at the back of the house; there were always scads of kids around, dancing up a storm. Marilu herself began dance and voice studies at the age of two-and-a-half.

After twelve years of parochial school, she won an Outstanding Americans Youth Foundation scholarship for being, I swear to you, Illinois's "Outstanding Teenager" for 1970; she used the dough to attend the University of Chicago as a political science major since the college didn't offer a drama degree. She added that during those years, she was resident choreographer for Chicago's Center Stage Group, and appeared both in local theater productions and in college shows.

All this caught the attention of Jim Jacobs, a Chicago theater legend who cocreated a little musical number called *Grease.* Jacobs had Henner audition for that new play (on November 21, 1970,

as Marilu's frighteningly photographic memory spits out and subsequent research confirms), and Henner won the role of Marty. When the show packed up to go to New York Jacobs invited her along, but Henner decided to stay in school. Yet not long afterward, when the first national touring company was getting organized, Jacobs called back, and this time Marilu got her act together and took it on the road.

She left the tour after a year to do the Broadway musical *Over Here!,* which starred The Andrews Sisters. She took an apartment on Broadway and 83rd Street, went on to a Broadway revival of *Pal Joey,* and, on and off, reprised her role of Marty in the Broadway version of *Grease.* She made a pretty good living from TV commercials, too—twenty-eight of them, she counts. "I did four Playtex bra commercials, two Playtex panties, and one Fruit of the Loom pantyhose commercial where I was the inside of an apple with my legs sticking out. I was a Samsonite Luggage girl, I went to Venice to shoot a ring-around-the-collar commercial, [and] I shot for Ponderosa Steak House, Barnett Bank, Schlitz Beer, Joy Dishwashing Liquid, and Reese's Peanut Butter Cups. And I got a Clio nomination for an Exxon Bicentennial Minute that was based on Annie Sullivan, Helen Keller's teacher."

Henner made an auspicious feature-film debut as a topless dancer in the cult-classic newspaper flick, *Between the Lines.* She went on to star opposite Richard Gere in *Bloodbrothers,* and she broke into episodic television with pilots for the series *Off Campus, Leonard,* and *The Paper Chase.* The latter pilot accidentally helped her land the role of Elaine Nardo.

"The producers of *Taxi* originally wanted Elaine as a tough, thirty-three-year-old Italian from New York, with a twelve-year-old daughter. And here I come, twenty-five, Polish and Greek from Chicago—technically not even old enough to have a twelve-year-old kid. But I was brought in because Joel Thurm, the casting director, thought I had the right energy. I looked like I would work in an art gallery and still be one of the guys. But they were undecided and kept asking me back. Now, at the same time, I had done the *Paper Chase* pilot and told them I was going to go with that. When they saw I had other options, they felt threatened, and it just happened. Elaine became Irish, they made her di-

Marilu Henner.

vorced from an Italian, and they gave her two little kids.

"Elaine went through everything—marriage, divorce, different relationships, weird hairdos, seeing a shrink. She was, like, Miss Commitment. She'd find something and go all the way with it. She'd beat the choice to death!"

Marilu confided that she saw Elaine as a more specific person than the writers often did. "Elaine was the only woman in a show with seven men. With them, you had to be specific so that they didn't overlap. With one woman, every female-type quality was given to me. So I felt my character wasn't as definite as it should have been. But it became more definite—Elaine became a real person." She smiled. "That's the macrobiotic in me. I see everything as yin and yang."

I saw everything as terrific. She may be a celebrity, but one-on-one, Marilu was warm and down-to-earth, as interested as she was interesting. And looks? She had the kind of smoldering looks that could make a priest reach through a confessional.

I ran a yellow light and got bold and brazen: I asked her if she thought her image was sexy. Y'see, since *Taxi,* Marilu has been in a lot of movies, including *The Man Who Loved Women, Johnny Dangerously, Rustlers' Rhapsody,* and always in very sexy roles. Marilu even burned a few tubes on my set when she guest-starred on buddy and one-time boyfriend Tony Danza's show, *Who's the Boss?*

"I dunno," she said, blushing. "I've been glamorous, plain, funny, sad. I wore sweat shirts *and* gowns on *Taxi.* I can't pinpoint one particular image and don't feel like I have to. It's more fun to be *all* those things.

"People who know me in real life or have seen me on talk shows say I'm more like Elaine than one of my feature-film characters. But all those characters are me. You take from all the different facets of your personality."

"Funny," I suggested. "They're all funny."

"But I'm *not* funny!" she playfully protested. "I was never the funny one in my family. I always tell people they should talk to my brother Lorin—*he's* funny! Comedy has always been hard for me, yet I always seem to get offered comedic roles. Maybe it's because I look like I'm always having fun, laughing. [*Johnny Dangerously* star] Michael Keaton's

Judd Hirsch and Marilu Henner.

nickname for me was 'Marilu I-can't-finish-the-sentence-without-laughing Henner.''

As I relit a stogie, I noticed she was opening all the windows. Figuring her for one of those anti-smoking fanatics, I went to flick my cigar out the window.

"No, no, if you want to smoke, go ahead," she insisted, though I noticed she didn't roll up the windows, either. "Do what you want. I never preach or give anyone a hard time. People have to do what they want to do. I have this 'gusto' theory: If you're going to smoke or eat red meat or drink or whatever, do it with gusto. Just *do* it!"

I figured the logical thing to do next was to put out my stogie and ask her about health.

"After both my parents died at early ages of degenerative diseases, I became very concerned about my own health and fitness. I became a self-taught nutritionist. I've read between three hundred and four hundred books on the subject," she asserted, "and I'd like to one day write my own book."

She went on, telling me about her preventive health program, which consists of rigorous exercise and a vegetarian, chemical-free diet. I remembered that she had even talked her way into the privately owned gym on the Paramount Studios lot at the time of *Taxi;* the owners had told her that in its twenty-five years, no woman had ever been allowed. "I convinced them they had no legal reason to keep me out," she told Liz Smith of the New York *Daily News.* I began to feel old and out of shape. I cursed my power steering. The only exercise I've had since I started hacking was raising and lowering the meter.

"I do three days of weight training and three days of aerobic exercise every week," Henner told me. "You adjust. You have to do it even more when you're working on a film, on location, because it keeps up your stamina. Bodybuilding has really improved the way I look and feel. I watch myself on *Taxi,* and I think I look so much older on them than I do now."

Believe it or not, she *did* look even better in person than on television, and on *Taxi* she was no creamed chip beef on toast, neither. And guys have always noticed; her *Taxi* costars, for instance, told me they did *not* think of Marilu as a sister, no sir. And who among us didn't feel a twinge of envy as we saw her squired about by longtime boyfriend John Travolta, whom she met while in the cast of *Grease* in New York. She was also married briefly to actor Frederic Forrest (the good guy in *The Rose* and her costar in *Hammett*), and she's presently married to director Robert Lieberman; their son, Nicholas Morgan, was born May 12, 1994.

We talked briefly about her latest work—a couple of made-for-cable things, a movie or two, and her scorchingly sexy memoirs, *By All Means Keep Moving*. And then, sadly, we arrived at her destination.

Even though I took a long-cut, I knew this moment would arrive. I told Marilu I'd watch her in anything she did. She smiled and thanked me; I smiled, too, knowing that with her *Guinness Book* total recall, she'd always remember me. As she got out of the cab, she asked for a receipt. She could've had anything she wanted.

JUDD HIRSCH

I was breaking in a new set of hubcaps by driving around the Broadway theater district. The after-theater crowd was becoming as visible as Claude Rains with bandages. It was a clear night and the stars were out. Hungry paparazzi were making sure to catch each one. Amid flashguns and cries of adulation, a man rushed into my cab. He was husky and tall, with a salt-and-pepper beard. He wore a baby blue safari outfit and a captain's hat. His eyes

were dark, hard, and tricky. I could tell he wanted to get away. I could also tell that this was the cab-driver's cabdriver: Alex Reiger, or, really, Judd Hirsch.

I was as thrilled as a kid eating a Hershey bar. I'd been lucky enough to talk to other members of the *Taxi* cast, but to talk to the man who played the ultimate cabbie . . . this was my night.

Right away things began to get as sour as milk left overnight in the microwave.

After I'd extended my fondness for *Taxi* and for his work on the show and congratulated him on his Tony Award for his performance in the hit play *I'm Not Rappaport,* Hirsch became curt. He wasn't fond of fans, and he was especially livid over the ones who took his picture.

"People come backstage and they ask to take your picture," he said in his *rat-a-tat* tones. "I say, 'I'd rather you didn't'—and they take it anyway. They think they own a piece of you. How do *you* know what they're gonna do with that picture—turn around and sell it to the *National Enquirer?* You know what I wanna do when they do that?" he continued, his voice getting even faster. "I wanna take that camera, break it into a million pieces, and shove it up their ass."

Hirsch's statement landed between us like a boulder. I'd heard rumors about his disposition and temper, but why take it out on me? When I told him how *Taxi* figured in my memoirs, he countered with, "Why would you want to write about *Taxi?* The show stands on its own."

I suggested that people write about the works of Shakespeare and T. S. Eliot. He said people didn't interview Shakespeare or T. S. Eliot. It was a nonsense reply; I could just as easily have used the careers of the well-interviewed Henry Fonda or Sir Laurence Olivier as examples (and besides, Eliot talked to *The Paris Review;* I happen to keep a copy in my glove compartment). Hirsch also was deeply puzzled why Danny DeVito or Tony Danza or Jim Brooks or anybody else from the show would talk to me.

"Are they getting anything out of it?" he asked. Before I could say no, he went on about how "the studios always screw you. They never give you a full accounting, and they take everything. Why should I help the studio by talking to you?"

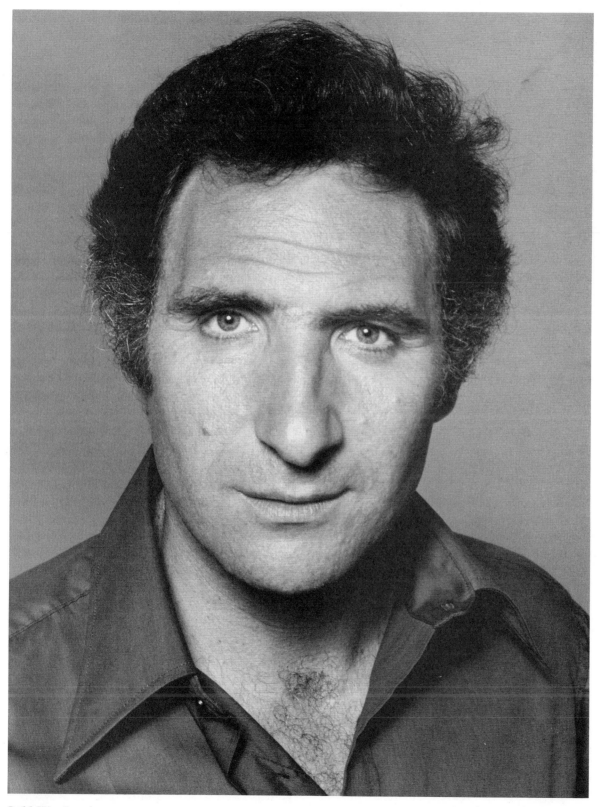

Judd Hirsch.

Judd Hirsch as Alex Reiger.

This was terrible. I would have felt more comfortable talking to Charles Manson. By now, I still didn't know where we were going, but I wanted to get there quick. Hirsch went on, defending his stand about honor without profit.

"I get approached all the time," he said. "Someone once came up to me, wanted to interview me for a book on acting. Why should I give away my time to do that? It's a commercial venture. Somebody's making money off it."

The rest of the ride was as quiet as a nun's confession. When we parted, he was genuinely polite, shook my hand, and wished me luck.

I sat there awhile, perplexed. I needed a drink. Hell, I needed a lot of drinks. Yet I also needed information. I'd become intrigued with Hirsch and was dogged and determined to learn more about him.

I drove back to the theater district and found a *Playbill* program for *I'm Not Rappaport.* After I wiped some melted Junior Mints off the pages and looked

at it, I'm telling ya, his life materialized in front of me. Maybe Shirley MacLaine is right.

He was born March 15, 1935, in New York City to Joseph Stanley and Sally Kitzis Hirsch of the Bronx. He studied engineering and physics at the City College of New York and also dabbled in architecture at the city's Cooper Union College. His exposure to the arts there led him to study acting at three different schools, including the prestigious American Academy of Dramatic Arts (which some years later Danny DeVito would attend).

As with virtually all young yobbos in the acting dodge, Hirsch had to odd job it to survive. He says he's been a busboy, a newspaper deliverer, a driver at a camp, a library clerk, and a law-office clerk. Though he's hard-pressed to admit it, Hirsch got married some thirty years ago, following a dalliance in the Catskills. He was young; it ended quickly. A second marriage, which ended in 1977, produced a son, Alex—coincidentally, as in Alex Reiger. Hirsch and his recent third wife, Bonni, had daughter Montana Eve on March 29, 1994.

For his first professional acting job, Hirsch spent the summer in Estes Park, Colorado, where a stock company performed in the back room of a restaurant. Afterward, Hirsch returned to New York and worked extensively in theater. From the mid-sixties on, he worked steadily if not particularly lucratively both off-Broadway and on, though making his living primarily from TV commercials.

It took a decade for his talents to be fully appreciated. His first big break was the acclaimed TV movie *The Law* (1974) and a short-lived spinoff series. Just then this tall drink of water sidled up to me on the sidewalk. At first I thought it was Alan Alda, but it turned out to be look-alike John Badham, the director of *Saturday Night Fever, WarGames, Short Circuit,* and—maybe this was my lucky night after all—*The Law.* He gave me a firsthand account of how Hirsch landed the role.

"The casting objective of that picture was we didn't want anybody in the show that was really well known. And yet we had people carrying major parts, so we couldn't get inexperienced actors. We came across Judd Hirsch through Eleanor Kilgallen [sister of journalist/wit Dorothy]. Eleanor was basically the New York casting department of Universal Pictures. She had been a big help to me before [and now] she wrote me a note saying the perfect person for this part in *The Law* is Judd Hirsch. I mean she might as well have said Hymie Schwartz. And she had enclosed a picture, and the picture looked like Frankenstein! It was not a good picture. And I said well, if I didn't know Eleanor, I would pay no attention to this and throw it in the trash.

"So I called up Eleanor and asked, have you got any film at all on him? She said the only things she could get her hands on were an American Airlines commercial and a Listerine commercial. So these arrived, we looked at them, and [*Law* producer-cowriter] Bill Sackheim said, 'They'll never take him, he's too ugly. But he sure could read [co-writer] Joel Oliansky's dialogue.' You could hear from that fast way of speaking that he has, that energetic thing, that he's gonna be terrific for this. So I said, let's get him out here, let's test him. [And Bill said] no, they'll never take him. I said, what can it hurt? It's not like George Segal, whom everybody at NBC wanted, or Elliott Gould is knocking down the door to play this part.

"So we bring Judd Hirsch up. He walks in the room and gives you a limp handshake like you wouldn't believe—which is not very encouraging—takes the script, starts to read it, and you go, 'This guy is really good! Let's test him!' I take him down to the *Marcus Welby* set, which is finishing work at five o'clock, and we get the crew to stay for an extra hour. And we shot this dialogue with him, and it was very good. Yet Bill would not show it to the network, wouldn't show it to the head of the studio—he kept worrying about it, until finally he had to do something. And the head of the studio said, 'Let's show it to the network,' and the network said, 'yeah, he'll be good!' So all his worrying was for naught."

After *The Law* came the 1976 police show *Delvecchio,* soon followed by a Drama Desk Award for his supporting role in Jules Feiffer's *Knock Knock.* He reached another career plateau the following year with his role as a Neil Simon surrogate in the playwright's semiautobiographical Broadway hit, *Chapter Two.* There were movies along the way, mostly small roles and no leads, though one supporting role, as psychiatrist Dr. Berger in *Ordinary People,* netted him an Oscar nomination. *Taxi* never did

make Hirsch a superstar, but even if *Taxi* hadn't come along, Judd Hirsch would still have had a good career.

I was getting facts without any soul. As I sat in a Tin Pan Alley bar and sipped an Absolut and tonic, I wondered about two things. The first was Hirsch. I'd learned all the essentials, but I still didn't know anything about *him*. The second was the shaky bartender. His lips were as dry as peanut butter on sandpaper. I couldn't imagine how it felt to be mixing drinks all night and never down one.

I left more curious than a dead cat.

It wasn't until I strayed into an after-hours joint that I got more information about Hirsch. The place was packed with insomniacs dancing, gambling, and drinking as if the Russians were at the county line. The jukebox kept playing the same song, but nobody noticed.

I struck up a conversation with a has-been director who likes casting nubile young runaways fresh off Greyhounds. He was hanging out with a couple of wire-service reporters and other muckrakers, and me, I'm a naturally friendly guy. People talk to me. I like to listen.

I learned that Hirsch had told Jerry Buck of the Associated Press about his start in summer stock in the Rockies. "[I]n order to get there, I answered an ad to drive a car to Colorado. It turned out to be a New York taxi cab," Hirsch had claimed. "Some poor sucker had bought it sight unseen from a catalog."

Tom Burke of *TV Guide* chimed in with something else Hirsch told him about those beginnings. "When I started acting professionally, in summer stock, I thought there had to be *scientific* ways to make an audience believe you. What's the equation for it? Well, there are as many equations as there are actors! You solve the problem of a scene you're playing the way you, the *person,* would solve them. I also knew that what I liked to see on a stage or screen was an actor who *thought.* I decided that when I played, the audiences would watch me *think.*" Standing there with my drink in hand, I was amazed at the memories these writers had.

Another one, a guy named Bill Kaufman of *New York Newsday,* mentioned that Hirsch had said his time with *Chapter Two* had taught him all about taxis. "I spent a hell of a lot of time riding in cabs,"

Judd Hirsch.

were nominated for Tony Awards, but not Hirsch. Hirsch got fed up, went on a diatribe about the Tonys being nothing more than a TV game show, and took up Jim Brooks's offer to do *Taxi.* Third time lucky.

"I've known some very talented people who have dropped out [of the profession], but when you really look at them and question why they dropped out, you realize that they didn't really drop out, they simply dropped onward," Hirsch said to Dick Maurice of the Copley News Service. "Their nature didn't intend them to do what they were going to do. In the theater, you probably have more people who probably belong elsewhere than in any other profession I know. It's not like being a doctor—you don't have to pass tests to get in. This happens to be a pet peeve of mine." Nevertheless, according to Maurice, Hirsch said, "I'm noncompetitive. The only person I compete with is myself. Competition really turns me off. I just don't like the idea of having to make it against anyone, over anyone."

Maybe. But Tom Burke of *TV Guide* thought Hirsch doth protest too much: Burke said Hirsch's "reactions are too bright, his smiles too urgent." Burke went on to say, "Though Hirsch says he has just quit smoking, he chain-smokes. His demeanor is that of a man who desperately needs to win. As a [*Taxi*] driver, he's unruffled, but as a man, Judd Hirsch looks keenly driven."

In such esteemed company, I had a few Hirsch stories of my own to tell, things the other *Taxi* people had told me. Marilu Henner, for instance, takes Hirsch's arrogance in stride. "I don't care what people say about Judd," she told me. "Judd was the only real star on that show from day one, and he never pulled a star thing. He was extremely generous with all of us. We had an ensemble show because of Judd, because he could have pulled rank many, many times."

Randy Carver described Hirsch as "always searching, exploring his character and the relationship his character had with the other people. It was a very sensitive type of creative energy he put out."

One senior TV executive, however, remembered that when ABC canceled *Taxi,* Hirsch had promised to do whatever he could to keep the show alive; yet when NBC picked up the show, Hirsch turned

Hirsch had said. "I lived in the West [Greenwich] Village, and took a cab twice a day. After seven months, you get to talk to a lot of cabdrivers. It's like osmosis—you pick up on their attitudes and mannerisms."

A jamoke named Cecil Smith from the *Los Angeles Times* said Hirsch told him how wary he was of doing television when the *Taxi* offer came around. Hirsch had said he'd become "very discouraged about television. I begin to feel like a nemesis, failing in shows like *The Law* and *Delvecchio.* But only a fool thinks it's failure. It's like getting rear-ended by cabs three times in one year; you begin to think it's your fault."

Hirsch clearly was ambivalent about going back to television, especially when it looked as if he were about to become a big star on Broadway. Then he got on the receiving end of a hard slap of water— all three of his *Chapter Two* costars and the play itself around and wanted a big raise, profit participation, a host of unreasonable things given the circumstances. Hirsch, said the executive, would not give an inch and the show might have died. Hirsch's situation was resolved, but only after intervention from the highest powers at NBC, who, the executive characterized it, "humiliated him into doing the right thing." Others who worked on the show confirmed these "negotiations."

I'd heard enough. Back outside, it wasn't even light yet, but I was tired and just wanted to get home. I'd learned that Judd Hirsch and Alex Reiger are miles apart, and yet, also the same side of a faded coin. Maybe that's what makes him a great actor and a lousy passenger.

CAROL KANE

It was the middle of June, and the Lincoln Center area was crawling with native New Yorkers and tourists. Panhandlers, musicians, mimes, and street merchants out of Marrakech were making more money than any taxi driver. On a breezy, sunny day like this, sightseeing on foot must've seemed to them much more enjoyable than running yellow lights in an un-air-conditioned hack.

Giving in and joining the parade, I parked my cab in a loading zone and put a "Do Not Disturb" sign on the windshield. There was a line outside the Lincoln Center Deli longer than for the contra hearings, and the sidewalk cafés were fuller than a fat man at a smorgasbord. I settled for the shade of a Sabrett's umbrella and was having the daily special of roast warthog and a bottle of *brefnish* when a familiar face walked by. She caught my attention like a twelve-gun salute at Fort Myers.

Her long blondish hair was piled up on her head like a turban, making her look much taller than the five-foot-two she actually is. Her features were ethereal—a pixie nose, high cheekbones, and full, red lips that held a devilish smile. I knew she had huge blue eyes under her wide green sunglasses. Her attire was second-hand chic—baggy slacks and a David Letterman T-shirt. Her thinness made her appear delicate, and the pug puppy dog she was walking didn't add any weight to the scenario.

Yet nobody bothered her, recognized her, or pat-

ted the dog. She was just another bouncy New Yorker out for a stroll. She reminded me of a grounded Peter Pan.

When she turned onto one of the side streets, I decided to follow her. My memoirs wouldn't be complete without talking to Carol Kane, who played Simka Dahblitz Gravas on *Taxi*.

As I crossed the street, vivid recollections of her past roles flashed in front of me: her film debut at 18, starring with John Carradine in a psychedelic horror film she'd like to forget; in *Carnal Knowledge*, sitting next to Art Garfunkel watching Jack Nicholson's slide show; in *The Last Detail*, as the fragile hooker picked from out of a buxom bevy by virginal sailor Randy Quaid; in *Annie Hall*, arguing over the Kennedy assassination with Woody Allen; in *Hester Street*, as the Old Country, turn-of-the-century wife (a role that earned her an Academy Award nomination); in *When a Stranger Calls*, playing a terrified teenager.

All these roles, plus a few dozen more, are all so unlike Simka Dahblitz, the feisty, energetic, loud, and occasionally ill-tempered girl friend and then wife of Latka Gravas. Simka could be manipulative, sexy, and stubborn. She didn't take any guff, even from Louie.

I was impressed. The wallflower had blossomed into a cactus. I recalled certain roles after *Taxi*. She was no longer the "cameo queen," as she's called herself. Although she still fits well in ensemble pieces, her roles have become meatier, bitchier—sort of like Simka with a green card.

There was all that hissing and yelling in *Transylvania 6-5000*. There was that great seduction scene in *Over the Brooklyn Bridge*, when a timid Carol comes through the door and all but forces herself on Elliott Gould. There was the fed-up wife in *Ishtar*, the sassy coworker in *Jumpin' Jack Flash*, and the thousand-year-old grandmother in *The Princess Bride*. One of my favorite recollections was Carol's role in the intermittently terrific, short-lived NBC series *All Is Forgiven*. Although Carol's Nicolette Bingham, the Southern head writer for a daytime soap opera, had all the snappy lines, the show's star was Bess Armstrong. A shame: Nicolette *was* the show.

It seemed that Carol was always a great team player, but not in the starting lineup. Yet on *Taxi*, every one of the actors had a leading role—that's

Carol Kane.

the kind of show it was. And when it was Carol's turn to star, she blazed.

My confidence was in first gear, and my curiosity revved to second. I boldly walked up to her to say hello—and the puppy tore at my pants. For a little pug (a well-named breed), he had a growl like Rambo. Carol smiled, apologized, and scolded George, the first attack-pug I'd ever seen. All that came out of my mouth was *ibeeda* and an assortment of other gibberish.

Luckily, Carol was a good sport and told me that people do that all the time. They think that Latka and Simka's language was real and codified, but it was nothing of the sort.

"The scripts were all in the English," she told me. "There were a few words, like *yaktabe*, that became translatable, but just a few. It was always changing, because we never wrote anything down. It was one of those things where you had to just take it and fly with it, because when you open your mouth and start talking, you hope that something comes out that sounds like something.

"But as you did it more and more, it became less and less frightening. For instance, now I couldn't do it, because I'm not in practice. I was on the Letterman show, and he asked me to say something in the language, and I opened my mouth and—it wasn't there. It'll come back, but it takes time."

Carol first appeared on *Taxi* as a guest star in the episode "Guess Who's Coming for *Brefnish*?" (episode #40). She returned as a guest star in the fourth-season episode "Simka Returns" (episode #81), and earned an Emmy Award as the Outstanding Lead Actress in a comedy. She had one more guest appearance, in the landmark episode "The Wedding of Latka and Simka" (episode #87). When *Taxi* opened on NBC for its fifth and final season, Carol came on as a cast member—and won another Emmy, this time as Outstanding Supporting Actress in a comedy.

Since Simka's place in the order of *Taxi* revolved around her relationship with Latka, I asked about her initial encounters with the manic and talented Andy Kaufman.

"The first time I did Simka, I met Andy and I was very worried about the language," she related to me. "I wanted to research it very thoroughly, and it was inconceivable to me that this show could happen in just five days. So I said to Andy and [director] Jimmy Burrows that I had to work on this over the weekend before we started, and they were wonderful about it.

"I first went out to dinner with Jimmy and Andy, which was lovely. They took me to the Imperial Gardens, and we talked and worked a bit. Then I went out with Andy alone so we could work solely on the language. I was to go to his house, but before I did, Andy said to me that he'd been thinking, and what we should do is go someplace where no one knows us, and I would speak only in [the Latka] language. He suggested we go to Mexico.

"Now, I had heard all this stuff about him, that he's kind of odd and stuff, so I figured I would just have to sort of try to be open to whatever he was going to come up with and go along with it, and that it would be very good for me. But when I got to his house, he was on the phone and playing bongos and trying to get me to mud-wrestle. And time was going by; it's like 8:30. I was trying to be real patient, but it was starting to get late. So I finally said, 'Well, you know, if we're going to Mexico we should get going.' " She laughed. "He looked at me like I was *out of my mind!* Just insane! 'We're not going to Mexico,' he said. 'That was a joke!' I guess I had this vision of something extreme and off, and *something* about Mexico must've seemed right to me. But he was completely joking. He was very high-strung; you could never tell if he was joking. In this particular instance he was surprised it had worked.

"So anyway, that night we ended up going to a Chinese restaurant, and when the waiter wasn't there, we would decide what we wanted to eat, and when the waiter came back I would speak the language and Andy would interpret for me. This was very wise of him, to know that if I broke it in in real life, that it would really lessen the fear in me of doing it for the camera. Oh, he was brilliant.

"For me, it was the same thing as dancing. When you start dancing, you are very self-conscious about it because you might look foolish. The language is the same thing. As Andy explained it to me, it's

Carol Kane as Simka Dahblitz Gravas.

what children do naturally—'Let's talk in Russian,' or 'Let's talk in French or Chinese.' They just open their mouths and start. They don't think, 'I have to learn the words' or anything, they just pretend. The only addition to this is that I wanted to maintain the same rhythm as Andy, so there was something to make me listen to him.''

I must have looked as confused as a baker at a vegetable stand. While the puppy did something I couldn't do for him, I regrouped and thought about Carol's roots. She was born Carolyn Laurie Kane in Cleveland, Ohio, on June 18, 1952. She saw her first play, a local production of *Alice in Wonderland*, when she was just seven, and realized that acting was to be her vocation; a precocious kid, she began organizing plays with her fellow moppets. The following year, she moved with her family to New York. By the time she was thirteen, and her architect father and jazz singer–pianist mother were di-

vorcing, Carol had lived not only there but also in Paris and, briefly, Haiti. She settled back in New York and, after a stint at the Cherry Lawn boarding school in Connecticut, was back in ''The City'' and diving into ''The Arts.''

Carol attended high school at the Professional Children's School in Manhattan; shortly thereafter, at the age of fourteen, she won her first professional acting role, touring with Tammy Grimes in *The Prime of Miss Jean Brodie*. Enamored of her career, Carol decided against college: She was accepted at New York's Bernard Baruch College, she said, but either dropped out or never went.

She did theater all over the Northeast, including her share of off-Broadway; she even appeared in a Lincoln Center production of *Macbeth* with fellow neophyte Christopher Lloyd. In Boston, she performed alongside Al Pacino in Bertolt Brecht's *The Resistible Rise of Arturo Ui*. On Broadway she performed in *Ring Around the Bathtub* and, alongside Shelley Winters, costarred in the Broadway revival of Paul Zindel's Pulitzer Prize–winning off-Broadway play, *The Effect of Gamma Rays on Man-in-the-Moon Marigolds*.

A little-known fact about Carol is that she's an international film star. She received critical kudos for her performance in the psychodramatic fantasy *Les Jeux de la Comtesse Doligen de Gratz*, which played at Cannes and was supposed to be pretty good if you like that sort of thing. She starred or costarred in the Spanish film *La Sabina*, another French film, *The Secret Room*, the Canadian *Wedding in White*, which won Best Film at the Canadian Film Festival, and the Australian sex-comedy *Norman Loves Rose*, for which she was nominated Best Actress by the Australian Film Institute.

We'd been walking along the same street so long, the puppy was becoming territorial. Carol, initially shy and modest about her career accomplishments, opened up when we discussed how she's become a full-fledged character comedienne.

''I used to approach [acting] with a great deal of seriousness and study,'' she told me, ''but I've been practicing putting more humor into it and every other aspect of my life. And it was directly because of *Taxi*. It was a really wonderful, rich show. The writing was so, ahhhh!'' she said, frustrated at not being able to come up with the right happy word.

"I got to say such great things! There were many times I thought I'd like to pay them for their lines. 'Peel me like a grape so I can get outta here'—how much do you want for that line?" she exclaimed.

"*Taxi* is just an irreplaceable part of my life. There are people in my life now from *Taxi* that I can't imagine living without. They gave me this awareness of humor. When I watch it now—and I'm seeing many episodes I'd never seen before—each one of them looks like a little motion picture.

"Let me tell you—and I don't think anyone who worked on it would disagree with me on this—*Taxi* was one of the most important parts of all of our histories."

It finally dawned on me that she lived on that street. It turned out she's lived in the same New York apartment since she was fourteen. She's had a second place in Los Angeles (home of former boyfriend Woody Harrelson of *Cheers*), but you could tell New York was her home. I thanked her for her time, tried to pet the puppy but figured I needed all my fingers, and told Carol that Simka might have been an immigrant, but she was a real citizen Kane.

When I got back to my cab, a flatfoot was giving me a ticket. I told him, *"Ibeeda."* He didn't find it funny. Maybe I should have had Simka come yell at him for me.

Carol Kane (with Andy Kaufman): "I got to say such great things."

ANDY KAUFMAN

Remember the song that went "Mama said there'd be days like this"? Mine started early last Halloween. My first fare was such a knockout, she woke me up quicker than intravenous coffee. She had such a cosmopolitan arrogance that I started to pay the fare *for* her.

Suddenly, a man ruptured the revolving doors of the Fifth Avenue hotel she was about to enter and did five things almost at once. He sped by the knockout, stopped in his tracks, eyed her like a coroner examining a corpse, kissed both her hands, and then jumped into my cab and directed me to Catch a Rising Star.

"Quite an eye-opener, huh?" I said, driving out into the afternoon traffic.

"Who, the doll?" he asked in a voice faster than the speed of sound. "Lemme tell ya, babe, in Vegas she'd be the countergirl at Wendy's."

"I thought she was gorgeous," I admitted.

"Then, babe, you got the taste of casino chips sat on by a fat lady." He sounded like a parrot being sandpapered. And the clothes! A peach-colored tuxedo, a baby-blue ruffled shirt, a black bow tie bigger than a vampire bat, shades, and an oversize toupee that made him look like a funeral director at Lake Tahoe. He looked oddly familiar, but then, this *was* Halloween, and stockbrokers believed in dressing down.

"You from Vegas?" I asked, trying to be friendly.

"No, monoxide-breath, I'm from Puerto Rico," he shot back. He began singing Elvis doing "My Way" in Spanish.

I was getting fed up. Luckily this wouldn't be a long fare. Catch a Rising Star was only a few long

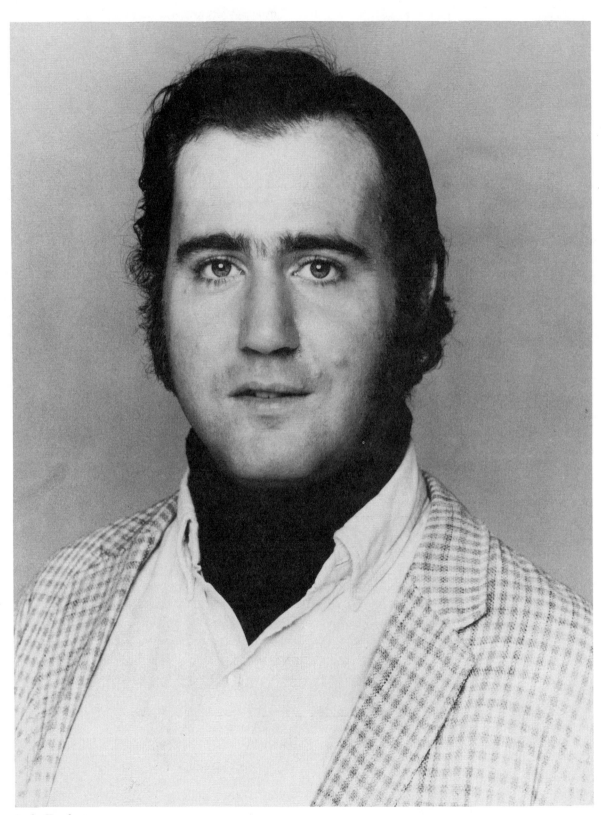

Andy Kaufman.

blocks over on the East Side, right around the corner from an old girl friend of mine. When we got there a few minutes later, I noticed a big banner displayed in the big window. It read: ''Trick or Treat Night with Tony Clifton.''

''Whoa!'' he chirped, flashing a grin like the Cheshire Cat. ''Looks like somebody blew a bundle at the Fun City Sears!'' He got out, pulled a pocketful of Monopoly money from his jacket, and gave me an autograph for a tip. As I drove away, I could still see him pounding on the doors and screaming for ''the babes!''

It didn't dawn on the dead recesses of my mind until I was clear across town. Tony Clifton. That name kept coming up, like taxes on April 15. Everybody I'd talked to from *Taxi* had alluded that Clifton and Andy Kaufman—*Taxi* mechanic Latka Gravas—were one and the same. But that was impossible. Kaufman—a performance artist masquerading as a stand-up comic, who would read *The Great Gatsby* to audiences to see how long they'd stand it, and who with purposeful outrageousness declared himself Inter-Gender Wrestling Champion and wrestled any and all female comers—had died on May 16, 1984, of lung cancer, at the young age of thirty-five.

My mind was going faster than a sick cat searching for its kitty litter. Kaufman, a native New Yorker who grew up in Great Neck, Long Island, was truly a comedic genius, a bizarre, irreverent, over-the-edge believer in living theater. Clifton, on the other hand, was an obnoxious, overweight lounge lizard—the Norman Bates of Vegas. I tried to piece together everything I'd heard about them.

James Burrows, who directed more episodes of *Taxi* than even *he* cares to remember, had called Kaufman ''a sweet kid from Great Neck who was probably one of the strangest, funniest comedians you'll ever see. His choice of ways to get laughs were choices no one else ever would think of. It was humor from wanting to kill him, from the nerve, from the audacity of what he did. That's how he got his laughs.''

Marilu Henner had a hard time talking about Kaufman, but she pulled herself together and told me, ''I loved Andy. I got to be so close to Andy, toward the end especially. I got to know him better

then than I did when we worked together on the show.''

Tony Danza had shot straight from the hip. ''I hated Andy at first. He drove me crazy. He'd be late all the time, we'd have to wait, he had a stand-in for rehearsal—Andy came half a day Tuesday and all day Friday, and [yet] he *never* made a mistake. You never see him on any of the gag reels. He always knew his stuff cold. He was really a genius.

''But I used to get mad at him, and I used to soak him with the fire extinguisher. Sad—he wouldn't *do* anything, he'd just stand there. Then [Jim] Brooks came to me and said, 'No soaking actors!' ''

Carol Kane, who played his wife, Simka, was probably the closest to Kaufman during *Taxi*, and many of her recollections about him were doused with emotion and tears. ''He had a master plan, but he didn't really complete it. You know those concerts where [afterward] he would take people by bus someplace for milk and cookies? What he wanted was for some of those concerts to be able to continue for weeks. People would make dates to meet for these things. That was his plan, and he would have carried it out.

''Andy was *so* passionate. On our first date when we went to the Chinese place [see Carol Kane's biography], I had asked him, before, to show me some [video] tapes. I watched the Carnegie Hall concert and the wrestling, and one of them upset me too much to watch, because it seemed that he was getting hurt. So I left the room, and that upset him so much. I think he wanted things to have an impact, and if you got upset watching this, that was good by him. But if you left the room, then he felt he stopped having impact.''

Randy Carver, who knew Kaufman most briefly, ironically summed him up most precisely: ''A very gifted, unique person. He just didn't know when the camera was off. He could be very giving and very spoiled in different ways. He *was* a genius, out there on the edge all the time. His life was like a happening—remember those sixties 'happenings'? Well, he brought that kind of energy into his work as an actor. He stretched the boundaries of art.

''You either loved Andy for what he did, or he

Andy Kaufman as Latka Gravas.

was just too crazy for you. He was sort of like a test pilot, probing the outer perimeters of the envelope. A comedic test pilot, if you will.''

''Remember that wrestling thing?'' asked Jim Brooks, who hired Kaufman after seeing him and Tony Clifton perform at The Comedy Store in Los Angeles. ''Where he took in the whole country that he had gotten hurt wrestling? The only time Andy ever conceded to me anything about anything he did was when he told me about that. And I said, 'How could you do that to all of us! And we were so worried about you!' And he said, 'Hey, do you know what it's like to be in traction?' He had gone into *traction* for this! So he always asked more of himself than anybody else when he did these things.''

Jeff Conaway's experiences with Kaufman were mixed. ''Andy *was* funny. Andy and I had a problem the first year, but we straightened it out. He had a good heart. We became friends, used to go out to dinner, talk. But one day we had some lunch, and we're walking, and these two girls come up to him and say, 'Hey, is this wrestling thing still on?' And he said, 'Sure,' and the girl said, 'OK, you and me, right here!' He said, 'Jeff, you referee.' I couldn't believe it, right there in the street! She

almost won, almost got him, but he won. Andy was something else.

''When he died, in the first and second editions of the *New York Post,* there was a picture of Andy and myself from *Taxi,* and some people who really didn't know which was which assumed I was Andy, and that it was me who died. When this got back to me, I felt really odd, like, was this a message or something? Am I the next to go?''

''I didn't realize he was as sick as he was. He tried cleaning up his diet, but it was funny, because he'd still eat candy. He never smoked, drank; he was into macrobiotics, meditation. He would come out and say he'd just levitated ten feet in the air. I always thought if anyone could do it, Andy could. It was fun seeing him through the years become comfortable with us.''

Something was definitely not kosher in the deli. There was that other thing Randy Carver had told me—a rumor that Kaufman wasn't really dead. ''A year after Andy had passed away,'' Carver had said, ''Tony Clifton gave a charity performance at The Comedy Store. And I know a lot of people showed up expecting Andy to be there. It's almost like they didn't take his death seriously, because it would not be unlike him to have done something like that, to fake his death.'' (The best information, incidentally, makes the Tony Clifton show a product of Kaufman's manager and coconspirator, George Shapiro. But who knows?)

''Someone had seen him near the end, at an airport,'' Carver had continued, ''and couldn't believe all the weight he'd lost. And they couldn't help wondering if he was doing it for effect or if in fact he was really dying. For one reason or another,'' he'd added somewhat spiritually, ''I still think he's out there.''

As young hooligans, goblins, and southpaws pitched eggs at my cab, I made a beeline back to Catch a Rising Star. Sure enough, the place was closed. There wasn't a Tony Clifton banner in sight. I felt like I was in one of the old black-and-white *Twilight Zone* episodes back when I was still young enough to be scared.

Dark settled in like a case of the vapors, and Dracula, Frankenstein, and Ollie North look-alikes roamed the streets. Down in the Village, you couldn't tell who was wearing a costume or their everyday attire. Andy Kaufman would have liked it. Judging from his bizarre sense of humor, Kaufman would have gone to a Halloween bash dressed as himself and spent the night denying it was really him.

Kaufman had been something of a performer way back, supposedly hiring himself out as a kids' party entertainer when he was only eight or fourteen or sixteen, depending on who you believe. After high school, he actually drove taxis (and trucks) and then enrolled at Grahm Junior College in Boston. He was entranced by television, and so naturally he wrote, produced, and starred in his own campus TV show, *Uncle Andy's Fun House*. Amazingly, like magic, he got to bring that same show (more or less) to network television for a 1979 ABC special. He once said he got his first "big break" at college, as the comedy relief at the black students' group's annual *Soul Time Revue* talent show.

I remembered seeing Kaufman on *Saturday Night Live*—where he'd gotten his first major TV exposure in 1975—doing his routine on the congas, which I found funny. Other bits, like lip-syncing the Mighty Mouse theme, were just nerve-racking. In his character of "Foreign Man" (which evolved into Latka), he'd do intentionally horrendous impressions of Archie Bunker, saying repeatedly, "Everyone is stupid meathead" until you became uncomfortably convinced it wasn't an act, that this was a real foreign amateur making a fool of himself up there. But then he'd do Elvis, he'd do it straight, and it wasn't like someone doing Elvis, it *was* Elvis.

On *Taxi,* his Latka Gravas character usually stayed in the background. Even then he could be irritating. Then in later seasons he'd turn into Vic Ferrari—swinger, playboy, self-centered but self-assured, paying homage to Jerry Lewis's Buddy Love in *The Nutty Professor*. He was great.

During those years that Kaufman did his wrestling routine, offering $500 to any woman who could pin him down ($1,000 if on-camera), I thought the whole ploy dangerous not only to him but to all us males. Then I thought back to my own roots, the early sixties in Sunnyside Gardens, Queens, booing and hissing villainous wrestlers like Karl Von Hess and Buddy Rogers. I wondered if Kaufman were there, too, only cheering them instead.

The late Andy Kaufman—performance artist, not just a comedian.

I was beginning to understand this eldest of three children from a well-to-do Long Island family. Like those wrestlers, who never broke character, Kaufman loved provoking fans and playing the bad guy. For most comedians, one minute onstage without laughter is a nightmare. Kaufman *relished* that minute. For a Capricorn (born January 17, 1949), Kaufman was more of a Gemini, a good-cop/bad-cop interrogating himself. To say that to Kaufman the whole world was a stage is an understatement. This was a guy who while doing *Taxi* once worked as a busboy in a Hollywood deli on Monday nights just to study people. Instead of trying out new material in comedy clubs, Kaufman took to the wintry streets of New York, immersing himself in character as a bag-person and fighting, arguing, and crying among real civilians.

Kaufman pushed, sometimes to the extreme, but he was an artist. Five years on a hit TV show wasn't a stepping-stone for Kaufman—it was a chore. He hated scripts and rehearsing. Creativity came from within, on the spot—Close Encounters of the Kaufman Kind.

It was getting late, and all the mental defectives were out now in full regalia. I drove by Catch a Rising Star, but up on the marquee wasn't Tony Clifton's name, but that of comedienne Elayne Boosler, one of Andy Kaufman's former lovers. I dug in my pocket for the autographed tip. That was proof—but proof of what? Kaufman used to swear that Tony Clifton was a real Las Vegas nightclub singer he saw in 1969 and that he used to imitate Clifton only at first for a little while. And while Brooks, Weinberger, original *Taxi* casting director Joel Thurm, and others admit the charade, Kaufman's old manager, George Shapiro, to this day faithfully denies that Kaufman and Clifton were one and the same. So who was in my cab?

I was as baffled as a grave-digger in quicksand. What a night. I was ready to call it quits and check into a saloon when a diminutive lady got into my hack. She reeked of garlic, wolfsbane, and the Old Country. I knew immediately this was no kid dressed as a gypsy woman, especially when she asked to be taken to the Bronx Zoo where she could hear her "children of the night." It being a full moon and all, I wished *anyone* else had gotten into my cab—even Tony Clifton.

At the mere thought of his name, the old woman asked about my puzzlement. My hands were shaking, rattling, and rolling on the steering wheel as she pulled out a shimmering ball. Her bony fingers hovered over it, and suddenly a voice spoke from inside. I kept telling myself she had to be the ventriloquist from Bellevue.

What I heard was the voice of Danny DeVito, telling me his account of the infamous Tony Clifton *Taxi* story. It was like she was reading my own memory of my ride with DeVito. Danny had told me about Clifton—hired to guest-star as Louie De Palma's brother Nick in episode #10—being so impossible to work with that Ed Weinberger had to publicly fire him. Now DeVito was saying that Kaufman was supposedly away that week doing a college gig. But then Danny tripped himself up. "Clifton comes in two hours late. Now, everybody at Paramount has got wind of the firing. Everybody's in the bleachers—secretaries, people in the film, TV, advertising end. They all come to see Ed fire Andy—I mean, eh, Tony Clifton. It's a prearranged thing."

A few seconds later, DeVito's voice said, "Ed's going, 'Tony, Tony,' and he's not letting Ed talk. Now Judd gets upset 'cause of the whole charade.' " Charade! Throughout the account, DeVito kept slipping, but he always stuck to his guns—that Kaufman and Clifton were not the same person. I needed more evidence.

Again that gypsy woman waved her hands over the ball, and this time Tony Danza's voice filled my cab.

"What happened that day," recounted Danza's voice, "is I happened to bring my [8mm] camera. They were going to fire him in front of everybody, so around two o'clock the place starts to fill up. I told one guy to put on the lights and I ran film. Then Andy [*Andy!*] comes in with these two girls, sits them on his lap, and says, 'I rewrote the script; I think these two girls should be sitting on my lap through the whole show.'

"Ed disagrees. Then he brings all these presents in—ya know, stuffed animals with remote controls, barking and moving. And Ed's saying, 'You're fired' and he's saying, 'You can't fire *me*.' And Judd is sitting the whole time in one of the mock-up cabs, watchin'. I just wondered how much he was going to put up with this. Remember, we had to pretend that Andy *was* Clifton, that he wasn't Andy. We all had to indulge him. So anyway, him and Judd get into a wrestling match. Judd tries to throw him off the stage. They get a little crazy. I don't know if he's in character or what, but they get into a thing about whose contract is bigger than whose. Finally, security comes and drags Andy off, and he's screaming, 'You'll never work in Vegas again!' Absolute lunatic.

"Then we're off, on hiatus. The next week we come back, and I got the film. So everybody goes into my little cubicle up on Stage 25. So I'm running it on the wall and we're dying laughing. There's Judd wrestlin' with Andy and Ed, and the dogs are barkin'—it's just hysterical! All of a sudden, who opens the door but Andy Kaufman. He walks into the room, an' we all got like kids—caught, ya know? But he just looks at the thing and he goes, 'Who's that asshole?' We say, 'Oh, this guy we worked with last week.' 'Yeah,' he says, 'don't look like too much fun,' and he walks out. And he never said anything else about it again."

As I pulled into the Bronx Zoo at a quarter to midnight, I felt a little better. I had my proof, and a deeper understanding of the genius of Andy Kaufman. Artists like him who don't play by the rules never die—their spirits live on eternally, encouraging us to laugh at things other than what the Nielsen ratings deem funny. I turned to thank the gypsy woman, but she was gone, and the "children of the night" were howling like tourists at a wet T-shirt contest. I tried to get out of there, but my battery went dead, and a husky man got into the cab and said his name was Lawrence Talbot. Remember the song that went "Mama said there'd be days like this"?

CHRISTOPHER LLOYD

It was a rainy night in New York City. People with the sense of waltzing mice were out on the town, and everybody wanted a cab. I didn't care. I'd put in long hours, and was half-beat from exhaustion and half-starved for food. So I sat in my buggy and ate a large take-out dinner. I was shoveling some *arroz con pollo* into my mouth when a lanky shadow fell over my yellow rice.

The man standing over my cab was quiet, patient, dressed in denim from head to toe, with horn-rimmed glasses and a crewcut straight out of Parris Island. In that part of town he looked about as unobtrusive as a mongoose on a slice of pizza.

It didn't matter where he wanted to go. I felt comfortable, bordering on blind trust. I could tell we shared an affinity for the sixties, those lost, difficult, but sentimental years, and we both were out of place in the eighties. His peace was not a sign, but from within, and that Ted Bundy grin couldn't mask his gentle nature.

Chris Lloyd in person wasn't anything like the Reverend Jim "Iggy" Ignatowski. He looked more like he did as Taber in the film *One Flew Over the Cuckoo's Nest.* As Jim, Chris was loud, wigged-out, and prone to long, sometimes meaningless orations. In real life, Chris was soft-spoken, eloquent, but hard-pressed to carry on any lengthy conversations. While the hot, black *café Cubano* had me speeding along Canal Street, Chris drank herbal tea.

Night and day, day and night—we connected, but sometimes missed the dots. . . . Until I started asking him about how he became Jim, a character we both loved.

"They sent me some pages, and I looked at 'em overnight. I remember there was a kind of attitude Jim had, a kind of basic attitude, which was suggested in the writing quite strongly," he recounted in a voice devoid of any "Jim-isms." "I've heard stories about how when I first came in to audition, because of the way I looked the secretary didn't know if I was supposed to be there or had wandered in off the street. Maybe that's true—I *did* come in character.

"I had an old pair of Levi's, an old pair of sneakers I inherited from my ex-father-in-law, and a blue shirt all torn, frayed, and old. A friend of mine who lives up in Laurel Canyon had found an old Levi's jacket with a peace sign on it, in the bushes. Laurel Canyon was a big hippie kind of place once. So he gives me this thing. It'd been hanging around in my closet for a couple of years, so I pulled it out and put that on. I used to wear Levi's Jackets all the time; that was my basic outfit. I didn't have any emblems on them, but this jacket obviously was a prized piece. I wore it on the show, and it stuck—it became Jim's uniform. I can't even get it back! I tried to get it back from the wardrobe department, but they can't find it."

The windshield wipers were making me groggy. Rain was coming down like from shattered fish tanks. The thunder was rumbling about in the distance like a bunch of elephants playing tag. It didn't faze Chris. He was getting into our discussion about Jim.

"Iggy was kind of a composite of a lot of different people. I had lots of years of doing off-off-Broadway down around the Bowery. There's a restaurant there named Phebe's that's gotten very uptown, but back then it was like a seedy place where actors hung out, all these people working for the Public Theatre, all these off-off-Broadway people. I was working for a long time for the theater next door. The top three floors were a flophouse, and the bottom floor was a theater. And you'd go there at night, and you'd have to walk over these guys sprawled out all over. Every once in a while during a performance, a guy would wander in and nobody would catch him. And they'd just wander in—it was a little arena theater—and they'd just walk right onto the stage! Living theater! You'd turn them around, point them the other way."

True to his nature, he said of his classic creation that "a tremendous amount of credit goes to the writers. I contributed, but I pretty much relied on them. I do generally as an actor. I'm not much of

Christopher Lloyd.

a creator or a writer. I like to take what's written and make it happen. These writers came up with some incredible stuff. I was just a neophyte in sit-com land. The one thing that bothered me was that they didn't maintain the reverend aspect. Because 'Reverend Jim' kind of explains the character.''

Born October 22, 1938, in Stamford, Connecticut, Chris Lloyd grew up in nearby New Canaan and went to high school in Westport. He was the baby in a wealthy family, the youngest of four girls and three boys. Somewhat like his character on *Taxi*, the heir skipped college and moved to the burnt-out Lower East Side of New York. He told me he had lived ''on 3rd Street between Avenues A and B,'' an area which lately is getting so gentrified that even the gentry have all moved out. ''I

was walking home one day and wasn't really thinking, walking by these worn-down lots. And I turned around and discovered I was in the middle of this gang war! Guys yelling at each other, bricks flying over my head, taunting each other across the street. I just said, 'OK, just keep walking!''' He laughs. ''It's like you're in the jungle and you see a lion—'Just keep walking!'''

He began acting at the famed Neighborhood Playhouse, and soon began appearing in summer-stock and off-off-Broadway productions. In 1969, despite no particular musical-comedy training or interest, he landed a small part in a Broadway musical *Red, White and Maddox*. By the seventies he was an off-Broadway regular, earning special accolades in 1973 for what New York theater-goers still consider a legendary performance, in the one-man, experimental German play *Kaspar;* he won Obie and Drama Desk awards for his work there and in other plays that year.

As luck would have it, I had had one of Chris's close friends in my cab the other day—Peter Weller, Mr. *Robocop* himself. Weller had told me a story about performing in *Macbeth* along with guys by the name of Christopher Walken, John Heard, Dan Hedaya, James Tolkin, a young woman named Carol Kane, and—Christopher Lloyd. "During rehearsals, he hadn't said anything to anybody in three weeks. But he had an old-time friend there, an actor named Clarence Feldner, and Clarence says, 'That's alright, don't pay any attention to him—his nickname is 'The Fog.' He doesn't talk much but he's a real good guy.'

"Now, we're standing offstage one time, there's a light problem. Me, John Heard, Chris Walken, all sitting on a bench in the vomitorium, which is sort of an offstage dark place. There's just one little blue light on. And so we start telling jokes. We tell jokes for maybe forty-five minutes. Finally Walken tells a joke about Frank Zappa. We start laughing. All of a sudden from underneath this bench the three of us are sitting on, we hear this [low and steady] ho, ho, ho, ho. We freak out, man—there's nobody there! And Chris Lloyd gets up from underneath the bench. This guy who doesn't talk to anybody, he's been lying there the whole forty-five minutes listening to jokes! This is the one he's chosen to laugh at. We all are stunned.

"So he comes out, now—like, wants to join the club. He says, 'I know a joke.' So he tells us this cartoon he saw in *The New Yorker*, which he was reading constantly. He always reads it, like an addiction to it. It was from around the time of the moon shots—these astronauts on the moon or some planet, looking at this being sitting on a rock. And this being has got four eyes and antennae and four arms, which are, like, conversational, palms up, and four legs, two of which are crossed, and the caption says, 'So enough of me, what about yourselves?' So we're all falling on the floor there, laughing at this. And this was my introduction to Chris Lloyd. Same with John Heard and Walken. We all bring it up—'Remember that time. . . .' "

Christopher Lloyd as Reverend Jim.

Before, during, and after *Taxi,* Chris did a lot of television. Some of it was silly—an adventure series pilot called *Stunt Seven,* for instance, and *Street Hawk,* a Rex Smith vehicle (literally—it was a motorcycle). But there were two episodes of *Barney Miller* and the well-regarded but short-lived *Best of the West* as well as a memorable two-part episode of *Cheers.* He did prestigious PBS work such as *The Adams Chronicles* and the anthologies *Visions* and *American Playhouse.* After *Taxi* he starred in an ABC series pilot called *Old Friends.* And his movie work—this guy had a rap sheet like Dillinger's. He's done three movies with his friend Jack Nicholson: *One Flew Over the Cuckoo's Nest, Goin' South* (both with Danny DeVito), and *The Postman Always Rings Twice.* For some reason, he's done more than his share of failed westerns—*Three Warriors, Butch and Sundance: The Early Years,* and *The Legend of the Lone Ranger.* But in 1983, with *Mr. Mom* and Mel Brooks's *To Be or Not to Be,* Chris established himself as a major character

The exquisite Chris Lloyd: "I could show up in any condition!"

actor in films. He cemented that reputation with *Star Trek III: The Search for Spock,* in which he played Jim as a Klingon, and with the enormously successful *Back to the Future* films. On the home front, he and his wife of about three years, Carol Ann Vanek, filed for divorce in July, 1991.

All this information made me wish I had a whole *Thermos* of Cuban coffee. On endless nights like these, the lines between my eyes were longer than the ones to buy Springsteen tickets at Madison Square Garden. Chris could relate. He said he wasn't a fast learner, and for episodes where he had a lot of lines, there'd be many nights he'd stay up memorizing. "But one nice thing about being Jim," he said, chuckling, "was that I could show up in any condition. It didn't matter! And nobody would ever know the difference! A once-in-a-lifetime role," he said wistfully.

Another nice thing about Jim was that he seemed to be the only character who actually *liked* Louie De Palma.

"I don't think Jim took Louie very seriously," he told me. "I think Jim thought he was cute—

amusing. He genuinely liked Louie. Part of it was that Louie was the boss, and Jim had a great deal of respect—he believed in it. Plus I think the writers wanted that contrast. Even though the boss was nasty to Jim, it went right past him most of the time."

I made one of my rare observations. The earth shook from the thunder outside instead. I told Chris that I felt Jim was very Christ-like, that he behaved the way he did on purpose so as to make people happy. He did it so much, that even at home, the spaciness became part of his nature. A high-falutin writer friend of mine calls it, "literature's noble fool, the idiot savant."

I looked through my rearview mirror and waited for an answer. Chris stared into space, contorted his mouth, and shook his shoulders. It was an eerie moment, and when it passed, there was no Iggy, not even a hint. Seeing this made me wonder if he were interested in ever playing Jim again.

"Only if there were a *Taxi* reunion," Chris said in his own voice. "See, I'm essentially a character actor, and I depend a lot on coming up with a new Chris Lloyd each time. To become identified with only one character dilutes possibilities. Often casting people will make choices based on how this person has become identifiable. So I'm sort of protecting what I do."

I understood and accepted. Everyone has to move on. Chris Lloyd was not Jim Ignatowski, only in reruns. I missed Jim, and when we reached his destination and he ran off into the rain, I missed Chris. Right then I would have settled for a cup of *Klingon* coffee. As I pulled out into the early-morning traffic, a gravelly voice bellowed out of nowhere, "Thanks, boss!" And I knew that reruns were a state of mind.

RHEA PERLMAN

The back door to my cab opened, and nobody got in. Or so it seemed, until this pixie-eyed, dark-haired woman sat up in the left corner and giggled. The giggle had a Brooklyn air about it that made me immediately recognize my passenger as the acid-tongued Carla Tortelli Lebec from *Cheers.* Or ac-

Rhea Perlman.

tually, actress Rhea Perlman, who in person is a lot more like Zena Sherman, the character she played in five prominent episodes of *Taxi*.

Zena was a sweet, tender, hard-working girl from Brooklyn (just like Rhea) who worked in Manhattan (also like Rhea) who could be tough when it came to putting her boy friend Louie De Palma (real-life husband Danny DeVito) in his place.

"I don't think I'm mild-mannered," she said quietly, but with an undercurrent of deliberation. "Not as mild-mannered as Zena. I mean, every character you play is an outgrowth of yourself, but I don't think I'm really 'the nice girl,' " she slurred sardonically. "I *can* be nice, but I'm not *that* nice." She giggled. "Zena's niceness was in contrast to Louie's insanity. They even gave me a reverend for a father! *That* was different—I'm Jewish, y'know? So that made my character even nicer! I was getting nicer and nicer!" She jokingly screams. "But it was fun. That's what I like about doing sitcoms, that they throw these things at you. *You* don't know your father is a reverend. *You* don't know your [i.e., Carla Tortelli's] sister is a nymphomaniac. *You* don't know any of this stuff until you get the script. That's what makes it fun: your character developing as the writers develop."

As my cab bounced along New York's melting potholes, we talked a little about her real life, the one without a script.

Back in January 1971, future husband Danny DeVito was performing as a stableboy in an off-Broadway play called *The Shrinking Bride*. Rhea was just breaking into experimental theater, supporting herself by working as a waitress, and had gone to see a friend in the production. But it was Danny she focused on. "It was love at first sight," she told me. "He had this maniacal energy that just dominated the stage."

They moved in together maybe two weeks afterward, and eleven years to the day from when they met they were married in the backyard of their house. With typical madness, they were married by a nondenominational minister/Los Angeles Philharmonic French horn player. Their wedding march was a record of "Our Gang's" Alfalfa crooning "I'm in the Mood for Love."

Me, I was in the mood for more information, and Rhea gave it to me.

She was born March 31, 1948, in the Coney Island section of Brooklyn and grew up in nearby Bensonhurst. The name Rhea comes from Greek mythology—the daughter of Gaea and Uranus, the mother of Zeus, Poseidon, and other assorted deities. (It's also the name of the South American ostrich, but I figure we could rule that out.) Rhea's mother was a bookkeeper, and her dad, Phil, is a retiree from a doll-parts company. Lately, dad's become an extra on *Cheers,* on which Rhea's younger sister Heide served as a story editor and a producer before going on to cocreate *The Tracey Ullman Show.*

Rhea told me she's worked both off-off-Broadway and off-off-the-wall. While studying theater at Hunter College, she made a living as an "eraser" for a publishing company that recirculated scribbled-on books and as an allergy tester for an orthomolecular psychiatrist. Unknowingly preparing for her role in *Cheers,* Rhea was a waitress in one of the city's most elegant eateries—I know *I've* never eaten there—the Rainbow Room at the top of the RCA Building. Rhea had the distinction, she claims, of spilling spaghetti on David Rockefeller's dining companion. Now there's an idea for a *Cheers* episode if I ever heard one. Any Rockefellers left to guest-star? Maybe she could spill oysters.

Rhea's first professional acting role was in an experimental play called *Dracula Sabbat*. With Danny, she has costarred in and/or helped produce several independent short subjects, including *Minestrone* (sponsored by the American Film Institute), *The Selling of Vince D'Angelo, Vinyl Visits an FM Station,* and, behind-the-scenes only, *The Sound Sleeper.* She and DeVito also helped found and build a small theater company in New York, the Colonnades Theatre Lab.

After moving to Los Angeles, Rhea got a fistful of work in the TV movies *Stalk the Wild Child* (1976), *I Want to Keep My Baby* (1976), *Mary Jane Harper Cried Last Night* (1977), *Having Babies II* (1977), *Intimate Strangers* (1977), *Like Normal People* (1979), and *Drop-Out Father* (1982). Funny, but they didn't sound funny.

"They were all dramas," she explained, "a bunch of these kinds of movies about social problems like unwed mothers and people who beat their kids and people who couldn't have babies." Serious topics—but the way she described them somehow made them sound *funny*. "They *were* funny!" she contended. "TV movies run in spurts. Lots of times they're all about diseases, or all about Vietnam vets, or all about homosexuals. They run in spurts and it gets, like, kitschy after a while." The kitsch extended to the movies, with a feature called *Love Child* (1982) that played like 19-inches diagonal. She also did a made-for-cable movie, *The Ratings Game* (1984), directed by husband DeVito, who also starred in it, and provided a voice for the animated feature *My Little Pony* (1986). She's lately added the 1987 TV movie *Dangerous Affection* and the 1988 PBS documentary *Who Cares for the Children?* to her rap sheet.

Rhea's five episodes of *Taxi* led in 1982 to *Cheers,* for which she won three consecutive Comedy Supporting Actress Emmys (1984–86). Obviously, she has plenty to cheer about.

As we reached Rhea's destination—in Brooklyn, of course—I let her out with a smile, and she smiled back at me. I felt lucky. Carla might have spit.

TITLE LIST

The 112 original and 2 retrospective episodes of *Taxi* are listed here in the order in which they were produced. Though broadcast in a different order (see "Original Network Airdates"), they are generally rerun in this order in syndication. The titles are from the original scripts.

#1	Like Father, Like Daughter
#2	Blind Date
#3	The Great Line
#4	Come as You Aren't
#5	One-Punch Banta
#6	Bobby's Acting Career
#7	High School Reunion
#8	Paper Marriage
#9	Money Troubles
#10	A Full House for Christmas
#11	Sugar Mama
#12	Men Are Such Beasts
#13	Elaine and the Lame Duck
#14	Bobby's Big Break
#15	Friends
#16	Louie Sees the Light
#17	Substitute Father
#18	Mama Gravas
#19	Alex Tastes Death and Finds a Nice Restaurant
#20	Hollywood Calling
#21	Memories of Cab 804, Part I
#22	Memories of Cab 804, Part II
#23	Honor Thy Father
#24	The Reluctant Fighter
#25	Louie and the Nice Girl
#26	Wherefore Art Thou, Bobby?
#27	Reverend Jim: A Space Odyssey
#28	Nardo Loses Her Marbles
#29	A Woman Between Friends
#30	The Lighter Side of Angela Matusa
#31	The Great Race
#32	The Apartment
#33	Elaine's Secret Admirer
#34	Alex's Romance
#35	Latka's Revolting

#36	Louie Meets the Folks
#37	Tony and Brian
#38	Jim Gets a Pet
#39	What Price Bobby?
#40	Guess Who's Coming for Brefnish?
#41	Shut It Down, Part I
#42	Shut It Down, Part II
#43	Fantasy Borough, Part I
#44	Fantasy Borough, Part II
#45	Art Work
#46	Alex Jumps Out of an Airplane
#47	Louie's Rival
#48	Fathers of the Bride
#49	Going Home
#50	Elaine's Strange Triangle
#51	Bobby's Roommate
#52	Tony's Sister and Jim
#53	Call of the Mild
#54	Thy Boss' Wife
#55	Latka's Cookies
#56	The Ten Percent Solution
#57	Zen and the Art of Cab Driving
#58	Elaine's Old Friend
#59	The Costume Party
#60	Out of Commission
#61	Bobby and the Critic
#62	Louie's Mother
#63	Louie Bumps Into an Old Lady
#64	Latka the Playboy
#65	Jim the Psychic
#66	Fledgling
#67	On the Job, Part I
#68	On the Job, Part II
#69	Vienna Waits
#70	Mr. Personalities
#71	Jim Joins the Network
#72	Louie's Fling
#73	Like Father, Like Son
#74	Louie's Mom Remarries
#75	Of Mice and Tony
#76	Nina Loves Alex
#77	Louie Goes Too Far
#78	I Wanna Be Around

* Titled "A Taxi Celebration" on-screen.

ORIGINAL NETWORK AIRDATES

AIRDATE	EPISODE TITLE AND SYNDICATION NUMBER

FIRST SEASON

ABC: TUESDAY 9:30 P.M.

9/12/78	Like Father, Like Daughter (#1)
9/19/78	One-Punch Banta (#5)
9/26/78	Blind Date (#2)
10/03/78	PREEMPTION: Baseball Playoff
10/05/78*	Bobby's Acting Career (#6)
10/10/78	Come as You Aren't (#4)
10/17/78	The Great Line (#3)
10/24/78	High School Reunion (#7)
10/31/78	Paper Marriage (#8)
11/07/78	PREEMPTION: *The '78 Vote*
11/14/78	Money Troubles (#9)
11/21/78	Men Are Such Beasts (#12)
11/28/78	Memories of Cab 804, Part I (#21)
12/05/78	Memories of Cab 804, Part II (#22)
12/12/78	A Full House for Christmas (#10)
12/19/78	PREEMPTION: *The Carpenters: A Christmas Portrait*
12/26/78	Blind Date (repeat from 9/26/78)
1/02/79	The Great Line (repeat from 10/17/78)
1/09/79	Paper Marriage (repeat from 10/31/78)
1/16/79	Sugar Mama (#11)
1/23/79	PREEMPTION: State of the Union Address
1/30/79	Friends (#15)
2/06/79	Louie Sees the Light (#16)
2/13/79	Elaine and the Lame Duck (#13)
2/15/79*	Bobby's Big Break (#14)

2/20/79	PREEMPTION: *Roots: The Next Generation*
2/27/79	Mama Gravas (#18)
3/06/79	Alex Tastes Death and Finds a Nice Restaurant (#19)
3/13/79	PREEMPTION: *The Ropers*
3/20/79	PREEMPTION: *13 Queens Boulevard*
3/27/79	PREEMPTION: *Three's Company*
4/03/79	Like Father, Like Daughter (repeat from 9/12/78)
4/10/79	One-Punch Banta (repeat from 9/19/78)
4/17/79	Come as You Aren't (repeat from 10/10/78)
4/24/79	Money Troubles (repeat from 11/14/78)
5/01/79	High School Reunion (repeat from 10/24/78)
5/08/79	Hollywood Calling (#20)
5/15/79	Substitute Father (#17)
5/22/79	Memories of Cab 804, Part I (repeat from 11/28/78)
5/29/79	Memories of Cab 804, Part II (repeat from 12/05/78)
6/05/79	Men Are Such Beasts (repeat from 11/21/78)
6/12/79	Sugar Mama (repeat from 1/16/79)
6/19/79	Friends (repeat from 1/30/79)
6/26/79	A Full House for Christmas (repeat from 12/12/78)
7/03/79	Elaine and the Lame Duck (repeat from 2/13/79)
7/10/79	Bobby's Big Break (repeat from 2/15/79)

TAXI

87

7/17/79	Blind Date (repeat from 9/26 and 12/26/78)	1/22/80	What Price Bobby? (#39)
7/24/79	Alex Tastes Death and Finds a Nice Restaurant (repeat from 3/06/79)	1/29/80	Shut It Down, Part I (#41)
		2/05/80	Shut It Down, Part II (#42)
7/31/79	Paper Marriage (repeat from 10/31/78 and 1/09/79)	2/12/80	PREEMPTION: Winter Olympics Preview
8/07/79	Hollywood Calling (repeat from 5/08/79)	2/19/80	PREEMPTION: The Winter Olympics
8/14/79	Substitute Father (repeat from 5/15/79)	2/26/80	Alex Jumps Out of an Airplane (#46)
8/21/79	Mama Gravas (repeat from 2/27/79)	3/04/80	Art Work (#45)
		3/11/80	Reverend Jim: A Space Odyssey (repeat from 9/25/79)
8/28/79	PREEMPTION: *240 Robert*		
9/04/79	PREEMPTION: *The Lazarus Syndrome*	3/18/80	Louie and the Nice Girl (repeat from 9/11/79)
		3/25/80	The Apartment (repeat from 11/13/79)

SECOND SEASON

ABC: TUESDAY, 9:30 P.M.

9/11/79	Louie and the Nice Girl (#25)	4/01/80	Alex's Romance (repeat from 11/20/79)
9/18/79	Honor Thy Father (#23)	4/08/80	A Woman Between Friends (repeat from 10/30/79)
9/25/79	Reverend Jim: A Space Odyssey (#27)	4/15/80	Nardo Loses Her Marbles (repeat from 10/02/79)
10/02/79	Nardo Loses Her Marbles (#28)		
10/09/79	The Reluctant Fighter (#24)	4/22/80	The Lighter Side of Angela Matusa (repeat from 10/23/79)
10/16/79	PREEMPTION: The World Series	4/29/80	Louie Meets the Folks (repeat from 12/11/79)
10/21/79†	Wherefore Art Thou, Bobby? (#26)	5/06/80	Fantasy Borough, Part I (#43)
		5/13/80	Fantasy Borough, Part II (#44)
10/23/79	The Lighter Side of Angela Matusa (#30)	5/20/80	The Great Race (repeat from 11/06/79)
10/30/79	A Woman Between Friends (#29)	5/27/80	Latka's Revolting (repeat from 11/27/79)
11/06/79	The Great Race (#31)		
11/13/79	The Apartment (#32)	6/03/80	Honor Thy Father (repeat from 9/18/79)
11/20/79	Alex's Romance (#34)		
11/27/79	Latka's Revolting (#35)	6/10/80	Louie Meets the Folks (repeat from 12/11/79 and 4/29/80)
12/04/79	Elaine's Secret Admirer (#33)		
12/11/79	Louie Meets the Folks (#36)	6/17/80	What Price Bobby? (repeat from 1/22/80)
12/18/79	Jim Gets a Pet (#38)		
12/25/79	The Reluctant Fighter (repeat from 10/09/79)	6/24/80	Alex Jumps Out of an Airplane (repeat from 2/26/80)
1/01/80	Wherefore Art Thou, Bobby? (repeat from 10/21/79)	7/01/80	Tony and Brian (repeat from 1/08/80)
		7/08/80	PREEMPTION: All-Star Game
1/08/80	Tony and Brian (#37)	7/15/80	PREEMPTION: Republican National Convention
1/15/80	Guess Who's Coming for Brefnish? (#40)	7/22/80	Elaine's Secret Admirer (repeat from 12/04/79)
		7/29/80	Art Work (repeat from 3/04/80)

8/05/80	Jim Gets a Pet (repeat from 12/18/79)
8/12/80	PREEMPTION: Democratic National Convention
8/19/80	Guess Who's Coming for Brefnish? (repeat from 1/15/80)
8/26/80	One-Punch Banta (repeat from 9/19/78 and 4/10/79)
9/02/80	High School Reunion (repeat from 10/24/78 and 5/01/79)
9/09/80	PREEMPTION: *Pearl*
9/16/80	Shut It Down, Part I (repeat from 1/29/80)
9/23/80	Shut It Down, Part II (repeat from 2/05/80)
9/30/80	Mama Gravas (repeat from 2/27 and 8/21/79)
10/07/80	PREEMPTION: National League Championship Game
10/14/80	Fantasy Borough, Part I (repeat from 5/06/80)
10/21/80	Fantasy Borough, Part II (repeat from 5/13/80)

THIRD SEASON

ABC: WEDNESDAY, 9:00 P.M.

11/19/80	Louie's Rival (#47)
11/26/80	Tony's Sister and Jim (#52)
12/03/80	Fathers of the Bride (#48)
12/10/80	Elaine's Strange Triangle (#50)
12/17/80	Going Home (#49)
12/24/80	PREEMPTION: *Eight Is Enough*
12/31/80	Alex Tastes Death and Finds a Nice Restaurant (repeat from 3/06 and 7/24/79)
1/07/81	The Ten Percent Solution (#56)
1/14/81	PREEMPTION: President Carter's Farewell Address (episode scheduled: ''Thy Boss' Wife'')
1/21/81	Call of the Mild (#53)
1/28/81	PREEMPTION: ABC News special: *The Secret Negotiations* (episode scheduled: ''Latka's Cookies'')

THURSDAY, 9:30 P.M.

2/05/81	Latka's Cookies (#55)
2/12/81	Thy Boss' Wife (#54)
2/19/81	The Costume Party (#59)
2/26/81	Elaine's Old Friend (#58)
3/05/81	Louie's Rival (repeat from 11/19/80)
3/12/81	Out of Commission (#60)
3/19/81	Zen and the Art of Cab Driving (#57)
3/26/81	Louie's Mother (#62)
4/02/81	Elaine's Strange Triangle (repeat from 12/10/80)
4/09/81	Bobby's Roommate (#51)
4/16/81	Louie Bumps Into an Old Lady (#63)
4/23/81	Tony's Sister and Jim (repeat from 11/26/80)
4/30/81	Bobby and the Critic (#61)
5/07/81	On the Job, Part I (#67)
5/14/81	On the Job, Part II (#68)
5/21/81	Latka the Playboy (#64)
5/28/81	Fathers of the Bride (repeat from 12/03/80)
6/04/81	Going Home (repeat from 12/17/80)
6/11/81	Latka's Cookies (repeat from 2/05/81)
6/18/81	Call of the Mild (repeat from 1/21/81)
6/25/81	The Ten Percent Solution (repeat from 1/07/81)
7/02/81	The Costume Party (repeat from 2/19/81)
7/09/81	Thy Boss' Wife (repeat from 2/12/81)
7/16/81	Elaine's Old Friend (repeat from 2/26/81)
7/23/81	Out of Commission (repeat from 3/12/81)
7/30/81	Zen and the Art of Cab Driving (repeat from 3/19/81)
8/06/81	Bobby and the Critic (repeat from 4/30/81)
8/13/81	Louie's Mother (repeat from 3/26/81)

8/20/81	PREEMPTION: *ABC News Closeup: The Monastery*	
8/27/81	Bobby's Roommate (repeat from 4/09/81)	
9/03/81	Louie Bumps Into an Old Lady (repeat from 4/16/81)	
9/10/81	PREEMPTION: NFL Football	
9/17/81	PREEMPTION: NFL Football	
9/24/81‡	On the Job, Parts I & II (repeats from 5/07 and 5/14/81)	
10/01/81	PREEMPTION: *The Manions of America*	

FOURTH SEASON

ABC: THURSDAY, 9:30 P.M.

10/08/81	Jim the Psychic (#65)
10/15/81	Vienna Waits (#69)
10/22/81	Mr. Personalities (#70)
10/29/81	Jim Joins the Network (#71)
11/05/81	Louie's Fling (#72)
11/12/81	Like Father, Like Son (#73)
11/19/81	Louie's Mom Remarries (#74)
11/26/81	Fledgling (#66)
12/03/81	PREEMPTION: NFL Football
12/10/81	Of Mice and Tony (#75)
12/17/81	Louie Goes Too Far (#77)
12/24/81‡	On the Job, Parts I & II (repeats from 5/07 and 5/14/81, and 9/24/81)
12/31/81	Vienna Waits (repeat from 10/15/81)
1/07/82	I Wanna Be Around (#78)
1/14/82	Bobby Doesn't Live Here Anymore (#79)
1/21/82	Nina Loves Alex (#76)
1/28/82	Tony's Lady (#80)
2/04/82	Simka Returns (#81)
2/11/82	Jim and the Kid (#82)
2/18/82	Take My Ex-Wife, Please (#83)
2/25/82	The Unkindest Cut (#84)
3/04/82	Tony's Comeback (#85)
3/11/82	Jim the Psychic (repeat from 10/08/81)
3/18/82	Elegant Iggy (#86)
3/25/82	The Wedding of Latka and Simka (#87)

4/01/82	Louie's Fling (repeat from 11/05/81)
4/08/82	Cooking for Two (#88)
4/15/82	Louie's Mom Remarries (repeat from 11/19/81)
4/22/82	Mr. Personalities (repeat from 10/22/81)
4/29/82	The Road Not Taken, Part I (#89)
5/06/82	The Road Not Taken, Part II (#90)
5/13/82	Louie Goes Too Far (repeat from 12/17/81)
5/20/82	Of Mice and Tony (repeat from 12/10/81)
5/27/82	Bobby Doesn't Live Here Anymore (repeat from 1/14/82)
6/03/82	Jim Joins the Network (repeat from 10/29/81)
6/07/82	Elegant Iggy (repeat from 3/18/82)

OFF ABC'S SCHEDULE

FIFTH SEASON

NBC: THURSDAY, 9:30 P.M.

9/30/82	The Shloogel Show (#91)
10/07/82	Jim's Inheritance (# 93)
10/14/82	Alex Goes Off the Wagon (#92)
10/21/82	Scenskees from a Marriage, Part I (#94)
10/28/82	Scenskees from a Marriage, Part II (#95)
11/04/82	Crime and Punishment (#102)
11/11/82	Alex the Gofer (#96)
11/18/82	Louie's Revenge (#97)
11/25/82	Travels with My Dad (#98)
12/02/82	Elaine and the Monk (#99)
12/09/82	Zena's Honeymoon (#100)
12/16/82	Get Me Through the Holidays (#103)
12/23/82	Cooking for Two (repeat from 4/08/82, ABC)
12/30/82	Take My Ex-Wife, Please (repeat from 2/18/82, ABC)

ON HIATUS

SATURDAY, 9:30 P.M.

1/22/83	Louie Moves Uptown (#101)
1/29/83	Alex's Old Buddy (#104)
2/05/83	Sugar Ray Nardo (#105)

ON HIATUS

WEDNESDAY, 9:30 P.M.

3/23/83§	A Taxi Celebration (#113–#114)
3/30/83	Alex Gets Burned by an Old Flame (#106)
4/06/83	Louie and the Blind Girl (#109)
4/13/83	Arnie Meets the Kids (#111)
4/20/83	Tony's Baby (#107)
4/27/83	Alex Goes Off the Wagon (repeat from 10/14/82; West Coast telecast only; East Coast telecast preempted; Originally scheduled: Jim's Mario's)

5/04/83	PREEMPTION: *The Facts of Life*
5/11/83	PREEMPTION: *The Facts of Life*
5/18/83	Jim's Mario's (#108)
5/25/83	A Grand Gesture (#112)
6/01/83	PREEMPTION: *Buffalo Bill*
6/08/83	PREEMPTION: *Buffalo Bill*
6/15/83	Simka's Monthlies (#110)
6/22/83	Crime and Punishment (repeat from 11/04/82)
6/29/83	The Shloogel Show (repeat from 9/30/82)
7/06/83	PREEMPTION: Baseball All-Star Game
7/13/83	Jim's Inheritance (repeat from 10/07/82)

OFF THE AIR

*Thursday airing due to preemption
† Sunday airing due to preemption
‡ 9 P.M.
§ a.k.a. ''Retrospective, Parts I and II'' in syndication

SERIES CREDITS

▪▫▪▫▪

TAXI

Created by James L. Brooks, Stan Daniels, David Davis, and Ed Weinberger

CAST

ALEX REIGER* ....Judd Hirsch
BOBBY WHEELER .... Jeff Conaway
                            (seasons 1–3)
LOUIE DE PALMA ....Danny DeVito
TONY BANTA .... Tony Danza
ELAINE O'CONNOR NARDO .... Marilu Henner
"REVEREND" JIM IGNATOWSKI ("IGGY"),
    NÉ JAMES CALDWELL
      .... Christopher Lloyd (beginning episode 33)
JOHN BURNS .... Randall Carver (season 1)
SIMKA DAHBLITZ GRAVAS ....Carol Kane
                           (season 5)
LATKA GRAVAS ....Andy Kaufman

Also seen as an extra, bit player, or guest star in virtually every episode: J. Alan Thomas as Jeff Bennett

EXECUTIVE CREATIVE CONSULTANT/EXECUTIVE CONSULTANT: James L. Brooks
EXECUTIVE PRODUCERS: James L. Brooks, Stan Daniels, Ed Weinberger, and (season 1) David Davis†
PRODUCTION EXECUTIVE: Ronald E. Frazier (seasons 1–4); James Wright (season 5)
ORIGINAL CASTING: Joel Thurm
MUSIC: Bob James
MUSIC AND SOUND EFFECTS: Ed Norton Music Inc.; Recorded by: Glen Glenn Sound; Production Mixer: Jim Wright; Opticals: Freeze Frame; Taxis provided by: Checker Motor Corp.
PRODUCED BY John Charles Walters Productions in association with Paramount Television

FIRST SEASON

PRODUCERS: Glen Charles and Les Charles
ASSOCIATE PRODUCER: Budd Cherry
DIRECTOR OF PHOTOGRAPHY: Edward E. Nugent
ART DIRECTOR: Tom H. John
FILM EDITOR: M. Pam Blumenthal
UNIT PRODUCTION MANAGER/ASSISTANT EDITOR/FIRST ASSISTANT DIRECTOR: Gregg Peters
SECOND ASSISTANT DIRECTOR‡: Dick Evans, Stewart Lyons, Michael Stanislavsky, Jack Clements
CASTING: Rhonda S. Young
SET DECORATOR: Ed Parker (first episode only), Joseph A. Armetta
TECHNICAL COORDINATOR: Gil Clasen
SCRIPT SUPERVISOR: Rosemary Dorsey
MAKEUP‡: Jerry Cash, Ray Sebastian II
COSTUMES: Ralph T. Schlain
ASSISTANTS TO MR. CHERRY§: Larry Foster, Richard Sakai
ASSISTANTS TO MR. DANIELS§: Robin Chambers, Andrea Davis, Larry Foster, Lea Goldbaum, Richard Sakai, Catherine Tessier, Donna Wheeler

SECOND SEASON

PRODUCERS: Glen Charles and Les Charles
ASSOCIATE PRODUCER: Richard Sakai
EXECUTIVE SCRIPT CONSULTANT: Barry Kemp
EXECUTIVE STORY EDITOR: David Lloyd (beginning partway through season)
STORY EDITORS: Ian Praiser and Howard Gewirtz (beginning partway through season)
PROGRAM CONSULTANT: Ken Estin
DIRECTOR OF PHOTOGRAPHY: Edward E. Nugent
ART DIRECTOR‡: Mary Dodson, Lynn Griffin
FILM EDITOR: M. Pam Blumenthal (with Jack Michon beginning partway through season)
UNIT PRODUCTION MANAGER AND ASSISTANT EDITOR: Gregg Peters
FIRST ASSISTANT DIRECTOR: Stewart Lyons

SECOND ASSISTANT DIRECTOR: Carlo Quinterio

CASTING: Susan Arnold

SET DECORATOR‡: Steve Potter, Fred S. Winston

TECHNICAL COORDINATOR: Gil Clasen

SCRIPT SUPERVISOR: Judi Brown

COSTUMER: Ralph T. Schlain

MARILU HENNER'S COSTUMES: Sharon Day

MAKEUP: Jerry Cash

TALENT COORDINATOR: Robin Chambers

ASSISTANTS TO MR. DANIELS§: Matthew Carlson, Cathy Clark, Elizabeth Hill, Dixie Reinhardt, Connie Schiro, Donna Wheeler, H. Adele Woodson

THIRD SEASON

PRODUCERS: Glen Charles and Les Charles

ASSOCIATE PRODUCER: Richard Sakai

EXECUTIVE SCRIPT CONSULTANT: Barry Kemp

EXECUTIVE STORY EDITOR: David Lloyd

STORY EDITOR: Ken Estin

DIRECTOR OF PHOTOGRAPHY: Kenneth Peach, ASC

ART DIRECTOR: Kenneth Reid

FILM EDITORS: M. Pam Blumenthal, usually with Jack Michon or Andrew Chulack

UNIT PRODUCTION MANAGER AND ASSISTANT EDITOR: Gregg Peters

FIRST ASSISTANT DIRECTOR: Mike Stanislavsky

SECOND ASSISTANT DIRECTOR‡: Carlo Quinterio primarily; also Brian Ellis and Michael Looney

CASTING: Joan Sittenfield

CONSULTANT [ART DIRECTION]: Tommy Goetz

TALENT COORDINATOR: Robin Chambers

WARDROBE: MacGregor Sportswear

SET DECORATOR‡: Sharon Thomas, Charles Tycer, Fred Winston

TECHNICAL COORDINATOR: Gil Clasen

SCRIPT SUPERVISOR: Judi Brown

COSTUMER: Ralph T. Schlain

WOMEN'S COSTUMES: Dolores Murray

MAKEUP: Jerry Cash

ASSISTANTS TO MR. DANIELS§: Catharine Clark, Barbara Duncan, Mark Harrah, Elizabeth Hill, Robin James, Jay Kleckner, Tina Levine, Sandy Lovelace, Patricia Marino, Greg Nierman, Chris Painter, Donna Wheeler.

FOURTH SEASON

PRODUCERS: Ken Estin, Howard Gewirtz, and Ian Praiser

COPRODUCER: Richard Sakai

EXECUTIVE CONSULTANTS: Glen Charles and Les Charles

EXECUTIVE SCRIPT CONSULTANT: David Lloyd

EXECUTIVE STORY EDITOR: Sam Simon

ASSOCIATE PRODUCER: Greg Nierman

DIRECTOR OF PHOTOGRAPHY: Kenneth Peach, ASC

ART DIRECTOR: Tommy Goetz

FILM EDITORS: M. Pam Blumenthal, usually with Douglas Hines, ACE, or Bernard Balmuth, ACE

UNIT PRODUCTION MANAGER: Gregg Peters

FIRST ASSISTANT DIRECTOR: Mike Stanislavsky

SECOND ASSISTANT DIRECTOR: Lorraine Raglin

CASTING: Jennifer Jackson Part

SET DECORATOR: Charles Tycer

TECHNICAL COORDINATOR: Gil Clasen

SCRIPT SUPERVISOR: Rosemary Dorsey

COSTUMER: Ralph T. Schlain

MEN'S WARDROBE PROVIDED BY: Botany 500

MAKEUP: Larry Abbott, SMA

ASSISTANTS TO MR. DANIELS§: Nat Bernstein, Catharine Clark, Barbara Duncan, Mark Harrah, Leslie Maier, Cary Matsumura, Lynne Nessel, Sandy Lovelace

FIFTH SEASON

PRODUCERS: Ken Estin, Richard Sakai, and Sam Simon

EXECUTIVE SCRIPT CONSULTANT: David Lloyd

EXECUTIVE CONSULTANTS: David Davis/Harvey Miller

STORY EDITOR: Katherine Green

ASSOCIATE PRODUCER: Cary D. Matsumura

STORY CONSULTANT: Al Aidekman (episode #109 only)

DIRECTOR OF PHOTOGRAPHY: Kenneth Peach, ASC

ART DIRECTOR: Ed La Porta

FILM EDITORS: M. Pam Blumenthal, with either Steve W. Schultz or Roger W. Tweten

FIRST ASSISTANT DIRECTOR: Mike Stanislavsky

SECOND ASSISTANT DIRECTOR: Susan Norton

CASTING: Vicki Rosenberg

SET DECORATOR: Charles Tycer

TECHNICAL COORDINATOR: Gil Clasen

COSTUMER: Annette Gagnon
MEN'S WARDROBE: Rudy Garcia
MAKEUP: Charlene Robertson
HAIR: Charlotte Harvey
SCRIPT SUPERVISOR: Rosemary Dorsey
TALENT COORDINATOR: Barbara Duncan
MEN'S WARDROBE PROVIDED BY: Botany 500
ASSISTANT TO MR. MATSUMURA: Patricia S. Marino
ASSISTANTS TO MR. DANIELS§: Kimberly Allen, Sharon Feldstein, Shawn Goodman, Charlotte Grey, Michael Griffith, Mark Harrah, Sue Herring, Sandy Lovelace

NOTES

*Some sources spell it "Rieger," and the name is found both ways in John Charles Walters and Paramount material; the great majority of scripts, however, spell it "Reiger."

†After the first season, listed in the closing credits under "Title Visualization"

‡Each on different episodes.

§Assistants variously added, moved around, and very occasionally dropped throughout the season.

ACE, ASC, and SMA stand for the professional associations American Cinema Editor, American Society of Cinematographers, and Society of Makeup Artists, respectively.

SCREENWRITER CREDITS

AIDEKMAN, Al
#109   Louie and the Blind Girl (w/Ken Estin and Sam Simon; story by Larry Scott Anderson)

ALLEE, Pat
#56   The Ten Percent Solution

BENNETT, Ruth
#16   Louie Sees the Light

BROOKS, Holly Holmberg
#110   Simka's Monthlies

BROOKS, James L.
#1   Like Father, Like Daughter (w/Stan Daniels, Dave Davis, Ed Weinberger)

CARON, Glenn Gordon
#31   The Great Race

CHARLES, Glen and Les
#4   Come as You Aren't
#8   Paper Marriage (story by Barton Dean)
#11   Sugar Mama
#13   Elaine and the Lame Duck
#18   Mama Gravas
#20   Hollywood Calling
#23   Honor Thy Father
#27   Reverend Jim: A Space Odyssey
#35   Latka's Revolting
#45   Art Work
#49   Going Home
#55   Latka's Cookies
#57   Zen and the Art of Cab Driving
#64   Latka the Playboy
#75   Of Mice and Tony
#78   I Wanna Be Around
#79   Bobby Doesn't Live Here Anymore

DANIELS, Dari
#107   Tony's Baby

DANIELS, Stan
#1   Like Father, Like Daughter (w/James L. Brooks, Dave Davis, Ed Weinberger)
#6   Bobby's Acting Career (w/Ed Weinberger)
#12   Men Are Such Beasts (w/Ed Weinberger)

DANZIGER, Dennis
#67   On the Job, Part I (w/Ellen Sandler)
#68   On the Job, Part II (w/Ellen Sandler)

DAVIS, Dave
#1   Like Father, Like Daughter (w/James L. Brooks, Stan Daniels, Ed Weinberger)

DEAN, Barton
#98   Travels with My Dad
#106   Alex Gets Burned by an Old Flame

ESTIN, Ken
#24   The Reluctant Fighter
#29   A Woman Between Friends
#37   Tony and Brian
#39   What Price Bobby?
#46   Alex Jumps Out of an Airplane
#47   Louie's Rival

#83	Take My Ex-Wife, Please
#87	The Wedding of Latka and Simka
#90	The Road Not Taken, Part II
#94	Scenskees from a Marriage, Part I
#95	Scenskees from a Marriage, Part II

ROSEN, Sy
| #7 | High School Reunion |

RUBINOWITZ, Barry
| #32 | The Apartment |

SANDLER, Ellen
| #67 | On the Job, Part I (w/Dennis Danziger) |
| #68 | On the Job, Part II (w/Dennis Danziger) |

SIMON, Sam
#60	Out of Commission
#72	Louie's Fling
#84	The Unkindest Cut (story by Holly Holmberg Brooks and Barbara Duncan)
#85	Tony's Comeback
#88	Cooking for Two (w/Ken Estin)
#89	The Road Not Taken, Part I (w/Ken Estin)
#91	The Shloogel Show (w/Ken Estin)
#97	Louie's Revenge
#103	Get Me Through the Holidays (w/Ken Estin)
#104	Alex's Old Buddy (w/Ken Estin)
#108	Jim's Mario's (w/Ken Estin)
#109	Louie and the Blind Girl (w/Ken Estin and Al Aidekman; story by Larry Scott Anderson)
#112	A Grand Gesture (w/Ken Estin)

WEINBERGER, Ed
#1	Like Father, Like Daughter (w/ James L. Brooks, Stan Daniels, Dave Davis)
#6	Bobby's Acting Career (w/Stan Daniels)
#12	Men Are Such Beasts (w/Stan Daniels)

STORY BASIS ONLY

BROOKS, Holly Holmberg
| #65 | Jim the Psychic |
| #84 | The Unkindest Cut (w/Barbara Duncan) |

DEAN, Barton
| #8 | Paper Marriage |

DUNCAN, Barbara
| #84 | The Unkindest Cut (w/Holly Holmberg Brooks) |

JACOBSON, Mark
| #41 | Shut It Down, Part I (w/Michael Tolkin) |

TOLKIN, Michael
| #41 | Shut It Down, Part I (w/Mark Jacobson) |

DIRECTORS

Most *Taxi* episodes were directed by James Burrows. The following are the exceptions:

CHAMBERS, Jeff
| #58 | Elaine's Old Friend |

DANIELS, Stan
| #97 | Louie's Revenge |
| #102 | Crime and Punishment |

DARLING, Joan
| #76 | Nina Loves Alex |

DEVITO, Danny
#99	Elaine and the Monk
#105	Sugar Ray Nardo
#108	Jim's Mario's

LESSAC, Michael
#77	Louie Goes Too Far
#85	Tony's Comeback
#96	Alex the Gofer

MACKENZIE, Will
| #57 | Zen and the Art of Cab Driving |

MILLER, Harvey
| #106 | Alex Gets Burned by an Old Flame |
| #110 | Simka's Monthlies |

PITLIK, Noam
#71	Jim Joins the Networks
#83	Take My Ex-Wife, Please
#84	The Unkindest Cut
#86	Elegant Iggy
#91	The Shloogel Show
#92	Alex Goes Off the Wagon
#93	Jim's Inheritance
#94	Scenskees from a Marriage, Part I

INDEX OF *TAXI* PERFORMERS

Numbers given are those of episodes, not pages.

T A X I

99

TAXI

100

TAXI
101

The ride begins: Episode #1, "Like Father, Like Daughter."

The Taxi Episode Guide

▉▉▉▉▉

#1 LIKE FATHER, LIKE DAUGHTER

WRITTEN BY JAMES L. BROOKS, STAN DANIELS, DAVID DAVIS, AND ED WEINBERGER. DIRECTED BY JAMES BURROWS.

In his wire-mesh dispatcher's cage at the Sunshine Cab Co., Louie De Palma takes in bookings from the returning night-shift drivers and barks cab assignments over the PA system to the day shift. He sarcastically asks cabbie Tony Banta, a struggling young boxer, how it felt to get creamed in his fight last night. Tony indignantly responds he didn't get creamed, he lost on a decision. Louie: "I'm impressed."

In walks Alex Reiger, a middle-aged career cabbie. He's obviously very popular, with lots of drivers asking if he wants to go out to breakfast. He's busy at the moment with a young out-of-towner named John Burns, who's just moved to New York with his last $150 and who needs to break a fifty in order to pay his $4.85 fare. After settling with Alex, John goes over to the garage pay phone to try to rustle up a place to stay.

Bobby Wheeler, a young actor, tells Alex about a promising audition he had for the play *Equus.* John, meantime, has discovered the pay phone is broken, and that the cabbies can make calls for free. A line immediately forms, with Bobby at the front. He rings up the National Theatre in London, and asks to speak to Sir Laurence Olivier. The great actor is busy taking a curtain call, but Bobby gives Olivier's secretary a message for him—applause. Tony calls Bangkok, where, as a Private First Class

on leave during the Vietnam War, he came across "the classiest lady I ever met"—#12 at the VIP Massage Parlor. As he waits for the call to go through, a pretty, red-haired woman walks into the garage. Louie is all greasy charm until he discovers she's "a *cab driver?!* Whaddya mean bustin' my chops here, makin' believe yer a *real person?!*" Alex tells Elaine not to let Louie get to her. "He's really a fine person, miss. He'd give you the scales off his back." Elaine says it's OK, she's not really a cabdriver anyway but an art gallery receptionist. Alex understands. "You see that guy over there? Now he's an actor. The guy on the phone? He's a prizefighter. This lady over here? She's a beautician. The man behind her? He's a writer. Me? I'm a cabdriver. I'm the only cabdriver in this place."

Tony finishes his call, and the cabbies urge Alex to make one. After first demurring, he mentions a daughter he hasn't seen in fifteen years. Elaine is appalled ("My ex-husband was right—he's *not* the worst there is"), but Louie more or less comes to Alex's defense: "Leave the man alone. If he doesn't give a damn about his kid, that's *his* business." Alex explains that his ex-wife married a prosperous South American who legally adopted their daughter, Cathy; he then resolves to call them in Rio de Janeiro. As he waits for his ex-wife, Phyllis Bornstein Consuelos, to come to the phone, a wide-eyed, vaguely Eastern European mechanic named Latka Gravas trundles down the stairs to ask Alex for help in English. The lesson is cut short when Alex's ex comes on and says their daughter is on her way to college in Portugal. She's passing through Miami tomorrow night. So sorry.

Alex about to meet his daughter in the premiere episode.

Alex gets the flight information from Phyllis and impulsively decides to drive to Miami. Over Louie's objections, he commandeers cab #1621 and, with the help of Tony, Bobby, John, and Latka, speeds off on the twenty-four-hour trip. They arrive at Miami International Airport just in time—Iberia's 7:30 (presumably A.M.) flight #936 is making its final boarding in five minutes.

Alex picks out Cathy from the crowd of school-girls in dress uniforms and tentatively introduces himself. A surprised Cathy says she's heard her mother talk of him—that he owns a big ranch and is thinking of running for the U.S. Senate. Alex tells her the mundane truth. They make polite conversation, until she finally tells him she's sorry, but he's *not* her father—her father was the man who raised her. Alex, hurt, says he was there for her first two years and that he remembers all these infant things—looks she gave him, the way she sneezed, foods she hated. As he remembers more

and more, he holds back tears and tells her not to say he doesn't know what it was like to be a father.

Cathy doesn't know what to feel. The last boarding call is announced. Alex gives her his driver's license so she'll have his address and a picture of him. She doesn't know whether to hug him or not. In a rush, she does, and misty herself, tells Alex, "I think I have your smile." Alex: "That's funny. I just got it two seconds ago."

Tag: The phone is repaired, to the cabbies' disappointment, and John announces he's got his hack license.

GUESTS:

Talia Balsam (Cathy Consuelos)
Jill Jaress (airline-counter attendant)

Quite unusually for a TV comedy's premiere episode, the debut of *Taxi* not only introduced the characters, told a story, and got in its jokes, but also immediately began revealing the characters' pasts. One of the reasons *Taxi* works so well as drama is that we know the characters as multidimensional people with well-developed personal histories. This helps make them whole, makes them recognizably like us, and gives the stories a ring of truth you don't expect from *Three's Company*.

One character's past was partially erased, however, since the episode filmed at about forty-five minutes and had to be trimmed. The original opening sequence showed John Burns taking Alex's cab to the apartment of his hometown girlfriend. With her voice supplied by Rhea Perlman, she tells John through the intercom that she's dating someone else. Heartbroken, John returns to Alex's cab.

The first part of this scene—John getting in Alex's cab and accidentally knocking down the safety shield between the front and back seats—turned up in part one of the first season's "pickup" episodes, "Memories of Cab 804." Another scene, showing the cabbies on the way to Miami, rotating drivers without stopping the car, was cut before the filming stage.

Guest star Talia Balsam, who plays Cathy and who reprises that role in episode #48, "Fathers of the Bride," is the daughter of actor Martin Balsam and actress Joyce Van Patten. Original casting director Joel Thurm remembers he only brought in two actresses to read for the part. One was Talia. The other was a young unknown by the name of Rosanna Arquette. Jill Jaress, playing the airline-counter attendant, had costarred with Kenneth Mars and Don Ameche in *Taxi* cocreator Dave Davis's 1971 CBS pilot, *Shepherd's Flock*.

Incidentally, the very first cab assignment we ever hear Louie give is, "Belson! You got cab 2452!"—an inside hello to producer Jerry Belson (*The Odd Couple*), who dropped out of *Taxi* in the planning stages.

#2 BLIND DATE

WRITTEN BY MICHAEL LEESON.
DIRECTED BY JAMES BURROWS.

In the garage, Bobby is on the pay phone with his answering service. It's the same as Gene Shalit's, he explains to the other cabbies, and when Bobby (client #131) doesn't have any messages, the sympathetic operator, Angela, gives him Shalit's instead. All the cabbies have spoken with "that great voice" when they phone Bob's service, and Alex in particular had a great conversation with her.

With Bobby's prodding, Alex gets on the phone and asks Angela out on a date. He's a little edgy about it since, he claims, he hasn't been romantically involved in eight years, but he does it anyway. Meanwhile, Latka, cleaning a cab, has found some money, which Louie, true to nature, immediately tries to scarf.

Later, Alex shows up at Angela's apartment (#3D) and knocks on the door. The "D" falls off, and as Alex is bending to pick it up, Angela (Suzanne Kent)—all 250 pounds or so—opens the door. She's in a dowdy flowered dress and as hostile as a Hun. She gives Alex several opportunities to cancel the date, but the perplexed Alex stoically insists on going out.

He takes her to Mario's (shown with a different exterior than in subsequent episodes), but her hostility and self-pity make her an ogre. She decides to leave and very loudly refuses to have Alex see her home. "They buy you dinner and they think they own you," she tells the on-looking crowd. The next day, Alex commiserates with Elaine about Angela: "I feel like I'm walking away from a car wreck with a person trapped inside." He resolves to get through to her. Going back to her apartment, he virtually dares her to drop her defenses. She angrily does. You wanna be my friend, she tells him, then you gotta stick around for the long run. Alex says sure. Angela starts to soften. Does this mean we can get together just to get together? Call each other on the phone just to say hello? Alex smiles and says sure. She breaks down and they hug—new friends.

In some ways, this episode is the quintessential *Taxi*. Maybe *too* quintessential—ABC didn't want it broadcast so early in the show's run, feeling it wasn't funny enough. It was plenty funny, and earned both an Emmy nomination and a Humanitas Award. Stan Daniels says the story grew from a real-life grain in Ed Weinberger's life. "Weinberger really had this terrific answering-service lady whom he talked with all the time. He never dated her, though," says Daniels. "If he did, he never admitted it!"

Suzanne Kent, a character actress who appeared in the TV movies *The Ordeal of Patty Hearst, Amazons,* and *Like Normal People* (with fellow *Taxi* guest Rhea Perlman), has most recently been seen on Showtime's *It's Garry Shandling's Show* and in the movies *Echo Park* and *Nuts*. And fans of the ubiquitous J. Alan Thomas will be pleased to know he has a line even this early in the series.

#3 THE GREAT LINE

WRITTEN BY EARL POMERANTZ.
DIRECTED BY JAMES BURROWS.

Mario's, the cabbies' hangout, is more boisterous than usual today. Bobby arranges a $50 beer-chugging bet between Tony and a strangely confident stranger—who beats the young boxer as badly as he ever was beaten in the ring. John, meantime, is smitten with a pretty brunette named Suzanne Caruthers (Ellen Regan) who is sitting with two friends. Casanova Bobby magnanimously hands him a patented come-on line, which John uses to unexpected success. "Let's cut the preliminaries," John bashfully asks the girl, "you want get married?'' She kiddingly answers, ''Sure!'' The two nice souls hit it off immediately, and, finding they share a passion for bowling, go off to throw a few frames.

Two days later, a shell-shocked John informs the cabbies that he and Suzanne actually went through with the wedding—caught up in the joke, they drove in her best friend's Volvo to Maryland for a quick ceremony. John helplessly tells Alex how terrified he is, that in his mind, ''it's all connected: You get married, you have kids, you grow old, and then you die. Somehow to me, if you didn't get married, you wouldn't die!''

While John commiserates at Mario's with Alex over what to do with Suzanne, Lou walks in, says hi to Rudy the bartender, challenges the chug-champ to a duel, and with a typical dirty trick wins the $20 bet. He then charges John a buck for a letter that Suzanne dropped off at the garage. She's written that she's an ''immature nut'' for going through with this silly joke, and that he's much too nice a guy to have to put up with her. Of course, she'll have the marriage annulled.

Now John decides he can't live without her and wants Alex to help him get her back. He reluctantly agrees and together they go to Suzanne's family's apartment. Alex asks her dad how he would react to find that his daughter fell in love at first sight and got married without telling him. Her father matter-of-factly replies that it goes against every moral and spiritual value he's ever tried to instill in his family. Oh. Somehow, though, Suzanne and John work things out themselves and love conquers all. More or less.

OTHER GUESTS:

Dolph Sweet (Mr. Mart[in] Caruthers)
Sheila Rogers (Mrs. Lillian Caruthers)
Rusdi Lane (Rudy, the bartender at Mario's)
William ''The Fox'' Foster (the beer-chugger)

The producers obviously were going for the un-predictable here—so often in episodic TV and movies, after all, the hero falls in love and gets married, only to have his bride killed or abducted. It's even happened to James Bond and The Incredible Hulk. Having John *stay* married was a way of knocking the pins of predictability out from under

us. Gosh. Maybe sometimes predictable's better.

Regardless, scriptwriter Earl Pomerantz—the source of such *Taxi* classics as ''Nardo Loses Her Marbles'' (episode #28) and ''Louie's Mom Remarries'' (episode #74)—calls his *Taxi* debut ''my favorite of all the ones I did. The idea came from Jim Brooks, and I thought it was very funny: the notion of a pickup line so good, the guy gets married!'' Pomerantz had hit the big time when fellow Canadian Lorne Michaels invited him to work on Lily Tomlin's first two TV specials. He shared a 1975–76 writing Emmy for the second, and went on to write Emmy-nominated scripts for *The Mary Tyler Moore Show,* create the series *Best of the West* and *Family Man,* and serve as *The Cosby Show*'s co-executive-producer for its first eight episodes.

Sweet-faced Ellen Regan had costarred as a paid escort on the very short-lived (April to May 1978) sitcom *The Ted Knight Show.* Around the same time, she appeared in the pilots *Almost Heaven,* with Jay Leno and Eva Gabor, and *The Lovebirds;* more recently, she costarred on the sitcom *Me & Mrs. C.* She's since been seen on *Cheers.* The *real* star of this episode, however, is the late character actor Dolph Sweet, who passed away in 1985 at age sixty-four; his blank-faced Mr. Caruthers is a hilariously stoic, solid wall of know-nothingness: Asked if he likes to receive bad news straight out or to have it gilded, the gruff-looking Caruthers strongly replies, ''Gilded.'' Sweet was best known as the world-weary but wisecracking cop, Capt. Carl Kanisky, in *Gimme a Break!*—a series cocreated by *Taxi* writer Sy Rosen. He'd previously played a cop on the 1960s Peter Falk series *The Trials of O'Brien,* and before his *Break!* was in the cast of two soap operas and the short-lived ABC sitcom *When the Whistle Blows.*

#4 COME AS YOU AREN'T

WRITTEN BY GLEN CHARLES AND LES CHARLES. DIRECTED BY JAMES BURROWS.

A rushed businessman enters Elaine's cab one rainy night, on his way to the Metropolitan Museum of Art. He politely asks a jabbering Elaine not to talk to him, and when she tries to explain herself, abruptly shuts her up. Then, when she turns off

Madison Avenue for what she says is a shorter route, the man accuses her of trying to jack up the fare. Insulted, she orders him out of the cab; when he refuses, she starts crying "Rape" in a stage whisper. The man, unfazed, says the police will have a hard time believing her when they discover he's the National Secretary of the Gay Liberation Force. Having no choice, Elaine takes him to the museum. The fare is $2.85; the man leaves $1 and, inadvertently, his briefcase. A vengeful Elaine drives it down the street and drops it in the rain.

When she gets back to the garage, Bobby has his own problems—the Qantas Airlines koala bear got sick in his cab. Elaine finds Alex and says she needs his help. It seems that her first window display at the Madison Avenue art gallery she works at is a hit, and she has impulsively invited the owners and patrons to a cocktail party at her place. Now she's terrified of making a bad impression and invites Alex (and, reluctantly, the other cabbies) for moral support. The hitch is, nobody knows she's a cab-driver—and she has to ask her friends to lie about their profession.

Four nights later, Alex shows up early at Elaine's apartment (#A), followed by Latka in fresh over-alls. Elaine's a bit concerned about the liquor she could afford—off-brands such as Betty's Vodka and champagne in cans. Regardless, her guests wind up enjoying themselves. Latka even picks up a mousy girl and leaves with her. Alex, mingling, meets Paul, a writer for *ArtNews,* who asks Alex what he does for a living. To cover for Elaine, he claims to put out oil-well fires. "All holocausts may look alike," he pontificates, "but each has a personality all its own." Rita, an exotic blonde attracted by his macho occupation, hints at sex. Alex is on a roll.

Just then, the man with whom Elaine fought the other night shows up; Mrs. Hazeltine (whom future episodes depict as the art gallery's owner) introduces him to their horrified hostess. Fortunately, the man doesn't recognize her. At first Elaine is relieved. Then she gets insulted. Angrily, she tells the guy exactly where they met—in her cab. And what's more, she says, pointing at Alex, *he's* a cab-driver, too! The blonde immediately excuses her-self.

After the party, a brooding Alex sits drinking a can of champagne. He refuses to be consoled, es-pecially since the blonde called him garbage and spit on his shoes. When Elaine tries to cheer him up by saying how well everything else turned out, with people admiring her for holding two jobs and the man giving her a large retroactive tip, Alex has had enough. He starts to leave—but Elaine is scared to death of his going away mad. "You're maybe my best friend," she finally admits. That does it. With a resigned smile, he turns and they hug.

GUESTS:

William Bogert (James Broderick, the man in Elaine's cab)
Andra Akers (Rita)
Paula Victor (Mrs. Hazeltine)
Clyde Kusatsu (Paul)
Treva Silverman (the young lady Latka picks up at the party)

This was the first episode to spotlight Marilu Henner and to establish the bond between Alex and Elaine. "Around the time we shot that episode, I had just moved into my first real apartment in L.A.," Marilu recalls, "and so I finally felt like I was really in the show. I had seen Judd on Broad-way in *Chapter Two* only six months before, and now to do an intimate, two-person scene with someone whose work I had admired and who was really a star to me, and here I am calling him 'maybe my best friend' . . . ! It made me feel like I'd arrived, or had begun to arrive."

Bit player Treva Silverman was a prolific script-writer for *The Mary Tyler Moore Show,* who won two Emmy Awards in 1974. Honolulu native Clyde Kusatsu appeared on episodes of *All in the Family, M*A*S*H, and Wiseguy,* and was a regular on *Bring 'Em Back Alive* and Dad in *All-American Girl.* And for Tony Danza fans, the end-credit shot of him addressing the camera is a remnant of *Taxi*'s original opening (see "Auditions and Audacity").

#5 ONE-PUNCH BANTA
WRITTEN BY EARL POMERANTZ.
DIRECTED BY JAMES BURROWS.

Louie finds Latka idle, a situation he refuses to ac-cept even when Latka informs him that all cabs are

Latka giving Louie some unwanted attention—and
vice-versa—in episode #5, "One-Punch Banta."

fixed and clean. In response, Lou spitefully rips out
an engine part from a taxi and tells Latka to get
busy. Tony enters with Bobby, who's telling him a
fish story about a $120 booking that evaporates with
Tony's skepticism until it reaches $80. John is busy
studying at the table.

Alex comes in, and Louie gives him the word
that John is being fired for his low bookings. Alex—
the garage's top booker—tells Lou to give John a
chance, and that if John goes, *he* goes. "Oo-ooh,"
Lou answers defiantly, "a threat that worked."
John can stay for now, but Alex knows he's got to
develop some street-savvy and starts to instruct
him. Meanwhile, Tony gets off the phone with exciting news—he's been picked to spar with Carlos
Navarone, the middleweight champ.

At the Downtown Gym, Elaine, Alex, and Bobby
meet Tony with a gift—a red, hooded boxer's robe.
Tony's touched—it's the first he's ever owned, and
he rushes to try it on. Navarone's manager, Jerry
Martin (Allan Arbus), comes by and tells Tony he'll
be going three rounds with the champ. The cabbies
help Tony on with his gloves—a mistake, since the
robe has small sleeves that Martin impatiently
rips—and the practice session begins. And incredibly, Tony knocks the champ down.

The news spreads, and many days later in the
garage (where we see Louie instructing Latka in the
relative merits of lust versus love), the cabbies cheer
their local hero, who has landed a pro fight the
following evening. Tony will make $1,500 and meet
major contender Frankie Wallace, whom *Ring* mag-

azine has ranked eighth in his division. The whole
garage is rooting for their boy—but only so much,
Louie implies: anybody wanna put their money
where their mouths are? Nobody does. Alex, in
Tony's defense, says he'll bet five bucks; Louie hu-
miliates him into a hundred.

The next night—Friday—is always busy, but all
the cabbies are at Madison Square Garden for
Tony's bout. Louie calls for Belson, Cohen, and
Benitez, but no one's there—so he takes his microphone and starts warbling "From This Moment
On" through the PA system. At the Garden, Alex
is giving Tony a last-minute rubdown. Navarone
and Martin come by to wish Tony luck—and to
thank him for "that trick in the gym." The champ,
it seems, was having trouble lining up opponents
until he pretended that some nobody had dropped
him. Tony doesn't believe it. The champ arrogantly says to go ahead and punch him in the stomach, which Tony does to no effect.

Tony gets angry and wants to fight, while Alex
desperately tries to intercede. The two boxers go at
it for the few seconds it takes Navarone to land a
one-two-three combination that decks Tony. The
champ and his manager leave him on the floor col-
lecting his marbles, and another boxer comes by
and helps Alex lift Tony to his feet. Unfortunately,
that other boxer is Tony's opponent.

Tag: As Bobby applies an ice pack to Tony's
bruised face, Louie comes by to collect his hundred
from Alex. The cabbies all swear they'll be there
for Tony in the future—and Louie happily swears
he'll be there to collect on his bets.

OTHER GUESTS:

World Boxing Council Welterweight Champion
    Carlos Palomino (Carlos Navarone)
Ron Rich (an attendant who pops in while Tony's
    on the floor)
Dwight Woody (Frankie Wallace)

Sharp-eyed fans will notice that after the champ
arrogantly knocks down Tony in the locker room,
his eyes go wide in an "uh-oh," and he covers his
mouth with his hands. This is because Palomino
accidentally popped Danza a *real* shot on the chin.
"He hit me good, too," Danza recalls with a
chuckle of admiration. To both his and Palomino's

credit, they kept on going with the scene.

Palomino, who was WBC Welterweight Champion from 1976–1979, later appeared as a boxer in the 1984 film *Strangers Kiss.* He's since been seen in light-beer commercials. "It was my idea to have him on the show," says Danza. "I'd said to them, 'Ya know, Palomino lives here and he was a big idol of mine'—in fact, I patterned myself after him—'and so why don't we get him? See, the thing is, you wanted it to be somebody who could make the boxing scenes look good. You didn't want a guy who would hurt you, and you didn't want a guy who wouldn't fuck around at all. And ya wanna know somethin' funny? After Palomino came on our show, he never won another fight!'' Fellow guest star Allan Arbus is familiar as army psychiatrist Dr. Sidney Freedman on *M*A*S*H.*

Louie's lounge act features "From This Moment On" from *Brigadoon* by Lerner and Loewe.

#6 BOBBY'S ACTING CAREER

WRITTEN BY ED WEINBERGER AND
STAN DANIELS.

DIRECTED BY JAMES BURROWS.

Alex picks up an obnoxious boor (John Lehne) and his dog, heading to 51st Street. The dog, a Great Dane, is called Hamlet; the owner patronizingly asks if Alex knows why. "Because he came from a small town?" Alex replies sarcastically. The man explains he won Hamlet in a poker game a few weeks back and wants to show Alex how smart the dog is. Hamlet fails to speak (though the theater-loving Alex contributes. "Oh, what a rogue and peasant slave am I''), and the angered man starts beating the dog. Alex tells him to stop, and when the man refuses, Alex throws him out and makes off with the grateful Dane.

When Alex arrives at the garage, he finds that Bobby isn't letting anyone use the pay phone. When the other cabbies confront him, he explains that when he came to Manhattan from his native Bronx, he gave himself three years to get a part. Tonight at midnight, those three years are up, and unless he hears from his agent about a part, he'll have to give up acting. The Great Dane's owner storms in, demanding the dog back. The cabbies

(to whom Alex has explained the situation) play dumb, and the man vows to return with the police.

The phone rings—Bobby hasn't gotten the job he was hoping for. Prodded by Alex, he takes to the streets and lands a few auditions on sheer luck and chutzpah. That evening, the cabbies join him in his apartment (#A) for an ostensible celebration, and Bobby opens champagne, exclaiming gleefully, "I didn't get a job!" He tells the curious cabbies he's so sure he will get one by his midnight deadline that he's celebrating already.

As the minutes tick down, Alex tries to buffer his actor-friend's upcoming trauma. He takes Bobby aside and tells him there are other jobs and maybe, just maybe, he's not meant to be an actor. Bobby, suddenly angered, tells Alex he would take that talk from anybody except a father-figure like him; he finally becomes so upset he orders Alex to leave and never speak to him again. Alex, shocked but resigned, starts to go. Bobby whirls him back and smiles: "Still say I'm not such a good actor?" Midnight finally comes: no acting job. The cabbies are heartbroken for Bobby; Latka is crying. But Bobby shrugs—so he'll give it another three years. . . .

Tag: The dog-owner drags in a policeman who, with Solomonic wisdom, separates the owner and Alex and tells each of them to call the dog: whomever the dog responds to gets to keep him. Hamlet chooses his old master—to the man's quick regret.

OTHER GUESTS:

Michael Mann (Peter Nicholson, a commercial director at an E. F. Hutton audition that Bobby landed; not the Michael Mann who is the executive producer of *Miami Vice*)
Robert Phalen (Tom Jeffries, the director's assistant; last name given in the end credits, not in the episode)
Taurean Blacque (the policeman)

This is the first time we see the brownstone-basement apartment that Bobby kept throughout the series. As happened so often with *Taxi*, art mirrored life. "For a while, Marilu lived in the same building as I did in Los Angeles," Jeff Conaway relates. "So she knew exactly how I lived and how I decorated. So after the set designer and I had talked about what Bobby's apartment would look like, Marilu went over and told him all about my ice skates and posters and all that stuff hanging all over my walls—those touches really came out of my apartment!'' He laughs. ''So when I go to see Bobby's apartment for the first time, I freak! It's like, 'Who's been telling tales out of school?' ''

As for Bronxite Bobby hanging up a prominent pennant for the Mets rather than his hometown Yankees, Conaway suggests that Bobby ''was a Mets *and* a Yankees fan, and if there was only a Mets pennant there, so what? He could've been a Cubs fan, even. I think the incongruity appealed to [the producers]—a guy from the Bronx who roots for a Queens team.'' Possibly. On the other hand, Conaway himself *is* from Flushing, Queens—site of the Mets' Shea Stadium.

Taurean Blacque's police officer evidently moved up the ranks after this episode: Blacque went on to portray Detective Neil Washington in *Hill Street Blues*. And John Lehne, who played the dog-owner, is one of Marilu's old acting teachers.

#7 HIGH SCHOOL REUNION

WRITTEN BY SY ROSEN.
DIRECTED BY JAMES BURROWS.

Louie comes into Mario's despondent over his twenty-year-high school reunion, taking place that night at the Lenox Hotel. Insinuating himself at a table with the beer-drinking cabbies, he recalls a particular humiliation at his senior prom, where prankster Stanley Tarses and the girl of Lou's dreams, Sheila Martin, invited him to sit at their table—and then led the diminutive Lou to an infant's high chair. He vowed then that someday he'd show them all up, but now confesses that coming back as a cab-company dispatcher probably won't do it.

The cabbies, who normally despise and fear Lou, begin to pity him. He doesn't want to hear it. Bobby, however, tells him what an irresistible acting challenge it would be to portray a successful Louie De Palma. Lou says it can't work, but Bobby—doing a serviceable impression of Lou even as they speak—quickly convinces him.

Meantime, Alex is trying to talk barmaid Beverly (Joanna Cassidy) into letting him walk her home. They've gone through this before, and Beverly simply doesn't want to date cabdrivers.

That night, at the reunion, a curiously tall ''Louie'' (who explains he had a late growing spurt after high school) surprises and impresses some old classmates, gets even with Stanley Tarses (Pierrino Mascarino), and dances up a storm with Sheila Martin (Arlene Golonka). Lou, Alex, and Beverly show up, against their better instincts, and Lou inadvertently sets in motion a spectacular slapstick finale.

OTHER GUESTS:

Angelo Gnazzo (George Wilson, an old classmate)
Sandy Holt (woman at the reunion)

ADDITIONAL CREDITS:

Choreography: Jeff Conaway
Stunt Coordinator: Lee Eileene Pulford

''That episode was fun,'' Jeff Conaway remembers, ''but it also scared the hell out of me. We were shooting 'Bobby's Acting Career' [episode #6] when Jim Brooks tells me they've got a great idea for another episode built around Bobby. I was thrilled, because on the first five I didn't do a hell of a lot. Then when they told me, 'You're going to be Louie next week,' my jaw dropped. I'm shaking, dying. What do they mean, 'be Louie'?'' Conaway climbed that particular Matterhorn by following DeVito around for a few days, observing him, and watching a videotape of Danny. The only problem, Jeff laughs, was that ''for a few weeks after that, it was hard for me to drop it. Every now and then somebody would say, 'Look! You're doing Louie again!' ''

The dance scene, which Conaway choreographed, came out looking smooth despite an injury on the set—he was doing a split and pulled his inner thigh muscles badly enough to need a nurse to come in and wrap them. DeVito remembers being in his dressing room ''when all of sudden Jim Brooks and Ed Weinberger come running by with fistfuls of ice, heading to Jeff's room.'' Conaway survived more handily than this episode, which strains credibility—not that Bobby would volunteer his services but that anyone would believe Louie had changed so much.

Arlene Golonka is best recognized as Ken Berry's girlfriend on *The Andy Griffith Show* and its spin-off, *Mayberry RFD.* Joanna Cassidy, who plays Beverly, was a steadily working actress for years before this, and achieved stardom soon afterward with co-starring roles in the movie *Under Fire* and in two TV series, *Codename: Firefox* and *Buffalo Bill.* (Speaking of which, *Buffalo Bill* cocreator and *The Bob Newhart Show* coexecutive producer Jay Tarses was the inspiration for the last name of Louie's high school nemesis.) Was there any thought of keeping Cassidy on as a girl friend for Alex? "We thought of it," says Jim Brooks. "There was, as you know, an awful lot of continuity with guest characters. I guess we thought that tying down our central character that way would take the series in a different, more male-female direction than we wanted."

#8 PAPER MARRIAGE

STORY BY BARTON DEAN.
TELEPLAY BY GLEN CHARLES AND LES CHARLES.
DIRECTED BY JAMES BURROWS.

Two officials from the Federal Immigration and Naturalization Service (INS) come to the garage looking for the supervisor. It seems there's a problem with Latka Gravas, so the cabbies stonewall till they can talk with their mechanic friend. The INS officials go out for coffee until Louie returns, and the cabbies rush to Latka. He shows them a letter he got two weeks ago, which states that his student visa ran out two weeks before that. He was supposed to contact the INS office four days ago, but he'd only (mis)translated "Dear Allen." Alex: "That's 'Alien.' "

Lou returns from cleaning graffiti from the men's room, growling to the cabbies, "What you wrote about me in there was disgusting. Some of it ain't even true." The cabbies explain that the INS wants Latka, and Louie, not willing to tangle with the Feds, says he has to turn Latka in. John asks how Louie can do that to someone he loves, and when the cabbies argue that Lou doesn't love *anybody,* Lou softens and calls Latka "the poodle I never had." He'll help—at least until the Feds return, whereupon he fingers Latka immediately.

Latka gives them the slip and shows up later in

the back of Alex's cab (#264) after a terrified woman passenger screams at finding him there. Latka explains to Alex he needs to get married to an American, and Alex vows to help. Sometime later in the garage, Latka proposes to Elaine, who politely refuses. Alex brings in Vivian Harow (Rita Taggart), a handsome, well-built call girl. They agree to stage a paper wedding on Thursday.

The big day arrives, with Louie dismayed that Latka still refuses to speak to him. The guys are all joking along the lines of the vice squad giving the bride away, which gets Elaine's hackles up. Vivian walks in, and Elaine insists she wear Elaine's old wedding gown. Vivian's agreeable: "I've dressed up as everything from Pocahontas to Darth Vader. You want me in a bridal gown, you got it." Now (and rather at the last minute) they need a minister. Bobby says there's one who hangs around Mario's and rushes to try to find him.

The INS officers return, and Lou, perhaps wanting to make up for before, tells a story about Latka and Vivian being in love, and that her wealthy family opposed the union so much that they'd offered a scornful Latka a thousand dollars to call it off. The agents don't really buy it, but they roll their eyes and let the gainfully employed and obviously well-liked Latka be. The cabbies congratulate Lou and ask him how he devised such a story so quickly. He answers that the story was true and had happened to him—except that the family had only offered fifty bucks and that he'd grabbed it.

Bobby returns with a bewildered-looking burn-out named Reverend Jim (Christopher Lloyd). The hazy ex-hippie assures them he's recognized by the state and was ordained in 1968 by The Church of the Peaceful, which, he adds, "was investigated and cleared completely." This is his first wedding, and except for Louie's less-than-accomplished violin playing, it goes off without a hitch. Vivian slips off the gown, tosses the bouquet to best man Alex, and splits for an appointment at the Hilton. Latka is disappointed to find there's no honeymoon. "Boy," he sighs, "America ees a tough town."

OTHER GUESTS:

James Randolph (INS agent Richards)
Woody Eny (the other, unnamed INS agent)
Michele Bernath (the woman in Alex's cab)

Aside from being a very funny episode in its own right, "Paper Marriage" is memorable for introducing the inimitable Reverend Jim (whose last name we don't learn until his return in episode #27). Christopher Lloyd remembers shyly that even on his first appearance in this episode, "there was some intimation that they sort of wanted me to come back as a regular. I kept that in my mind from then until my second episode, the one with the driver's test."

Jim at this early stage is played straighter and less gravelly-voiced than later on. "I remember seeing some of the early shows and then the later ones, and I could see the contrast. I was smoking at the time, which probably made my voice more gravelly than it is anyway." He smiles. "As time went on, I just got more and more into the character, became more 'Jim-my.' " (For the story of Chris's audition and the real-life inspirations for Jim, see "Awake, A Wake" and Christopher Lloyd's biography.)

Rita Taggart has played sexy, sassy broads and earnest everyday women for more than a decade. Her TV movies include *James Dean, Rape and Marriage: The Rideout Case., Mae West,* and HBO's *Steambath.* Some of her most recent series guest shots have been on *St. Elsewhere, Cagney and Lacey, Night Court,* and *Kate and Allie.*

Longstanding *Taxi* director Jim Burrows is rightfully acclaimed as one of television's best. This makes all the more fun a very strange scene transition here. In easily the weirdest shot in *Taxi*'s run—maybe in all of television—we see a closeup of tires, pulling back to a closeup of a hanging wedding-bell decoration, pulling back to the decorated garage. Watch for it—it'll make you wonder if maybe Reverend Jim was working the camera that day!

#9 MONEY TROUBLES

WRITTEN BY EARL POMERANTZ.
DIRECTED BY JAMES BURROWS.

Alex is helping prep Latka for dinner with the newlyweds, John and Suzanne. Latka is repulsed when he hears the old saying of being "hungry enough to eat a horse." Hungry enough to eat a dog, however—*that* he understands. During dinner at John

and Suzanne's small but nice studio apartment (with a skylight, yet!), a crisis develops: Suzanne's parents phone to say they're retiring and can no longer afford to pay the young couple's rent. Now either Suzanne will have to drop out of nursing school or John will have to give up his forestry education. Dinner, naturally, becomes an uncomfortable experience, though Latka at least makes the best of it with what little English he knows at this point.

Later at the garage, Alex is wrestling with his good intentions. He has $2,000 he can spare, but says he's always found that loaning money creates suspicions and resentments that can ruin a friendship. He finally decides it's worth a try, and, besides, John will probably be too proud to accept the loan anyway.

Meanwhile, John and Suzanne are desperately seeking a way to keep both of them in college while making enough money to live on. As newlyweds do, they decide to "sleep on it." Alex chooses that moment to come in and offer the loan. John doesn't want to accept it, but Suzanne suggests they talk about it in private, and asks Alex to step into the bathroom. Suzanne wants to know why it's OK to take money from her parents but not from Alex. John refuses to budge, and he suggests they flip a coin—the winner of the toss stays in school. Suzanne hesitantly agrees. John flips and catches the coin and sadly informs his wife that's she lost. But then, seeing her dejected face, John breaks down, throws himself on his knees and admits he lied, that *she* had won the toss. Together, they decide to accept Alex's loan. They call Alex out of the bathroom (where to his relief he'd heard only the "won't accept" part) and surprise him by saying cheerfully, "We'll borrow as much as you got!"

A bland sitcom premise—young newlyweds run out of cash; who can they turn to?—is partially redeemed by the antiheroic notion that, yes, the square-jawed young man *will* ask for help, and, furthermore, he's desperate enough to try to scam even his own wife. But somehow, the domestic plot line doesn't have the punch that it should. As some of *Taxi*'s creators found out with *Rhoda*, it's hard to make married childless couples funny. (*The Bob Newhart Show* doesn't count—Howard the navigator and Bob's wacky patients were surrogate kids.)

As was briefly considered for Joanna Cassidy (episode #7), "There was some talk about having Ellen Regan become a semiregular," Randy Carver reports. "They were going to use our characters to explore the marriage relationship in a comedic way. That didn't pan out, but they did do it later when Latka and Simka got married."

#10 A FULL HOUSE FOR CHRISTMAS

WRITTEN BY BARRY KEMP.
DIRECTED BY JAMES BURROWS.

Christmastime at the Sunshine Cab Co.: As young carolers come by and get shooed away by the Grinchlike Louie, an unexpected visitor arrives—Louie's younger brother Nicky (Richard Foronjy), whom he hasn't seen in six years. Nicky is a well-to-do professional gambler based in Las Vegas. While in New York to see his mother, he naturally sits in on a few hands of poker with the garage gang. Just as naturally, he wins all their money in what starts to become a marathon session. In fact, Nicky becomes so intent on the game that he doesn't have time to visit Ma.

Louie then hits upon the idea that garage poker-champ Alex play Nicky one-on-one in a high-stakes match: The cab company's receipts versus a Vegas vacation for Ma, complete with stage shows and dinners out. It's a close one, but Alex wins it.

Tag: The ever-resourceful Louie finds a way of making a buck off the carolers.

OTHER GUESTS:

The Benny Powell Singers (the carolers)
Darren Milton (the entrepreneurial caroler)

This rarely screened episode is more prominent for what happened off-screen than on. Andy Kaufman agreed to be cast on a TV series only on the condition that the producers also hire his obnoxious lounge singer alter ego, Tony Clifton, for a couple of episodes. Clifton's first appearance was to have been in this episode, portraying Louie's brother Nick.

DeVito recalls being in "the ol' commissary at Paramount when Ed Weinberger came up to me and said, 'We're preparing a Christmas show and I wanna talk to you about it.' Now, 'I wanna talk to you about it' sounds to me like something's up, and it was."

"We were all called in," Randy Carver recounts, "and told that Andy Kaufman was not going to be in this episode, that they've signed another actor from Las Vegas named Tony Clifton. He may resemble Andy Kaufman, they told us, but he's not Andy Kaufman. On Monday at read-through I found Clifton to be a very obnoxious person, but I figured, well, he's from Vegas. So I sent him a telegram to the studio, which said 'This is just to welcome you to the show, and I'm really looking forward to a great week. Your friend, Randall Carver.' So on Tuesday, he told me thanks for the telegram, that he'd appreciated it."

This was probably the only good note in that entire discordant day. "Clifton" arrived late, and after growling at production executive Ron Frazier to get away from the door of his motor home, he finally exited with a couple of heavily made-up women for whom he demanded roles. "Guy comes in," recalls DeVito, "he's got two babes, one on each arm, with tiny miniskirts, lipstick up to their noses, right? And he's got gifts for everybody. Gave us all these tiny mechanical toys—beep, beep, beep! *Chip-chip-chip-chip.*'" he embellishes, acting it out.

Jeff Conaway, for one, refused to go along with the charade and stormed off the set. Judd Hirsch lost his patience as well. Coexecutive producer Ed Weinberger then told Clifton he was fired. Clifton, angered, alternately shouted threats and begged for another chance. Paramount security guards arrived and—not having been let in on the stunt, which was staged in front of a *Los Angeles Times* reporter—physically rushed him off the lot.

"The last image I remember," says DeVito, "was they hadda call security to get him off the lot. They hadda pull him out, backwards, like this." He demonstrates. "Guy on this arm, guy on that arm, babes screamin' and hollerin'. And he's going like this [pointing his finger viciously]: 'I'll remember you guys! None of youse will ever work in Vegas again!'" By late Wednesday, Richard Foronjy was filling-in as Nick.

"Kaufman had agreed with Weinberger that Clifton had to leave the show," recalls Gary Nar-

A light moment on the set: Conaway and Hirsch.

dino, then head of Paramount Television. "Clifton was a disruptive force. So Kaufman made Ed agree that Clifton would be fired publicly in front of a rehearsal audience. And that's exactly what they did. Madness!" Nardino adds appreciatively, "Kaufman was a genius. But strange."

#11 SUGAR MAMA

WRITTEN BY GLEN CHARLES AND LES CHARLES. DIRECTED BY JAMES BURROWS.

It's a full moon out, and Louie warns Alex over the radio to watch out for the usual crazies. But Alex (cab #264) has just dropped an airport fare at staid 79th Street and Park Avenue and brushes aside Louie's superstition. Then a sprightly octogenarian named Dee Wilcox (Ruth Gordon) hops into Alex's cab and asks to be taken to Shea Sta-

dium. Alex helpfully advises her there's no game tonight. "I didn't ask for a schedule," she shoots back. Full moon indeed. After reminiscing at Shea about the old Brooklyn Dodgers' Ebbets Field, she directs the cab to La Guardia Airport to watch the planes land.

Alex finally drops her off at the Plaza Hotel (shown but not named), where she tips him $26 on a $74.25 fare—to beat his previous record of $25, she joshes. Later on, Dee explains that she was a candy clerk at Woolworth's for thirty-five years, and a few months before she retired, a wealthy old man named George fell in love with her. Four months after they were married he died, leaving her "filthy comfortable."

The next night at the garage, John is wandering around stoned, a contact high from the pot smoked by some musicians in his cab the previous night. Dee comes into the garage, saying she wants to hire

Alex to drive her around again tonight. Alex demurs, but she slips Louie five bucks for a quick cab. That night, she gives Alex a hundred bucks and says she appreciates what money can buy: "Nice food, nice clothes, nice people."

At the garage the following night, the cabbies all ride Alex. Elaine says that when she heard the best fares were in the eighties, she thought they meant streets, not years. Lou, of course, gets his dig in, and Alex, rather cruelly, has him gulp scalding coffee when Lou gets a coughing fit. That night, Dee gives Alex a couple of gifts—a cashmere sports coat and a tie. She slyly talks him into going to the Enchanted Island Ballroom with her. At this older-folks hangout, she dances with her would-be beau, Weldon Manning, while Alex waits around the punchbowl. There he meets a pleasant gigolo who calls himself Ramon, who wants to talk shop. Alex realizes that he's becoming Dee's paid companion.

When he takes Dee back home to the fourth floor of the Plaza—the two of them having won the rhumba contest—Alex insists they just be friends, that he won't be bought. At that, Dee bids him adieu. She likes paying her way with people. "I know people [who] gave their lives to their children. Those children don't even come to see 'em. If I had any kids . . . I would put them on my payroll—and they'd come see *me!*" Alex gives her a "Joan Crawford" speech about dignity and feeling used and convinces her that the next time they go to lunch, she not pay. Dee smiles and gives in—and hopes her stomach can handle "the kind of dumps *you* can afford."

OTHER GUESTS:

Herb Vigran (Weldon Manning)
Aharon Ipalé (Ramon)

The ever-delightful Ruth Gordon (1896–1985), a celebrated actress, playwright, and screenwriter, was brought in for a dose of star power. Since her asking price was higher than the first-season budget could afford, ABC kicked in a supplemental $5,000 to nail her down. The effort paid off. Gordon's impish charm and the echo of her signature role in *Harold and Maude* (1972) give Dee Wilcox's essentially self-centered attitude an eccentric heart. It's to Judd Hirsch's credit that he keeps pace with her,

and while this episode is clearly "The Ruth Gordon Show," the big final scene between Alex and Dee is by no means played in Gordon's shadow.

Several of the cast members recount one of the funniest offstage incidents of the series. When setting up the ballroom scene, director Jim Burrows called for "Judd, Ruth, and Aharon." Gordon, shocked, asked him to please repeat what he said. Burrows repeated, slowly, "Give me Judd, Ruth, and Aharon." Gordon, suddenly relieved, broke out in peals of laughter. Everybody else broke into laughter when she explained why: "I thought you said, 'Give me Judd, Ruth, and a hard-on!' "

Gordon's stellar performance in this episode earned her an Emmy; she'd gotten nominations in two previous years, and could finally add the award to her Best Supporting Actress Oscar for *Rosemary's Baby* (1968). And then there's the lovable Herb Vigran (1910–1986), a character actor we all know from childhood as the natty comic crook in many episodes of the fifties TV-series *Superman*.

#12 MEN ARE SUCH BEASTS

WRITTEN BY ED WEINBERGER AND
STAN DANIELS.
DIRECTED BY JAMES BURROWS.

Tony is dating a cute-as-a-button Bronx cabbie named Denise (Gail Edwards). Yet she's becoming too cloying, and Tony—who says his absentee father left him to be raised by his mother and three older sisters—doesn't handle cloying so well. He breaks it off with Denise, who responds by taking a job at Sunshine. No matter what Tony says or does, the obsessed Denise hovers around him—which is fine by Lou, who loves having her around since she books like a maniac. One reason for this, Tony notices, is that she pops amphetamines to keep her awake and hopping through long shifts.

An obliging Denise says that if that's what's bothering Tony, she can throw them away anytime—which she does, to the delight of several cabbie extras who (in a wonderfully choreographed scene) dive onto the floor to retrieve them. Tony finally tells Louie that either she goes or he does. "Get ridda her?" Lou snorts, "I wanna breed her!'' The whole garage unites behind Tony, however, and a cornered Lou tells Denise she's out of a job. She doesn't take this lightly. Glaring at Tony, she vows to haunt him at work, at home, at the gym—everywhere.

With options running out, Tony finally tells Denise he's involved with somebody else—Louie. Denise, insulted and astonished by Tony's ploy, dares Lou to admit he's gay; Lou, bending to the will of the majority, grudgingly tells her he prefers to think of it as ''an alternative life-style.'' Denise is amazed that Tony expects her to believe this. Tony answers that to get rid of her, he'd marry the guy. This doesn't sit well with Louie, but it finally chases away the clinging Denise.

OTHER GUESTS:

George Reynolds (an unnamed black cabdriver)

''This episode was based on something that happened to somebody's friend—which is how a lot of episodes came about,'' chuckles Stan Daniels. ''Somebody's friend did have a girl friend like this, who used this tactic of just hanging on.''

Amazingly, the episode triumphs over a sitcom premise. A lot of it has to do with the caliber of the performances. The somewhat-slow Tony is wonderfully hangdog and perplexed, and Gail Edwards carries an appropriately creepy mix of wide-eyed innocence and *Fatal Attraction.* If there's anything wrong with this very funny episode, it's that we can't quite accept (a) that palooka Tony thinks he's too good for this sweet, gorgeous, ambitious girl and (b) that she *doesn't* think she's too good for him.

Miami native Gail Edwards, one of the most arresting-looking actresses on television, costarred with Ann Jillian and fellow *Taxi* guest star Susan Sullivan in the sitcom *It's a Living* a.k.a. *Making a Living.* You can catch her on reruns of *M*A*S*H, Benson,* and *Three's a Crowd;* her more recent work includes the premiere episode of Steven Spielberg's *Amazing Stories.* On commercials she's doled out common sense to Jack Klugman for Canon copiers and to a couple of whiny coworkers for Sizzler steakhouses.

#13 ELAINE AND THE LAME DUCK
WRITTEN BY GLEN CHARLES AND LES CHARLES.
DIRECTED BY JAMES BURROWS.

Alex's fare is a real schlemiel whose naively boorish behavior alienates his date. She asks to go home, leaving the dejected man (Jeffrey Tambor) to pour his heart out to Alex. He introduces himself as U.S. Congressman Walter Griswold, romantic loser, and Alex, sensing a matchmaking possibility, decides to try and fix him up with Elaine. Alex brings Griswold to the garage, where the congressman sadly explains he got elected only because his father is a major party contributor and his opponent was convicted of murder; even so, they had to hold a runoff election. And now he's facing a recall.

During dinner at Mario's, his self-pitying brings out the mother in Elaine. Later—and even though Griswold accidentally set the table on fire—Elaine brings him home to bed. The next morning, a very pleased Griswold wants to share a relationship with Elaine, but she talks him out of it. The night has bolstered his self-confidence, however.

Tag: Alex, giving Griswold a ride to the airport, congratulates him on his male conquest.

OTHER GUESTS:

Rusdi Lane (waiter/bartender at Mario's)

This episode puts the ''lame'' in lame duck. Substitute ''The writers and everyone else involved'' for ''Elaine'' and you'll get the idea.

Jeffrey Tambor, one of the actors who'd auditioned for the role of Alex, went on to play a recurring role as a judge in *Hill Street Blues* and the lead role in *Mr. Sunshine.* Among his other series roles is Murray, the beleaguered news chief on ABC's *Max Headroom* adventure series.

#14 BOBBY'S BIG BREAK
WRITTEN BY BARRY KEMP.
DIRECTED BY JAMES BURROWS.

Bobby finally lands a professional acting job: two appearances on the upcoming Friday and following Tuesday episodes of the soap opera *For Better For Worse.* He plays the long-lost boyfriend of the soap's leading lady and thinks it means a part in the regular cast. Feeling confident and having finally had enough of Louie's taunting, he rips up his cabbie license and throws it in the dispatcher's face. Louie is incensed. "You'll be back!" he says, sneering. "They ALL come back! Only one guy ever made it in the whole history of this garage, and that was James Caan. And HE'LL be back!"

On Friday, the cabbies huddle around a TV set, watching the soap. They see leading lady Olivia (Amanda McBroom) in a hospital lobby. She is talking nervously with her wheelchair-bound friend (Michele Conaway) about her upcoming reunion with her boyfriend, Skip. As the show ends, we see Bobby as Skip, bandaged and prone on a hospital gurney.

On Tuesday, to their astonishment, the cabbies see Skip killed off—Bobby's out. That night, Alex demands that Louie be gentle with the despondent Bobby when he comes in for his job back. "You think you're pretty cute, don't you?" Alex challenges. "I *am* cute!" Louie defends. Alex threatens him, but finally says only that Louie shouldn't tear apart what dignity Bobby has left, simply because—he shouldn't. Louie can't believe this grade-school stuff. "I shouldn't? I shouldn't?!" He laughs himself sick over it and continues to laugh when Bobby walks in. Louie finally composes himself and says stiffly that it's nice to have you back, Bob.

Tag: Louie speculates with Bobby on the way he *might* have gone about publicly humiliating him. "And then I might have turned on the PA, like this . . ."

The last name isn't coincidental—Michele Conaway, who plays an actress in the soap opera hospital scene, is Jeff Conaway's sister. As Jeff recalls, "Rhonda Young, who was casting *Taxi* that year, was my sister's and my agent when we were teenagers. She told me there was a part that week that maybe Michele could do—she'd been a regular on *General Hospital* for a while and had done some other things. So she auditioned for the part of Olivia, my girlfriend in the soap, and Ed [Weinberger, an executive producer] came by and said, 'Hey, Jeff, your sister is real good and everything, but we can't have you kissing her on the show!' I laughed—he was right. They offered her the other role instead."

#15 FRIENDS

WRITTEN BY EARL POMERANTZ.
DIRECTED BY JAMES BURROWS.

Latka has a toothache, but can't get Louie to let him go to the dentist. Meanwhile, Tony is telling the cabbies what a rotten blind date he got stuck with over the weekend. He took it as a favor to Bobby, since Bobby's date, Dominique, had an out-of-town cousin she didn't want to leave alone. It turned out the only thing Tony had in common with his date was that she wanted to be a boxer. The cabbies are divided on whether or not Tony should have put up with such a miserable night out of friendship.

John says friends always have to help each other out; why, he remembers one childhood friend with whom he even shared a distress signal, which he demonstrates: "Yak-a-bye! Yak-a-bye!" An alarmed Latka responds to it with a fire extinguisher; when Bobby and Alex walk in, he tells them they just missed the "yak-a-bye" drill.

Tony chats with them for a minute before going to the phone, and Bobby invites the cabbies to his place Sunday to watch a football game. "Hey, Latka," he calls out. "You wanna watch the football game in my apartment?" "No," says Latka, "I rather watch it on television." Tony returns with big news: Tomorrow he's fighting a state champ in Scranton, Pennsylvania—the state champ of New Hampshire, whose only other big fighter is this guy's dad. He asks Bobby to take care of his fish, George and Wanda, while he's away. Tony and the fish go back four years; he bought them with the big $3 he says he got from the purse of his first win. Bobby doesn't want the responsibility, but Tony reminds him of all the favors he's done for him. Bobby reluctantly agrees. Louie also reluctantly agrees to let Latka see the dentist.

On Sunday, Alex and Latka arrive at Bobby's apartment. He's not in, but he always leaves a key hidden somewhere near the door. They go in, turn on the set, and hope Bobby's only gone out for some munchies. He does return, but has been on a date with Dominique. While the three of them are watching the game, Tony phones. He hasn't fought yet, and the cabbies wish him luck. Latka says how much he likes American television's instant replay. "In my country, they just make them do it again." Bobby goes over to feed the fish, which he forgot to do yesterday, and finds them dead. He's horrified, but doesn't want to take the blame. He tells Alex, "Maybe it was one of those murder-suicide things."

Soon afterward, in the garage, the cabbies, except for Bobby, wait for Tony to return. He lost the fight, it turns out, but, "The guy said I gave him a much better fight than his dad." Tony brought back a present for his fish—a little castle. He says he knows it's silly, but the fish are a symbol of survival to him. While Tony's putting his stuff away, Bobby enters with a goldfish bowl and two look-alikes. Tony thinks they look great—now where are *his* fish? Bobby painfully confesses they're gone—but he saved them, in a zip-lock bag. A hurt Tony says, "I don't wanna have anything to do with you—friend."

Days go by; Tony refuses to talk to Bobby, and Louie calls the actor "Fish Killer." Alex finally convinces Tony that he should accept Bobby's invitation to meet at home and talk things out: "The fish would have wanted it this way." Alex and Tony show up the next day at Bobby's, but he's out. All around are things Bobby's borrowed from Tony and never returned—including the "lucky shirt" he wears to auditions. Tony can't understand why he likes Bobby: "I mean, there's guy's I don't like who treat me better. One guy I hate treats me almost as good." Then Bobby enters with Dominique. After all his begging to have Tony come over and talk, he forgot all about it.

Dominique goes into the other room, and Alex explodes at Bobby, calling him irresponsible, inconsiderate, undependable, selfish, insensitive . . . it's so bad even Tony comes to Bobby's defense. Alex is so riled, he tells Tony it's *his* fault anyway that the fish are dead; he left them in the care of a guy who forgets to feed himself half the time. Now Tony gets mad at Alex, and Bobby intervenes.

The situation finally strikes them as funny, and Bobby announces he's going to take his friends out for conciliatory steak and Löwenbräu, followed by tickets to the Knicks game. Then he remembers he has to tell Dominique. He goes in to the other room to tell her that a man's gotta do what a man's gotta

do, etc. Tony and Alex wait for him. And wait. And wait. Resigned to Bobby's quicksilver traits, they head out. But not before Tony helpfully cares for the fish.

Tag: In the garage, Bobby presents a grateful Tony with George and Wanda, mounted on a plaque.

GUESTS:

Liz Miller (Dominique)

"It's a goldfish show," says writer Earl Pomerantz matter-of-factly. "Everytime I write for a series, I put a goldfish in there. Remember the goldfish episode on *The Cosby Show* [where the Huxtables gather 'round the toilet for a funeral]? What happened was, I went out of town once, when I was still single, and I gave my goldfish to Les Charles and his wife to take care of. And when I came back, one of them was dead—the fish, not Les or his wife. They've always felt awful about that. And so what comedy writers do sometimes is to write a story about it. Basically, 'Friends' is about friendship and about counting on a guy—and then that guy kills your fish!" He cackles.

Conaway blushingly remembers a behind-the-scenes occurrence that he figures, in retrospect, says a lot about how far he's come in terms of self-confidence. "Ed Weinberger was always goofing, and we're rehearsing this show, and I'm kissing Dominique, and Ed's giving me," he says, gesturing, " 'No, naw, you're not kissing right.' And I'm saying to myself, what's wrong with *him*—I went to [the] NYU Theatre Program, I had a lot of kissing scenes. I know how to kiss for real, I know how to do it for the screen. So I'm getting pissed off because Ed keeps telling me I'm doing it wrong, and the girl is looking at me like I don't know what I'm doing. Finally, Ed says, 'I'm gonna have to come down and show you how to do it right.' So what it was, was that being a little insecure, I never realized he was *playing,* that he just wanted to come over and lay one on the chick. It didn't dawn on me to have fun with that." From a feminist viewpoint, of course, Jeff's position was admirable. We wonder how guest Liz Miller took it.

"The way my mind was working back then,"

Conaway reflects, "I was always trying to be perfect, because if I wasn't perfect that meant I wasn't good enough, and that meant I was going to be fired and my whole life was going to go down the tubes." He's since realized, "When you torture yourself like that, it's hard to have a good time. I used to drive my wife crazy."

He needn't have worried. Conaway's reactions to the fish deaths, to finding Tony and Alex in his apartment, and to Louie's taunts are priceless. Insecurity plagues nearly *every* actor—nearly *everybody*—and Conaway's insecurity, which gave life to Bobby's, just made the character's reactions when he was pulled out of his own little world all the more meaningful.

As great as this episode is, there are a lot of needless logic and continuity problems to it. Logic, first: Bobby, who grew up in the Bronx, would never leave a key hidden outside his door. Nowadays, most people who grew up in *Peoria* wouldn't leave their keys outside their doors. It makes more sense for Alex to have had a key to Bobby's place, as friends sometimes give their keys to one another for security reasons, etc. Also, goldfish generally don't die after one day of no feeding unless they were sick. Maybe the script should have had Tony stay away longer. Now, continuity: The cabbies ask Tony about his date over the weekend, he gets a call to fight "tomorrow," and tomorrow turns out to be Sunday. Sloppy. The cabbies in the opener could have just asked Tony how his date went, without confining it to a weekend.

#16 LOUIE SEES THE LIGHT

WRITTEN BY RUTH BENNETT.
DIRECTED BY JAMES BURROWS.

When John comes in with yet another typically low booking, Louie begins yet another typical tirade. This time, however, he suddenly clutches at his stomach. The cabbies, alarmed, tell Lou to go to a doctor right away. "What?" he replies defiantly. "See a doctor for [groans loudly] a simple, gut-wrenching pain?" He checks himself into University Hospital where the cabbies, improbably, come to visit him the night before his operation. As they shuffle out, he asks Alex to remain. Lou wants to promise God that if He gets him through surgery alive, he'll become the best person he can possibly be—Alex as his witness.

The operation comes off fine, and Louie, back at work minus a gallstone, is living up to his promise. Bobby, however, offers the cabbies a $50 bet that Louie can't keep his oath for a whole day. Alex, who initially refuses on principle, takes the bet at 2-1 odds. Bobby proceeds to goad and taunt Louie until the enraged dispatcher finally hoists Bobby on a giant engine-block hook and vows to make him "the second most miserable cabdriver in New York City! The *most* miserable cabdriver in all of New York City is whoever lets him down, or feeds him."

Tag: At Mario's, Lou asks if Alex believes in hell. "Believe in it?" Alex snorts. "I work there." Lou is convinced that he welshed on God and that God is waiting for him outside with brass knuckles. Alex reminds Louie that he only promised to be the best person he possibly could be—and if that person is a low-down rat, then that's the way it goes. A relieved Lou thanks Alex sincerely for his theological insight.

GUESTS:

Fay Hauser (nurse)
John Dukakis (Goodwin a rookie driver)

Note: The end-credit shot of Danza is from the original, discarded *Taxi* opening.

People were always having operations and concurrent religious crises on MTM shows, so why not on *Taxi?* Danny DeVito's portrayal of a devout creep makes this performance come off with more vigor and quite a few more laughs than usual. And thank goodness scriptwriter Ruth Bennett (later a *Family Ties* producer and a creator of *Sara* and *Duet*) didn't build the episode around "Let's watch Louie try to be good." Forget it. We *know* it's not going to stick, so let's play around with the best way to make it *unstick*. Great! Still, it goes to show that in the first season of *Taxi,* they were still writing episodes that could be "typed." Try pigeonholing "The Shloogel Show" (episode #91).

DeVito's most vivid impression of that episode

"was the amount of candy Andy Kaufman ate at the bedside. These things were like cotton candy, kind of—same texture, but it wasn't exactly that." He laughs. "He had to eat 'em on camera and, like, God forbid he'd have to eat regular chocolates! He wouldn't eat anything like that unless it was total sugar. He would've done it if he'd had to, but they made up these special spun-sugar candies for him that looked like chocolates, which you could keep on popping in your mouth, and they'd dissolve. He ate 'em at the run-through, during rehearsals, during filming, *and* pickups! He must've eaten six boxes of those things, God bless him."

Among the biographical tidbits we learn from this episode is that Louie was delivered on a kitchen table by a midwife, and Latka has a cousin named Baschi—presumably the Baschi from episode #35, "Latka's Revolting."

#17 SUBSTITUTE FATHER

WRITTEN BY BARRY KEMP.
DIRECTED BY JAMES BURROWS.

Elaine's sick aunt in Buffalo needs her right away, and though daughter Jennifer is going along, Elaine doesn't want to pull son Jason (Michael Hershewe) out of the district finals of a spelling bee. Alex agrees to watch him while she's away, but when she runs out to the car where Jason's waiting, Alex realizes he made plans to have dinner with his sister on Thursday and a date on Friday. He talks Bobby into taking Jason on Thursday, Tony into part of Friday, and John to switch around some plans—it all gets very complicated. Elaine brings Jason in and hugs him and while Alex goes upstairs to get his stuff, an uncomfortable Bobby tries to make conversation. "So. You're a kid, huh?" Jason asks Bobby's advice about stage fright and makes an immediate friend. The two go out to breakfast.

In the garage a couple of days later, Louie is on the phone with a customer who has a complaint. "Yes, ma'am, I hear you. You say one of our drivers was rude to you. Well, what was it he said, exactly? I see. And how fat *are* you?" Tony brings in Jason, after the two enjoyed a fun boxing lesson. The kid is so personable even Louie tells him, "I

don't dislike you as much as I do most kids." He says they have in common the fact they were both raised by a single mother. "Tell me something," he says to Jason, "do you smoke? You drink? You use foul language?" Negative on all counts. "Yeah, it sure is tough without a father to teach you."

John takes Jason to see *Death on the Nile,* and Alex plans to take him to see the Knicks. The night before the spelling bee, Louie and his mother take him to a wrestling match. Jason's not getting any studying done. The day of the spelling bee, the cabbies show up to lend their support—and Louie to place some bets. The moderator introduces Jason, who represents P.S 33 in New York. The spelling bee comes down to him and a girl named Christa from P.S. 25 in Bronxville. She snags it when she correctly spells *vermeil* after Jason misses. He takes the loss nobly, though Louie calls out, "Fix! Fix!"

At the garage right after the spelling bee, the guys all blame themselves for not letting Jason study. Elaine gets back in, and after Jason gives her the news, he tells her it was his own fault for not studying, that he was old enough to be responsible. Elaine's proud that he learned a lesson—though she'd still have preferred that he'd won. As the two of them leave, the guys all talk about wanting kids of their own.

Tag: The guys are all drunk on Louie's twelve-year-old Scotch (Alex: "It says eight years old." Louie: "Right, and I bought it four years ago"), and sing "Sonny Boy."

OTHER GUESTS:

David Knapp (the spelling bee moderator)
Tan Adams (Christa Fowler)
Suzanne Carney (Marilu Hartman)
Carl Byrd (Boyd Fowler, a parent)

Michael Hershewe grew up too quickly to stay in the role of Jason, and David Mendenhall eventually took over the part. Like many child actors, Michael looked younger than he actually was, and many episodes later, when the scripts called for a ten-year-old Jason, Michael looked like the teenager he was.

The name "Marilu" given to one of the little

girls in the spelling bee should tip off viewers that family or friends were involved. As a beaming Marilu Henner explains, ''That's my niece Suzanne. What happened is that at first they wanted me to have a [ten-year-old] daughter. Then when they wrote the episode, they thought it'd be better to leave a son to hang out with the guys. I told [the producers] I had already brought my niece out here to play my daughter, because I thought she looked so much like me, and so they had her play the little girl in the spelling bee. She's adorable, isn't she?''

Since P.S. 33 is specified as ''in New York,'' rather than a borough, it means that the Nardo clan lived in Manhattan (around 27th Street and Ninth Avenue, where P.S. 33 is located). Elaine and her kids moved a couple of times throughout the show's run; at this point, they'd been living for a long time in a white-faced brownstone (as confirmed in episode #33); the building type is typical in that Chelsea section of Manhattan.

By the final season, the Nardos were living in an expensive-looking East Side high rise. Given Elaine's two modest jobs and the fact her ex-husband has a ski chalet in Aspen (see episode #103), a pattern emerges: Hubby must've been loaded, and it took her years of just getting by financially (as seen by her not being able to afford her apartment when it turned co-op [episode #51], and flying charter on a trip to Europe [episode #69]), before she received a divorce settlement. That settlement apparently helped her hold on to the apartment that turned co-op, and later, to move on up to the East Side.

#18 MAMA GRAVAS

WRITTEN BY GLEN CHARLES AND LES CHARLES.
DIRECTED BY JAMES BURROWS.

Latka is dressed up for his mother's visit to America. She's coming straight to the garage from the airport so that Latka who's gotten the rest of the day off, can show her the sights. Louie, however, rescinds Latka's time off—over the cabbies' protests, of course. ''Hey, I'm not doin' this because I enjoy it,'' Louie tells them. ''I *do* enjoy it, but that's not the reason.'' Latka asks a reluctant Alex,

who's exhausted after a fourteen-hour shift, to take his sweet old mother to Mario's for a bite. Alex tries to get out of it—until he sees that Latka's mother Greta (Susan Kellerman) is a statuesque peasant beauty with cleavage deeper than the Grand Canyon.

At Mario's, she tells Alex she can't wait to see the New York City she's heard so much about—''garbage strike, blackout, urban blight . . . Yankee Dog Stadium!'' Alex comments on her youthfulness, and she explains she was just fifteen when she married Latka's father, who died two years later ''in struggle for liberty and freedom.'' ''Oh,'' says Alex, ''he was a freedom fighter shot by the police.'' ''No,'' she replies proudly, ''He was police shot by freedom fighters.'' She starts coming on to Alex—whose name in her language, she says invitingly, means ''one who makes *nik nik* during harvest!'' Latka comes by and gives them two tickets for the Rockettes at Radio City Music Hall. He asks his mother about old-country friends: Grishmel, who had a horrible operation; Schmopsi, who went nutso, and Luurgid, who shot himself. ''It's always nice to get news of back home,'' he tells Alex.

The next night at the garage, John and Tony are discovering that—according to their logic—it will be impossible to ever get fresh apples in the vending machine. Alex comes in and asks Elaine for some advice. To hear him tell it, Greta ripped his shirt off, threw him down, and had her way with him. ''After we were alone for a while, she turned into an animal—a *great* one.'' Elaine suggests not telling Latka—but from the sound of Latka's voice, as he demands to speak with Alex ''man to face,'' it's too late. Yet instead of being upset, he calls Alex ''Daddy.'' Alex explains there's some mistake, and when Greta enters the garage, she tells Latka she doesn't plan to marry Alex. The offended Latka says his mother is nothing but a dirty *kakbolt,* whereupon she slaps him and then sits him down to explain her loneliness. Latka accepts this, but refuses to be friends any longer with Alex.

In the tool room, a despondent Latka pulls a bottle of homemade *brefnish* from his locker and takes a swig. Alex enters and apologizes for hurting Latka, but insists he did nothing wrong. Latka doesn't buy it and refuses to bump rears with Alex (his country's equivalent of a friendly handshake between friends). Alex can't believe Latka doesn't want to be friends anymore—no more poker, no more TV football, no more breakfasts at Mario's? But Latka remains firm—it's a matter of honor. Alex reluctantly turns to leave. Then Latka suggests they *globnik,* meaning, as Alex reads from a dictionary, " 'to pretend or assume some event or occurrence never took place.' Do you think that would do it—just pretend it never happened?" "Pretend what never happened?" Latka asks. Quick on his feet, Alex smiles and says he doesn't know. The two bump rears, friends once again.

OTHER GUESTS:

T. J. Castronova (Tommy, the bartender at Mario's)

Note: The end-credit shot of Jeff Conaway is from the original, discarded *Taxi* opening. The shot of Danza is from episode #21 and was filmed the same day as the Queensboro Bridge opening eventually used.

This is one of the funniest, most memorable episodes of the first season, and also one with a great deal to say about the little lies and selective memories we allow ourselves between friends. It touches upon another aspect of friendship as well, namely the locker-room bragging we need for our egos: Does grown boy Alex really need Elaine's advice, or is he just looking to tell someone about his conquest? Or *maybe* he wanted to make Elaine a little jealous.

And Alex reveals that his mother is living, and is sixty-seven years old. But she must have died soon afterward, since in episode #23, Alex mentions her funeral as a thing of the past.

The talented Susan Kellerman, a walking Statue of Liberty, has appeared in a host of TV movies and as a guest on such series as *Remington Steele, Knight Rider, The Jeffersons,* and *Cagney and Lacey.* She returned to *Taxi* twice, for "The Wedding of Latka and Simka" (episode #87) and "The Road Not Taken, Part II" (episode #90).

#19 ALEX TASTES DEATH AND FINDS A NICE RESTAURANT

WRITTEN BY MICHAEL LEESON.
DIRECTED BY JAMES BURROWS.

Louie is mechanically giving out cab assignments, and in between names and cab numbers matter-of-factly tells the shocked cabbies that Alex has been shot and robbed. He was taken to Mount Sinai Hospital and, as it turns out, is relatively OK; as the cabbies rush out to see him, he calmly walks into the garage. The bullet nicked his ear, causing a scratch and temporarily diminished hearing. Elaine: "But there's nothing else wrong?" Alex: "No, it didn't take long. He just put this little bandage on here and let me go." After he explains what happened, Bobby comments it's the kind of thing "you never think could happen to you." Alex: "What makes you think he was a Jew?" Before he goes home to rest, he tells them all he remembers about how the guy looked: He was big and had "kill" tattooed across his fist. Louie reminds him never to pick up people with tattoos: "They're all morons, maniacs, and lowlifes." Tony points out the "Keep on Truckin' " tattoo on his arm. "Oh yeah, and losers."

The next night, Alex has climbed right back on that proverbial horse. Over the radio, Louie tells him to be careful and not feel any pressure to book big tonight—then asks Nardo for the five bucks she promised him to read that little speech. Alex passes up fares until he picks up someone safe—a young priest. But the priest is going to Front Street, by Pier Six, and when he can only name ten of the twelve apostles, Alex throws him out of the cab. "Whew! Close one." At the garage, all the cabbies are growing paranoid after Alex's experience. Bobby suggests one tactic to scare off a robber—fake a heart attack. He can do it, he says; he's an actor. To demonstrate, he gives a convincing performance. On being told of Bobby's attack, Louie merely says, "Well, move him. I could have tripped and broke my neck." Bobby: "See—I convinced him."

Alex comes in, having booked nothing. "Not too good, Alex," says Lou. Alex: "I quit." Louie: "You're not used to criticism, are you?" A fright-

Episode #19: "Alex Tastes Death and Finds a Nice Restaurant."

ened Alex has made up his mind. Bobby points out that Alex has been driving a cab for ten years. Alex replies he can do other things—he used to be an upholsterer, a bartender, a waiter. They can't convince him to stay, so they wish him well. Louie even shakes his hand.

Sometime later, we find Alex working as a waiter at a posh French restaurant called Genevieve's. The cabbies come in to visit and have dinner, but they're all really uncouth; when other patrons complain that Alex is ignoring their table, Bobby even mouths off to them. And Alex, though he's making great money and has a good work atmosphere, impulsively decides to quit and go back to cab driving with his friends.

Tag: Alex is back at work. Cautiously, he allows a Girl Scout into his cab.

GUESTS:

James Staley (the priest)
Byron Webster (the maître d')
John Petlock (a waiter)
Charles Thomas Murphy, Mavis Palmer (the other patrons)

Note: The actress playing the Girl Scout is uncredited.

Alex has only been driving for ten years? C'mon. He was driving part-time back when he was still married and had a kid, and he hasn't seen the kid in fifteen years (see episode #1). Probably what happened is he quit driving for a while to upholster, etc., and went back to cabbing after that—making it the last ten years straight, plus some driving a few years before that.

Episode #20: Louie, not moving to Queens, in "Hollywood Calling."

#20 HOLLYWOOD CALLING

WRITTEN BY GLEN CHARLES AND LES CHARLES.
DIRECTED BY JAMES BURROWS.

Hollywood director Roger Chapman (Martin Mull) has the garage all excited: He wants to make a movie about cabdrivers and is at the Sunshine Cab Co. on a research trip to gather material. He ingratiates himself with the drivers by offering to have breakfast brought in every day his crew is there. Soon the star, Michael Patrese, arrives. Alex is the only one not excited by all this. A real curmudgeon, he refuses to contribute any of his great cabdriving stories. Chapman is undaunted, leading Alex to demand help from the shop steward. No one knows who that is, so Louie looks it up: Ben Garetsky—who's been dead for two years. Elaine nominates Alex to replace him, but though the ayes are overwhelming, Alex demurs. Tony nominates the dead Garetsky, who wins in a landslide.

As the days go by, the cabbies acclimate themselves to the movie team's presence. Soon, fancy catered breakfasts are the order of the day; even the cook from Mario's shows up to eat there. Chapman gets Tony tickets to a sold-out title fight and a date with his secretary, Lea. Alex finally relents and tells Chapman some cab-driving stories.

Later, the director informs the cabbies that not only will Bobby have a role in the movie, but that garage-owner Mr. McKenzie has agreed to let him shoot on-location there, provided Louie gives his OK. Louie does—for $15,000 and the title of Location Coordinator. To celebrate, Chapman invites the cabbies to a party at the Plaza Hotel, the exterior of which we see. At the party, a phone call comes from one Peter Koppelman, the (fictional) head of production at Paramount. (As Chapman's assistant Richard explains it, Koppelman, who used to be with Universal, has replaced Paramount's John Muncie; Hawthorne from Columbia is now with Universal; Lou Green from M-G-M is now with Columbia; and Muncie is now with—or maybe at—Burger King.) Koppelman is calling to cancel the cabbie picture. Chapman tries every angle to save it. He asks Lea for help, since she used to date Koppelman. Lea says she dated Muncie and Hawthorne, not Koppelman—it was *Patrese* who dated Koppelman! Neither Alex nor Louie can sway the new production chief; Louie even tells the man he's promised his mother that the money means they can move to Queens. As the sun slowly sinks on the project, everyone departs, one by one—though Louie hangs back long enough to steal the towels.

OTHER GUESTS:

Joey Aresco (Michael Patrese)
Christine Dickinson (Lea, the director's secretary—perhaps named after *Taxi* assistant Lea Goldbaum)
Gary Imhoff (Richard, the director's asistant—perhaps named after *Taxi* assistant, and later coproducer, Richard Sakai)
Rik Colitti (the cook from Mario's)

Note: George Reynolds is listed in the end credits, where we see a snippet of him delivering a line, but his part was cut.

That's the problem with late-season shows—the producers are so desperate for scripts that episodes like this one result. Waiter! Send it back! And Martin Mull, a whitebread TV and film comedian who specializes in satirizing middle-American life-styles, is so stereotypically smarmy here it's surprising that even the most naive cabdriver wouldn't just say, "Later . . ." Jim Brooks insists the episode bears little resemblance to the *Taxi* team's similar research trip, and it's easy to believe him. If they had been as jerky as Chapman, they might have ended up alone in the South Bronx after midnight.

For the record, Mull got his first major exposure playing twins Barth and Marth Gimble on Norman Lear's syndicated satire, *Mary Hartman, Mary Hartman.* He reprised the role of Barth on the talk-show parodies *Fernwood 2Night* and *America 2Night.* His movie credits include *My Bodyguard* and *Mr. Mom.*

#21 MEMORIES OF CAB 804, PART I
WRITTEN BY BARRY KEMP.
DIRECTED BY JAMES BURROWS.

Alex, Tony, and Bobby impatiently wait for John so they can go to the track, as Elaine looks on disapprovingly. But Louie gets a phone call that John has had a wreck. Worse, he's cracked up cab #804, a beloved old war-horse. The cabbies are shocked. Tony notes that in one more month, 804 would have been the company's first cab to hit a half-million miles. Alex recalls it was in 804 he first met John, picking him up near Grand Central Station. The young out-of-towner, who was headed to 222 East 64th Street, accidentally knocked down the safety shield between the front and rear seats—an omen, Alex figures in retrospect.

Bobby flashes back to the night he locked horns—and gun barrels—with a pragmatic thief (Scoey Mitchlll). After hours of debate at gunpoint over the propriety of the robbery attempt—during which time the fogged-up cab is ticketed—the crook finally decides to leave. Bobby, holding the guns, which are jammed but still potentially useful as bludgeons, demands the thief pay him the $38 fare plus the $10 ticket. The crook pays up. Now, he says, he doesn't have enough money for cab fare

home. Bobby asks him his address (447 West 23rd Street), but rather than take him home, Bobby speeds off to the police. Back in the present, he shows his coworkers a newspaper clipping about the incident.

Tony recalls the day he was cruising Northern Boulevard around Queensboro Plaza, when he picked up a guy with no particular destination. On the Queensboro Bridge headed toward Manhattan, the guy asks Tony to pull the cab over and gets out to jump. "Hey, don't do that!" Tony yells at him. "OK," the guy says, getting back in. So much for dramatic talk-downs.

Louie contributes a story about his cab-driving days. A rich father deposits his con-man twelve-year-old in the back of the cab and gives Louie $20 to take the kid to the Walden School. He hands the kid $600 for tuition and books and says he'll see him at Thanksgiving and will apologize to his mother for him. The kid gives Lou thirty bucks to let him drive, then wins $200 on a couple of sucker bets. But Lou gets even, of course: The kid wants to bet $800 on who can hold his breath the longest, and Lou, pulling the same sneaky tactics as the kid, wins. He softens up, however, when the kid starts to cry—and gives him twenty bucks.

As the story finishes, John walks in and announces he's alright. The cabbies rush past him to the towed-in 804, which is crushed like a modern sculpture.

OTHER GUESTS:

Rod Browning (the father)
Chris Barnes (the rich kid)
Ed Weinberger (man on bridge, uncredited)

#22 MEMORIES OF CAB 804, PART II
WRITTEN BY BARRY KEMP.
DIRECTED BY JAMES BURROWS.

As Latka struggles valiantly to repair the beloved cab #804, the cabbies share reminiscences. Alex remembers the night he picked up a young pregnant woman (Regie Baff) and her boyfriend (Mandy Patinkin) and helped deliver the baby when the (partially) Lamaze-trained husband panicked. In gratitude, he tells the cabbies, they

TAXI

T A X I

125

would've named the baby after him—but they hated the name "Alex."

Elaine remembers the night she picked up the rich, handsome, and extraordinarily nice Mike Beldon (Tom Selleck). She agrees to take him to an early-morning art auction 140 miles away. Beldon turns out to be such a good guy that he helps Elaine with the driving and opens up to her, explaining he'd been married and had wanted kids though his wife didn't, and that maybe he's a little old-fashioned that way. "Y'know," Elaine tells him, "here we are, sharing the same experiences, the same interests. Sorta maybe feeling a little attracted to each other?" "Maybe a little," Beldon admits. "Maybe a lot?" Elaine asks. "Maybe a lot!" he confirms. Elaine (half to herself): "Good!"

When they arrive at the mansion where the auction is to take place, Beldon tenderly asks Elaine to sleep with him. Very regretfully, she turns him down. He understands, and Elaine, seeing the hurt look on his face, gives him a long kiss. As they part, he pays the fare and adds $100 for a tip. Elaine, astonished, can't bring herself to take it; he presses it in her palm and tells her to think of it "as a down payment on your art gallery." "What would you have given me if I'd stayed the night?" she asks half-jokingly. "A very sweet memory," he replies. Over the radio, Louie comments, "Yer better off wit' the hundred."

Tag: Latka has done his best, but #804 is going to that great garage in the sky. Maybe, speculates Alex, it was #803. . . .

Some of the first *Taxi* scenes ever filmed were shot for this two-part "pickup" episode, which, like the later "Fantasy Borough," "On the Job," and "The Road Not Taken," is composed of bits and pieces shot here and there and then assembled for economical, two-part, end-of-season shows. The very first scenes shot were of Tony Danza. *Taxi* cocreator Dave Davis—who directed the opening and closing sequences and most of the on-location "connectives," such as shots of Times Square—shot Danza and cocreator Ed Weinberger on the Queensboro Bridge the same day he shot the opening sequence. In fact, when Banta talks about

cruising Queensboro Plaza—a Queens crossroads at the foot of the bridge—we see the actual location. That seldom happens in television.

As mentioned in the background for episode #1, a scene removed from the premiere showed Alex picking up John Burns at "Grand Central Station"—although the initial shot of the cab has it turning onto Times Square from 45th Street, with the Astor Plaza building and the distinctive lights of tourist-café Lindy's in the background. Part of the leftover footage is included here, up to the point where John's tap knocks down the safety shield. We don't, however, get to hear Alex comment sarcastically that the shield "wasn't built to take that kind of abuse," or to see John get shot down by his old girl friend.

The quirkily named Scoey Mitchell appeared in the *Taxi* creators' TV movie *Cindy*, and for one season was a cast member on *Rhoda*. Child-actor Chris (C.D.) Barnes went on to the series *Starman* and *Day by Day*. And two soon-to-be major stars made memorable early appearances in this episode: Many Patinkin and went on to his Tony Award–winning role as Che in the Broadway musical *Evita*. He's since gone on to continued success on Broadway in *Sunday in the Park with George*, and has appeared in such movies as *The Princess Bride*, *Ragtime*, *Daniel*, and *Yentl*, and in TV's *Chicago Hope*.

Selleck—whose first TV appearance was as an unpicked bachelor on *The Dating Game* circa 1970—had previously appeared on *The Streets of San Francisco*, *The Rockford Files* (twice as Jim Rockford's rich, galling rival, Lance White), and the soap operas *Doctor's Hospital* and *The Young and the Restless*. After two failed TV movie/pilots (1978's *The Gypsy Warriors* and 1979's *Boston and Killbride*), Selleck connected with the popular *Magnum, P.I.* in 1980—which, ironically, helped to kill *Taxi* in the ratings.

"I'd met Tom Selleck before," recalls Marilu Henner. "When I started doing *Taxi* I was living with an actor who was in an acting class with Tom, and I knew Tom from there when he couldn't get a job. My boyfriend would say, 'My god, I can't believe this guy's not working, he's so good-looking!' " Selleck's sweet, convincing performance, which might have been subtitled *Magnum, Art Dealer*, turned out to be a prototype for the screen

Episode #23: Alex pointedly refusing advice from his sister (guest star Joan Hackett) in "Honor Thy Father."

image that finally brought him success. Initially nervous in front of *Taxi*'s studio audience, his winning performance was shot as a pickup—appropriately enough, given the scene.

#23 HONOR THY FATHER

WRITTEN BY LES CHARLES AND GLEN CHARLES.
DIRECTED BY JAMES BURROWS.

A cheerful Puerto Rican cabbie (Richard Beauchamp) is irking Latka by mooching his tools, leading to a bilingual argument that Louie has to break up. Lou's attention is distracted by a tall, cool woman in a black dress (Joan Hackett) who's come looking for Alex. She tells Elaine she's his sister, Charlotte, whom he doesn't see often: She lives in East Hampton, a posh Long Island resort community, and is only in town for a fund-raising dinner. Elaine: "What are you raising funds for?" Charlotte: "Starving . . . something." She chats with Latka in his native tongue and remarks afterward, "Too bad his grammar is so poor. . . . He's from the lower classes. My guess is his family herded sheep." Louie: "My guess is they dated them." She finally can't wait any longer and asks Elaine to tell Alex his father is sick and in the hospital, and that she'll be back tomorrow.

When Alex is given the news, he reacts indiffer-

ently. Prodded, he explains that his father, Joe, was a womanizer who deserted the family when Alex was small. They survived on welfare, and Alex had to forgo college—although Dad helped to pay for Charlotte's tuition. And when Alex's mother died, Joe brought a date to the funeral. Now, Joe and Alex haven't spoken in almost thirty years. When Charlotte returns the next day, she takes Alex to Latka's tool room for privacy and tries to convince him to see their father. Alex eventually relents and goes with Charlotte to The New York Hospital

On Taxis in New York City

In real-life, New York City's taxicab industry goes like this: There are 11,787 "medallions," or taxicab licenses. The number has been fixed since 1937, and, subsequently, a medallion can cost as much as a co-op apartment in Manhattan ($100,000 and up). About 5,000 of these medallions are in the hands of private owner-operators, guys who own and maintain their own cabs. The rest are owned by "fleets." (There's also a semi-regulated livery-car or "gypsy cab" industry, but a strange caste system keeps these 35,000 cars in the less affluent neighborhoods.)

At the time the article that formed the seed for *Taxi* appeared in *New York Magazine*, fleet drivers earned a commission on their bookings. That's what the crew on *Taxi* did. If they were hacking today, they'd be leasing cabs from a fleet, paying for their own gas, and keeping the profit. They wouldn't be responding to radio calls either; that aspect was phased out between 1981 and 1985 in favor of private car services. They also wouldn't be driving those classic Checker cabs—they're no long manufactured, and except for a handful of hardy survivors, are no more to be seen on the streets of New York.

One thing hasn't changed: Then as now, the lengths of shifts were loose. At the time of *Taxi*'s conception, the night shift lasted from about 5 P.M. to 5 A.M. It's no wonder then that when Alex, Bobby, Tony, Elaine, Jim, and John came stumbling in after twelve hours, they didn't have the strength to fight off Louie's barbs.

(room 682). While Charlotte waits outside, Alex walks in and sees a frail old man, bedridden and surrounded by ominous machines. Alex tries to think of pleasant things to say, but has little luck. Finally, he gives up, and breaking down, discovers how much he really missed his father. He hugs the old man, then he hears from behind him, "Hello, Alex." It's Joe (Jack Gilford), who was out of the room. The mortified Alex is so shocked he can't think of anything to say. He and his father part, with Alex newly stung by the idea of family versus the reality of it.

Tag: The Puerto Rican cabbie again takes one of Latka's tools. Latka objects and a fight brews. Suddenly, from the cage, Jeff announces it's quitting time. The two drop their stances until tomorrow: "Take it easy." "OK, bye-bye."

OTHER GUESTS:

Ian Wolfe (old man in the hospital)
Margaret Ladd (Miss Stallworth, another hospital visitor)

Alex doesn't miss *his* father, but *a* father. The image of a traditional father-figure is what brings him to the hospital and what makes him profess his filial love—to the wrong person, i.e., anybody. As soon as Alex does meet his father, reality sets in, and the two have nothing to say to one another.

"I always had a couple of shows about my dad in every series I did," Brooks confesses. "In *The Mary Tyler Moore Show,* he was Ted Baxter's father. My dad was away a lot." He told Kevin Sessums of *Interview* that, "I was early latchkey. My father wasn't a regular financial contributor in the home and my mother worked very hard. So I was alone a lot. My mother was an enormous influence on me." Brooks's father even abandoned the family on occasion. "[Abandonment] is a big issue with me," Brooks told Sessums. "The word itself sends little shivers over me."

The episode is lifted almost literally from real life, he adds. "The joke—'Dad! Oh, it's not him'—was literal. I went to the hospital, saw this frail-looking old man there, and I said 'Daddy!' and it turned out to be the wrong guy." Brooks's long-unseen father was in the next room, relatively healthy.

Joan Hackett, so excellent as the strong-willed sister who'd named the family cat Scheherazade over Alex's suggestion of Taffy, came to prominence as one of the eight highly touted newcomers of *The Group* (1966). She received a 1981 Oscar nomination for her final screen role, in Neil Simon's *Only When I Laugh,* playing an aging Park Avenue beauty similar to Charlotte Reiger. A respected character actress whose sophistication often surpassed her material, she died of cancer in 1983.

Ian Wolfe (1896-1992) was a venerable movie character actor since 1934, making notable appearances in such films as *Witness for the Prosecution* and *Rebel Without a Cause.* He's been on *Cheers,* and as late as 1990 performed in the movie *Dick Tracy.* For background on Jack Gilford, see episode #73, "Like Father, Like Son."

#24 THE RELUCTANT FIGHTER
WRITTEN BY KEN ESTIN.
DIRECTED BY JAMES BURROWS.

An old, punchy guy named Vince from Tony's gym comes by the garage looking for "Tony Banta, the boxer." Louie asks if he'll settle for "Tony Banta, the bum." Tony, sitting with Alex and Elaine, who are playing chess, greets Vince and introduces him around. After Alex and Elaine head off for breakfast, Vince tells Tony that Benny Foster, the thirty-eight-year-old ex-champ, is trying to make a comeback. He's going to start with some unknowns and work his way up. Tony is dismayed—the ex-champ, fighting unknowns. "How low will this guy sink?" he wonders. Vince: "He wants to fight *you.*" "That low?" Tony is reluctant, but comes around when Vince explains what a big chance it is and how much publicity there'll be. Tony begins to get excited. "It's kinda like a painter gettin' a chance to beat up on Rembrandt!"

Sometime later, Tony brings his friends to Bobby Gleason's Gym, where Foster is holding a press conference. The former champ comes in with a woman on each arm and explains that the big thing bringing him back is a wheelchair-bound kid named Brian Sims. Brian had written to him, saying Benny was his hero, and the ex-champ took a liking to the boy. Brian has gotten through one operation OK, but has a bigger (and apparently very expensive) one ahead (a kidney operation, we discover later). Tony's spirits go right down the tube.

Later that day, when Tony's picture appears in the paper, Louie snickers, "Wouldn't that be somethin', beatin' the ex-champ? Crushin' the comeback of one of America's most beloved athletes and breakin' the heart of a sick little kid all in one fight!" Regardless, Lou still considers Tony a loser and dispatches Jeff in cab #316 with $500 for his bookie to bet on Foster. Tony doesn't want to go through with the fight, but Alex convinces him he owes it to all those other fighters who'll never have this chance.

At the Felt Forum, Tony wins by a decisive knockout. He feels so terrible about it, he won't let the referee raise his arm. In the locker room afterward, Alex suggests Tony might feel better if he spoke to Brian. Brian wheels himself in, and Tony apologizes and asks the cute little boy's forgiveness. Brian opens his arms to hug Tony—and then socks him with a fistful of ball bearings: Doesn't that dumb palooka know how hard it is to get fighters to come to the hospital? "We keep gettin' singers!" Brian complains. Tony, keeping his distance, offers to be the kid's new hero. Brian takes him up on it, but only "until you lose one." Tony says honestly, "That could be weeks."

Tag: Tony wheels Brian to the garage after having taken him to his first hockey game. Louie berates Banta as usual, and Brian offers to give Louie a hug for that. He does, with no sock in the jaw. Even better—he stole Louie's wallet.

GUESTS:

Marc Anthony Danza (Brian Sims)
Armando Muniz (Benny Foster)
Michael V. Gazzo (Vince)
Gene LeBell (the referee)
John Dennis (a maintenance man)

Art imitates life: In one acting debut is Tony Danza's real-life son from his first marriage, and in another acting debut is Armando Muniz, a real-life welterweight who twice fought fellow *Taxi* boxer/guest star Carlos Palomino.

Marc Anthony's debut came about, remembers Daddy, after the youngster had made an impres-

Louie putting "The Reluctant Fighter" on the ropes.

sion—literally—on the set of "One-Punch Banta" (episode #5). "You know that bit where Louie gets Alex to bet on me, and Alex only bets five dollars and Louie tells him, 'Oooh, big spender'? My son Marc, seven years old, is on the set, watching us all week. Now, I was going out with Marilu at the time, and on Wednesday night, the three of us went out to dinner and Marc did Louie's part *exactly*—all the intonations, all the 'oohs' and 'hee-hee-hees'! The next day I asked Marc if he'd do it for the crew and he said sure. And he was great and got a big hand from all the camera guys and everybody. Friday night comes, and we blow a light circuit, which almost *never* had happened before. So Burrows comes to me and asks if Marc would do his Louie impression for the audience while we're waiting. So Marc said sure, and he ended up getting a standing ovation from the audience! And after that I got a couple of offers for him to do shows! Paramount was really hot for him. I didn't want him to act, though, but Ed [Weinberger] said, 'Why not let him do a show here?' and I figured that much was OK."

The episode also marked the introduction of a future *Taxi* coproducer, Ken Estin, who'd never before had a script produced. Today he's the Emmy-winning cocreator of *The Tracey Ullman Show*. "It's a Cinderella story, alright," he says with a grin. Estin, who'd graduated with an English degree from the University of California at Davis, was a professional trucker, holder of a Class I tractor-trailer license. He drove mostly around his native Los Angeles, and sometimes also played banjo and sang for small audiences. "What happened is that I wrote a spec script [one written "on speculation" with no guarantee of any payment] for Glen and Les Charles, who were producing the show at that time. At that point I didn't know anything about television, or what was expected of a script, or how much they were going to pay me—nothing!" He's not kidding: That script was for *The Bob Newhart Show,* which was already off the air.

"But I sent it anyhow, and they liked it well enough to ask if I wanted to attempt a script for *Taxi.* My first meeting with them I was very nervous, and all I got out of it was an agreement to do one outline. So I wrote it, and then they asked me for a first-draft script and then a second draft, and before I even finished the second draft they asked me to write two more. And then that same week, they asked me if I wanted to be a staff writer." He shakes his head at all this, still amazed by it after years of Emmy and Writers Guild awards. "I figure that I'm very, very lucky," he says. "I know I'm talented, but there are a *lot* of talented people out there waiting for a break."

#25 LOUIE AND THE NICE GIRL

WRITTEN BY EARL POMERANTZ.
DIRECTED BY JAMES BURROWS.

When Jeff announces that Zena (Rhea Perlman) is here to fill up the candy machines, the cabbies rush to form a line. But Louie, as usual, pulls rank and gets the honor of "the first Baby Ruth. MMMmmm!" he smacks his lips in pathetic victory, "Why does the first one always taste the best?" Zena pulls Elaine aside and says she's infatuated with Louie, only she's too shy to say anything. Elaine is repulsed, and Zena, after being convinced Elaine isn't interested in the powerful man who runs the garage like a well-oiled machine, allows Alex to introduce her to the dispatcher. Louie invites Zena to his cousin's wedding the next evening, and she accepts.

Weeks later, Louie struts into the garage with a raincoat and no shirt, boasting of how the insatia-

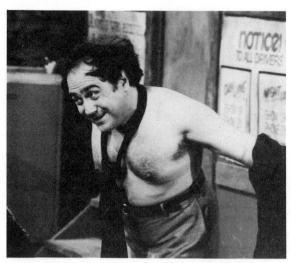

Episode #25: Louie lying about his wild nights with Zena in "Louie and the Nice Girl."

ble Zena keeps ripping the shirt off his back. The cabbies are revolted and refuse to listen to Louie's obnoxious comments. He nudges Alex, who pointedly tells Lou not to keep sneering "heh, heh, heh" whenever anyone mentions Zena—Louie doesn't even know he's doing it. Bobby and Elaine are equally disinclined to hear him. Only a smiling Tony is interested, but Lou thinks not.

When Jeff calls out that Louie's wanted upstairs, Lou instructs the cabbies to tell Zena when she comes by that he'll see her for dinner that evening at eight. Zena arrives and seeks advice from Alex. It seems she and Louie have been dating for five weeks, and he hasn't touched her. Alex, somewhat rudely, can barely contain his laughter. That evening at Mario's, Lou is hanging around the cabbies before his date. Alex tells Lou what Zena said, and Lou confesses it's true. Now he, too, wants advice. "Alex, I gotta open up to someone," he pleads. "You're the only one I can almost stomach. If you won't do it out of compassion, out of pure humanity, would you do it for money?" He would—$20 to start, and $10 extra after Lou explains he was raised to believe in "nice girls" and "the kind you have fun with," and that he has had fun indeed with hookers. Alex sarcastically tells him that in that case, he should leave Zena. Lou thanks him for the good advice and leaves to break off the relationship.

At Zena's apartment (on the third floor of a gray-brick building), Lou abruptly informs her, "We're splittin' up, good-bye." Zena, shocked, asks why. Lou: "You really wanna drag this out, don't cha?" He tells her there's someone else—disco diva Donna Summer. Zena, naturally, doesn't buy it. She says she knows the real reason—she's too "nice" for him. As Louie sits absorbing it, she explains she's in love with him, even though she's not sure why, and that she's been crying herself to sleep. Lou looks up, moved, and tells her, "Take me to the place you cry."

Schmaltzy ending? No, for when she goes into the bedroom, Lou slams the door behind and screams he can't go in there. Zena talks him into a good-bye kiss, which turns out to be a real barn-burner that literally sweeps him off his feet. Lou is overwhelmed, and Zena, shutting out the light, snickers to him: "Heh, heh, heh."

OTHER GUESTS:

T. J. Castronova (Tommy, the bartender at Mario's)

Note: Zena's last name, Sherman, is given in the end credits and in the subsequent episodes, but not in this one.

"At first it was nerve-racking," remembers Rhea Perlman of her on-screen *Taxi* debut. (She'd previously done a voiceover that was excised from episode #1, and, along with Marilu Henner, "Taxi will be back in a moment" voiceovers.) "Not just because of playing opposite Danny or because it was a hit show, but because I knew all these people as friends. They didn't know me as an actress. They knew I *acted* [with several TV movies to her credit], but it wasn't like they really knew my work. I really felt like I had to be good and not let anyone down and all that kinda crap."

Rhea's description of Zena's attraction for Louie sounds almost like her own for Danny. "I think she was physically attracted to him—she thought he was really cute. I think she saw that really sweet underside, and all that outer stuff was just defense. It was just sort of an immediate attraction—that one-in-a-million girl!"

Interestingly, when Louie seeks an audience for his vulgar stories, Tony shows a childlike enthusi-

A concerned Alex wondering "Wherefore Art Thou, Bobby?"

asm from which Louie turns away. The moment clearly presages the reintroduction (episode #27) of Reverend Jim, who, similarly, always lent an innocent ear to Louie's ravings.

#26 WHEREFORE ART THOU, BOBBY?

WRITTEN BY BARRY KEMP.
DIRECTED BY JAMES BURROWS.

At the garage, Bobby is peeved because he's just landed a local TV commercial—he wants to be a serious actor, he tells Alex, and not do this kind of junk. Enter Tony with Steve Jensen (Michael Horton), a young out-of-towner who's come to New York to seek his own fortunes as an actor. Tony helpfully introduces him to Bobby, who tells Steve what a rotten profession they're in. Yet Bob's taken with the young actor's sincerity and offers to introduce him to his agent. "And then *you* can introduce *me* to my agent," he half-jokes.

A day or two later, while Bobby's elsewhere, a stunned Steve wanders into the garage with good news—his first day out, he's landed an off-Broadway role as Romeo! (A congratulatory Tony asks, "In what play?") The cabbies are happy for him, but they are worried about how Bobby will take it— he's been trying for a break like this for years. Sadistic Louie offers to tell him, and the cabbies practically have to assault him before he promises not to phone; he starts to send a telegram instead.

Later, the cabbies meet at Bobby's apartment for a surprise party celebrating his suntan lotion commercial. Bob walks in with his face half-tan. Breaking open beers, the cabbies gently try to tell him about Steve's good fortune. Steve finally blurts it out, and a congratulatory Bobby takes him by the shoulders and then gradually begins to strangle Steve until the cabbies pull him off.

The next day, Bobby seems overly humble with Louie; in an apparent bid for sympathy, he announces he's quitting acting. Alex craftily suggests that Steve, whom he's helping to memorize lines, try a scene with Bobby. They perform part of act V, scene III, where Paris (Bobby) is slain by Romeo (Steve). The cabbies applaud this genuinely moving bit, but Bobby says that if he can be this good and still not find work, something's wrong with the profession. At this, Louie gloats louder than ever—leading Bobby to change his mind, telling Lou in plaintive terms that he'll stay an actor if for no other reason than to someday shove Louie's laugh down his throat. "Thank you, Lou!" he gushes gratefully. To which a very perplexed Louie can only reply, "Yer welcome."

Tag: In a fit of pique at Bobby's victory over him, Louie overturns the candy machine.

One of this great episode's funniest moments occurs when the cabbies, gathered at Bobby's apartment, try to play down the importance of Steve's having landed the role of Romeo. They mumble to the tune of "yeah, OK, that's nice," and Elaine tosses off, "Well, if you like revivals." It works hilariously—and it wasn't even in the script. "It

was an ad-lib," says Marilu Henner. "I came up with it during rehearsals, but I didn't want to say it out loud because I figured they'd give it to somebody else or they'd cut it. So I just said it during filming. That one was *mine!*"

Michael Horton is a familiar face from *M*A*S*H* and other shows in syndication, and previous to appearing in *Taxi* had costarred in the short-lived NBC detective series *The Eddie Capra Mysteries*.

#27 REVEREND JIM: A SPACE ODYSSEY

WRITTEN BY GLEN CHARLES AND LES CHARLES. DIRECTED BY JAMES BURROWS.

Around a table at Mario's, the cabbies are discussing a boxing match that Tony actually won, albeit by default when his opponent fell and knocked himself out climbing over the ropes. Latka arrives, apologizing for having missed the fight; he'd taken the wrong subway train and wound up in Harlem. There, he says, he walked into a bar and said that he was looking for a fight. Several patrons offered to help, but then, Latka continues, decided they were related to him: "They thought I was their brother!" As he exits, lightly singing James Brown's "(Get Up I Feel Like Being a) Sex Machine," the cabbies spot the burnt-out Rev. Jim (Christopher Lloyd) alone at the bar. They invite him to sit with them; after he accepts and gets comfortable he asks if he's supposed to know who they are. They remind Jim that he officiated at Latka's paper wedding (episode #8).

They ask him about himself. Slurring and hazy, Jim declares that he has a function in life. "I am the living embodiment of the sixties," he begins, rather heavy-handedly. "Everything that came along, I went with. Even if I didn't know what it was, I went with it. I marched and protested against that crummy war," he continues. Tony interrupts, sneering, "Izzat so?" "Pardon me?" Jim asks innocently. "Y'know," Tony says angrily, standing and pointing, "the only reason why guys like you got to stay home, protest, and get loaded is because guys like me were over in 'Nam doing your fightin' for you. What do you say to that?" What else?

Episode #27: "Reverend Jim: A Space Odyssey." Andy Kaufman (*far left*) did not appear in this scene as filmed.

"Thank you." Tony, deflated, can only answer, "Yer welcome."

The cabbies finish their beers, and as they leave decide to help this wayward soul. Jim has no skills, no qualifications, nothing—a perfect cabdriver! They bring him to the garage, but Louie doesn't even want him in the building, let alone on the payroll. As the cabbies go over their options, they spot Jim slip some kind of pill into the unwary Louie's coffee; he says innocently that it's a harmless sedative. It turns out to be a very strong "harmless sedative," as an extremely relaxed Louie begins singing "Moonlight Bay." He glides giddily across the room, joined by the cabbies in harmony, and Bobby slyly asks if Jim can have the job. "Surrrre," Louie said smiling, "everybody works on Moonlight Bay." He curls up for a nap on a taxi hood.

At the Department of Motor Vehicles later, the cabbies help Jim fill out his driver's license appli-cation. He gives his name as Jim Ignatowski; just like Chris Lloyd, his height is 5′ 10″ and he has brown eyes. Bobby reads the application to him briskly: "Have you ever experienced loss of con-sciousness, hallucinations, dizzy spells, convulsive disorders, fainting, or periods of loss of memory?" Jim: "Hasn't everyone?" Bobby: "Mental illness or narcotic addiction?" Jim: "That's a tough choice." They finally get through it, and Bobby tells him he's ready for the test. Jim is shocked: "I thought this *was* the test!" Once the actual written test begins, Jim gets stumped on a question. "What does a yellow light mean?" he loudly whispers to Bobby, who responds, "Slow down"—thereby set-ting up perhaps the single funniest routine in the annals of *Taxi*. Reading it here won't do it justice; suffice to say, Jim takes Bobby literally—three times. Later, having muddled through and gotten his license, he arrives at the garage and takes Alex on his maiden voyage.

OTHER GUESTS:

T. J. Castronova (Tommy, the bartender at Mario's)

A classic—probably one of the best episodes of any TV comedy ever. Like Norton's "addressing the ball" on *The Honeymooners* or Lucy's being told "you gotta havea you passaporta" at the France-Italy border, Jim and Bobby's "slow down" scene is a must for any TV time capsule. Incredibly, it was a scripted routine—no ad-libs or improvisations, just brilliant interpretation of what was on the page. And while Christopher Lloyd well deserves the credit he's gotten for this acting equivalent of a trapeze triple-somersault, Jeff Conaway's increasingly agitated Bobby is the perfect foil—neither sensible Alex nor maternal Elaine nor somewhat-dim Tony could have conveyed the desperate struggle of the self-centered Bobby when a well-meaning gesture keeps flying back in his face.

"If you look closely at that scene," says Marilu Henner, "you'll see me stabbing my hand with a pencil to keep from laughing. I could barely stop myself." Recalls Jim Brooks, "Chris with his driver's test got one of the biggest laughs I'd ever heard. It was like, your money or your life—I mean, just when you think it can't go on, it does! We just had to bring him back onto the show."

Chris Lloyd remembers "being disappointed when they cut it. I wanted to do it *again*—get up on my feet this time and *really* make it slow!" In any case, it worked perfectly, and with episode #33, Lloyd returned as a recurring guest and soon afterward was made a member of the cast.

For you music buffs, "Moonlight Bay" was a popular 1912 vaudeville song. That it's still fairly well known today is the result of two movies: 1943's *Tin Pan Alley* and 1951's *On Moonlight Bay*.

#28 NARDO LOSES HER MARBLES

WRITTEN BY EARL POMERANTZ.
DIRECTED BY JAMES BURROWS.

The guys haven't seen Elaine much lately. She's been working overtime on the exhibit her gallery is opening the coming Saturday at 7 P.M.—it's the first time she's in charge. The guys have been busy

as well: Tony was knocked out in the second round of the Gomez fight, and Bobby had appeared in a quick-closing experimental play. As for Alex, "I went to a bad play and a short fight." Feeling bad about neglecting her friends, Elaine sits in on a garage poker game while fielding a million phone messages about the gallery and her kids.

It quickly becomes apparent she's spreading herself too thin: At the opening, she loses her cool when a temperamental artist decides to remove one of his large canvases then and there, and when a gallery co-owner complains that the champagne is flat, Elaine finally goes nuts and angrily starts blowing bubbles into his glass. Alex rushes her out and drives her home; on the way he advises she seek professional counseling. The distraught Elaine, however, begins coming on to Alex, and despite his protests about sex as a psychological crutch, moans, "I love it when a man accuses me of unconsciously avoiding therapy." Summoning all his willpower, Alex finally convinces her to seek help. Soon afterward, she appears at the curiously luxurious (given her finances) office of Dr. Bernard Collins (Tom Ewell). He's an avuncular old gent who shrugs off Elaine's inquiries about whether she should talk about her parents, scream, etc., encompassing the list of psychiatric clichés. Collins just wants to talk.

After a couple of false starts, Elaine explains how she's "the kind of person *other* people come to for help," and how she'd grown up with three younger brothers whom she helped take care of when she was just eight years old. Finally she breaks down—and *still* wants to skip further therapy! Evidently, though she kept at it—we next see her in the garage on the way to an appointment, telling Alex it's been ten visits and she's coming along fine. She's wearing an incredibly low-cut red-and-white striped dress that Alex had told her had once tempted him. Perhaps as revenge for getting her to see a shrink, she shoots him down before he even knows it.

Tag: Elaine tries to explain to Latka that she's seeing a psychiatrist, not a podiatrist.

OTHER GUESTS:

Mary Woronov (Fran Strickland—"one of our [gallery's] best artists," according to Elaine)
Robert Picardo (Philip Polevoy; last name given in the end credits, not in the episode)

William Callaway (Sandor Kovacs, the gallery co-owner; name given in the end credits, not in the episode)

Note: The end credits list Paula Victor as Mrs. Hazeltine (the gallery owner), but she doesn't appear in the episode. Also, Dr. Collins is miscredited as Dr. Richmond.

ADDITIONAL CREDITS:

Strickland paintings by Vivan Kerstein.
Sculptures by Vasa

A great episode that reveals much about Elaine—not only factual things like her large family and early responsibilities (echoing Marilu Henner's own childhood with two brothers and three sisters) but also her essentially maternal, nurturing outlook on life.

Writer Earl Pomerantz says the idea for this episode derived from his habit of watching a show "and saying, 'What's wrong with this picture?' Here I saw a woman who works at night driving a cab, who works in the daytime at an art gallery, and who has two small kids besides. When does she sleep? At a time when women were trying to do everything, she was trying to do more than everything. It seemed like a very theoretical life-style that didn't fit into normal standards of behavior. So I decided to examine what that's like.''

This episode is also key for what it says about the relationship between Elaine and Alex, which got more and more complex as the series wore on. From the start, she sensed a kindred spirit. Yet their friendship never became a romance, and except for a brief tryst their last night in Europe (where Alex and Elaine had gone as platonic companions in episode #69), there's no indication they were lovers more than once or twice. Alex eventually grows to resent this, as seen by his sniping when Elaine dates Simka's cousin (episode #99) and elsewhere. In the end, the avuncular Alex appeals to Elaine neither as a dashing lover (a la her ex-husband and her usual boyfriends) nor as a puppy dog (a la Arnie Ross in episode #91 and #111) whom she can mother and, unlike her ex-husband, control.

Turning in a graciously dry and expressive performance is Tom Ewell (1909–1994). TV audiences know him best as Billy Truman, the kindly but razor-sharp hotel clerk in *Baretta,* but for movie buffs, Ewell is a rooted part of Marilyn Monroe's legacy. After having won a Tony Award for *The Seven Year Itch* on Broadway, Ewell reprised his role in the classic 1955 movie costarring Marilyn; in her trademark scene, he watches as she stands atop a subway grate, letting the cool breeze billow her skirts. Fellow guest Robert Picardo went on to recurring roles on *The Wonder Years* and *China Beach.*

Incidentally, Marilu's overwhelmingly sexy red-and-white striped dress came from her own wardrobe. Does this woman know how to dress or what?

#29 A WOMAN BETWEEN FRIENDS

WRITTEN BY KEN ESTIN.
DIRECTED BY JAMES BURROWS.

Over beers at Mario's with the cabbies, Alex discovers he has a bad tooth. Everyone tells him to see a dentist, but Alex asserts he has a phobia about men who use sharp instruments to poke through mouths. Elaine says she'll set up an appointment for him; Alex agrees to it only if she doesn't tell him when until it's time to go.

As they talk, Bobby and Tony spot a willowy blonde (Constance Forslund) enter and sit at the bar. The two immediately fall in lust. They both want to ask her out, but Bobby claims he saw her first. They start arguing about it until they get so loud Alex orders them to sit down and be quiet. They decide they'll *both* ask her out, with the girl choosing her favorite after the first date. Now they argue over who's going to speak to her first. Alex flips a coin to settle it. Bobby wins and hits it off with her immediately. A frustrated Tony watches and greets the girl (in his own fashion) from across the room.

At the garage a few days later, Louie is congratulating Latka for having fixed ten cabs in one day. As a reward, Latka can tune up Louie's mother's car. Latka says wait a minute, and Louie explains that this is a bonus. Latka asks Elaine and Alex if a bonus is good. Sure, they say, not having heard the rest of the conversation. OK, then—*tenk you veddy much.* Tony comes in with his bookings, and Alex and Elaine ask about the blonde, whose name is Janet. He says he took her out Friday and Bobby

TAXI

dated her Saturday. Elaine sarcastically asks if the friends will now compare notes, which the two proceed to do when Bobby comes in. It's a draw so far, and so Tony wants to take Janet to the fights; Bobby wants to take her out as well, but neither has asked her yet. They rush to the phone, where Tony gets the receiver and Bobby kindles a fight when he commandeers the push buttons.

The cabbies break up the imminent battle, and Bobby remembers Janet's not home now anyway. He also tells Tony he's not right for Janet—implying, as Louie gleefully confirms, that Tony is too stupid for her. Naturally, this sets Tony off, and he wants to punch Bobby out. Quick-thinking Bobby offers to punch *himself* out. He demonstrates with a theatrical blow to the stomach. Tony actually sort of buys it—"Not hard enough," he says. Bobby "hits" himself again—"Now, Tony," he sputters, "that really staggered me." Tony growls at him, "In the face"—it's all Alex can do to wrestle Bobby's arm away from himself. "What am I doing," Alex asks himself breathlessly, "breaking up a fight between one guy?" The two friends agree on war.

As the week goes by, each borrows date money from an annoyed Alex, and Elaine gets so tired of the adolescent rivalry that she confronts Bobby and Tony and asks what does Janet think about all this? They don't seem to know or care, and Alex tells them to sit down and discuss this with her.

When Elaine tells Alex it's time for his dental appointment, he quickly volunteers to go over to Mario's (where Janet's due to meet Bobby for a date) to help them out. While they wait, Louie comes in for a ringside seat; Alex pays him ten bucks to go away. Janet comes in, and the guys explain the problem and tell her to choose between Bobby and Tony. She's taken aback by the sudden demand, but says, OK, here goes—whereupon Tony and Bobby ask her to take a minute and think about it. She does so while a disgruntled Alex leaves.

Alone for a moment, Bobby and Tony realize their friendship hinges on Janet's decision, and they reluctantly decide to drop her. Janet is understandably upset at having her feelings taken for granted, and she vengefully coos that the guy she was going to choose would have had "the time of his life tonight—the kind of night that makes a man *real*

happy he's a man." And chew this over, she adds, leaving—her choice was Bobby. Bob cringes while Tony says he thinks they did the right thing.

Tag: Elaine enters the garage and tells Alex he has ten minutes to get to the dentist—a visit he initially, but unsuccessfully, tries to avoid.

OTHER GUESTS:

T. J. Castronova (Tommy, the bartender at Mario's)

Connie Forslund's delightfully understated bewilderment makes her boyfriend-juggling seem the natural course of things. She craftily plays Janet one large step away from dumb blonde—but only one step nonetheless. Adding a realistic edge, Jeff Conaway had known her from way back. "I went to college with Connie, and we went out together and everything. It was fun sort of reprising our roles from real life." Unlike real life, he adds, he and Danza didn't compete for women off-camera. He laughs, "It was always, 'Well, you saw her first, go ahead, I don't care.' And I was with my wife, so I didn't go after anyone anyway until we split up. Still, Marilu used to call Tony and I 'The Lust Brothers' because we did like to run around and have a good time!"

Connie's Janet primed her for spotlight roles in two TV movies: 1980's *Moviola: This Year's Blonde,* in which she played the lead role of Marilyn Monroe, and 1981's *The Harlem Globetrotters on Gilligan's Island,* which, critical snipes aside, allowed her to play one of the great teenage fantasies of the sixties, starlet Ginger Grant. Connie also starred in a 1979 TV movie/pilot *Pleasure Cove,* a sort of South Sea island *Love Boat* that still airs occasionally on late-night television. More recently, she's guested on *Murder, She Wrote* and other TV shows, and played the pot-smoking mom in *River's Edge.*

#30 THE LIGHTER SIDE OF ANGELA MATUSA

WRITTEN BY EARL POMERANTZ.
DIRECTED BY JAMES BURROWS.

While Tony tries to drum up players for a softball game against the day shift, Alex finds a phone message from Angela Matusa (Suzanne Kent), the very overweight woman he dated in episode #2. Alex tells the cabbies that though he and Angela became friends, they lost touch with each other about six months ago. Angela shows up at the garage, and the cabbies are shocked to see she's lost about 100 pounds. Louie, who'd been writing fat jokes for the occasion, is disappointed but gracious—if she ever gains the weight back, look him up so the jokes won't go to waste. An example: "Some men climb mountains; others date 'em.''

Angela and Alex go to dinner at Mario's. She orders chicken, no skin; broccoli, no butter; salad, no dressing; and no dessert. He has a salad with Thousand Island dressing; veal Marsala, with linguine and clam sauce on the side; and garlic bread. Alex explains how proud he is of her, and that he himself used to smoke but had quit. Angela replies that she did it all for him and touches his hand meaningfully. Panicking, Alex grabs a lit cigarette from a fellow diner and begins puffing away. He excuses himself, saying he has to think all this over, and when the food arrives, a depressed Angela spins the table around and starts munching on Alex's high-calorie meal.

At the garage later, an overweight guy named Wayne Hubbard (Phil Rubenstein) comes looking for Alex. He's a member of Angela's weight clinic and is kind of sweet on her, and he tells Alex she's missing. Alex and Wayne scour all her old eating haunts, finally finding her at a greasy spoon scarfing pork chops. Alex tells her she's being silly. Can't she see that Wayne's really the one for her? After some convincing, she decides he's right, and she invites Wayne home with her—something she's avoided up to now because Wayne is married with four kids.

Tag: At Mario's in between innings: Even with Elaine's grandparents from Buffalo in the outfield, the cabbies are still getting slaughtered.

OTHER GUESTS:

Dick Miller (Ernie, the waiter at the greasy spoon)

T. J. Castronova (Tommy, the bartender at Mario's)

As Jim Brooks remembers, this episode came about after "we heard that the actress had lost weight. We wrote specifically to that fact.'' Suzanne Kent's reappearance is an early example of the intricate continuity that helped set *Taxi* apart from most other TV comedies to that time. (For more on Suzanne Kent, see the background on episode #2.)

Dick Miller, the greasy-spoon proprietor, is one of the most recognizable and well-liked character actors in the business; his hangdog face has added humanity to countless movies and TV shows from the fifties on. He even appeared on *Taxi* again in another role, proving to be the best thing in episode #98 ("Travels with My Dad''). Dick Miller's everyman appeal might best be summed up this way: When Arnold Schwarzenegger kills gun-shop owner Dick in *The Terminator,* you *know* Arnold's an irredeemable bad guy.

#31 THE GREAT RACE

WRITTEN BY GLENN GORDON CARON.
DIRECTED BY JAMES BURROWS.

Louie is sick and tired of the low bookings the cabbies have been toting lately—tonight, Nardo made just $41, and Banta only $52. Lou belittles them with tales of his own great bookings back when he was a lowly hack. Alex unenthusiastically confirms Louie's bragging. But Bobby, fed up, suggests a race between Alex and loudmouthed Lou: whoever makes the most money in eight hours wins. Bobby puts $100 where his mouth is; Jeff collects the bets. Lou agrees to all this only after Elaine consents to a side bet—$500 versus a date.

The two drivers set off, Alex in cab #132, Louie in cab #781. Alex picks up two nuns who can't decide which film to see—*The Muppet Movie* or *The Sound of Music.* They argue about it until Alex decides for them. Then a rich Asian businessman gets in. Either unknowledgeable or unconcerned about American money, he flashes a wad of hundreds at Alex, who struggles with his conscience before taking the correct meter amount. (Elaine, on the cab radio, half-jokingly calls him stupid.)

Lou, meanwhile, has tried to rip off an undercover inspector from the Taxi and Limousine Commission and then mouths off to him. The angry inspector revokes Lou's license—only it's Banta's;

At the starting gate of "The Great Race."

Lou also has Wheeler's in hand. Alex then hits the jackpot—a kindly, apparently well-to-do lady who's delivering groceries (nonperishables, hopefully) to several spots from Long Island to New Jersey. We finally see Lou try to bilk a blind passenger $22.50 for a $6 ride, only to have it backfire—the guy was counting the meter's clicks.

At daybreak, the combatants return to the garage. Alex has booked $197. Lou has booked $212.30. He's apparently won, and Alex accepts his loss—a lot more gracefully than a terrified Elaine, who now has to go out with the despotic dispatcher. However, it appears their tips haven't been counted yet, and, as Bobby had said, "whoever brings in the most money wins." Alex had been tipped forty bucks altogether. Lou, just eighty cents—a record high for him. Latka is called on to decide whether tips count. Of course, they do. And joy reigns.

GUESTS:

Julie Payne, Kres Mersky (the nuns)
Scott Brady (taxi inspector Ryan, misidentified as "Melnick" on the end credits)
James Hong (Asian businessman)
Jean Owens Hayworth (lady with groceries)
Fred Stuthman (blind passenger)

This is an episode about moral choices, about not becoming a Louie De Palma. Alex is led into temptation, not only for himself but also for all the other cabbies—especially Elaine, who'd have to endure what she sees as a night of horror with Louie.

Yet even with the rich foreigner's huge money roll in front of him, and a ready-made rationalization that he could skim a little for his friends' sake, Alex sticks to his conscience. Partially this is his nature, but also, as he suggests obliquely, it was also a way of fighting the "competitiveness" that had led him in the past to habitual gambling.

Guest star James Hong is one of film and television's best-known Asian actors. His movies include *Blade Runner, Black Widow, Year of the Dragon,* and *Big Trouble in Little China,* and his TV credits are immense. Old-movie fans will recognize the late Scott Brady (1924–1985), the younger brother of actor Lawrence Tierney and a tough-guy in movies since 1948. some of his pictures include *Johnny Guitar, $ [Dollars],* and *The China Syndrome.* Brady also starred in the old syndicated series *Shotgun Slade,* a sort of cowboy *Peter Gunn.* And screenwriter Glenn Gordon Caron went on to create the hit TV series *Moonlighting.*

#32 THE APARTMENT

WRITTEN BY BARRY RUBINOWITZ.
DIRECTED BY JAMES BURROWS.

While gullible Tony is discovering that it wasn't really Neil Armstrong in his cab just then, and that his tip isn't really a moon rock, Louie is making a discovery of his own: Latka has been living in the garage and sleeping on boss Mr. McKenzie's couch. It seems Latka's apartment building is being torn down. The cabbies want to know why. "Because it could not be burned," Latka answers. Alex says he'll help Latka find a place. Sometime later, Latka announces he's snagged one on his own. He invites Alex up to see it.

The apartment turns out to be gorgeous—an ultramodern penthouse with a Jacuzzi, a high-tech audio system, a remote-controlled hideaway bar and a live-in maid. Latka is very pleased with himself: It cost him his life savings of $3,000, but it was worth it to own a place like this, he says proudly. Alex sadly breaks the news that $3,000 is just one month's rent. (At least apparently—usually an additional amount equal to the rent has to be put up as a security deposit.) Alex is about to call the realtor, a Mr. Martin, to cancel the deal, but Latka plays with the remote-controlled lights, music, and bar, and level-headed Alex is seduced by the place. He decides to move in for one month with Latka (though neither says anything about splitting the rent).

The month passes by wonderfully, with the cabbies frequently visiting and staying over. Tony (who's seeing a girl named Cathy) and Bobby have a choice of bringing their dates into the bedroom or the game room. Even Lou drops by, only to be quickly thrown out—with purloined Scotch. Not wanting to give up their luxurious playhouse, the cabbies decide to throw a rent party. But when a couple of dozen men and no women except Elaine show up, the mood turns ugly. Alex refunds the men their money, and the cabbies vow to help Latka find a new place. In the meantime, they leave him to spend a final night in his wonderful apartment in private—except for the tall, blonde maid, who shyly asks him, *"Nik nik?"* (See "Latka-isms," page 165.)

GUESTS:

Nancy Steen (the maid; Louie calls her ''Inga,'' but since he's never been there before, we can assume this is just his way of being cute)
Dick Butkus (a hostile partyer)

This is not a good episode. The cabbies uncharacteristically take advantage of Latka's mistake, with no one offering to help pay rent for what becomes their private amusement park. It also defies believability that Latka could have rented the place to begin with, since landlords of luxury apartments in New York City invariably check references, income, etc.—very much a sitcom.

Dick Butkus is the former NFL Chicago Bear and frequent TV guest star. Nancy Steen was a regular on the variety show *Tony Orlando and Dawn* and in 1980's *Steve Allen Comedy Hour.*

#33 ELAINE'S SECRET ADMIRER

WRITTEN BY BARRY KEMP.
DIRECTED BY JAMES BURROWS.

The guys all show up at Elaine's apartment to help paint it. It seems every time she breaks up with a

Elaine relaxing in "The Apartment."

guy, she paints her apartment. Tony: ''Elaine, there must be twenty coats of paint here.'' Elaine: ''It's been a rough year. Let's see—the blue one is Tom, under Tom is Roger, under Roger was Eric, and under Eric was—I forget.'' Tony: ''Looks like a dull gray.'' Elaine: ''My ex-husband.''

They turn on the television to catch the New York Jets while Elaine goes out to get the mail; sure enough, the guys soon get engrossed in the game and forget all about painting. Elaine returns with a strange letter; it's a romantic poem: ''I saw you standing in a Manhattan sunset/Your auburn hair blowing from Atlantic winds/Your eyes were smiling at thoughts far away/Dancing to sonnets only you could hear/If I could, I would build you a castle/In a world of some other time/A castle I can only imagine/A castle only you could inspire.''

The next day at work, she finds another poem in her locker. At first she thinks Alex wrote them. He says no: ''I once wrote a poem for my wife. She grated it.'' Louie names himself as the author, and in response to a challenge, proceeds to try and make up a poem—with full body language: ''Cascading/ Cascading water. A waterfall. Clouds. Lots of them. Light and puffy. You know—clouds! And flowers, covered with dew. And trees hangin' over. And you and me naked on a rock!'' It's not him.

Jim then confides to Alex that it was he who wrote the poems. He'd only done it, he says, to make Elaine feel better since she'd just broken up with a guy named Steve. Elaine, however, is convinced that a vacuous but handsome cabbie named Don Reavy wrote them. She asks him about it, and after a very funny sequence where virtually all he says is ''Yeah'' in different, meaningful ways, they go out for a bite to eat.

A couple of weeks go by. Bobby concedes to Elaine that the guys have unsuccessfully tried four times to paint her apartment. (The Jets are apparently having a great season.) In the meantime, Elaine and Don have been going out a lot, and Louie informs the cabbies that she and her new beau are planning a ski weekend in Vermont. Alex is finally pushed to tell Elaine the truth, that it was ''burn-out'' Jim who wrote those poems. A suddenly somber Elaine sadly answers that she'll never learn—that dream-princes and magic castles don't exist, that she's nothing more than a cabdriver with big ideas. ''You finally got it through my thick skull—there aren't gonna be any castles in my life.'' But one night soon afterward, she comes home to her pleasant, whitefaced apartment building and finds Jim finishing up a huge metal sculpture in her living room. It's a castle. Yet sweet as that gesture is, she and Jim quickly realize they're not going to fall in love. A stoic Jim walks down the front steps of her building and gets into his van. The roof has been torn off for metal for the sculpture.

GUESTS:

Michael DeLano (Don Reavy)

This poignant episode provides a strong reintroduction for Reverend Jim. All the elements of Jim's appeal are already apparent: his generous spirit, his childlike soul, his sloppiness, his stubble (years before Don Johnson!), and his eccen-

tric thought patterns. A druggie joke was scrapped, however. ''Ed Weinberger was pretty hip,'' Chris Lloyd recalls, ''and he was pretty adamant about going as far with a character as he could. When they showed us all up at Elaine's apartment, they originally filmed me sniffing paint.'' He laughs. ''I was sort of hovering over a can and I had paint all over me from leaning in and [SNNNNIFFFFFFFF!]. I think a remnant of that shot ended up in the credits. They got away with a lot, but they couldn't get away with that one!''

Guest Michael DeLano had played singer Johnny Venture on several episodes of *Rhoda*. The convincing-looking apartment front where Jim parks his van wasn't a location shot, but a New York street set Paramount had at the time. And the names Elaine reels off when she's trying to guess the identity of her secret admirer included those of the cameramen, friends, relatives of friends, and people for whom she used to baby-sit.

#34 ALEX'S ROMANCE

WRITTEN BY IAN PRAISER AND HOWARD GEWIRTZ.

DIRECTED BY ED WEINBERGER.

Bobby has his hands full with a crying Joyce Rogers (Dee Wallace), a long-popular soap opera villainess who's just been dropped from her series—the producers think she's become too old to play a home-wrecker. (The soap opera is *For Better For Worse*, the same one Bobby appeared on in episode #14.) Alex walks into Mario's where they're sitting, and Bobby, who's late for an appointment, sees a way out of his predicament. Alex, Joyce; Joyce, Alex. Bye!

Alex is at first reluctant to listen to *strangers'* problems now, on top of all those of his friends, but Joyce is attractive and he finds he can make her laugh. They decide to have dinner together, but not at Mario's, Alex warns. ''Even Mario doesn't eat at Mario's.'' Afterward, they go to Alex's place, and despite Joyce's warnings that she's unstable and nothing but trouble, they obviously are physically and romantically attracted to each other.

A romance blossoms, with Alex rather arrogantly

priding himself on being a stabilizing factor in Joyce's hectic life. But in the midst of all his cheer, Joyce arrives at the garage to tell Alex she may have a part in another TV series, this one shot in Los Angeles. She has to go pick up the script at her agent's right now, but she'll drop by Alex's apartment later. At the thought of losing her, Alex decides to propose marriage.

At his place later, Joyce gets suspicious when he greets her in a suit and starts talking about having known her a short time but having seen and loved all her moods and . . . Joyce: "Oh my God, Alex, you're not proposing, are you?" "Who, me? No, of course not. Marriage? Farthest thing from my mind!" Joyce asks him why in the world he'd want to marry her. He tells her how stable he is and how good he'd be for her. She can't believe this. "You've known me three weeks," Joyce yells at him, "and you're hearing *wedding bells!*" With that, she picks up and rings a small bell on Alex's coffee table. In response, tuxedoed violin players stroll from his bedroom, playing "As Time Goes By." An embarrassed Alex hustles them out. Even Joyce is touched and amused. She's still going off to Los Angeles for the TV show, but she and Alex can still spend a couple of days together before she goes. Then Joyce hears a bump from a closet. Alex pretends it's nothing, but Joyce determinedly opens the closet door to be greeted by dozens of helium-filled balloons (blown about by a fan Alex keeps in his closet for just such an occasion, it seems). Amid the billowing balloons, Alex hugs Joyce to him and yells above the fan, "Will you marry me?" To which Joyce laughs and yells, "No!" To which Alex yells, "Just checking!"

In the garage later, Alex sits alone, Joyce a memory. The cabbies all feel sorry for him. Jim offers to speak to Alex; he is, he reminds them, a man of the cloth. Elaine suggests he take Bobby along to help. Jim says OK and grabs Latka. They bring Alex into the tool room, where Jim tries to buck him up with an inspirational talk that climaxes with the thought that life is like an ice cream cone: You've got to eat it when you get it, and you got to eat it fast or it'll melt all over your arm. Latka jumps up, inspired, and pledges to live his life right and eat his ice cream and oh boy, oh boy. He

leaves, and Jim tells Alex he knew he could help out Bobby. The guy's had it rough, trying to make it as a boxer. Yeah, Alex agrees—and raising those two kids as well. "By the way," Jim asks, "how are *you* doing?" Alex: "Fine, Jim. I'm fine." Jim: "Okey-doke." And what do you know? It helped.

This is yet another example of the practical, pragmatic Alex getting burned by emotion and spontaneity. Ironically, it's all in character. Part of Alex is always straining to be impulsive, to let loose— hence, his sudden drive to Miami to see his daughter in episode #1, his spur-of-the-moment trip to Europe in episode #69, his on-the-spot decision to go camping with other wilderness neophytes in episode #53, and his gambling throughout the series. And rather than being friends with blue-collar career cabbies like himself, Alex chooses fledgling actors, boxers, and art mavens—hardly "practical," "pragmatic" types. Joyce here is an actress; another serious romance (episode #73) involves a commercial artist. And though he consciously fights the affections of perky young actress Nina Chambers (episode #76), he falls for her in the end despite himself. Even in this early episode, we can already see that Alex's pragmatism may be less self-described than self-inflicted.

Dee Wallace Stone (at the time still known as Dee Wallace) had her first major exposure in the 1981 cult film *The Howling*, soon followed by major success as the mother in 1982's *E.T.* "I don't think Joyce Rogers is anything like me, other than the fact we're in the same profession," says Dee. "I think she really bought into her own publicity: She thought she really *was* a soap opera character, and that this was a big, melodramatic plot twist. If I had fallen in love with someone like Alex, I would have made my career work there [in New York]. Because acting's only what I do, not who I am. Because one of these days, acting's going to stop, and you want to have other fulfilling things in your life." Dee, who's married to fellow actor Christopher Stone, continues to hop between features and TV movies, and costarred in the 1986–1987 series *Together We Stand*.

This episode was the only one of the first fifty-six that Jim Burrows didn't direct. Burrows was busy that week trying to get another John Charles Walters show—the much-acclaimed, short-lived *The Associates*—off the ground. *Taxi* cocreator Ed Weinberger filled in. "They were having trouble on the other show because somebody had been ill or something," says Dee, "and poor Ed had the weight of the world on his shoulders." Laughing, she adds, "And he told me, 'Dee, just get me through this week!' "

At least Ed didn't have to get through the door: Alex's closet door (from behind which the balloons emerge) somehow becomes Alex's front door in later episodes. Did Mary Richards's closets ever move around like that?

#35 LATKA'S REVOLTING

WRITTEN BY GLEN CHARLES AND LES CHARLES. DIRECTED BY JAMES BURROWS.

A busy Latka is tuned to a radio station that broadcasts in his native language a couple of hours a day. As Jim arrives, Latka hears an announcement that revolution has broken out in his country. He panics for his family and says he must go back and fight. Alex sits him down and gives him some useless advice, and then a visitor shows up at the garage: the gravelly-voiced Baschi (Lenny Baker), an old-country friend of Latka's (evidently his cousin; see episode #16) who had emigrated with him. Baschi, who dreamed of becoming a movie producer,went to Hollywood and now works at Sid's Car Wash; he's come to New York to collect Latka and return home to the revolution. Latka declines the invitation, but Baschi softens him up with the national anthem. And besides, Latka explains to his friends, he was a general in the old country.

At Mario's, the cabbies throw a farewell party for Latka, who's wearing his general's uniform. Tony offers a toast and tries to talk about the camaraderie of war: "I remember one night, it was just before the Tet Offensive. I was sitting with two of my best buddies, Chuck and Matt. And Chuck said, 'There's no way the three of us are gonna make it through this thing. . . . ' We cried that night . . . we hugged that night." Bobby somberly asks if they made it. "They made it," Tony answers dismissively. "A year later they married each other. I heard they opened up a roller disco in L.A."

Latka breaks out a bottle of his native drink, *brefnish*. Alex, who's had it before and ought to know better, takes a big gulp and falls back in his chair. Jim: "The line forms behind me." The farewell party eventually breaks into singing and dancing, and Jim announces he's going to go fight side by side with Latka. "Death to the revolutionary rebels!" he yells, raising aloft his mug of beer. "But I am fighting for the revolutionary rebels," Latka tells him. Jim cries, "Death to the imperialist stooges!" Latka: "But they were thrown out long ago." Jim: "Death to the puppet regime!" Latka: "But there *is* no puppet regime." Jim, annoyed: "Who the hell are we fightin'?" Latka: "The tyrannical despot." Jim: "Well, the tyrannical despot will soon know the name Jim . . . ummm . . ." Alex: "Ignatowski." Jim: "Right! Already it's spreading!"

Louie drops by to give Latka his severance pay. He's in a foul mood and accuses Latka of deserting America. He brings Latka to the foyer for a further chewing-out, but by their silhouettes and Louie's whispers, the cabbies see it's actually an emotional farewell. Latka comes back in tears. Louie tells the cabbies to get Latka a beer, he was rough on him. Alex, not letting on, exhorts Louie to stay.

After more toasts, Baschi and six comrades come marching into the bar. It's time to go. A tearful Elaine promises to write and asks Latka to draw a map so they'll know what's where. Baschi does so on a menu blackboard. It soon becomes disturbingly evident that hordes of government troops surround the rebel stronghold—and this handful here are the only reinforcements! Latka quickly tells Baschi to "kiss my *yaktabe*." In response, Baschi and the troops start singing their national anthem to persuade him, but the cabbies quickly overwhelm them with George M. Cohan's American classic "Yankee Doodle Dandy." One by one, Latka's countrymen break ranks—even Baschi, who tap dances to the song's finale.

OTHER GUESTS:

T. J. Castronova (Tommy, the bartender at Mario's)

Note: The actors playing the fellow rebels are uncredited.

The brilliant Lenny Baker, who died of cancer on April 12, 1982, at age thirty-seven, was well on his way to becoming, like Tom Hanks and Tom Selleck, yet another major star passing through *Taxi* on the way up. Best known outside the theater community for his sensitive and funny performance in the film *Next Stop, Greenwich Village* (1976), he was one of New York theater's most acclaimed good citizens. Though winning the 1977 Tony Award for Featured Actor in a Musical (*I Love My Wife*), he continued pursuing offbeat nonstar roles off-Broadway, on television, wherever he found them. His old-country Baschi (last name Krepitz in early scripts, though dropped by shoot day) is eccentric by American standards, but is far, far away from the typical "cute foreigner" you see in most sitcoms. Baker created Baschi as an individual.

For this very funny and insightful tale of national loyalty versus knowing when to quit—a current history metaphor, perhaps?—*Taxi* cocreator Stan Daniels wrote the music and lyrics to Latka's national anthem (see below). George M. Cohan's "Yankee Doodle Dandy" is best remembered, of course, from James Cagney's show-stopping performance of it in the 1942 film *Yankee Doodle Dandy*. And the "dueling-anthems" routine comes, of course, from *Casablanca*. As what doesn't?

Incidentally, the voice of the Latka-language radio newscaster is that of Judd Hirsch.

LATKA'S NATIONAL ANTHEM

Ibeeda Ibee-dorfnish, Ibeeda
Ibeeda Malka-morfnish, Ibeeda
Ibeeda Ibee-Dabee
Yaktabe Yakta-Babee
Bilfkayo Bilfka-Yabee
Kerkaflick Kerka-Flumsmarch
Ibeeda
I-bee-daaaaaaa.

—words and music by Stan Daniels

#36 LOUIE MEETS THE FOLKS

WRITTEN BY BARRY KEMP.
DIRECTED BY JAMES BURROWS.

It's a normal day—more or less—at the Sunshine Cab Co. Tony is getting ready to fight a Rocky Sinacori, who'd knocked him out in the second round the last time they met. Bobby is reading a letter from a fan of one of his commercials. Zena Sherman (Rhea Perlman), the candy vendor who's dating Lou, comes into the garage and is introduced to Jim, with typical bizarreness. She tells Lou something, and after she leaves, Louie begs Alex for two minutes of his time, which Alex grudgingly gives him, counting it down on his watch the whole time. Louie humbly explains that Zena wants to take him home to meet her parents, and that he's scared to death at the prospect. Zena is "the first non-pro I've ever been out with," he confesses. "Before I met Zena, the longest relationship I ever had was thirty minutes." Alex finally accepts Louie's offer of $200 to accompany him to dinner at Zena's folks.

At the home of the Reverend and Mrs. Sherman, Alex is mistaken for Zena's boyfriend. Her parents are taken aback at the real one, but try to put on a nice face. Louie, despite Alex's attempts to keep him from saying anything crude, sinks deeper and deeper into trouble as he mistakes the parents' polite demeanor as acceptance.

After dinner, he takes up Mrs. Sherman's invitation to help clear the table while the rest go into the living room. Out of earshot, she explains Lou is free to see Zena, and have dates and go out. But, she adds sweetly, if he ever contemplates anything like marriage, "I'll have you killed. I think I can do that, can't I? I mean, I read about that in a book once. You can hire people to do that for you, can't you?" Louie, shocked and terrified, confirms that you indeed can. He vows to keep "our little secret." As the guests depart, Mrs. Sherman hugs Alex and shakes Louie's hand—after which Zena insists that they kiss. . . .

OTHER GUESTS:

John C. Becher (Reverend Nathan Sherman)
Camila Ashland (Mrs. Beth Sherman)

TAXI

143

Rhea Perlman's second appearance as Zena takes a typical sitcom premise—bringing home an unsuitable suitor—and brilliantly twists it inside out before dunking it in a cup of black humor. It's safe to say that Robert Young probably would have handled it differently had Kitten or Princess brought Louie home. Then again, maybe not.

Though Rhea's character had come back for an encore fairly quickly in the same season she'd been introduced, Rhea herself insists ''there was never a possibility of my becoming a cast member. It was just, 'Hey, we like you, do another show.' There was never any intention that I knew of as with Chris Lloyd, who was brought in slowly as a regular.''

Guest Camila Ashland soon played opposite Rhea Perlman again, but in a more antagonistic role—the horrifying high-school teacher who encounters ex-student Carla Tortelli on *Cheers*.

#37 TONY AND BRIAN

WRITTEN BY KEN ESTIN.

DIRECTED BY JAMES BURROWS.

Bobby is moving up as an actor. At the garage, he displays newspaper reviews of his performance as Biff in the 88th Street Actor's Workshop production of Arthur Miller's *Death of a Salesman*. One critic hated everything about the production except Bobby (which seems to happen to him a lot). *The Long Island Bulletin,* however, hated everything, *including* Bobby. But Bobby's not worried—nobody in Manhattan reads that rag anyway. At least not until Louie wheels in a bundle to distribute.

Tony enters the garage with his nine-year-old friend, Brian Sims (Marc Anthony Danza), the youngster who'd been in a wheelchair back when Tony fought Brian's idol (episode #24). Brian is out of his wheelchair now, but is as cynical and conniving as ever. Brian's living in a foster home now, and Tony cherishes those times when Brian can visit. The cabbies believe Tony would make a good father and urge him to adopt the kid; they all troop over to his Brooklyn apartment—a large, sparsely furnished one-bedroom on the fifth floor of a brick apartment house—to lend moral support. Brian, however, has other ideas—like being adopted by the wealthy Brennans, whose nephew is a friend of his.

Tony, accompanied by the ever-faithful Alex, goes to the Brennans' mansion to check things out. The people are so nice, Alex tells them that if they're ever thinking of adopting a forty-two-year-old cabbie. . . . Brian thinks he's on easy street. To his dismay, however, the Brennans reject him for someone cuter. He shows up at Tony's with the idea that, hey, if you want me, here I am. A hurt Tony isn't so sure he wants Brian now. He suggests that they cut cards to decide whether or not Brian can stay. Tony wins: Brian can stay after all.

OTHER GUESTS:

Michael Fairman (John Brennan)
Barbara Stuart (Mrs. Brennan)
Shane Butterworth (Tommy, the Brennans' nephew)
Mary Betten (the maid)

This is not a great episode. Brian's conniving is so distasteful, you keep wondering what Tony sees in him. Plus, we know in the back of our minds that adoption involves a rigorous process, thus torpedoing the plot: Tony, a young, single man in the dangerous and time-consuming profession of boxing, couldn't possibly have adopted Brian. An episode about Tony facing up to that prospect would have been much more *Taxi*-like.

Writer Ken Estin, who was a script consultant that season and who went on to become a *Taxi* story editor and coproducer, admits, ''We kind of dropped the adoption thing. We liked Brian and we liked Marc, but we decided it wasn't good for Tony to be a father. In my own mind, what I assumed happened is that Tony didn't qualify with the adoption agency. So Brian went to a good family and grew up very healthy and in a good environment, and Tony went to see him regularly. Either that,'' Estin cracks, ''or he died.''

#38 JIM GETS A PET

WRITTEN BY DAVID LLOYD.

DIRECTED BY JAMES BURROWS.

Alex, Tony, Jim, Bobby, and Latka are just getting back from a day at the races. This is a sore point with Elaine, whose ex-husband's gambling helped ruin her marriage. Jim, however, is in love with this newly discovered thrill: When Jeff goes to get coffee from the vending machine, Jim bets Bobby that a vodka gimlet will come out. He loses, but, he adds vigorously, it was worth it for that delicious moment of uncertainty. Right. Lou, spotting a sucker, offers Jim a loan at 85 percent interest. Jim accepts and starts visiting the track regularly.

One day Alex tries to wake him up to the realities of loan-sharking and does an absolutely marvelous bit acting out a series of mobster scenarios. Jim sees the light and swears he'll never borrow gambling money again. In the meantime, it's a good thing he's just won $10,000 so he can pay Lou back. It seems Jim had bet $35 on a 300-to-1 shot named On Dasher and felt so strongly for the old, valiant horse that he bought him. In fact, a trainer is just now bringing him by. Jim promptly renames the horse Gary: On Dasher, he explains, was his slave name.

With misguided generosity, he decides to set the poor unfortunate creature free. New York City not being the Great Plains, the cabbies convince Jim to find another home for On . . . er, Gary. Jim chooses his apartment—the top floor of a condemned loft building. But when Tony, Bobby, and Alex come to check up on Jim and his horse, Gary is dead. Back in the garage, Jim is despondent. Alex suggests that Jim (ostensibly still a reverend of his old hippie church) hold a service. He does so, giving an eloquent and touching memorial that brings Elaine to tears and even moves Louie to ask Jim to do the service for his mother when the time comes.

Note: The actor who brings the horse into the garage is not listed in the end credits, though he has a line.

This early showcase for Jim was the first *Taxi* script by the curmudgeonly comedy writer David Lloyd, one of television's best known and most prolific. Amazingly, his even-dozen *Taxi* episodes include both some of the best (the Emmy-winning "Elaine's Strange Triangle," "Jim Joins the Network," "Alex the Gofer") and two of the absolute worst ("Louie Bumps Into an Old Lady" and "The Costume Party"). He also served as a story editor/script consultant for the last four seasons of

Taxi, a spot he's held on other shows, including *Cheers.* Lloyd (no relation to Christopher Lloyd) got his start writing for Jack Paar and Dick Cavett. He went on to *The Mary Tyler Moore Show,* writing thirty episodes plus cowriting the finale, taking an Emmy Award for "Chuckles Bites the Dust" and a nomination for "Lou and That Woman." After *The Mary Tyler Moore Show* went off the air, Lloyd cowrote and coproduced a very bad, failed CBS pilot, *Your Place or Mine.*

Though his building is condemned, Jim gets electricity via an extension cord evidently plugged into a generator. Despite appearances, this is realistic. In New York City, abandoned buildings are sometimes taken over by "homesteaders" who slowly fix them up. One real-life veteran of this is actor William Converse-Roberts (*The Days and Nights of Molly Dodd*), who explains, "The City doesn't like it so much anymore, but [during the fiscal crisis of the 1970s], when people homesteaded a building, they could buy it from the city as a co-op. I paid two hundred dollars for my apartment in 1978," he says. "But then I spent ten thousand dollars to fix it up."

Tony Danza's bare-handed walnut-cracking in this episode was real, the actor swears. "That's me, pal!" He laughs. "It wasn't in the script, but then they got the idea and asked if I could do it. I said I thought I could; it depended on getting the right walnuts. There were a couple I couldn't do, but then we got ones I could." And though it would've made sense to score the walnuts for easier breaking, Tonys says they didn't bother.

As for the horse: The cast members never really got to know him or most of the other trained animals used on the show. According to one *Taxi* star, the trainers often kept their animals partially sedated—"not in a coma or anything, just calm"— or else continuously kept practicing tricks with them. Generally, these days, an ASPCA observer is on hand.

#39 WHAT PRICE BOBBY?

WRITTEN BY KEN ESTIN.
DIRECTED BY JAMES BURROWS.

Bobby, cruising the theater district, picks up an attractive woman (Susan Sullivan) heading to 634

East 62nd Street. Bobby can't believe his luck—it's Nora Chandliss, one of the biggest personal managers in the theatrical profession, a real starmaker, and she's here in his cab! He pitches her, but she's not interested in hearing another actor talk about how good he is and what a break this is. Still and all, she seems to see something in Bobby. He tells her about a play he's doing in Brooklyn, a piece of drivel called *Stalled,* about a bunch of people stuck in an elevator. Nora tells him she'll try and see it. Bobby takes this as a polite no. Nora is a little put off by that. Bobby says it's OK, he understands how busy she is. They go back and forth until she says she'll be there already. Bobby drops her off and drives away feeling triumphant.

At the garage a few nights later, Elaine is telling the cabbies that Alex phoned from his ski vacation to say he's having a great time and isn't coming back. Bobby comes in and announces that Nora came to his play last night. He explains that unlike an agent, a personal manager would take control over his whole career. "If she can find it," Louie interjects nastily. Bobby says he's doing OK so far; after all, his foot can be seen in a current athlete's-foot medication commercial. The phone rings and it's Nora on the line. She wants to see Bobby in her office right away. Ecstatically, he rushes over. Nora tells him that yes, the play stank, and yes, he was marvelous. She wants to work with him. Bobby's in heaven. Right away, she gives him the phone numbers of a photographer and a hair stylist he's to use, and she tells him to come back later so that her secretary can take him out to choose some new clothes. Bobby thankfully tells her he can't wait to prove how good he is. She says he can start tonight—and gives him the key to her apartment.

The next day, Bobby comes into the garage uncharacteristically quiet. When the curious cabbies ask him how it went with Nora, he just shrugs and says Nora's going to represent him. When they press him for details, he says there's nothing much, we did this, we did that, we talked business, we went to bed. At first, the cabbies are happy that Bobby's found a new romance as well as a manager, but they soon realize it's not quite like that, that Bobby feels cheap and used.

He goes to Nora's apartment later, after having auditioned for the role of Brick in a Broadway re-vival of Tennessee Williams's *Cat on a Hot Tin Roof.* He overhears the tough Nora discussing an unacceptable deal on the phone: "I'll tell ya, why don't we both sleep on it.... Well, I can't agree to lunch until we sleep on it.... That's right, let's sleep on whether we have lunch." Bobby is despondent over the horrible audition he gave, but Nora tells him he got the part—that in order to get one of her star clients, they had to take Bobby as well. Bobby is still upset. He doesn't like the fact he's sleeping with his manager. Nora says she understands. In that case, let's keep it strictly...she says "personal" at the same time he says "business." That's it, she tells him. Please leave. Very coldly, very businesslike, she drops him as a client. Bobby is in shock, but he tells her proudly that no matter what, he's still got his self-respect. "No, you don't," she says matter-of-factly. "If I said come back, you'd come back in a second." Bobby: "Try me." Nora: 'Come back." Bobby: "OK." Nora: "Now you don't have your self-respect. Good night."

Bobby is down to having lost his manager, his self-respect, and his pride. But at least, he announces defiantly, "I have my *shoes!*" Nora doesn't understand that. Neither does Bobby, but it was the first thing that popped into his head. And, of course, Nora doesn't allow him even that. This makes Bobby so angry, he threatens to destroy a lamp. Alarmed, she returns the footwear. Bobby exits proudly, telling her that nobody, but nobody, messes with his shoes.

Tag: Alex on the phone from the ski resort tells Bobby he's sorry about what happened, and he'll talk with him about it at length tomorrow when he gets back. Even Louie is sympathetic toward Bobby's bad luck. But they both know there's only one thing he can say: "Wheeler, Cab 544."

NOTE: Nora Chandliss misidentified as "Nora Sutton" in end-credits.

This episode is a great big slice of show-business reality, built upon audaciously real-life practices that most rags-to-riches biographies ignore. All of Bobby's talent and hard work are secondary to Nora, just as his momentary lack of them at the audition are meaningless to the Broadway producers who are forced to take him in order to get an actress they want. Think about that the next time you see performers strangely out of place in a TV show or a movie or even a celebrity magazine. Then play guess-which-star's-manager-also-manages-them.

"You talk to people about it when that sort of situation comes up," Jeff Conaway notes. "I don't really know first-hand because I've never done it, but the other day I was talking to my agent and told him, 'You know, I think this producer wants something from me.' And he said, 'Well, so what?' That kind of thing wasn't news to him. And I just felt like I don't have to do that. It would mean that I really joined the whore race, and I don't ever want to do that. In the end, you have to have self-respect."

Playing the brutal and beautiful Nora was Susan Sullivan, a prolific, well-regarded actress and former Playboy Bunny who hopped almost immediately from soap operas and *Taxi* to a costarring role in the sitcom *It's a Living*. After that came TV stardom on *Falcon Crest* and ubiquitous Tylenol commercials. Jeff Conaway had actually played *her* manager in a pre-*Taxi* TV movie, *Breaking Up Is Hard to Do*. As he remembers, "The producers came to me and asked how I'd like to work with Susan, and I said great, 'cause she was a real pro, we communicated, no problems. They were really great that way, asking like that. I look back now and I realize how much they really cared about us."

Observes the beauteous Ms. Sullivan of her *Taxi* appearance: "Now that I'm on the other side I try to remember this, but it's always strange to come onto a series where everybody knows everybody else and you feel like such a stranger. So it's always nice to come in like I did on *Taxi* with some kind of compatibility with somebody I already knew. I liked working with Jeff again. We had a good time. I think when people are really talented and secure in their talent, as the *Taxi* cast was, they're the kindest to people coming in." She saw the hardball manager she played as "a part of myself I don't get cast as very often. I suppose I should take that as a compliment since it's a cold, hard part of myself—that tough, using, manipulative side, which I clearly have in me and don't like to show. But it's always nice to have it in your grab bag!"

Except for the phone call in the tag, which was filmed as a pickup sometime after the rest of the episode, Judd Hirsch missed this show. At the time (the first week of December 1979), he was shooting what would be an Oscar-nominated role as psychiatrist Dr. Berger in the film *Ordinary People*.

#40 GUESS WHO'S COMING FOR BREFNISH?

WRITTEN BY BARRY KEMP.
DIRECTED BY JAMES BURROWS.

A group of hopeful secretaries are hanging around the garage waiting for job interviews with cab-company owner Mr. McKenzie. Louie, trying to score brownie points with the eventual winner, confidently whispers to each that he just *knows* she's the one who'll get the job. When the position becomes filled before all the applicants have been interviewed, the women go away grumbling—one of them (Carol Kane) grumbling in Latka's native tongue. Hello, what's this? Latka and the pretty young lady start jabbering away, both astonished and delighted to find someone else from their home country. Latka introduces her to the cabbies as "Simka Dahblitz—but not *the* Simka Dahblitz."

They go out to lunch together, after which Latka will show her New York, including, as he comically confides in the cabbies, "the apartment of a lonely, lonely man." The two hit it off well, but at Mario's, Latka can't resist making "mountain people" jokes—how many mountain people does it take to milk a goat, etc., etc. Latka, it seems, was a flatlander. Simka laughs weakly at his jokes: She is a mountain person, and though she likes Latka, she's reluctant to tell him.

After a few weeks of dating, which includes taking in the Broadway musical *Grease*, Simka finally decides to break the news about herself to Latka. But when she tries, Latka is on a roll with mountain-people jokes, and the sweet, volatile Simka finally explodes and tells him her secret. Then she demands that Latka look her in the eye and say it doesn't matter. He tries but cannot. Deeply hurt, she leaves. After several days, Latka is feeling miserable. The cabbies convince him that his prejudices are hurting a big chance for some happiness in this life. He finally agrees and vows to accept

Simka as she is. Simka agrees to meet him at Mario's and arrives looking radiant. Latka tells her, in essence, that she's ''good enough'' for him even though she is a mountain person, and that he knows he can live with the disgrace because he loves her.

But Simka doesn't need his pity or his love. She's found a job (albeit a menial one at a racetrack) and has a serious relationship with a handsome surgeon, Dr. John Hannon, who comes to meet her there. Latka asks what kind of life that will be—surgeons are never home. John explains that he only works a couple of days a week. Well, says Latka, he'll be underfoot all the time. John answers politely that he has a house quite big enough for privacy. Well, Latka tries, look at all that cleaning. John replies that he has a cleaning staff. Well, Latka says—you have a sister? Unfortunately, no. Simka leaves Latka there as gently as possible, and Latka sits alone at the bar, his lesson learned. He plays the now ironic ''Summer Lovers'' from *Grease,* and despondently tells Tommy the bartender one last mountain-person joke: ''How does a mountain girl make love? Like an angel.''

OTHER GUESTS:

T. J. Castronova (Tommy, the bartender at Mario's)
Teresa Baxter, Edith Fields (applicants)

Note: Dr. John Hannon played by Frank Ashmore per production notes, Phil Coccioletti per end-credits.

This episode marks the debut of Simka, played dazzlingly by Carol Kane. Kane, the multifaceted, Oscar-nominated ''queen of cameos'' experienced some comical misconceptions on the set. Not that they were so comical at the time, she remembers. As a movie actress unfamiliar with the up-to-shoot-night rewriting common to TV comedy, she went through a rite of passage that week. Even by Friday night, she still wasn't sure who Jim Brooks was.

''On shoot night, they were still making changes—there were notes right up to the last minute! And I'm thinking,'' she recalls with a laugh, '' 'Don't they understand this is the time when an actor must prepare? And must be alone?' I thought it was supposed to be like the opening night of a show. Oh, my, I was just completely in another world! I had no idea what was going on. Jim was knocking on my door, trying to give me some no doubt extremely helpful notes, and I'm thinking, 'Who does he think he is, talking to me about my work when it's time for the show!' I thought he was like the money-man producer; I had no idea he was a writer—a brilliant writer—and a director himself!

''Jim was always too gracious to tell me about this. Other people told me. Little by little I began to turn green, because I began to realize who these people were and what their contributions were. I was just mortified! But looking back, I'm sure they realized I didn't know television, because they were all so very kind.''

Though this was Simka's first appearance, she'd been brewing in the writers' minds for some time. In a never-used speech from an early draft of ''Alex's Romance'' (episode #34), Latka tries to console a despondent Alex:

Alex, in my country I had a girl. Simka. Golden-haired beauty. We love ourselves. *(remembering the hot times)* Wow. She say: ''Latka, I love you. I want to spend life together. I want little Latkas.'' I say: ''OK, thank you very much.'' We plan wedding. When big day come, I wait, and wait . . . but no Simka. Only Dear Krepke letter. The years pass . . . I come to this country. Then one day in Central Park, there's my Simka! I run, yelling, ''Simka! Simka'' She no hear. Two babies take her to the swings. She kiss them and smile. She look very happy. I walk away. *(During Latka's story, he becomes increasingly emotional, until he is reduced to heaving, wailing sobs.)*

The version of ''Summer Lovers'' we hear on the jukebox was recorded especially for this episode by two *Grease* alumni—Marilu Henner and Jeff Conaway.

#41 SHUT IT DOWN, PART I

STORY BY MARK JACOBSON AND MICHAEL TOLKIN.

TELEPLAY BY HOWARD GEWIRTZ AND IAN PRAISER.

DIRECTED BY JAMES BURROWS.

Tony storms into the garage looking to break Latka's neck. His brakes just went out on him, causing a near-collision. The cabbies hold him back, however, and tell him that Latka can only do so much with what he has, that the cab company is dangerously cheap when it comes to replacement parts and new cabs. Louie comes out of the restroom and all eyes turn on him. The cabbies tell him they're sick of putting their lives in danger every time they get behind the wheel. Louie shrugs; is that all? But the crowd turns ugly, and Louie promises to "write up a report." He tries to get into his cage, but the mob won't let him. The situation gets nasty, and Louie is forced to use a "secret passageway" to try and elude the angry cabbies.

Elaine says enough is enough, that they should take their complaints to the shop steward. Unfortunately, nobody seems to know who that is. Louie is gleeful in their disorganization, and even more so after Alex shies away from the responsibility and Tony volunteers himself as new shop steward. Well, why not? The cabbies vote him in. Louie, sensing a pigeon, homes in for the kill. Tony demands to talk to Louie right away. Louie is all greasy charm—why, sure, pal. He invites Tony to The Tidepool, a nearby restaurant where "us executives" talk over weighty matters. Tony gets all gushy, doesn't get anything accomplished, and gets voted out of office.

Bobby, fed up, says they should all go on strike. Elaine, trying to keep a cooler head, convinces the cabbies that they should pursue diplomatic means instead, and inadvertently convinces them to elect her shop steward. Realizing that skinflint company-owner McKenzie is the real problem, she storms upstairs to confront him. When she returns, having had no luck, the cabbies are on strike!

A very cold couple of days go by. Bobby comes in to get coffee from the (nonworking) machine, and Lou tortures him with an important phone message about a big movie audition—yesterday. As Bobby goes numb, the cabbies come in with big news of their own: The union has agreed to hold a hearing on their grievances and plans to subpoena the company's maintenance records. Louie scoffs. He's cooked the books to make it seem as if Sunshine spends as much, if not more, for upkeep and maintenance than any other cab company in New York. The cabbies are taken aback and can only hope the arbitrator will be able to sift out the truth.

They go back on the picket line, all except Alex. He stays behind with Lou, and gradually convinces the Italian-Catholic dispatcher that lying under oath will result in "eternal damnation."

Lou finally gets so terrified of God's vengeance (as he was before in episode #16, "Louie Sees the Light") that he agrees to negotiate with Elaine. (McKenzie has told him to end the strike in whatever way he sees fit.) Elaine comes in and is surprised to hear that Louie's willing to go along with their demands on one condition: a date with Elaine. As he puts it, "One date! To save cabbies' lives!" They negotiate the circumstances back and forth: Elaine wanting lunch at separate tables with lots of people around and to meet him there, Louie finally getting her to agree to dinner with him picking her up and dropping her off. And in earshot of at least two people, she must call him "Stallion." That part, he tells her, is nonnegotiable. Elaine finally agrees.

Note: Paperboy uncredited

#42 SHUT IT DOWN, PART II

WRITTEN BY HOWARD GEWIRTZ AND
IAN PRAISER.

DIRECTED BY JAMES BURROWS.

Flashbacks to the last episode bring us to the end of the strike. The cabbies don't know of Elaine's sacrifices for them—that she's agreed to a dinner date with Louie. While Elaine is at home getting ready, Louie brags to Alex about the hot date he has. As Louie goes off to primp for it, Alex figures out what's up. He rushes over to Elaine's new apartment (#5B). She's frantic, borderline-hysterical, drinking liquor straight from a blender. (We learn later that her exaggerated behavior that evening comes partly from mixing alcohol with Valium. Lou: "I thought something like that could kill a person." Elaine: "So did I.")

Louie arrives, dressed to the nines and doused with Cruel Cavalier cologne. He's a bit irked by Alex's being there; Alex warns Lou not to try anything. Lou seems genuinely surprised and even a little hurt by all the hysterics. Elaine doesn't help matters when she emerges from the bedroom *sans* makeup, with her hair pulled back tight, and dressed in a roly-poly down jacket. This isn't ex-actly what Lou had in mind. In fact, what he had in mind he wrote in a script he hands Elaine at a garish Polynesian restaurant called The Tidepool; it's their conversation for the evening, he tells her, having helpfully figured she wouldn't know what to say to him.

The two of them toss back plenty of the restau-rant's specialty drink—"monsoons"—and Louie, who'd previously paid off the band, the maître d', and, it seems, the rest of the customers, dances the tango with Elaine. At her door later, Louie con-fesses how disappointed he is that she wouldn't even open herself up to the possibility of a nice evening out. It's half a con-job, though, and after two false exits, he finally gets the expected "Just a second, Louie." They negotiate a goodnight kiss. It starts out innocently, but then Louie jumps her and she slams the door in his face. Lou kind of expected that all along: He knows what he is and what he looks like, and Elaine is out of his league. But before he goes home, he tenderly leaves the doggie bag of shrimp puffs and garlic bread by her door.

GUESTS:

Lee Delano (the maître d')

Note: Maryedith Burrell is listed in the end credits as a hatcheck girl, but her part—wherein Louie had hired her to rush from her post, give him a big kiss, and tell him, "I'm still trembling from our last date"—was cut.

This was an accidental two-parter. "As we got into it," recounts Marilu Henner, "they didn't know what to cut, so they said, 'Let's do a two-parter and shoot it all in one evening.' This was right before Christmas—the twenty-first of Decem-ber [1979]."

Mark Jacobson, who wrote the *New York Magazine* article on which *Taxi* was based, had negotiated a deal to write some scripts. Not being a scriptwriter, he collaborated with one, his friend Michael Tolkin (whose father, Mel Tolkin, wrote for Sid Caesar and others in TV's golden age). They turned in several story ideas and eventually got the nod to write a strike episode. The script went through the usual TV comedy rewriting process, which in this case relegated outsiders Jacobson and Tolkin to "story by" status; the Writers Guild allows this in certain cases of rewriting.

"The original story," says Jacobson, "had Tony learning about and espousing Marxist philosophy, and eventually recanting. We saw the finished ep-isode, and it was like, the dispatcher will end the strike if he can have a date with some chick. We said to ourselves, 'What is that?' " But Jacobson insists he's not bothered. "People always call up my friend [*New York Magazine* writer] Michael Daly, wanting him to write screenplays about things he's got some expertise in. He does, then they always say it's too realistic. I've had about six or seven articles optioned like the *Taxi* piece," he says, "and it's fine with me what they do with them after that. I don't mind getting two thousand dollars and never hearing another word."

Since so many drafts of this script exist, and since it's such a visible example of the way a comedy script changes, a tour through its incarnations might be instructive:

In the December 12, 1979, Mark Jacobson-Michael Tolkin script marked "First Draft. Re-write: Gewirtz and Praiser," the first act is essen-tially the same as the final on-screen version: Tony comes into the garage after his near-collision; he is appointed shop steward; Louie bamboozles him. He's replaced by Elaine, who calls for a strike.

Act two is much different, however: We're in a hearing room where an arbiter named Jacoby takes testimony first from Bobby, and then from Louie on behalf of Mr. Leland P. (rather than Ed) MacKenzie (as it's spelled throughout these two scripts, though it was "McKenzie" on-screen in episode #54). Louie shows the arbiter his cooked books, and the arbiter orders the cabbies back to work until he can sort through that evidence. At the garage, Alex refuses to take a cab, and, as in the finished episode, puts the fear of God in Lou—down to the "eternal damnation" bit. Louie re-pents and phones Jacoby to tell him the truth. We dissolve to a despondent Lou getting his things ready in preparation for being fired, and the cab-bies trying to be sympathetic. Alex reminds Lou that MacKenzie "was abusive and had you scared out of your wits." Louie: "Just like dad." Fortu-nately for Lou, however, he gets a call that

MacKenzie has just shot himself.

Tag: MacKenzie's widow has come through with "new" rattletrap cabs from the Mount Cisco [sic] Cab Co.

A second "first draft" from December 14, credited only to Jacobson and Tolkin, is essentially the same, though Jacoby has become Turner, and Louie's description of a sadistic elementary school nun has expanded. Regarding eternal damnation: "Sister Porchnik had the worst version of it I ever heard. She used to do diagrams with colored chalk. She'd pick the hottest, humidest, ugliest day of the year, and she'd say (*imitating Sister Porchnik*) 'This is a wonderful day compared to eternal damnation.'"

By the December 17 draft, the arbiter is out and the strike is in full swing. Elaine tells the cabbies the union will hold a meeting on their grievances, and Louie brags about his phonied records. Alex counters with "eternal damnation," and Louie agrees to negotiate with Elaine. They go back and forth until she agrees on going out for a date. The next draft (December 18) extends the story to Elaine's hallway after the date, where she and Louie enact a harsher, shorter version of the eventual on-screen routine. The final scene, scrapped, takes place in the garage, where Elaine more or less convinces her friends that nothing happened on her date with Lou. The script breaks into two parts on December 19, and takes gradual shape from there.

Tony impresses him with his idea for world peace: Our leader and the Communist leader duke it out in the ring. Sevareid thinks it's so brilliant, he invites Tony to join the group. Latka daydreams of being a heartless dispatcher who condemns lowly mechanic Lou De Palma to the firing squad.

Bobby sees himself as a big singing star who comes home to Mario's, where a crowd has gathered to watch the seventh showing of his hit TV special. Bobby further pictures Louie as a bum who can't get anyone to believe he once knew the cabbie-cum-star. Taking Bobby aside, Lou begs him to tell the crowd the truth; in a bit of poetic justice, Bobby tells Louie it'll cost him a buck. It's his last dollar, but Lou figures it's worth it for the sake of his pride. Accepting it, Bobby turns to the crowd and blithely tells them he's never seen the guy before.

Finally, Jim envisions sitting at home when a decidedly cheesy looking alien craft appears outside his window. Amid an eerie light, an alien voice invites him to fly away with them.

Tag: A tuxedoed Herve Villechaize shows up to pick up his photos and thank Tony personally. Louie does a bad impression of him. Previews of part two follow.

OTHER GUESTS:

Warren Munson (Mario's customer #1)
Carl Lumbly (Mario's customer #2)

#43 FANTASY BOROUGH, PART I

WRITTEN BY BARRY KEMP.
DIRECTED BY JAMES BURROWS.

Tony rushes into the garage with a large manila envelope, breathlessly informing his friends that Herve Villechaize, the diminutive costar of ABC's *Fantasy Island*, left the package of photos in Tony's cab. Tony contacts Villechaize at his hotel, and the cabbies share their secret fantasies with each other as they wait for him to come by.

Tony's fantasy involves picking up the famous commentator Eric Sevareid (who portrays himself). Sevareid is going to New York University for a GOSG Conference—Gathering of Smart Guys.

#44 FANTASY BOROUGH, PART II

WRITTEN BY BARRY KEMP.
DIRECTED BY JAMES BURROWS.

Herve Villechaize from *Fantasy Island* has come and gone, but the cabbies are still inspired to daydream—except for the sober, practical Alex, who insists it's pointless, and something he's not very good at anyway. But his friends playfully prod him, and so he tries. He pictures himself behind the wheel of his cab. A breathtaking young woman named Tawny (Priscilla Barnes) hails his cab. As they ride, she chats with him. It seems promising. But—she's married. Cut!

Alex tries again. Taking it from where he left off,

Episode #44: ''Fantasy Borough, Part II.''

it seems she isn't really married—just teasing. The well-to-do Tawny is feeling wanderlust—and probably other kinds—and distracts Alex so much he has an auto accident. Cut! One more time. It turns out to have been only a fender bender. Alex and the girl are at a fantasy version of his apartment, complete with romantic lights and a roaring fire. They begin nuzzling, getting romantic. The girl says Alex is so warm, so nice—he reminds her of her favorite uncle when she was a little girl. Funny she should mention that. . . .

Louie's fantasy has him as the last rich man in the country. It's the Great Depression all over again; in the freezing garage, Alex reminds the cabbies about President Rizzo's dictum that thermostats should be kept at 28°. The sharply dressed Lou tells them to keep a stiff upper lip and retires to his mansion. There waits Elaine in a clingy, low-cut nightgown. But business must come before pleasure, and Lou orders her to bring in the family pet. It's Lassie. The famed collie just isn't pulling in the bucks like Snoopy and Benji, and so (after a marvelous bit of canine pleading), Louie sends Lassie out into the cold.

Finally we come to Elaine's fantasy: It's another boring day in the garage. The guys are playing cards. Elaine sits on the stairs in a raincoat. Softly, she begins singing that great old movie-musical number, "Lullaby of Broadway." As the song builds heat, so does Elaine: She whips off her raincoat to reveal a sexy, form-fitting blue dress. The cabbies and even Louie simply shrug and join her in song and dance. Elaine then leads them around a pole, and in a special effect, they emerge in top hats and tails. Elaine descends the stairs in showstopping tuxedo tights. Latka, like an oversize Baby New Year, trots across the floor with a sparkler in each hand. The garage is a riot of lights and music, and the full orchestra arrangement is even reprised over the closing credits.

OTHER GUESTS:

Lassie (owned and trained by Rudd Weatherwax)

The second-season pickup episodes proved to be witty showcases for most of the characters. A couple of the fantasies, however, seem a little lame: for instance, Tony's is unconvincingly against type,

Louie's Fantasy—not Elaine's—in "Fantasy Borough, Part II."

and Jim's is so far the other way it seems silly rather than insightful. Louie's and Latka's fantasies, on the other hand, are astonishingly in character, as is blue-collar Alex's *Penthouse*-letter cabbie's dream (with guest star Priscilla Barnes, who went on to costar in *Three's Company*).

On the other hand, Bobby's rock star and Elaine's movie-musical number come largely from Jeff Conaway's and Marilu Henner's own real-life, professional dreams. In fact, the song Bobby performs in his fantasy is "City Boy," the lead track of Jeff Conaway's Columbia Records album (see page 42). And Marilu—a trained singer-dancer—is lip-syncing to her own vocals. (Incidentally, Marilu's three outfits—a fancy nightgown in Louie's segment, and a clingy, satiny number plus a very brief tuxedo/leotard in the musical finale—have undoubtedly inspired many fantasies of their own!)

Bobby's fantasy was originally *Bobby's* fantasy, though. As Jeff relates, "I love makeup effects, and in the fantasy episode, I was playing Bobby as Laurence Olivier or someone like that, a very distinguished, eighty-year-old actor. I put on hours and hours of makeup, but it took too long, and so they changed it to me singing and meeting Louie at the bar. What it was, was I had ended up finally winning all these Academy Awards and stuff, and I get in a cab and it's this young cabdriver who recognizes me. And it turns out that I ask him to let me drive, and he sits in the back and we have this conversation of what it's like to be an actor and a cabdriver. It was fun, but we didn't end up using it 'cause the makeup took four, five hours to apply.''

Chris Lloyd—who in Jim's segment was beckoned by a distorted alien voice supplied by De-Vito—remembers the big musical number as "great—great fun. I could just schlep through it, because that would be in character. It's funny—I've been on Broadway only twice in my life, and both times in musicals [*Happy End* and *Red, White and Maddox*]. That's ironic. I mean, I never went to classes for that. I took voice lessons and all that stuff you're supposed to do as an actor, but I never made any attempt to be in the musical side of it.''

The producers, too, seemed to have had fun with the ''Lullaby of Broadway'' finale: The Al Dubin–Harry Warren classic from the film *Gold Diggers of 1935* is reprised over the end credits. The only other time Bob James's end theme was nudged aside was in episode #52 (''Tony's Sister and Jim'').

TAXI

154

#45 ART WORK

WRITTEN BY GLEN CHARLES AND LES CHARLES. DIRECTED BY JAMES BURROWS.

Tony bursts into the garage with a big fight tip—a light heavyweight named Johnson has a broken right hand. Elaine, as usual, objects to the cabbies' gambling, especially now that they're getting Latka involved. Not that it matters this time—*both* fighters are named Johnson. ''I see you guys miss every day,'' Elaine laments, and tells the cabbies that smart rich people invest in art. Well then, counters Alex, why don't we? Elaine resists, but Alex begins quoting from Rudyard Kipling's poem ''If''—which Jim spontaneously finishes. (''Where the hell did I learn that?'' he wonders aloud.)

Elaine relents and advises them to pool their money on a soon-to-be auctioned painting by an elderly, ill artist named Max Duffin; the strategy is that when Duffin passes away, the painting's value will skyrocket. They need $2,000, she estimates. Unfortunately, the cabbies haven't anywhere near that amount. But now Lou wants in, after, of course, examining the practical aspects of the situation: ''Is there a plug someone might accidentally trip over?'' Against their better judgment, they accept Louie's entreaties and, more important, his dough.

The day of the auction, Lou is more obnoxious than usual. But it's effective—his tortured coughing clears out the whole front row. When an untitled Duffin painting comes up, however, the bidding goes faster and higher than Elaine (bidder #445) expected. Bidder #498 gets the canvas for $2,900. The auctioneer almost immediately is handed a message that Mr. Duffin has passed away. Lou hollers in impotent rage at the rich man who got richer. Alex suggests trying to make the best of things—if nothing else has happened, at least they've been exposed to fine art.

Tag: The cabbies have each bought a reproduction and display them in the garage for an approving Elaine. Tony's is a hotel-wall seagull print. Bobby's is a modern, photorealistic electrical-outlet closeup. Louie's is a cheesy velvet bar-nude.

GUESTS:

Marvin Newman (auctioneer)
Richard Derr (buyer #1)
Peg Stewart (buyer #2)

Note: No artists are given in the end credits for this episode as they were for ''Nardo Loses Her Marbles'' (episode #28).

The paintings in the tag coincide, naturally, with each character's personality. The actors were given their choice from a small selection. Jeff Conaway says he picked the large, photorealistic closeup of an electrical outlet since ''I thought at the time that was kind of a Bobby thing, something kind of sexual to show a chick when she comes over.'' He laughs. ''Like, she'd ask about the painting and he'd say, 'Yeah, it's an outlet. You stick something in there and electricity happens!' ''

#46 ALEX JUMPS OUT OF AN AIRPLANE

WRITTEN BY KEN ESTIN.
DIRECTED BY JAMES BURROWS.

The cabbies are relaxing at Mario's when Lou comes in and wants to join them. Naturally, they resist. They soften, however, when he says he has a problem—which turns out to be he's so bored that he's willing to talk to even them. But Louie has to leave after Tommy the bartender tells him that boss Mr. McKenzie wants him right away, and the discussion turns to Alex's ski trip last weekend to Lake Placid. A pretty girl had dared him to take the treacherous ''Banzai Run.'' Maybe or almost by accident, Alex did—and survived, to the girl's admiration. Now the exhilaration of risk has seduced him. He gets up and bashes out a showtune (''Being Alive'') on the piano—to applause, yet. Later he has Tony teach him how to box, though his spar with a disdainful black boxer named Carl leaves him horizontal.

Then at Mario's sometime afterward, Alex announces he'll take the ultimate challenge—skydiving. Lou, ever sympathetic, urges Alex to make him his beneficiary. In the airplane later, with Bobby for moral support, and Louie watching over his ''investment,'' Alex weaves back and forth over his decision to jump. (Bobby, a big help, spends the time trying to pick up the female jump master.) Pragmatic, practical Alex finally loses his nerve—and then suddenly decides, ''Aw, what the hell,'' and just sort of goes. He starts screaming, ''I'm gonna die! I'm gonna die!'' But after the chute opens, he changes that to, ''I'm *not* gonna die!'' followed by a reprise of ''Being Alive.''

Tag: Alex is at Mario's, boring the cabbies with his skydiving story; the camera pulls back over New York, making even his courageous feat insignificant in the grand scheme of things.

GUESTS:

T. J. Castronova (Tommy, the bartender at Mario's)
Beverly Ross (jump master)

Note: The actor who plays Carl, the boxer, isn't identified in the end credits.

Alex's sudden love of risk-taking is perfectly in character, given his gambling background. Writer Ken Estin says he thought of Alex ''as a guy who's given up on the thrills of life, who's accepted life in a very simple way. I thought, how can we light a fire under him? It occurred to me that people sometimes decide to change when they come close to death. The ski run, complicated by his desire to look good in front of the woman, took care of that part. So then where do you take it? Well, jumping out of an airplane is a logical extension—it's the pinnacle of risk, and yet it's something just about anybody *can* do. I always research things pretty thoroughly before I write, and I called up a jump school and found you could learn skydiving and make your first jump all in one weekend.

''That episode was unusual in that we normally didn't do variations-on-a-theme type shows—we usually had a very strong plot that went from A to Z. But they trusted me enough to let me write and outline, and they liked it, and we took it from there.''

Executive producer Stan Daniels, whose first love is musical theater, played piano offstage while Alex bashed out ''Being Alive'' at Mario's. The song comes from Stephen Sondheim's Broadway musical *Company.*

#47 LOUIE'S RIVAL

WRITTEN BY KEN ESTIN.
DIRECTED BY JAMES BURROWS.

Elaine has a hot date with one Doug Johnson from her art gallery, and she ropes Bobby into baby-sitting her kids on Saturday night at eight. Elsewhere in the garage, Louie confesses to Alex that he's becoming scared of losing Zena (Rhea Perlman)—she's acting funny, aloof. Alex, rather brusquely, suggests a romantic date. Lou tries, but he and Zena have a spat that continues all the way to her apartment (on the top floor of a red-brick building).

There, she finally tells him that she's met someone else. Louie is dumbstruck. Zena explains that two weeks before, she met Dwight, the day bartender at Mario's. She relates how their relationship grew from friendly lunches to finally sex—at which point Louie is so shocked he can't breathe and hastily scribbles a note to that effect to the horrified Zena. She rushes him a glass of brandy, which he splashes harshly against his face to recover. Wet, broken, and disheveled, Lou staggers to the door. "Y'know somethin', Zena," he begins accusingly. "Someday yer gonna come back to me, crawlin' on yer knees, beggin' me to take you back. And when you do, you know what I'll say? I'll say—thank God." And he walks away.

The same night, Louie walks into Mario's, shattered. The cabbies, who are leaving, don't care; Bobby says, "Oh. See you tomorrow." But Alex asks Louie to sit and talk. Lou thinks that Dwight is working the bar this very moment. After a masterful comic scene in which Alex repeatedly tells a growling Lou to heel, Alex goes up to the bar. Almost before he gets a word out of his mouth, Dwight casually describes to Alex his whole affair with Zena, how she got too serious, and how he's going to have to let her go.

Alex tells Louie about it, and the groveling dispatcher returns to form: He shows up at Zena's just as Dwight's delivered his rejection and, in one of the best sandwich-making scenes ever filmed, makes himself right at home. But Zena says she still wants him out, that she doesn't love him, that she "doesn't know what love is." But Louie, deftly grasping at straws, says he does, and he's the only one who can tell her, because he reads about it and watches talk shows, and nobody knows what he knows: "Love is the end of happiness—Neeymph! Because one day, all a guy's gotta do to be happy is to watch the Mets. The next day, you gotta have Zena in the room watchin' the Mets with you. You don't know why—it's the same Mets. It's the same room. But you gotta have Zena there!" Against her better judgment—*way* against—she forces herself to take him back, to once again enter this stinking, rotten relationship. Lou blubbers how glad he is to hear her say that.

OTHER GUESTS:

Richard Minchenberg (Dwight)

Though we've seen Louie's insecurities regarding his profession (episode #7, "High School Reunion"), and his social graces (#36, "Louie Meets

the Folks"), this is the first time we see—almost in extremis—Lou's despair over finding someone to love. Now his shock at discovering that maybe the one girl in his life he'll ever have may be falling for someone else literally numbs him so that he can't breathe. It turns out that the nice-seeming Dwight was just another user (albeit one with enough class to be honest afterward), and that Zena is available to Lou once again. Yet the possibility of the incident recurring is so frightening to Lou that his brain refuses to accept it, and so he reverts to his usual crude behavior. Everything is "normal" again, "the way it used to be"—isn't it? When Zena thinks not, Lou's forced to confess how he feels, and in a way that shows he's been thinking about it for a long time. Stripped down to such an extreme character as Louie De Palma, the double-helix dance of love, sex, and insecurity becomes blatantly universal. It's a brilliant episode.

It's also one with a continuity error. In trying to console Lou, Alex mentions a girl he dated *four years ago* that he was crazy about. This statement contradicts his assertion in an earlier episode that he's had no "serious relationship in eight years."

Speaking of eight years, it was about that long ago that Hirsch and DeVito had performed together in a play called *The Line of Least Existence.* Danny had played Judd's dog, Andy—an experience that probably had some bearing on the great "Sit, Louie! Sit!" routine they go through in this episode at Mario's.

#48 FATHERS OF THE BRIDE
WRITTEN BY BARRY KEMP.
DIRECTED BY JAMES BURROWS.

Louie shows Alex a startling wedding notice in the newspaper: Alex's daughter, Cathy Consuelos, who lives in Brazil with her mother and stepfather, is about to marry a UN ambassador's son at St. Patrick's Cathedral; the reception is at the Waldorf-Astoria. Alex is furious at not being invited. He tries to call his ex-wife, Phyllis, in Rio de Janeiro, but her personal secretary explains it's no mistake—Phyllis specifically refused to invite him.

Alex angrily announces he's going to the reception anyway; Elaine, seeing him so upset, insists on

TAXI

156

going with him. At the Waldorf, Elaine uses her feminine charms to get past the attendant, and Alex spots his daughter. Cathy (Talia Balsam) lights up when she sees him and asks why he never responded to her invitation. She'd wanted him to be a member of the wedding, she says. She brings him around to meet her stepfather, Carlo, and Phyllis (Louise Lasser). Alex's ex has gained thirty pounds since she and Alex split up eighteen years ago, and a bitter Alex remarks on it.

Later, as his anger subsides, he feels guilty and asks Phyllis if she'll speak with him in private. He ushers her to a big janitor's room—*tres* atmospheric—where he apologizes, and they begin to reminisce. The two of them dance the verbal dance of the old married couple they somehow still are— swinging from happiness to hate, each knowing what the other is thinking. They remember how, despite everything, their sex life at least had been great. He always knew how to push her buttons, she says. Now she's not sure anybody can push her buttons—or *find* her buttons.

They hug for old times' sake, and Phyllis begins to get hot. As a flustered Alex starts to panic, he hears Cathy looking for them. He and Phyllis break from their clinch, hilariously, just in time. Cathy says how terrific it is to see them be friendly to one another, and what's more, it'd make her so happy to see them hug. Alex mumbles in *that* case, she'd have been ecstatic had she come in a couple of minutes later. Fortunately, Cathy doesn't hear that, and though Phyllis gets momentarily playful once again, they go back to the reception, reconciled.

OTHER GUESTS:

Carlo Quinterio (Carlo Consuelos)
Harvey Skolnick (reception attendant)

This episode gives us our first glimpse of Phyllis. Once we see it's the brilliant, idiosyncratic Louise Lasser, we know we're in for a *tour de farce*. She and Judd Hirsch connect as if they'd been married and divorced themselves, trading and sharing with all the intimate anger and secrets that build between couples. Lasser, who gained fame and notoriety as star of the syndicated satire *Mary Hartman, Mary Hartman* in 1976, learned all about intimacy when she was married to comedian-filmmaker Woody Al-

len from 1971 to 1976. Lasser still pops up on occasion as a TV guest star.

Talia Balsam reprises her role as the twenty-year-old Cathy, who seems quite decent if not much for following through on lost invitations to long-ago fathers. And that's second assistant director Carlo Quinterio playing Cathy's stepfather, Carlo Consuelos. Michael Looney filled in as second assistant director for this episode. "Carlo was so perfect for the part," says Ken Estin, "that we just had to use him. Everybody was saying, 'We gotta get somebody just like him.' And somebody finally said, 'Hey! You can't get any more like him than him!' "

Incidentally, Marilu Henner's exquisite evening dress was her own. If you were lucky enough to attend the 1979 Golden Globe Awards, you would have seen her wearing it there, too.

#49 GOING HOME

WRITTEN BY GLEN CHARLES AND LES CHARLES.
DIRECTED BY JAMES BURROWS.

A private detective named Spencer arrives at the garage, looking for Jim Ignatowski—a.k.a. James Caldwell, son of the wealthy Bostonian who hired him to track Jim down. It's been a fascinating trail, he tells the cabbies: Jim's last-known address was a '63 Volkswagen. It seems Dad wants Jim to come home, and has sent along two plane tickets. After Spencer leaves, Jim tells the cabbies how he'd dropped out of Harvard ten years ago when in his teens, after having done well his first semester and virtually ignoring his second. Elaine asks Jim why anyone would change his name *to* Ignatowski. Iggy explains that in the sixties, everyone changed their names to things like "Sunshine" and "Free" and (in a topical reference to Frank Zappa's daughter) "Moon Unit." Jim further urges Elaine, "Try sayin' it backwards!" She does so. Jim's horrified—he always thought it was "Star Child."

Jim decides to give his family a shot, and though no one, at first, wants to go with him to Boston, Alex finally relents. At the Caldwell mansion, Jim is reunited with his overweight, pompous brother, Tom, and his chunky though voluptuous sister, Lila, who seems to suffer from a touch of nymphomania. A butler sees Jim and Alex to the library, where Jim is reunited with his rich, long-suffering father (Victor Buono). Over the mantel is a portrait of Jim's mother, a slim brunette who passed away when Jim was very young; his father gazes at it when he's troubled. (Jim recalls being raised by a nanny, "a fat, sweet-tempered black lady"—who, he adds somewhat improbably, used to call him "Miss Scarlett.") Dad tries to be gracious and understanding with Jim, who through the years has remained his favorite child, but it's difficult.

At dinner, a scene ensues, and Jim's father orders him to leave. Alex follows Mr. Caldwell to the library to try to ease tensions. There he learns that Caldwell must, for tax reasons, leave the bulk of his estate to his kids as soon as possible. He'd wanted so much to give it to Jim rather than to the fatuous others. "You should have seen him as a child," he tells Alex. "I do," Alex answers, tenderly if patronizingly. Dad calls Jim in to offer him the money; Jim doesn't want it. Dad urges Jim to come home and "lead a decent, normal life." Jim's response: " 'Bye, dad." Jim departs, Alex and Caldwell follow, and father and son share a poignant albeit very loud farewell.

OTHER GUESTS:

Walter Olkewicz (Tom Caldwell)
Barbara Deutsch (Lila Caldwell)
Dick Yarmy (Spencer)
John Eames (the butler)

This episode is another of the all-time greats, as so many featuring Jim seem to be. Based to some extent on Chris Lloyd's own experience as a socially prominent scion who rejected college and went to New York's then burnt-out Lower East Side to pursue acting, "Going Home" explores a recurring Brooksian theme of the relationship between father and son. Jim's father—a rich, evidently self-made man, a pragmatist—is bonded to his youngest son in a way he can't explain and doesn't understand. In some ways, it's the reverse of Alex's inexplicable bond with his own father.

By now, too, we've discovered that virtually all of the protagonists were raised by single parents: Jim's mother died when he was young, Alex's father deserted the family early on (episode #23),

Latka's father was killed when Latka was little (episode #11), and Louie was raised by his widowed mother (episode #17). Tony, we discover in episodes #12 and #98, was raised by his mother and sisters while his father was away at sea for months at a time. Bobby's father, we're told in episode #51, apparently has long since passed away. And though Elaine's parents are never mentioned, she abruptly flew to an aunt's bedside in another city on a moment's notice (episode #17)—might that aunt have raised her?

Jim's dad was played by Victor Buono (1938–1987) whose last name, in English, is truly apt: He was *good*. Oscar-nominated for *Whatever Happened to Baby Jane?*, Buono spent most of his later career adding his larger-than-life presence to numerous TV shows and plays. Walter Olkewicz, who played Jim's older brother, Tom, had made memorable appearances on *Barney Miller* and elsewhere before *Taxi*, and had been in the cast of *The Last Resort*. He went on to costar in the series *Wizards and Warriors* (with Jeff Conaway) and has appeared on *Newhart*, *Family Ties*, *Cheers*, and other shows.

#50 ELAINE'S STRANGE TRIANGLE
WRITTEN BY DAVID LLOYD.
DIRECTED BY JAMES BURROWS.

Over beers at Mario's, Elaine is complaining to the cabbies about her rotten love life. They're sympathetic, and when a pleasant-looking, well-dressed man named Kirk (John David Carson) approaches Tony and Elaine, a well-meaning Tony hustles him to their table where he and Alex get Elaine to give Kirk her phone number. Kirk and Elaine wind up going out several times, but one day, Kirk tells Tony privately that he's got a problem that involves Elaine, and he feels real bad about it since he doesn't want to hurt her. When he approached them at Mario's, he confesses, "She wasn't the one I was after." In one of the best comic takes in the series, a quietly stunned Tony politely inquires, "No?" It seems Kirk is bisexual, and, well. . . .

Tony tracks Alex to Mario's and tells him the whole story. Alex is incensed that Kirk would, as he sees it, play with Elaine's emotions, and feels that somebody "should set him straight—as it were." Tony pleads with Alex to go with him to meet Kirk and clear the air. Alex reluctantly agrees, and soon he's sitting nervously in a gay bar with Kirk, waiting for Tony. Kirk tells Alex that everything's OK, that he's told Elaine and she understands. Relieved, Alex orders a beer and starts to relax a little. Then, before he knows it, he's pulled onto the dance floor by a hulking man who cuts a mean step. Trying desperately but politely to get away, Alex finally decides what the heck, and soon he's dancing on the bar surrounded by a clapping throng. Tony comes in and berates Alex for having such a good time when Elaine's heart is broken.

Tag: Alex is sitting dejectedly in the garage with a trophy in front of him. Jim asks what he won it for. Sarcastically, Alex replies it was for making a fool of himself. Jim wonders aloud why no one ever tells *him* about contests like that.

OTHER GUESTS:

Michael Pritchard (the gay dancer, identified as Kenny in the end credits)

ADDITIONAL CREDITS:

Choreography: Jeff Kutash

This gutsy episode is pulled off with humanity and three-dimensionality. The script won a well-deserved Emmy, aided by John David Carson's utterly believable performance. And as over the top as the final big dance number may have been, in context it works as joyously as a similar scene in the movie *Fame*.

Jim Brooks gives much of the credit to hulking dancer Michael Pritchard. "It was a very important bit of casting," he says. "Michael had to be comical without being threatening or offensive, and he and Judd played off each other wonderfully." In 1987, Pritchard, who's both a stand-up comic and a nationally known youth counselor, was the subject of a PBS documentary for his work with kids. And, honest to goodness, he was the opening act when Pope John Paul II addressed the people of San Francisco.

Now, what about Kirk approaching tough-guy Tony? Mario's is by no means a gay bar, but if the Sunshine Cab Co. is in the same Greenwich Vil-

lage neighborhood as the Dover Garage, it almost certainly has a fair number of gay customers. So, accepting Kirk's approach of Tony takes no great leap of faith.

#51 BOBBY'S ROOMMATE

WRITTEN BY EARL POMERANTZ.
DIRECTED BY JAMES BURROWS.

Elaine faces a typically desperate New York situation: Her apartment building has gone co-op (an indigenous version of turning condo), and she not only can't afford to buy in but she can't find another place to rent. She tries explaining to Jim that she's lost her apartment. "Have you looked in Brooklyn?" he asks. "That's where mine usually turns up." Complicating matters, she's dating a guy named Steve and feels nowhere near ready to move in with him. Bobby comes to the rescue: He's going on a month's tour of *Under the Yum-Yum Tree* in Florida and offers her his place while she looks for a new apartment. (Her kids are apparently with their dad.) Elaine accepts and soon has his basement apartment looking better than ever.

But after just a week, Bobby unexpectedly returns. Tony and Alex are at his apartment, visiting Elaine. It seems Bobby was caught fooling around with the costume girl—the director's daughter—on the bus ride to Florida; it took him this long to get back to New York. Obviously not wanting to turn Elaine out into the snow, he offers to let her stay; she can have the bed, he'll sleep on the couch. Elaine says OK, though Alex and Tony get ridiculously upset about the situation.

Sometime later, in the garage, Elaine confides to Alex how sweet and understanding Bobby can be, even though he likes very much to talk about himself. Suddenly she gets a phone call from Steve: He wants to meet her for dinner to talk about something important. She insists on discussing it now. He wants to break up. Dazed about losing another one, she goes home to Bobby's, looking forward to his solace. After Elaine leaves, Bobby strolls into the garage. Alex briefs him on the situation and warns him that she'll be vulnerable and may went some physical companionship. Bobby, genuinely alarmed, promises to be on his guard.

That night at 3 A.M., Elaine wakes him up to talk. She's feeling warm toward her friend and goes to get a "special bottle of wine" from her suitcase. In a panic, Bobby calls Alex for help. Elaine returns with the wine and wonders why Bobby's on the phone. He says he's calling his father; she answers that he told her his father was dead. Bobby finally confesses his fears about the situation. Elaine is insulted: Bobby has completely misinterpreted her actions. Doesn't he value their friendship any better than to think that? Bobby turns sheepish, and things return to an even keel—except for Alex, who's just run twenty-six blocks from his apartment to crash through Bobby's front door in his pajamas and a winter coat. After Elaine chastises them for their chauvinism, the three friends share a toast.

TAXI
▪▪▪▪▪▪▪
160

This story is about paternalism, about otherwise modern men relying on old-fashioned sex roles. Elaine gets upset at her friends because they automatically assume that "frail," "emotional" women need men to protect them from themselves. "Women always lose control, men don't," she challenges them sarcastically. One does suspect, however, that Alex was less upset about Bobby and Elaine rooming together for paternal reasons than for competitive ones: Although he constantly fought it, Alex obviously was attracted to Elaine and even said as much in some episodes. He even acts the same bitchy way when Elaine dates Simka's cousin in episode #99.

Before we see Bobby's apartment, we see a shot of Times Square. This ostensibly is to establish the theatrical mood of Bob's place, but the type of building he lives in—a converted brownstone from the looks of it, with his basement apartment partway below street level—just doesn't exist in that neighborhood. Converted brownstones are all over Manhattan, however, and Jeff Conaway says he always imagined Bobby's place as being on the Upper West Side.

By the way, that look of astonishment on Judd Hirsch's face when he crashes through Bobby's door is real, not acting. The trick door wasn't set up properly to break away: When Judd smashed through it, he *really* smashed through it, pulling it off its frame—and almost pulling himself off his *own* frame!

#52 TONY'S SISTER AND JIM

WRITTEN BY MICHAEL LEESON.
DIRECTED BY JAMES BURROWS.

Monica Banta Douglas (Julie Kavner), one of Tony's sisters, has returned to New York after five years in Spokane, Washington. The wonderfully deadpan Monica was married for four years to, as Tony bitterly puts it, "an Electrolux salesman with every allergy in the book, who painted turtles for relaxation." She's been divorced for about a year and has left her job as a flutist with the Spokane Symphony. Tony had planned, rather fantastically, for her and Alex to meet, fall in love, and get married; when Monica comes by the garage, he prods Alex to ask her to lunch. She accepts, but while she's waiting for him to get ready, she and Jim get to talking—first about Spokane (where Jim says he was born, which is unlikely since his family is Boston Brahmin), then about classical music. It seems Jim's favorite instrument is the gong and his favorite composer is Vivaldi, and soon he and Monica are humming a passage from "The Four Seasons." In response, Louie issues a new rule over the PA system: "I never thought I'd have to say this, but— no Vivaldi in the garage!" Jim and the very droll Monica agree to attend the symphony sometime.

Later, Tony stops by Monica's studio apartment (a $500-a-month sublet), and while he's there Jim phones to make a date. Monica accepts. Tony's horrified—his sister and burnt-out Jim? Jim shows up very late for the date at a fancy French restaurant. He explains that Tony had stopped him at the garage and warned him not to see Monica anymore after tonight. But for now, he's looking forward to it. He starts by haltingly, but quite effectively, ordering an exquisite meal in French. Monica is impressed. "I just learned what I should order," Jim admits. "That was the easy part. The hard part was phoning all over town trying to find a restaurant that serves that."

At the garage a couple of weeks later, Tony apologizes for breaking up Jim's romance, and in ma-

Episode #52: "Tony's Sister (guest star Julie Kavner) and Jim."

cho style offers to let him "plant one" on his face. Jim kisses him. "You're right, Tony, I feel much better." At Monica's apartment, she and Jim are sharing a pleasant evening: She plays the flute and he accompanies her by blowing into a bottle. Tony storms in, picks up Jim to physically throw him out, and gets into a big debate with Monica about maturity and the way family relationships change as everybody gets older. "Ya know," Monica tells him, "you been doin' this your whole life, Tony. Getting yourself into tight spots, then finding out you were wrong when it was too late to know what to do." Tony finally realizes she's right, and he puts Jim down and apologizes—a first, says Monica.

Tag: After dinner, Monica plays flute and Jim plays bottle as before. Tony, listening to the music, picks up a bottle and joins in.

OTHER GUESTS:

Andrew Bloch (the waiter)

It's hard to imagine anyone other than Julie Kavner playing Monica. Her droll, seen-it-all delivery is tempered by her understandable wonderment at being back in New York after all these years and meeting a character like Jim. Monica is independent, knows what she likes, and has enough control over her life to find an average-priced sublet in New York and to pick and choose the men she dates. Kavner's unglamorous looks add immeasurably and help fight the TV stereotype that only youthful model-types à la Joyce Davenport and Claire Huxtable can be strong, together women. Incidentally, that's Kavner herself playing the flute.

Kavner, the longtime companion of *Taxi* cocreator Dave Davis, helped launch the Fox TV network as a costar of *The Tracey Ulman Show*. She'd come to prominence as Valerie Harper's schlumpy, wisecracking sister on *Rhoda*, earning three Emmy nominations before winning the statuette in 1978. Her dry-witted versatility made her part of Woody Allen's floating repertory company, in such films as *Hannah and Her Sisters* and *Radio Days*. And of course, she's the voice of Marge on *The Simpsons*.

This was the last of Michael Leeson's three *Taxi* scripts. He later went on to cocreate *The Cosby Show*.

#53 CALL OF THE MILD
WRITTEN BY KATHERINE GREEN.
DIRECTED BY JAMES BURROWS.

The cabbies are gathered around a TV set, watching Bobby play a lumberjack in a commercial for Brickhauser, "America's boldest beer." Bobby recalls for them the clear air and fantastic scenery of the mountains where the TV spot was filmed. Tony, Alex, and Jim get inspired to go out to the woods like "real men" and rough it—even though it's the dead of winter.

Over the admonitions of Elaine and a laughingly skeptical Louie, they hire a guide to take them to a snowbound hunter's cabin 106 miles away from the nearest phone. (None of them hunt, but that doesn't seem to intrude on their "roughing it" fantasy.) The guide is a bit worried about them, no matter how much they reassure him, so he leaves them a rifle and ammunition and says he'll be back in a day or two to check on them. They scoff and tell him not to come back for a week.

After he's gone, the four adventurers discover there's no electricity in the cabin, and all their groceries will therefore spoil. They decide to store the groceries outside in the frigid snow, where animals get into them during the night. Alex offers to fish, and Jim goes foraging, but to no avail: Alex's catch looks like freshwater sardines. When Sunday arrives and the week is up, they're famished, barely coherent. What's worse, the guide fails to show up. A wild turkey wanders in and out of the cabin, and the guys send Vietnam vet Tony out to kill it. He finds he can't do it, so Alex takes the rifle and sol-

emnly does the job; Jim says a beautiful, thankful prayer over the resulting turkey dinner.

Back at the garage, a frantic Elaine is sick with worry. Then Louie gets a phone call—it's Alex, they're alright. Elaine runs into Louie's cage and grabs the phone. Louie deftly pulls down the shades. The next thing we hear is a yelp from Elaine, followed by a brief struggle. Elaine storms out so hard the blinds shoot back up, and we see Louie hung up to dry.

GUESTS:

Harvey Vernon (the guide)

To be kind, let's say an extremely *basic* plot device is at work here—strand the main characters on a desert island/snowbound cabin/Pirandello netherworld, and see what happens. A big problem with "Call of the Mild" is that we can't believe that Alex, at least, would be so stupid about food, or that the obviously concerned guide wouldn't have pointed out to them the cabin's lack of refrigeration. Granted, you have to set the story in motion, but these kinds of things are pebbles in your shoes. Make that thumbtacks.

This largely ineffectual episode does offer, regardless, some funny variations on tried-and-true sitcom routines—being stranded and trying not to mention food; city slickers in the country; and (very Buster Keatonesque) having no luck attempting to bring in packages.

Then, of course, there was the turkey. "It wasn't particularly well trained," remembers *Taxi* producer Richard Sakai. "I mean, turkeys are pretty stupid." To make it go where they wanted, the producers attached a thin, invisible leash to it. The turkey didn't seem to mind.

54 THY BOSS'S WIFE
WRITTEN BY KEN ESTIN.
DIRECTED BY JAMES BURROWS.

Bobby comes in from mime class and performs the classic "man in a glass box" exercise, which naturally befuddles Jim. Meanwhile, Louie is on the phone with his boss, Mr. McKenzie. McKenzie instructs him that if Mrs. McKenzie shows up, Louie should say her husband's out. The stern-looking Ruth McKenzie (Eileen Brennan) walks in a few minutes later and strides upstairs to have an argument with her husband. To the cabbies' curiosity, Louie chortles in strange glee. He tells them about a garage curse called "Mrs. McKenzie's Revenge," wherein the boss's wife, to get even with her husband, invites some unsuspecting young cabbie to dinner. If the cabbie refuses, she'll tell her husband he came anyway. After that, says Louie, it's like the driver never even existed: "I can't even find his records the next day." They don't buy it. Louie tells them Curly Melnick didn't buy it either until he disappeared.

The cabbies are still scoffing as an exhausted Alex staggers in after working a double shift; they ask him what he thinks about Louie's stupid Curly Melnick story. Just then Alex hears Mrs. McKenzie coming his way; newly energized, he dives into his locker and slams the door behind him. Now the cabbies are worried. Mrs. McKenzie surveys the prospects, finally settling on . . . Louie—if her husband hates the good-looking young ones, she reasons, he'll go crazy about this.

Shortly thereafter, Louie breaks into Alex's apartment, waking him and begging for advice. They can't come up with anything. Lou decides to confront Mrs. McKenzie and talk her out of her plan. But she greets him in a low-cut, clinging black nightgown, and Lou sweats out a struggle between refusing her and diving right in. Mrs. McKenzie flatters him and plays on his insecurities. Then she slips into the bedroom to wait for Louie, who, after initially refusing, literally leaps into bed. When it looks like Lou's finally given in, he and Mrs. McKenzie hear her husband at the door—his flight's been fogged in. He washes up as she tries to get Lou out of there, but he's hidden himself in a panic. The McKenzies decide to make up, and the cabbies don't see Lou around the garage for three days.

Tag: Bobby mimes pulling a rope, with Jim's "help." Bobby explains there really is no rope, and that it is just pantomime. Jim seems to understand, and then immediately "runs into" the glass box that Bobby had mimed the other day. Jim tells

Bobby that he should get rid of it right away—it's dangerous sitting there.

OTHER GUESTS:

Stephen Elliott (Ed McKenzie)

Here, Danny DeVito takes literally the phrase "leap into bed": He bounced himself off a small trampoline to fly in through the McKenzies' bedroom door. The stunt works, supremely visualizing exactly what Lou felt like doing. The bed, incidentally, was beyond king-size—at the cost of more time and trouble than anyone expected, the extra-large bed was specially constructed for the scene.

Eileen Brennan, the perfect mix of stern sensuality, had just made her mark as Goldie Hawn's tough sergeant in *Private Benjamin* (1980), for which she'd earned an Oscar nomination. Her TV work previously had included *Laugh-In*, the Norman Lear satire *All That Glitters*, the miniseries *Black Beauty*, plus starring roles in two short-lived ABC sitcoms, *13 Queens Blvd.* and *A New Kind of Family*. The episode netted Brennan an Emmy nomination for Best Actress in a comedy; that same year, she won as Best Supporting Actress in a comedy for the TV series *Private Benjamin*. Most recently, she costarred in *Off the Rack* with Ed Asner.

By the way, it's inconceivable that the missing Louie stayed under the bed for three days: Mr. McKenzie had to sleep or go to the bathroom *sometime*.

#55 LATKA'S COOKIES

WRITTEN BY GLEN CHARLES AND LES CHARLES.
DIRECTED BY JAMES BURROWS.

Latka's grandmother has died, but far from being mournful, Latka is ecstatic that she's bequeathed him the cookie recipe that made her famous throughout the old country. She's even left him a supply of her secret ingredients. The cabbies all try some of Latka's first batch, but find them virtually inedible. Despite this, Latka takes the opportunity to quit the garage and go into business for himself. Taking a cue from his American entrepreneur idol, cookie king Famous Amos, Latka begins marketing

Mixing a batch of "Latka's Cookies."

'Grandma Gravas' Old Fashioned Oatmeal Cookies.''

Back at the garage, where Louie is having little luck breaking in Jeff as a replacement mechanic, the cabbies find the cookies are growing on them. They also find themselves unusually euphoric and energetic: Bobby bounces across the garage, dancing what he says is the ballet *Afternoon of a Faun;* Alex has spent the night writing an opera, and Elaine is having religious epiphanies. Louie can't quite understand it, until Jim comes in, fresh from a vacation in Omaha. (He'd been hitchhiking to Washington, though it's not clear if he means the city or the state.) Jim samples one of Latka's cookies like a wine connoisseur and declares it's made with the natural source of cocaine: "Coca leaves . . . from South America." Sniffing again, he elaborates: "Peru, I believe. Southern Peru. 'Seventy-four, before the rain." Nibbling and then swirling a piece of cookie in his mouth, he adds, "Poignant, but not overbearing." When he describes the dangerous drug's euphoric and, to some, aphrodisiac effect, Louie springs into action with Elaine, who dazedly tells Louie he has the cutest ears.

After Alex gets wind of all this, he rushes over to Latka's apartment. There he finds a delirious Latka baking and mumbling and baking and speeding and baking and muttering, "twenty-four bags by tomorrow. . . ." Alex grabs him and tells him the secret ingredient is coca; Latka says he understands now why his grandmother was so popular with musicians. Alex offers to stay with Latka until he comes down from his high.

Sometime later, Alex nods off, and Latka hallucinates a visit from celebrity cookie maker Famous Amos (who descends on some very visible wires). Famous has come, he says, because he'd like to tell Latka that money's not a big deal, that the truly important things in life are nature and family and friends: "But I can't 'cause it's a crock. It's a crock! Hey, success is wonderful, man!" And flashing a crumpled bit of currency, he adds, "And cash is outasight! Do *whatever* you can to be successful!" The Reagan-era implication is unmistakable. Amos splits, and Latka excitedly wakes Alex up to tell him about his capitalist revelation. Suddenly he realizes: "Today I am an American."

GUESTS:

Famous Amos (Wally Amos) as himself

Funny and put together well, "Latka's Cookies" is a very daring episode. Alex and Latka eventually realize the dangers and illegality of cocaine: Latka, in fact, finds himself on a mumbling jag that's about to drive him nuts. Yet in the meantime, the short-term euphoric and aphrodisiac effects are very honestly (through exaggeratedly) presented.

"Ed [Weinberger] was pretty adamant about going as far with the cocaine-cookie routine as he could," remembers Chris Lloyd, "and he told the censors at the network it was vital to the joke, which it was." He adds with a chuckle, "He'd push things as far he could." Which no doubt is a signature of Weinberger's great success as a comedy producer.

The episode also gives us a comic turnaround on the usual noble theme of money not buying happiness. Ingeniously employing a self-made and self-proclaimed celebrity (personal-manager-cum-cookie-king Wally "Famous" Amos), the writers address what to many people is "being realistic"—that money *is* the most important thing in life. (The

A GUIDE TO LATKA-ISMS

Actual words and phrases in Latka's language, as transcribed from the episodes and, where available, cross-checked with printed material.

ABEE, DABEE, ICKEE, BICKEE	(Ah′-bee, Dah′-bee, Ik′-ee, Bik′-ee)	One, two, three, four
ADEE-FEEBEE	Ah′-dee fee′-bee)	Revolution
ANEE	(Ah′-nee)	Now
BEEMPO	(Beem′-po)	Woman
BLEEKO	(Blee′-ko)	Look (imperative, to look)
BREFNISH	(Bref′-nish)	A syrupy, green, alcoholic native drink
BUSHKALAY	(Boosh′-ka′lay)	"Congratulations!"
BYEFNIK	(Byef′-nik)	Eye
CATCH NEE VA?	(Katch′-neevah′)	Whom do you save (rescue)?
CATCHNEE LIMORSEE?	(Katch′-nee Lih-mour′-see)	How bad can it be?
CLAKCLUK	(Klak′-kluk)	Chicken
FORMWITZ	Form′-witz)	Something
GEWIRTZAL		A surrogate who must propose for a groom-to-be
GLOB	(Glahb)	To disappear
GLOBNIK	(Glahb′nik)	To pretend an event or occurrence has never taken place
GRETCHNEEPA	(Gretch′-nee′pah)	Good-bye
GROCK	(Grock)	An eight-string instrument
IBEEDA	(Ih′-bee-dah′)	1. That is right 2. Please
KAKBOLT	(Kak′-balt)	Whore
KRIMKAPOOSH		Premenstrual Syndrome (PMS)
LAVORSH	(Lah-voursh)	To work
LEEKA	(Lee′-kah)	Skinny
MERTZIG	(Murt′-zig)	The traditional imparting of wisdom from the man's mother to the prospective bride
NECREMENT	(Neh′-krehment)	Providence; fate
NIK NIK	(Nik Nik)	1. Love 2. Make love (colloquial)
PEETA	(Pee′-tah)	Yes
PLOTZ	(Plotz)	Sit (imperative, to sit)
POOSHKA	(Poosh′-kah)	Met (past tense of, to meet)
REKLAMENTEE	(Rek′-lah-men-tee)	Stay (imperative, to stay)
SOLA	(So′-lah)	To leave be
SHLOOGEL	(Shloo′-guhl)	A tradition in which newly married couples share their happiness by setting up their friends with perfect matches
VEESYANAL	(Vees′-yah-nahl′)	Raised (past tense of, to raise) one's voice
YAKABYE	(Yak′-a-buy)	Fire
YAKTABE	(Yahk′-ta-bay)	Rear end; ass
YARGO	(Yar′-go)	Eat (imperative, to eat)
YATKOS?	(Yaht′-kohs)	Who?

euphemism for that is usually "fiduciary responsibility" or "looking out for number one.") Hopefully, the crass sentiments expressed by Amos in Latka's hallucination come off as the satire they were intended to be.

#56 THE TEN PERCENT SOLUTION

WRITTEN BY PAT ALLEE.
DIRECTED BY JAMES BURROWS.

Bobby has just lost another acting gig—he wasn't the right physical type for the role. Casting directors want earthy types, he loudly complains—guys like Tony. Tony, naturally, takes this to heart and decides he wants to try his hand at acting. Bobby thinks the whole thing is ridiculous, but Tony drops by Bobby's apartment and cajoles him into becoming his manager.

At the garage later, the two of them practice lines from a script. Latka sees this and asks Bobby to be *his* agent, too, and proceeds to do a bit from an Italian movie, *Here Come the Huns,* that was shot in his native village. Bobby passes. Just then a call comes in for Robert Wheeler Management. Bobby plays it cool, telling the casting director on the other end that Tony is up for a part in Jane Fonda's new picture, but that he'll squeeze in this audition. Bobby hangs up, excited for Tony; Tony, a bit dim, wants to know more about this "Jane Fonda movie."

At the audition, Bobby and Tony trade lines from the movie, a drama about an Italian father and his sons. Bobby gives it his all; Tony gamely but woodenly handles his one-word lines. Incredibly, the two producers are satisfied, and Tony gets the part. Bobby's shocked, and his already shaky faith in the acting profession pretty much dissolves. Yet Tony's first day on the movie's Long Island set turns out to be his last. Even though most of the people were nice and he got to watch George C. Scott eat a jelly doughnut, the director began saying things like, "not right for the part" and "over my dead body." Bobby's faith is restored: Tony's rejection, he tells his friend grandly, means that quality and integrity aren't dead. "Gee," Tony answers, visibly impressed by his martyrdom.

Tag: A subplot throughout the episode concerned Louie's and Jeff's battles with a monstrous cockroach. Finally, Louie sets up hamburger bait at the end of a fishing pole. Alex tells him he's crazy, but as Louie describes the vicious insect, we see the fishing pole bend and the line finally break. Louie and Alex beat a hasty retreat.

GUESTS:

Sarina C. Grant (casting assistant)
Jim Staskel (Arthur Kramer, a movie producer at the audition)
Ed Weinberger (Jerry Lowell, a movie producer at the audition)

"No, I never felt that episode mimicked my career," Tony Danza maintains. "The only time I felt that was when we would do boxing shows." This episode *did,* however, mimic the career of *Taxi* producer Ed Weinberger, who, in one of his many cameo and bit-part appearances, appropriately plays a producer.

#57 ZEN AND THE ART OF CAB DRIVING

WRITTEN BY GLEN CHARLES AND LES CHARLES.
DIRECTED BY WILL MACKENZIE.

Jim, in cab #321, picks up two businessmen at the airport (Kennedy, because of the International Arrivals sign) and overhears them discussing a self-help theory called Dynamic Perfection. Newly inspired, Jim decides to take charge of his life. Step one: To become the perfect cab driver. And darned if he doesn't do so. When his shift ends, he immediately goes on another and eventually brings in a whopping $373. On another evening, he treats a Carnegie Hall–bound passenger to coffee, sandwiches, and a Sinatra retrospective (of sorts—Jim does the singing). Louie is ecstatic, but after a few weeks of this, Jim gives it up: He says he's made the money he needs to achieve his *real* goal.

He invites the cabbies up to his place to share his conquest with him. They arrive to find a huge sheet covering something mysterious. He unveils it, and they see . . . a complete audio/video system! There are televisions, VCRs, videodisc players, cable, and video games. To the astonished and disappointed cabbies, however, all this is "just television." They can't believe this is what Jim has worked so hard for. Jim can't even believe it himself at first: "What am I, nuts?" But then he collects himself and explains that he's bought his ticket to the global village: 24-hour news, movies, sports, everything! "The whole world comes through these screens. I watch the great events of this world. Just this afternoon, I was watching the Delaware legislature debating whether they should call themselves Delawarians or Delawarites. Personally, I'm rooting for the Delawarians—although the Delawarites put up a good argument. (Pause) Delaweenians didn't stand a chance."

The cabbies are still unimpressed. They get up to go, and Jim dejectedly turns on the audio/video bank. Then the mesmerizing power of television takes over: Bobby sees *Apocalypse Now* on one set and decides to stay and watch it. On another set, Elaine sees a symphony. Latka gets drawn in by *Submarine Command* with William Bendix; Tony, by a New York Islanders hockey game. Alex is disgusted by all this. Television is second-hand experience, he says, and presents a false picture of reality. "Real Life" is the only honest experience, he pontificates. Just then, a Delaware state assemblyman announces that henceforth the people of Delaware shall be known as Delawarians. Alex, as if he'd seen an umpire's bad call, loudly objects. He, too, gets sucked in by the simultaneous thrill and danger of video voyeurism.

GUESTS:

Nicholas Hormann (passenger talking about Dynamic Perfection)
Michael Mann (his friend; not the Michael Mann who is the executive producer of *Miami Vice*)
Jim McKrell (Carnegie Hall–bound passenger)

This is one of the most insightful and powerful of all the *Taxi* episodes—not so much for Jim's espousal of cure-all pop psychology, but for the forceful symbolism of Americans as media junkies. It is a rare episode of a TV series that dares to examine its own addictive nature, or the way television trivializes rioting, slavery, and war by cutting these things into "visual bites" and oversimplifying complex situations—and conversely, as the episode

shows, ascribing unjustified importance to trivial events ("Delawarians" versus "Delawarites"). It can't be said of many television shows—that an episode demands you read up on it. Two suggestions are *Demographic Vistas* by the insightful and entertaining social scientist David Marc, and the cleverly titled perennial, *Four Arguments for the Elimination of Television* by Jerry Mander. This episode's title, by the way, is based on that of one other book: the popular philosophical novel, *Zen and the Art of Motorcycle Maintenance*.

This was the second episode of *Taxi* not directed by Burrows; filling in was the respected Will Mackenzie, who among other things later directed the Shakespearean parody and the black-and-white *film noir* homage episodes of *Moonlighting*. As an actor, he played the boyfriend-husband of Carol, the receptionist, on *The Bob Newhart Show*. Mackenzie recalls his episode of *Taxi* as "a tremendous break for me. That *Taxi* led to several *Best of the West*s, and that really gave my directing career a boost." He'd gotten the assignment, he says, because "I'd known Jimmy [Burrows] when I was an actor in New York and he was a stage manager. We'd become friends, and [years later] he went to [Ed] Weinberger and said, 'let's use this guy.' " Mackenzie recently made his feature-film debut directing Mark Harmon in *Worth Winning*.

By the way, *Submarine Command* (1951) is a real movie that did indeed star William Bendix and William Holden—maybe "Bendix" sounds funnier.

#58 ELAINE'S OLD FRIEND

WRITTEN BY SUSAN JANE LINDNER AND NANCY LANE.

DIRECTED BY JEFF CHAMBERS

At the airport, Elaine drops an inebriated fare who says he's late for his plane. "Bu' thass OK," he slurs, putting on his cap, "I'm the pilot." While Elaine chews that over, a rich-looking blonde gets in and directs the cab to ritzy 63rd Street and Park Avenue. The woman spies Elaine's picture on the taxi license and suddenly starts up a cheer for East Side High School. Turns out it's Elaine's old high-school rival, Mary Parker (Martha Smith), who was

Episode #58: Elaine and Alex as make-believe lovers in "Elaine's Old Friend."

beau, and says he'd love for the four of them to get together Saturday night. Come Saturday at a fancy restaurant, "Bill" ravishes Elaine with his affection. He orders the best champagne, tells a touching story of how they met, dances with her, and in general behaves like the perfect romantic. Elaine is mesmerized; Mary is properly jealous.

Later that evening, Alex sees Elaine to her apartment (in a continuity error, still #5B—see below). She teasingly asks Alex if he wasn't maybe feeling a little romantic toward her for real. Alex scoffs at the idea. Him and Elaine? Don't be ridiculous. To prove it, he kisses her goodnight. See? No sparks. Elaine retaliates with a kiss that would curl Casanova's toes. Well? Nothing, Alex replies—in a voice about six octaves higher than usual. Her conquest complete, she smiles and rather abruptly bids him goodnight as he dazedly tries to decide what to do.

OTHER GUESTS:

John Considine (Michael)
Myron Natwick (maître d')
John Yates (inebriated pilot)

Cutting in half that famous *Honeymooners* episode, "A Man's Pride," wherein Ralph and his old high-school rival each pretend at a fancy dinner to be something they're not, "Elaine's Old Friend" has an unusual but probably realistic moral in America's free-market frenzy in the eighties—it's *not* alright to be a cabdriver, and money and success *are* important. It seems otherwise, at first, because the rich Michael and Mary aren't as in love as or as romantic as Elaine and "Bill"—but then, "Bill" is a sham! He doesn't exist. In real life, Michael and Mary *are* the happy couple, and it's *Elaine* who has the hard life. What's the story here? Money *can* buy happiness? Cabdrivers and cooks and clerks have to pretend to be something they're not in order to pretend to be happy? On top of that, we also see sexy Elaine's brutal teasing of Alex at the very end. It's an ugly, insecure side of her for which the writers deserve a pat on the back. Like the rest of us, and like too few TV characters, she's part dark and part light. For all its laughs, this is a very disturbing episode.

Martha Smith had recently made the leap from soap operas (she was one of the actresses playing

elected homecoming queen while Elaine O'Connor became head cheerleader and took the lead in the "senior class play."

Mary asks how Elaine is doing, which is just a windup to her telling Elaine that she's head of an advertising agency, owns a co-op in Manhattan, and has a boyfriend, Michael, who is a rich international lawyer. Elaine, somewhat stung, makes up a story about her own wonderful, witty, romantic boyfriend—Columbia University professor Bill Board. (It was almost Carmen Ghia, she tells Alex later.) Mary insists the four of them get together, but Elaine puts her off.

Later, at the garage, the cabbies talk about high school. Bobby says he was voted "most talented." Tony says he had perfect attendance in his junior year and was president of the biology club. Mary phones, still wanting to set up a date. Elaine, feeling hurt, starts to demur, but Alex suddenly grabs the phone from her, introduces himself as Elaine's

Sandy Horton on *Days of Our Lives*) to prime time, having starred with Debbie Allen in a 1979 TV movie/pilot, *Ebony, Ivory and Jade.* She later played Francine Desmond on *Scarecrow and Mrs. King.* John Considine is another soap veteran (*Another World* and the 1969–72 *Bright Promise*) who's lately appeared on *Remington Steele* and other prime-time shows.

This was the only *Taxi* episode by the Lane/ Lindner scriptwriting team. Lindner became a story editor, with the first season of Flip Wilson's *Charlie and Company* to her credit. The very attractive Nancy Lane doubles as an actress, having had a recurring role on *Rhoda* and costarring as film-editor Andrea Lewin in *The Duck Factory* (which also featured MTM veteran Jay Tarses and *Taxi* guest star Jack Gilford).

As for the continuity problem: Elaine lived in apartment #5B in episode #42, but then lost that apartment by episode #51 and was forced to room with Bobby. Now she's in #5B again—and since the hallway exterior is the same, it's *not* a different apartment #5B. Really, now. Even just switching around the number and the letter would have made a difference. But hey, let's stretch things and suggest that maybe her divorce settlement came through while she was rooming with Bobby, and she was able to buy her apartment after all.

#59 THE COSTUME PARTY

WRITTEN BY DAVID LLOYD.
DIRECTED BY JAMES BURROWS.

Bobby finds an expensive-looking briefcase in the back of his cab. He'd like to return it to its owner, but it's locked, and there doesn't seem to be any way to open it and look for some ID. Louie, however, using the near-mystical means of an expert pack rat, gets it open. Inside, the cabbies find an appointment book that apparently belongs to somebody in the entertainment field. In fact, the mysterious Mr. "N. Z." looks like a personal friend of Woody Allen's and has even been invited to a costume party that weekend on a yacht. The starstruck cabbies decide to crash—they'll be in costume anyway, they figure, so it'll work.

On Saturday night, Bobby shows up as Cyrano de Bergerac. Elaine comes in looking smashing in a strapless Scarlett O'Hara gown. Jim wears funny glasses. Alex, Tony, and Latka arrive in drag as the Andrews Sisters, respectively, Patti, Maxene, and LaVerne. They start to mingle. Bobby, who gets seasick, thinks he threw up on Broadway producer Hal Prince. Latka gets an autograph from someone he thinks is Henry Kissinger, but who turns out to be a nonentity named Gus Bates. It suddenly dawns on the cabbies that maybe this isn't a yachtful of celebrities after all. In fact, the party turns out to be thrown by Neal Zuckerman, a realtor.

The disappointed cabbies prepare to leave, when Alex abruptly stops them. Why go? Just because there are no celebrities? He tells them that these people are just as worthy of their respect. Alex nobly ventures over to Gus Bates, and, after a brief introduction, decides that maybe these people are too boring to party with after all.

Tag: Still in costume, the cabbies have brought a pizza back with them to the garage. The "Andrews Sisters" sing a bit of "Bei Mir Bist du Schoen" to try to cheer everybody up.

GUESTS:

Louis Guss (Maxie Melcher, a cabbie retiring after forty-one years with Sunshine Cab. Louie presents him with a calendar.)
Hector Britt (Gus Bates)

The cult of celebrity: Maybe famous people really *are* intrinsically more interesting than everyday folks. But take it from the authors, who do plenty of celebrity and noncelebrity interviews: Being famous doesn't make a dull person any less dull, and some of the wittiest and most admirable people in our acquaintance are unknowns. Incidentally, Hector Britt, who plays Kissinger-clone Gus Bates, is a professional Kissinger-impersonator from Ron Smith Lookalikes. The cult of celebrity can't be made any more tangible than by having people make a living playing off it.

"Bei Mir Bist du Schoen (Means That You're Grand)" was not only a smash for the forties vocal trio The Andrews Sisters, but also the first hit for the legendary tunesmith Sammy Cahn, who with Saul Chapin translated Sholom Secunda's popular Yiddish song.

#60 OUT OF COMMISSION

WRITTEN BY SAM SIMON.

DIRECTED BY JAMES BURROWS.

Alex helps a bloodied, beaten Tony into the locker room after a boxing match against a middleweight nicknamed "Shotgun." The loss was worse than usual: a knockout in the first round. The examining doctor seems exceptionally concerned, prompting Alex to ask what's wrong with Tony. The doctor responds: "He leads with his right." It turns out that this is Tony's third knockout loss in his last five fights, and his fourteenth in a career of eight wins and twenty-four losses. The doctor tells Tony he's going to recommend the New York State Athletic Commission suspend Tony's license. Tony rebels—boxing is all he has. Despite this, he's stripped of his license. Louie is almost as upset as Tony: without him to bet against, Lou has lost a major source of income.

Sometime later, Tony's manager, Lou-Lou Pantusso, comes by the garage with alarming news: Tony has bought the license of a boxer named Kid Rodriguez and plans to fight under that name. In fact, he tells the cabbies, Tony's fighting in an hour-and-a-half at the Brooklyn Armory. Louie's ecstatic—money time!

At the Armory, where "Kid Rodriguez" is the third bout on the card, Lou-Lou tries everything he can to make Tony (who's sporting a fake mustache) miss the fight. Alex, Bobby, and Jim show up to help; Bobby gets the bright idea of tearing apart what he thinks are Tony's trunks, but which actually belong to a hulking black bruiser who's not amused (but who accepts cash).

Tony explains to Bobby why he's going through all this when he knows "I ain't no great fighter. I can't even say I had one great fight. Not even one great round. But there've been moments. Y'see, not a day goes by when I don't think about this fight in Jersey. In the second round I throw a three-punch combination—left, right, left hook. It was perfect," He continues wistfully, "I heard the crowd gasp. For that one second, Tony Banta was as great as Muhammad Ali or Sugar Ray or *any* of them! I always thought that maybe I'd put a few of those moments together someday and have that

Episode #60: Tony in the desperate guise of Kid Rodriguez, as Alex looks on in "Out of Commission."

great fight. I mean, when I look back on it, I feel kinda special. Without it, I'm just a cabdriver. I'm just a lousy cabdriver." Bobby points out career cabbie Alex nearby. Tony starts to apologize, but Alex says it's OK. "I'm not really a cabdriver," he assures Tony. "I'm just waiting for something better to come along. You know. Like death."

On that note, the fight gets under way—Kid Rodriguez, "The Pride of San Juan," 23 wins, 8 losses, 162 pounds, versus Alberto "El Gato" Martinez, 14 wins, 6 losses, 159 pounds. All the while, Alex keeps trying to talk Tony out of boxing. He finally convinces him by saying that the way Tony had gotten hurt, all fighters get hurt, and would big-hearted Tony want to do that to other fighters? It's a specious argument, but Tony finally goes along. As the bell rings and the round starts and Martinez goes after him, Tony tries to explain he's giving up. Understandably, he can't get Martinez to listen. He starts fighting back and finally decks the other boxer—a knockout! But Tony was serious, and he leaves the ring, thereby losing by default. The referee raises the arm of the unconscious Martinez to declare him the winner. Tony, in his locker room, hangs up his gloves.

GUESTS:

Al Ruscio (Dr. Webster)
Carmine Caridi (Lou-Lou Pantusso)
Jessie Goins (Shotgun)
Mauricio Aldana (Alberto ''El Gato'' Martinez)
Vince Delgado (referee)
Jon St. Elwood (boxer whose trunks Bobby rips)
Jimmy Lennon (as himself, the ring announcer)

The first script by future *Taxi* coproducer Sam Simon came out of a real-life tactic by desperate boxers. ''I think if you went back and looked at *Sports Illustrated* for the week I wrote the script,'' says Simon, ''they had a cover story on violence in boxing and the prevalence of brain damage, and how there're fighters under license who shouldn't be. I just immediately spun a story off of it.'' It must have hit close to home—Danza himself, in his real-life middleweight career—was twice temporarily suspended for injuries.

It hit close to home for Danza in other ways, too. ''The whole monologue about the two-three combination, that's right out of my life,'' he confides. ''I helped write that, because it was *so* close to me. Ed [Weinberger] was great that way, great that he'd let you do that.''

Sam Simon, after coproducing *Taxi,* went on to coproduce the third season of *Cheers.* Lately, he's been working on screenplays and consulting on *It's Garry Shandling's Show* and *The Tracey Ullman Show.*

By the way, is it mere coincidence that ''Kid Rodriguez'' is also the name of a boxer in Stanley Kubrick's seminal film, *Killer's Kiss?*

#61 BOBBY AND THE CRITIC

WRITTEN BY BARRY KEMP.
DIRECTED BY JAMES BURROWS.

Bobby's gleeful: The one-man play in which he's starring, *Charles Darwin Tonight,* has made enough money its first two weeks for his theater group to actually buy a newspaper ad. As he sits in the garage, showing the cabbies the ad and getting worked up over a prominent critic's scathing review of another play, Tony comes in with some fast food and

some instant-win contest cards; Latka finds he's won ''a complete men's wardrobe.''

Meanwhile, Bobby has gotten so worked up over the critic, John Bowman, that he writes a vicious, insulting letter to the editor about him. After getting the anger out of his system, Bobby realizes he might be committing career suicide and chucks the letter into the garbage can. After the cabbies leave, however, Louie uncrumples the venomous missive and sends it on its way. The newspaper publishes it, and when the cabbies wonder who would have retrieved and mailed Bobby's letter, Louie proudly accepts credit. Bobby, furious, tries to blowtorch his way into the dispatcher-cage, but just then his agent calls to congratulate him on his courageous stand. Louie, in fact, tells him his plan may have backfired: Congratulatory messages have been coming in all morning. So has one other call, which Louie gleefully delivers to the happy Bobby in pantomime: John Bowman is coming to review Bobby's play tonight. Heh heh heh.

That night, during intermission, Bobby tells Alex backstage that the play stinks, that his acting stinks, that his career is over. Tony and Latka (dressed in a newly won yachting outfit) come to wish Bobby luck, to say how much they like the play, and to leave early before they start yawning; Jim comes in to pronounce the drama wonderfully hilarious. Bobby, who evolves from a middle-aged Darwin to an elderly one in the course of the ninety-minute play, goes back on stage gamely for part two—to Jim's well-meaning laughter and, he's sure, Bowman's approbation.

Afterward, at Mario's, Bobby continues his negative appraisal of his performance. Then Bowman (John Harkins) himself walks in; he was told at the theater that he might find Bobby at Mario's. At the bar Bowman has a word with the erstwhile Darwin. He pulls out a freshly written review that dismisses the play but lauds Bobby—a star in the making, a breath of hope for American theater. Stunned, Bobby humbly apologizes to Bowman for his letter and, in his mind, sees the start of a bright new phase in his acting career—up to the moment Bowman shreds the review in front of him, explaining that ''a bad review could make you a hero, a good review could make you a star. No review will keep you anonymous. And you can keep on acting in church basements and supermarket openings and your own mirror for the rest of your life. Ahhh! I enjoyed seeing you, Mr. Wheeler.'' He sighs and remarks, ''I had a *wonderful* evening.''

As Bowman starts to leave, Bobby falls to the floor mumbling futile thoughts of taping together the pieces. Then he realizes he is on his hands and knees groveling, and he stands and announces to Bowman that the man and all he stands for is a fraud, that powerful celebrity critics such as he do theater a disservice. ''It doesn't matter what some critic thinks,'' Bobby proclaims. ''It only matters what *I* think of my performance!'' Bowman leaves with his victory compromised. The cabbies cheer Bobby and agree in unison—especially Jim, who proudly reminds him, ''And *you* thought you stunk!''

This episode presents another strong theme, ably delivered. There are critics—who analyze a work of art within a social-historical context and look through the years, down the ages: And there are reviewers—who tell you whether the flick at the local mall is worth five bucks (or six, or seven) in terms of immediate gratification. Then there are those who try to be both. They not only damn the long-term significance of, say, a new play, but tell you how stupid you are if you pay money for what may well be entertaining to audiences unfamiliar and thus unoffended by its obvious eighteenth-century antecedents and the shadow of the definitive 1957 version. John Bowman (whose name bears a striking resemblance to the brilliant but deadly cynical *New York Magazine* critic John Simon) is one of these. Yet unlike Simon, who's at least willing to support a fresh young face because he loves theater so much, Bowman is vindictive to the extent that he'd destroy Bobby's career out of sheer spite. But what the hell—what with all the publicity (and Bobby's many witnesses at Mario's), maybe Frank Rich of the *Times* or Clive Barnes of the *Post* would've wandered on down to Bobby's play. On the other hand, maybe Bobby really did stink and Bowman wrote he was great just to get his goat.

John Harkins is one of the most familiar faces on

television, though he's only been a regular cast member on one show, the Weinberger/Daniels creation, *Doc*. Usually playing smug lawyers and pompous businessmen, he's appeared in about two dozen TV movies and countless films and TV shows, perhaps most notably in the Alger Hiss TV-docudrama *Concealed Enemies*.

#62 LOUIE'S MOTHER
WRITTEN BY KATHERINE GREEN.
DIRECTED BY JAMES BURROWS.

It's raining and Louie loves it—lots of people need cabs. Adding to his glee, he announces over the loudspeaker, is that he's installed his mother, with whom he's lived all these years, in a nursing home. Now he's throwing a party to celebrate, and none of the ''miserable cabbies'' are invited—except for Alex, who agrees to go out of morbid curiosity. When Alex arrives at Louie's fourth-floor apartment, the party consists of a half-eaten pizza and three catatonic scuzzos on the couch—Lyle, Huey, and Daytona Dave. Louie met them, he explains, at the scene of a sidewalk heart attack—they were the last four to leave. Yet at 7:30, even these party animals depart. Alex wants to go also, but when the two of them are alone, Lou breaks down and confesses that he hadn't sent his mother away—*she* left *him*. Out of pity, as he makes it understood, Alex invites Louie out for a beer.

In the garage sometime later, Louie is a zombie. The cabbies feel so sorry for him that they actually invite him, for the first time ever, to play poker with them. Unfortunately, Alex, who stepped away from the table for a moment, inquires as to who bet last: ''Who raised Louie?'' he asks. Lou's ears burn. ''Who raised Louie? *Ma* raised Louie!'' he sobs. Alex snaps him out of it. The good old mean, vile Lou is back and sneering as he stomps off to go get ''my mommy.''

At the nursing home, Lou knocks on his mother's door (Room #14). He asks her to come home. In Italian, the tough old lady resists. She asks him about all his girl friends—this Elaine Nardo and this Susan Anton? Lou finally confesses to her, ''Ma, I'm a lonely man.'' In Italian, he tells her

Episode #62: "Louie's Mother."
"Who raised Louie? Ma raised Louie!"

he loves her. "If I come home, will you be nice to me?" she asks. Louie pauses, then answers truthfully, "For a while." She comes out, blows smoke in his face, and the two of them depart together.

GUESTS:

Julia DeVito [Danny DeVito's mother] (Gabriella De Palma; first name given in end credits, not in episode)

Note: The actors playing Lyle, Huey, and Daytona Dave are uncredited.

With its echoes of *Marty,* Paddy Chayefsky's live TV drama and later movie, this episode is one of two that give us the strongest insight about Louie De Palma. (The other being "Louie Goes Too Far," episode #77, in which he finally breaks through the defensive wall that makes him so gross and insensitive. He doesn't become much *less* gross and insensitive right away, but he gets on the right road.) Here, he admits to his mother, with whom he lives and who knows him well, how empty his life really is.

In real life, DeVito's late mother was just as feisty as Mrs. De Palma. As Danny tells it, his ma—seventy-seven at the time—took to stardom with the aplomb of the late Clara Peller. "Weinberger said, 'Let's give it to your mother—she's gotta play the part!' It was Weinberger's idea. He called me into the office and asked how I felt about it. I was stunned. He asked me to call her. I told him, '*You*

call her and ask her!' So he talked to her, explained the role, etc., told her it would be a lot to learn. And she told *him,* 'Hey, I can do dialogue!' So he hired her, picked her up in a limousine, brought her to the studio. She was smoking like a fiend, hadda have her cigarettes in the room. He got her set up with a nice reclining chair since she has arthritis. And she wanted a TV so she could watch her soap operas—her stories, as she calls them. They gave her everything she wanted. She did better than me!"

#63 LOUIE BUMPS INTO AN OLD LADY

WRITTEN BY DAVID LLOYD.
DIRECTED BY JAMES BURROWS.

Louie has the hots for the pretty new female cabbie, a blonde named Janine. Prompted by her feeble booking receipts and her cooing innocence at not being able to grasp the fine art of cabdriving, Louie offers to take her for a spin and personally show her the ropes. Moments later, however, a sputtering, condescending Louie carries the injured Edith Tremayne (Iris Korn) into the garage, having apparently just struck her as she stepped off a curb. In rather typical sitcom fashion, Louie rents her a wheelchair, buys her roses, and figuratively wines and dines her, hoping to head off a civil suit. No go. Edith sweetly tells him she hopes her $1 million lawsuit won't affect their friendship.

Alex has noticed something strangely familiar about Edith. As Louie is discovering that Sunshine Cab won't spring for any legal expenses, Alex remembers that a cabdriver named Sonny Bergmeyer ran over the same lady a couple of years earlier. Sonny discovered she was a con artist, and Alex cuts a deal with Lou that he'll find Sonny and get him to testify if Lou will act more civilized.

The day of the trial, early-bird Jim overhears Edith and her lawyer talking. It seems that this time, at least, Edith's injury isn't faked: She's really broken her leg in two places. Sonny Bergmeyer has heard for whom his testimony was intended and has decided not to come, so Louie goes for broke. Dismissing his lawyer, he starts questioning Edith himself and stages a disastrous demonstration of her "faked" injury—pushing her wheelchair down a flight of stairs (shades of *Kiss of Death!*).

Tag: Alex, at the garage, informs the cabbies that Edith is OK. He has a list of cabbies she's conned and will try to contact them in order to get Lou out of jail. Or, he wonders, will he?

OTHER GUESTS:

Lane Brody (Janine)
Sam De Fazio (Lou's lawyer)
Joe Medalis (Edith's lawyer)
Jay Flash Riley (the judge)

This is one of the worst, most sitcomy episodes of *Taxi*. The less said. . . .

#64 LATKA THE PLAYBOY

WRITTEN BY GLEN CHARLES AND LES CHARLES.
DIRECTED BY JAMES BURROWS.

There's another monster cockroach at Sunshine Cab, or maybe the old one is back. As Louie describes it to the exterminator, "I'm tellin' ya, he barks at the mailman." Meanwhile, at Mario's Latka is having problems of his own. He's attracted to a pretty woman named Karen (Robin Klein), a frequent patron, but has never felt comfortable enough to approach her. But today, in his broken English and his overalls, he decides to give it a try. Politely but predictably, she shoots him down. Bobby self-righteously decides to give her a piece of his mind for that and winds up driving her home instead.

Latka decides to embark on a crash course in swinging Americanism: He takes some time off and immerses himself in *Playboy* and other magazines, and even (apparently) goes to sleep listening to English language audiotapes. In a foreshadowing of the split personalities Latka develops later on, his plan works too well. He loses his accent, begins wearing designer clothes, and turns into a fatuous lounge lizard named Vic Ferrari. At Mario's, as the cabbies watch, Latka/Vic picks up the once-unapproachable Karen.

Some days later, at the garage, Karen calls up Vic. Vic tells Bobby, who answered the phone, to lie and say he's out. Alex gets so disgusted by his dishonesty and boorishness that he tells Vic off. That night, Vic goes to Alex's apartment (#A2). He tells Alex he doesn't want to be Vic anymore, he wants Latka back. With Alex's urging, Latka comes back completely, broken English and all—or does he?

OTHER GUESTS:

George Wendt (the exterminator)
T. J. Castronova (Tommy, the bartender at Mario's)

Andy Kaufman's Tony Clifton was a parody of showbiz glitz and self-important celebrityhood. His Vic Ferrari narrowed the distance a bit between the audience and the despicable character: Vic was merely the embodiment of all the worst stereotypical traits of the American man. Less obvious is the fact that Karen, by falling for him, embodies a trait of the American woman that self-help authors make a mint writing about—falling for rats because their self-image won't allow them to accept the love of genuinely nice guys. Vic would make return appearances in "Mr. Personalities" (episode #70), "Louie's Mom Remarries" (episode #74), "Louie Goes Too Far" (episode #77), "Tony's Lady" (episode #80), and "Simka Returns" (episode #81). Latka's other multiple personalities include a cowboy and Alex Reiger (episode #70) and, in a bit cut from syndication, the upper-class Brit Sir Geoffrey Hypen-Hill ("Of Mice and Tony," episode #75).

Second City comedy-troupe alumnus George Wendt went on to costar as the underemployed accountant Norm Peterson in *Cheers*. He's also appeared in several movies lately, among them *Gung Ho* and *Fletch*. Before *Cheers*, he costarred in the short-lived CBS series *Making the Grade*.

#65 JIM THE PSYCHIC

STORY BY HOLLY HOLMBERG BROOKS.
TELEPLAY BY BARRY KEMP.
DIRECTED BY JAMES BURROWS.

A very distraught Jim arrives at the garage with good news and bad news. It seems that Jim has psychic dreams that often come true, and he's dreamed about Alex. The good news is that a beautiful blonde will fall for Alex. The bad news is that Thursday night at 7 P.M., Alex will be alone in his apartment; drink a glass of water; someone will mistake him for a woman; he'll be dressed in a green shirt and catcher's mask and dancing the cancan. "And then comes the crazy part!" There will be a knock on the door—and then . . . the end. Elaine wonders what Jim means: the end of the dream or the end of Alex? Both, sobs Jim. Pragmatic Alex doesn't buy it, but the cabbies tell him that Jim's predictions have a habit of coming true.

Later at Mario's, the good news does indeed happen: There's a brawl, and an attractive blonde named Peggy literally falls into Alex's lap. On Thursday Alex tells the cabbies how happy he feels about dating Peggy. He won't let Jim's "superstitions" bother him; nevertheless, the cabbies are worried. Louie even shows up at Alex's apartment (#A2) that night to get him out of there before the terror arrives. (Judging from the fact his apartment is in a high rise and that we see many cabs rushing back and forth on the street, Alex lives in Manhattan.) Yet Alex, despite Lou's entreaties, refuses to budge. This is crazy, he says, eating some munchies. Just crazy, he continues, coughing as the munchies go down his throat badly. Crazy, he says again as he quickly swallows some water to relieve his throat. "Ah HAHHH!" Louie screams, pointing at the water glass. "It's comin' true, Reiger!"

Alex doesn't buy it and starts to tell Louie how annoyed he is when the phone rings. It's a wrong number; somebody calling for "Mary." "No, this isn't Mary," Alex snaps. "Do I sound like a Mary?" He hangs up and starts to address Lou again, when it suddenly hits him—somebody mistook him for a woman. That's enough for Lou: He wants Reiger out. But Alex (in a nice illustration of the free will versus determinism debate) decides that if he gives in to some prediction of "fate," he'll betray his most steadfast beliefs.

He runs into his bedroom and returns with a green pullover shirt and a catcher's mask, and to Louie's horror starts dancing the cancan. The chimes of Alex's grandmother clock sound seven o'clock. Nothing happens. With little, nervous laughs of relief, Louie settles down. He laughs. "Ignatowski's a boob." Then comes the knock.

Louie jumps to his feet and tries to barricade the door. He pleads with Alex not to open it. Alex is determined to die as he lived, the captain of his fate. He flings the door open and . . . suffice to say, it's not the Jabberwock, my son.

GUESTS:

J. P. Bumpstead, Bob Larkin (the brawlers at Mario's)
Kiva Dawson (the entity at the door)

Note: The actress who plays "Peggy," who has no lines, is uncredited.

Ironically, Alex talks about being the self-determining master of his destiny, and yet he does exactly what the fates predict.

Chris Lloyd remembers some initial misgivings about what could have—but didn't—turn out to be a silly episode. "When I got the script, I thought it was gonna be a tough one to make work. I don't know that I thought it was silly, just hard to make believable that Jim had this dream and believed in it. But the writing took care of that." And so did the performance, Chris.

This was the last of fourteen *Taxi* episodes written by Barry Kemp; he went on to create *Newhart* and to produce *The Popcorn Kid*.

#66 FLEDGLING
WRITTEN BY KEN ESTIN.
DIRECTED BY JAMES BURROWS.

The Hazeltine, Elaine's art gallery, has sent her to authenticate a painting by the renowned artist Craig Eagen (Paul Sand). With Alex accompanying her, she visits the reclusive Eagen at his skylit loft. At first he politely but firmly refuses to let them in, but Elaine finally convinces him that she needs to actually see the painting and confirm it's indeed his. He finally lets them in, but fearfully keeps to the other side of the room. Eagen eventually admits he's suffering from agoraphobia, a fear of the outside world. Motherly Elaine decides to try and cure him, against Alex's better judgment.

At the garage sometime later, Alex and Elaine have an argument about it while Louie observes the proceedings like a novelist: "Alex walks away from Elaine. Elaine follows. Could there be a problem?" Elaine convinces Paul to come to the garage. She drives him in, and he sits in the front of the cab (#460) while the cabbies take turns trying to coax him out. He finally leaves the cab and enters the world. Elaine tenderly dances with him as Louie, in a moment of rare romance, hums a slow tune over the PA system and gets the drivers on their way.

This not-so-great episode starts with a sitcomy premise and ends with a blah. Like amnesiacs, there have probably been more agoraphobics on television than in the history of humankind. The episode does point out Elaine's maternal streak, and, on cue, Alex is typically bitchy when he thinks she's attracted to another man.

The appealing but one-note Paul Sand won a Tony award in 1971 for the musical *Story Theatre* and starred in his own half-season MTM sitcom after playing a memorable IRS auditor on *The Mary Tyler Moore Show*. He's since been a cast member of MTM's *St. Elsewhere* and was a guest on Tony Danza's *Who's the Boss?*

#67 ON THE JOB, PART I

WRITTEN BY DENNIS DANZIGER AND
ELLEN SANDLER.
DIRECTED BY JAMES BURROWS.

Sunshine Cab has gone bust. Louie clumps down the stairs after a last-ditch meeting in owner Mr. McKenzie's office and berates the cabbies for having bled the company by their demands for such frills as tire tread and brake linings. The cabbies take it as an omen and vow to get new, exciting jobs. They decide to meet a month later at Mario's to talk about what they've found. Louie calls them deserters and pronounces that McKenzie is right this minute coming up with the perfect solution: A shot rings out from McKenzie's office. (We discover that McKenzie really didn't shoot himself. He shot his accountant.)

A month later, the cabbies are gathered around a pitcher of beer at Mario's and begin to relate their adventures. Tony talks about having had to take a job as a collector for a bookie. Cue the flashbacks. Tony feels guilty about his job, even though he hasn't actually hurt anyone yet. He visits a priest, who recommends penance; Tony recommends that the priest cough up the $300 owed to Lou-Lou the bookie. Unwilling to break bones, Tony brings the priest to Lou-Lou, who grudgingly accepts a gold watch in payment. Lou-Lou, in return, pays Tony his wages by handing him an Emmy Award and sending him on his way.

Elaine then tells of her energetic attempts at being an executive secretary. At her outer-office desk on her first day, a blustery gentleman comes up and demands to speak to her boss, George Givens. Elaine, sensing trouble, makes up a good excuse for her absent employer. The visitor appreciates it: It seems *he's* George Givens, and for twenty-three years he's made a deliberate career of being a lost cog in the bureaucracy. "No one quite knows who I am," he boasts. "Oh, some people know my face, some people know my name. But very few of them put them together." Elaine, however, has been reading Givens's memos and finds them brilliant; she pushes him to speak up at the next board meeting. He does so, to less than optimum results for both of them.

Jim describes his efforts as a door-to-door salesman for the Magic Carpet Wizard vacuum cleaner/shampooer. As an increasingly shocked housewife looks on, Jim sprinkles paper, ashes, and finally grease on her carpet. He assures her not to worry, the Magic Carpet Wizard will get it clean. Let's not ruin the gag, and just say she has cause for worry. As Jim finishes his reminiscences, Latka gets up from the table and says his break is over now, and that he has to go wait on more tables and clean up. "I wouldn't be insulted by a tip," he says. He changes his mind when he sees their idea of one.

Tag: Previews of Part II.

GUESTS:

John O'Leary (the priest)
Carmine Caridi (Lou-Lou, the bookie)
Bill Wiley (George Givens)
John Petlock (chairman of the board at Givens's firm)

Robert Balderson (Barrett, Givens's coworker)
Alice Hirson (the housewife)
T. J. Castronova (Tommy, the bartender at Mario's)

#68 ON THE JOB, PART II
WRITTEN BY DENNIS DANZIGER AND
ELLEN SANDLER.
DIRECTED BY JAMES BURROWS.

After flashbacks to Part I, we return to Mario's, where the cabbies are sitting around a table, commiserating on new jobs and ill luck. Louie walks in, gloating about his great success in the outside world, until Tommy the bartender comes by to tell him he forgot to sign his unemployment check. Louie decides to tell his story, despite the cabbies' protests. Cue the flashbacks. With chutzpah by the gallon, Louie barges into a Wall Street brokerage firm and through sheer audacity gets the president to hire him. Using sleazy, high-pressure tactics, he becomes a top money-maker. Unfortunately, he's too sleazy even for the brokerage house and gets fired. He does profit from the experience, however, in his own inimitable way.

Bobby then tells of the "acting" job he landed: as an Easter bunny for children's parties. He hops into one such affair and discovers that the mother is a big-name director. To try and impress her, he gathers the kids for a monologue from the play *Whose Life Is It, Anyway?* ("Now, you have to pretend that the Easter bunny is paralyzed from the neck down.")

Finally, Alex tells of getting a low-key job as a night watchman. After the first couple of weeks, he begins going a little boingy: We see him counting the hairs on his head. Then it's time for some excitement as he does his rounds—by shining his flashlight onto a bank of video screens. After that, he aims a security camera at himself and pretends to be the star of "The Alex Reiger Show!" As he's finishing up a "National Anthem" sign-off, the next shift's watchman comes in. He's an old-timer who assures Alex that everything's OK, that all the new guys get this way at first. After Alex leaves, however, the old-timer does his own TV performance with a disturbingly cynical puppet.

Back in the present, Louie gets word that Sunshine Cab has been bought by new owners. Anybody who wants his or her old crummy, miserable job can have it. The cabbies are indignant: Haven't they proven there's life beyond the garage? No, they decide, they haven't. And they all go back to work.

Tag: Back at the garage, the cabbies accept their unpleasant but secure and familiar fate.

GUESTS:

Michael McGuire (Mr. Gray, president of the brokerage firm)
Dana Halsted (Ms. Lang, Gray's secretary)
Clint Young (a security guard at the brokerage firm)
Claire Malis (Cynthia Beck, the director)
Howie Allen, Heather Hobbs (two of the eight children at the party)
Al Lewis (Henry, the second night watchman)
T. J. Castronova (Tommy, the bartender at Mario's)

The third season's pickup episodes demonstrate once again the strength of each of the characters. Hirsch, in fact, is called upon to do essentially a solo performance, and his boredom and believability are astonishing. Conaway, too, is especially good in his bit, taking what might have been a silly situation and making the ludicrous opportunism of it uproarious simply by conveying how much Bobby loves his art.

Not to take anything away from the regular cast, these two episodes sported some of the most expressive guest performers in the business. As always, the unmistakable Carmine Caridi is so calm and purposeful, you wonder why he's never gotten to headline his own series. Caridi, who did in fact audition for the role of Alex, was a regular on *Fame* during its first season, and played Cloris Leachman's boss on *Phyllis* during its second; he'd previously costarred as her husband in an unsold 1974 pilot, *Pete 'n' Tillie*. Interestingly, the bookie he plays is named Lou-Lou, leading to the reasonable assumption that this is Lou-Lou Pantusso, the boxing manager who Caridi played in "Out of Commission" (episode #60).

The astonishing, unsung Bill Wiley, who steals

the show as Elaine's elusive boss, went on to steal every scene he appeared in on an episode of *Cheers,* and did the same in his regular role as the soap opera director in *All Is Forgiven.* A great find. John O'Leary, the all-too-human priest, is a familiar figure in TV movies and episodic series. Michael McGuire, playing one of the most three-dimensional and sympathetic big-businessmen seen on television, may best be known for his three appearances on *Cheers* as Dr. Sumner Sloane, the sleazeball English professor in Diane Chambers's life. And taking a small moment and sprinting with it to the finish line is the inimitable Al Lewis—Grandpa on *The Munsters* and, of late, a Greenwich Village restaurateur.

#69 VIENNA WAITS

WRITTEN BY KEN ESTIN.
DIRECTED BY HOWARD STORM.

Elaine bursts into the garage with great news: Her ex-husband, Vince, has shown up out of the blue and taken the kids on a long vacation with him. Now Elaine wants to do something special and crazy. She decides to go to Europe. And what's more, she wants her best friend Alex go with her. Alex says he can't: There's his job (which is extremely flexible, Elaine reminds him), the money (they'll fly charter and stay in inexpensive hotels, she says), and finally, there's what Alex perceives as the history of attraction between the two of them. How's Elaine going to feel, then, when he's off with "Monique" or whomever? Elaine assures him they're just good friends and that everything will be OK. So, they're off!

On the plane, Alex wants to get started on his romantic fantasy trip. Unfortunately, when he tries to start up a conversation with a good-looking woman on the flight, he's told to get lost. When he gets back to his seat, feeling dejected, he finds a handsome young troubador named Todd playing guitar for Elaine. He remains very polite to "Mr. Reiger" despite Alex's defensiveness, and at Elaine's request starts playing the Billy Joel song "Vienna." Alex realizes he isn't off to a great start.

In London, the first stop on the trip, Alex and Elaine are in a pub. Elaine is having fun and wants

to get together for a while every day at the same time. Alex isn't so sure—there are all these sultry European women to consider. Elaine understands. Her date, James, comes to take her out, and Alex, left alone, starts throwing darts. Next stop: Greece. At a picturesque fisherman's tavern, Elaine is dancing wildly with her date, Oumas, and his companions. Everybody likes everybody—except for dour Alex—and the whole bar is one big party. But just when he's at his bitchiest, he notices that a beautiful French model he'd invited earlier has, despite his expectations, actually come to the bar. Elaine, happy for Alex, leaves with Oumas. The model, Desiree, is dressed for a trip to the casino and expects Alex to take her there. When she finds out he can't afford that kind of date, she dumps him. Alex hits the ouzo.

The final stop on the trip is Vienna. Alex—broke by now—sits in a fancy restaurant waiting for Elaine. All he can afford to order from the stern waiter is clear broth. Elaine comes in, wearing a breathtaking designer gown, and feels the brunt of Alex's bitterness. From his description, she's been having one hell of a time—dating exotic men, meeting royalty, making a monk break a thirty year vow of silence to say "Wow!" He finally admits to her that he feels like a broken man. Elaine feels so sorry for her good friend that she decides to cancel her date so that she and Alex can spend their last night in Europe together. They've known each other for years, have seen the other neurotic, hurt, stupid, and angry, and have still remained friends. Maybe their friendship is strong enough to survive one night of love. Alex is overcome. To the strains of "Vienna," he goes off with Elaine arm-in-arm into the starry Old-World night.

GUESTS:

Gary Phillips (Todd)
Warwick Sims (James)
Reuven Bar-Yotam (Oumas)
Cassandra Gava (Desiree)
Rob Hughes (waiter in Vienna)
Patch Mackenzie (woman on plane)

In the culmination of a will-they-won't-they relationship almost as tense as the one on *Moonlighting,* Alex and Elaine finally go to bed together. In fact, fans of the show often refer to this episode as "Alex Gets Laid." It's hard to say whether they ever made love again, especially judging from Elaine's cryptic nonanswer to Simka's query about her love life in "Scenskees from a Marriage, Part II" (episode #95). In any case, this is the only time there was a definite on-screen reference to the event. By the way, that incredible white gown Elaine wears in Vienna belongs to Marilu Henner. She wore it to the Emmy Awards later that season.

Like many other *Taxi* episodes and incidents, "Vienna Waits" was based on real-life events. *Taxi* cocreator Jim Brooks "had just come back from Europe and had had a very good time," remembers Ken Estin. "He felt so good about it that he wanted to send some of the *Taxi* characters there. That part about getting together every day to write postcards, that was from Jim's experience." And in case there's any doubt, that is *not* Billy Joel performing his song "Vienna."

#70 MR. PERSONALITIES

WRITTEN BY IAN PRAISER AND HOWARD GEWIRTZ.

DIRECTED BY HOWARD STORM.

The cabbies are once again sitting around Mario's. Tony's thinking about applying for college and Elaine's getting fed up with Latka's multiple personalities, which lately have grown to include not only lounge lizard Vic Ferrari but also a cowboy. She says she's taken the liberty of setting up an appointment for Latka with her psychiatrist, Dr. Jeffries. (Her first psychiatrist was Dr. Collins [episode #28]. Alex, curiously, resents her doing this, saying he doesn't believe in psychiatrists—a complete turnaround from his stance in that earlier episode.) Just then, Elaine's babysitter phones her about some minor emergency, and Alex gets volunteered to shepherd Latka to Dr. Jeffries.

At the psychiatrist's office, Latka talks about his childhood fear of mean Uncle Babka, who inadvertently tortured him while trying "to make a man" of Latka. Then Latka assumes yet one more identity—Alex!

In the garage a month later, Latka/Alex is pulling in more bookings than Alex/Alex. He even gives better advice than Alex. In fact, when Elaine asks the real Alex if he'd like an extra ticket to see Lena Horne with her, he demurs in favor of a hockey game; Latka/Alex says of course he'll go—he had hockey tickets, but he'll just give them to some kid. Alex wonders why *he* didn't think of that.

Sometime later, Alex sits with Latka/Alex at Dr. Jeffries's office. Latka/Alex talks about his life: how his wife was cheating on him, how he doesn't like to be his friends' father figure, how his satisfaction with his lot perhaps masks a lack of ambition. Alex nods in astonishment and recognition. Yes! That's it! Latka/Alex then tells Dr. Jeffries that he's figured out the answer to all his problems—that he knows just what Alex Reiger should do with his life. And it's . . . oh, hello. Latka's back. Alex is frantic, but Latka can't reinstate his other self. Latka leaves, quite content, and Alex hangs around for the rest of the appointment.

GUESTS:

Barry Nelson (Dr. Jeffries)
Bernadette Birkett (Doris Marie Winslow, another patient)
Wendy Goldman (Lynne, Dr. Jeffries's secretary)
T. J. Castronova (Tommy, the bartender at Mario's)

Whose life is it, anyway? Though a showcase for Andy Kaufman—whose Alex doppelgänger is dead-on—Judd Hirsch nonetheless holds his ground. The final scene in the psychiatrist's office, where Latka/Alex articulates Alex's suppressed disappointments and his resignation to his lot is a hilarious heartwrencher—maddening, too. What the *hell* was he about to say?

Barry Nelson was a leading man in Broadway comedies of the fifties and sixties, and star of the old TV series *The Hunter* and *My Favorite Husband*. One of his most memorable appearances was in the classic *Twilight Zone* episode, "Stopover in a Quiet Town."

Incidentally, it's unclear who the mechanic is while Latka/Alex is off driving cabs. But knowing Louie, it's probably Latka himself on a different shift, wondering why he's so tired all the time.

"Babka," incidentally, is a type of Polish baked good.

#71 JIM JOINS THE NETWORK

WRITTEN BY DAVID LLOYD.
DIRECTED BY NOAM PITLIK.

Two TV executives—Mitch Harris (Martin Short) and his boss Janine (Melendy Britt)—are having a discussion in the back of Jim's cab. Janine says she faces an unpleasant task and doesn't know if she can handle it. Mitch tells her that of course she can, that her sense of responsibility will make her. "OK, here goes," she says, taking a breath: "I'm gonna have to fire you." She tells a stunned Mitch that the ratings have got to come up—and by the way, thanks for always being there for her. She laments as she leaves the cab, "I don't know what I'm gonna do without you." Mitch is in shock. Jim leads him haltingly into a conversation about TV scheduling and asks why they took off *Star Trek,* his favorite show. "The only guy I didn't like," Jim declares, "was the leader of the Romulans. It wasn't the actor's fault—it was the scripts. They gave him things to say that no Romulan would ever say."

Mitch asks Jim to take him to Central Park West and 68th Street. Chatting, he mentions that the network has two specials on tonight: *Hometown Girl,* a one-hour prime-time version of their most popular soap opera, and the problematic musical-variety special, *The Pittsburgh Steelers at Marineland.* Jim gets a psychic flash that the latter will be a hit and the former will get clobbered everywhere but Chicago. Mitch pointedly tells Jim to stick to cab driving—not a great piece of advice in this case.

The next day at the garage, the cabbies notice a white powder sprinkled around Louie's cage. Jim naturally investigates, even though his horrified friends think it's rat poison. Turns out it's flour. It seems that an obviously bored Louie has spotted a mouse in the garage and can now follow the rodent's footprints to his lair. "I'm gonna surround the place with mousetraps," he cackles. "As soon as that little sucker moves a muscle (*smack!*), Minnie's a widow!" A sympathetic Elaine convinces Lou to let her get rid of the mouse in some humane—and, importantly for Louie—cheap way. Mitch barrels into the garage, looking for Jim. It seems his predictions were exactly right, and Mitch

begs him for more help. Jim refuses, and Mitch tells him that, if given this chance years ago, Jim might have saved *Star Trek:* "What do you say, Jim? Shall we boldly go where no man has gone before?" You bet.

At Mitch's office, Jim sees a show called *Stunt Wife;* he likes it. Before he can say much more, however, Mitch asks the unkempt Jim to pretend to be a shoeshine boy in case anyone comes by. Okeydoke. Next he shows Jim a vulgar sitcom with a pasted-in laughtrack, followed by a new game show where a tub of melted cheese sits precariously over Paul Lynde's head. Jim loves it, and says to put it on Friday night at 9, even though the competition has a James Bond movie and a special, *Brooke Shields Turns Seventeen.* "I can't believe I'm letting a cabdriver off the street do my job for me," Mitch says dejectedly. Patting Mitch on the back, Jim tells him not to feel bad: "If you could do your job, you would!"

At the garage a few days later, Elaine displays a Rube Goldberg mouse-catcher her son, Jason, cooked up. Mitch calls and tells Jim he was right again. The cabbies are ecstatic for him—this is his big ticket out. Their joy quickly turns to anger when Jim explains he's unpaid and gets treated like a shoeshine boy. Alex explodes, and in a classic exchange with Jim exhorts his friend to finally stop letting himself be taken advantage of. A fiery Jim storms into Mitch's office with a few remarks about human dignity, and a humiliated Mitch apologizes and decides to come clean. He starts to phone his boss, but Janine breezes in with news of a victory party for him. Mitch confesses to her that Jim is the programming genius. Janine brushes that aside. We take advice from everyone, she tells him, "our friends, our lovers, the man on the street—even the shoeshine boy. I've gotten advice—darned good advice—from my hairdresser. My nephews picked our six o'clock news team." The only thing that counts, she says, is that Mitch made the final decision. Now, c'mon—the champagne is getting warm. Jim can't attend the party, but Mitch promises that come Monday, he'll get Jim an office and a job. Jim turns him down, and says he doesn't want to profit from his God-given gift. He asks for $150,000 for the shoeshines, though.

Tag: In a second classic bit in one episode, Louie delivers a brilliant man-to-mouse monologue.

Not only is this episode a clever jab at treacly, formulaic TV shows, but it's also a very accurate look at powerful media executives. Janine is no monster, though she dismisses Jim and refuses to give him credit. In fact, she's pleasant to the ostensible shoeshine boy and even shakes his hand. Yet she's blinded by her own rationalizations, a common—and double-edged—trait among many upper-management and government types. Who knows? Were the executives based on ABC programmers the *Taxi* producers had known? Nah.

Martin Short came out of Canada's Second City comedy troupe and had first worked for Brooks et al. on the short-lived but critically lauded legal sitcom *The Associates*. After this *Taxi* appearance—which would be his only guest shot ever on episodic television—Short made his mark on *SCTV* and, especially, *Saturday Night Live*. He's since gone into movies, among them *Three Amigos* and *Innerspace*.

"Y'know," says Short, "I have never seen that *Taxi!* People tell me it's repeated all the time and it's funny and all, but I've just never seen it. Gotta get a copy of that!" Landing the role wasn't a big struggle, Short recalls; since the producers already knew his work on *The Associates,* they simply called him up and offered it to him. The producers' style of working fit him just fine. "You're encouraged not so much to come up with specific bits, but just to have an attitude. It's hard to describe. You know that great big laugh Jim Brooks has? The one you hear on all his shows? Well, he'd never do it for the jokes—he knew all the jokes. He'd do it for the acting, the attitude. That's what he was responding to." Short's observation makes an interesting point: Playing the straight man here, rather than his typical comic fop, Short turns in what may be his best performance as an *actor*.

Incidentally, we don't know about *Stunt Wife,* but Chris Lloyd had costarred in an unsold pilot called *Stunt Seven*. Wonder if the writers knew that?

#72 LOUIE'S FLING
WRITTEN BY SAM SIMON.
DIRECTED BY JAMES BURROWS.

When Louie shows up at his girl friend's for an evening of wine and the Miss Universe contest, he finds Zena (Rhea Perlman) consoling her friend Emily (Andrea Marcovicci). Emily is in a sorry state: Her boy friend Adam, whom she supported through art school, has graduated and split to marry another woman. Emily's now a bit drunk and has taken some tranquilizers, and she's questioning why all this should have happened. Louie, with on-target street-smarts, tells her it's simple: She's attracted to unstable men who victimize her. Emily is impressed; he's given her a handle on her emotions. "Why are you always apologizing for him?" she asks Zena. Zena, momentarily proud of Louie, has him escort Emily home; Lou calls Alex to taxi them. At Alex's insistence, Lou accompanies Emily to her apartment. There, in the grip of drinks and drugs, Emily seduces him.

The next day Alex is angry and astonished that Louie could do such a thing behind Zena's back; he'd waited an hour in his cab, so sure that even Louie wasn't that low. Louie, however, is bragging about his conquest. Totally disgusted, Elaine plans to do Zena a favor and tell her the truth, thus getting Louie out of her life. Lou beats Elaine to the punch, however. Crushed, Zena still tries to understand him as "a weak man who hasn't had much pleasure in his life." He says he's glad Zena understands and won't mind sharing him. At that, Zena finally throws him out. Stunned, Lou goes to Emily. In the clear light of day, however, and after strained attempts at politeness, she informs Louie that he's "gross and disgusting." Moreover, she's spoken to the errant Adam, who's ringing her buzzer downstairs even as they speak.

Emily hustles Lou out via the fire escape, and he returns to the garage. There, thank God, he finds Alex. Alex is disdainful, but Lou begs him to listen and even begins crying. Giving in, Alex tells him that he should apologize to Zena and sincerely promise to make it up to her. Having been given the right solution, Lou reverts to form, and snickers that all it took were a few crocodile tears to do

Episode #72: "Louie's Fling."

the trick. Alex starts kicking himself: He should have known better than to believe that despicable worm. But as Louie is leaving, he stops, turns to Alex, and, all defenses down, confesses, "The tears were real."

"Louie was probably the most villainous character ever loved in a sitcom," says Sam Simon. "I have to say most of the reason for that was Danny. There's something about that guy people were sympathetic with, and so he could get away with murder. But not always. The first ending we filmed for this episode, we went over the line with him." In it, Louie returns to Emily's apartment, only to have her throw him out when she hears her crazy jealous boyfriend coming. She exits to spruce herself up, and then, as the original draft reads:

> Very quickly [Lou] starts to gather his things together, and then smiles and puts them down. He pours himself a glass of wine, making two glasses of wine on the table. He takes a little sip and sets it down. He takes a cigar out of his pocket, takes two puffs, and grinds it out in the ashtray, leaves it, and then puts a pair of shorts under a cushion, hanging out. He *exits* cackling, and we: fade out.

"The audience had been with us all the way, but then they were appalled at that last scene. So we came up with the scene that was eventually used on the show and shot it a couple of weeks later. That great final line—'The tears were real'—Jim Brooks came up with that. And it was great because it showed that Louie had misgivings about what he'd done."

Rhea Perlman remembers the episode being great fun "because I got to scream my head off in the last scene, when I kicked him out and told him he was garbage. I really liked doing that." She giggles. "It was the one time Zena wasn't 'the *niiice gir-ulll*'!"

#73 LIKE FATHER, LIKE SON

WRITTEN BY DAVID LLOYD.
DIRECTED BY JAMES BURROWS.

At the garage, Tony is bemoaning the fact that he's been called for jury duty. Alex points out that he shouldn't complain, that this is an important civic responsibility—one which, knock on wood, he himself hasn't had to take part in. Just then, Jim takes a phone call for Alex—it's Alex's father. Alex at first refuses to take the call. He tells the cabbies that he and his dad—a compulsive ladies' man who ran out on Alex's mother—have barely spoken in decades (see episode #23). When Alex finally does take the call, his father, Joe (Jack Gilford), says he's coming by to take Alex to lunch. When he arrives, Joe explains that he's been back in New York a little while—since 1974—and decided he missed his son.

At Mario's, Joe apologizes for having deserted his family, though he won't go so far as to regret not having sent money. Then, like a typical parent, he asks why Alex never remarried. Alex says he's never found the right woman: "Someone who's interested in the world and doesn't take it too seriously. Someone who's not afraid to ask for what she wants." A pretty woman sitting at the next table interrupts: "Excuse me, if you're through with that newspaper, could I borrow it? I want to see the Doonesbury cartoon on Alexander Haig." Alex hands her the paper and turns back to Joe. "Someone who's not afraid to be happy," he continues.

Behind him, the woman laughs at the cartoon. "And someone who appreciates me," Alex says finally. "Thank you very much," says the woman, handing the paper back to him, "that was nice of you."

With a little prodding from Joe—make that a lot—Alex meets the woman, a commercial artist named Karen (Barbara Babcock). They make plans to meet the next evening at eight at Mario's for drinks and a movie. But after Alex leaves, his father, posing as Joe McGinty, sets up a date with Karen for a political-comedy lecture featuring Jules Feiffer, Art Buchwald, and Russell Baker, which is being held at The New School, a real-life "alternative" college in Greenwich Village.

Louie overhears Karen make dates with both Alex and Joe, and many dates later, relishing the irony, breaks the news to Reiger. Flabbergasted, Alex runs over to Mario's to confront Karen. She tells him not to be ridiculous: She's not dating his father, she's dating that cute little man Joe that Alex was having dinner with. Alex tells her the truth, and Karen, shocked, confesses she and Joe have gotten, ahem, physical. Now Alex is livid. He tells Karen he'll see her later and rushes to Joe's apartment. It's gorgeous, and Alex is startled: He had no idea how his father lived, that his second wife, a doctor he'd married fifteen years ago, had (apparently) died and left Joe wealthy. Joe, picking up a framed photo, says to Alex "This is your stepbrother, Mel." Alex can't understand what attracts women to his father. Joe, in response, does his impression of thick pea soup bubbling to a frantic boil—ridiculously cute. Alex gets ready to leave, angry at Joe, for, along with everything else, changing Mom's "too salty" tuna casserole recipe. But Joe, doling out two plates of casserole, deftly plays on Alex's familial guilt. In a beautiful bit of symbolism, he sprinkles some salt on Alex's portion, and urges his son to come back for dinner.

As in "Honor Thy Father" (episode #23), Alex is once more drawn to his father despite all the rotten things Joe had done to him and his mother. Joe Reiger explains the bond best when he tells Alex that what it comes down to is this: Alex *has* to love him, because he's old and he's his father and who knows when and if they'll ever see each other again.

Legendary Jack Gilford (1907–1990) is exceptional as Alex's wayward pater. The sweet image he's cultivated over the years in countless movies, TV shows, and Cracker Jack commercials serves *Taxi* well: No matter how sneaky or self-centered Joe Reiger is, we all feel the same way toward Jack Gilford as Alex feels toward his dad. The casting of Gilford added one other bonus—the pea soup routine, which he contributed.

Although a little stiff and somewhat larger than life as Karen, Barbara Babcock has the look and feel of someone who'd fall for Alex despite her different social station. Babcock, who won an Emmy for her recurring role as Sergeant Esterhaus's steamy lover on *Hill Street Blues,* has continued to play the erotic man-eater on *Cheers, Mary,* and other shows and most recently costarred in *The Law and Harry McGraw.*

"We cruised *Hill Street Blues* a lot," Jim Brooks recalls. "As a matter of fact, Veronica Hamel wanted to do the show, and we wanted to write an episode for her, but [*Hill Street Blues* production company] MTM wouldn't let her. It would've been interesting, though." (As it happened, *Hill Street Blues*'s Taurean Blacque appeared on *Taxi* before he became Detective Neil Washington, but that's another story—episode #4, to be precise.)

#74 LOUIE'S MOM REMARRIES

WRITTEN BY EARL POMERANTZ.
DIRECTED BY JAMES BURROWS.

Vic Ferrari, schizoid Latka's other self, is all set for a winter vacation at Sugarloaf resort condo. The cabbies are sorry to see Latka's personality disorder flare up, but they console themselves with the fact that Vic's having a wonderful time. Louie, on the other hand, comes into the garage quite upset. He tells the cabbies that he won a big fight with his mother last night. She belongs to a club called Life Begins at Seventy and has fallen in love with a guest speaker, the eighty-three-year-old Itsumi Fujimoto (Jerry Fujikawa). Lou brags that he bullied her into not marrying the guy, as one by one the disgusted cabbies get up and leave—except for Jim, who urges Louie on with a bit of beer-commercial camaraderie.

As he gloats about his "victory," the tiny, tough Ma herself (Julia DeVito) walks in. As the cabbies make their introductions, she responds knowledgeably with information Lou's given her. To Elaine "Oh, Louie's girl." To Alex: "Oh, you're the Jewish fella Louie's always helpin' out." To Tony: "I can't believe what Louie says about *you*. What city are we in?" Tony: (pause) "Is this a trick question?" Ma: "Well, I'll be darned."

She tells Louie she still wants to marry Itsu, that she wants companionship. "Companionship!" Louie snorts. "Is that all you old people ever think about?" Reluctantly, he agrees to meet Itsu at Mario's. The dapper Japanese man turns out to be a nice guy, but Louie still withholds his blessing and tells his mother if she goes through with it, he's disowning her. Ma decides to go ahead with the marriage anyway. "Sayonara," she tells Louie.

On the day of the wedding, Jim and Alex go to the garage to convince Louie (who's been sleeping in his dispatcher's cage) to be with his mother. He refuses; he's been hurt. "Let me tell you somethin'," he screams at Reiger. "You get used to a way of life—you don't pick it. Me and Ma had a deal. We had an agreement. It was unspoken, there were no papers signed, but it was a deal just the same. . . . [Now] Ma is leaving me," he says helplessly. "She's bustin' us up."

Louie finally decides to go, after ascertaining for himself that no matter what awful, disgusting thing he does, it's all Alex's fault for talking him into going. The ceremony takes place at a Shinto temple. Jim, a self-described student of the world's religions, explains that the poetry of Shinto weddings makes them one of the three best kinds; the others are Polish, for the dancing, "and Vegas, for the glitter." Lou can't stand it and tries to stop the wedding. It's too late: Ma has drunk from the ceremonial bowl three times and is wed. Reluctantly, Louie bestows his blessing.

"She loved gettin' dressed up in that Japanese outfit," Danny DeVito recalls of his mother, who reprised her role from episode #62. "She has pictures of herself in it at her house. Just the other day, the kids, Lucie and Gracie—they hadn't talked to her in a while, and I said, 'You wanna see Nanny?' and they said yeah, and so I put on that episode for them to see Nanny in the show with Daddy. And when it got to the point where she comes out with the wig and the hat and everything, Gracie walked up to the TV and said, 'Who's that?'!"

Scriptwriter Earl Pomerantz accurately reflected the customs of Japan, where the majority of the population are Shintoist or Buddhist. "I did some reading, some research," he remembers. "Jim was the natural one to explain about it, since he was always this kind of guy who knew things he didn't know he knew."

Latka/Vic's vacation had originally been set for "Louie's Fling" (episode #72), and the upshot of it originally served as that episode's tag until the ending was changed. It was a very funny bit: Latka enters the garage, after having returned from "Vic" 's ski trip. "The strangest thing happened to me," he tells Jim. "Yesterday I woke up and I was in a ski cabin surrounded by a bunch of good-looking guys, and they put me in a tub full of boiling water and beautiful women. I thought they were going to cook us." To which Jim replies, "A not unfamiliar feeling, Latka. When you suddenly don't know where you are and who you're talking to, the most important thing is to stay calm. Make small talk, but if someone says something really confusing to you, simply laugh knowingly and walk away." Jim then proceeds to demonstrate this technique with Alex. Jim's bit proved so good, it was rescued for episode #86, the classic "Elegant Iggy."

#75 OF MICE AND TONY
WRITTEN BY GLEN CHARLES AND LES CHARLES. DIRECTED BY JAMES BURROWS.

Tony has a problem, but Alex is too happy to pay much attention: He's just won $1,300 on yesterday's football game. Elaine is disdainful about "you guys and that gambling thing," until she hears he won it from Louie. Then she blows him a kiss. Louie comes in and threatens to yank off the ear of an unmindful Jim with pliers if anyone laughs. ("Hmph," says Lou at Jim's lack of reaction, "no brains, no pain.'') Lou presses Alex to bet him double or nothing on that night's Oakland-Houston game, and Alex accepts. Tony finally gets a minute of Alex's time. It seems there's a promising young heavyweight down at the gym, an Olympic bronze medalist named Terry Carver (Ernie Hudson). Tony wants to manage the kid, but has self-doubts that Alex tries to dispel.

At Mario's later, a well-dressed Tony asks Tommy the bartender to try to make him seem important. Tommy readily agrees, and when Terry comes in, the bartender calls Tony ''Mr. Banta'' and even brings the phone to his table—a ploy that almost backfires when it rings and Tony, brilliantly fighting back nervousness, takes an apparently big-deal call and then nonchalantly tells Tommy to send a giant mushroom pizza ''to my friend Pantusso, on me.'' Over meatball subs that play an amazingly integral part in the pitch, Terry agrees to have Tony manage him.

That night, Elaine, Jim, and Alex watch the Oakland-Houston game at Mario's. So does Lou, who gets upset when Latka—whose multiple personalities have yielded the *veddy* proper Sir Geoffrey Hypen-Hill—changes channels on the television. After pouring beer in Sir G's bowler hat, Louie switches the game back on to see his team lose on a muffed field goal; now he owes Alex $2,600. Terry walks in and tells Tony that a mysterious ''syndicate'' has been pressuring him. Tony tells Terry not to get involved with mob guys, but Terry says he already told them they could come to his upcoming fight.

The night of the bout—with $5,200 of Louie's money riding on Terry's opponent, and Alex helping out in Terry's corner—the young heavyweight wins by a whopping first-round knockout. But in the locker room afterward, the syndicate shows up—five doctors looking for an investment. ''All we want,'' they say straightforwardly, ''is front row seats, a good tax break, and a chance to delude ourselves that we're part of the sports scene.'' They offer Terry the sun and the moon, and Tony reluctantly gives up his management. It's best for Terry; they both know that. Besides, the syndicate's paying Tony $5,000. Louie, very noisily and bitterly (''Die with festering boils! Die! Die! Die!'') pays off Alex, and the newly flush Tony and Alex decide

to celebrate with the ''greatest meal of their lives''—and for some reason head for Mario's.

OTHER GUESTS:

John Christy Ewing (Dr. Frazier, ophthalmology)
Andrew Winner (Dr. Gilman, obstetrics; misidentified as ''Dr. Baker'' in the end credits)
Howard Gewirtz (Dr. Baker, ears, nose, and throat; misidentified as ''Dr. Smith'' in the end credits)
Nat Bernstein (Dr. Stokely, internal medicine; misidentified as ''Dr. Stewart'' in the end credits)
Ian Praiser (Dr. Hardin, anesthesiology; misidentified as ''Dr. Harmon'' in the end credits)
Jimmy Lennon (the ring announcer; as himself)
Gene LeBell (the referee)
T. J. Castronova (Tommy, the bartender at Mario's)

Note: Charles James is credited as character Bill Thompson, but his scene was cut before airing.

This episode is a terrific showcase for Tony Danza. His scene inside Mario's, as he pitches his management to young contender Terry Carver, is filled with priceless looks and pauses as well as an unbelievable dialogue stunt performed with mouths full of meatball sandwiches. Interestingly, Tony takes a pizza order for a phone customer named Pantusso, which was not only the last name of Tony's manager/bookie but also of the late Coach in *Cheers.*

Guest star Ernie Hudson, who's perhaps best known as one of the *Ghostbusters,* had shaved his head and gotten in shape for the boxing play *The Great White Hope.* Yet as utterly natural and believable as he was in the role of Terry, Hudson remembers that in his audition, he was down for the count and saved by the bell. ''When I went to read,'' he says, ''they thought I was too small! Attitude has a lot to do with how you're perceived,'' he explains, ''and I was still pretty new to Hollywood and maybe a little unsure and all, though I *knew* as an actor I could make myself appear big or small. On my way out of the Paramount lot, I met Tony Danza, whom I'd never met before, and we got to talking about my audition. He said, 'How'd you do?' I said, 'Well, I dunno. . . .' He said, 'C'mon,' and he took me back up and read with me. And it was a really good reading and I got the job. That's sure something, isn't it?'' Yep. Hudson has stayed busy ever since, as a cast member in two sitcoms (*Highcliffe Manor* and *The Last Precinct*), and in loads of movies, including *Congo, Weeds, The Wrong Guys* and *Spacehunter: Adventures in the Forbidden Zone* with fellow *Taxi* guest star Andrea Marcovicci.

Though the end credits are a mishmash, a little investigation reveals *Taxi* writers/coproducers Ian Praiser and Howard Gewirtz played two of the doctors. ''And you know what else?'' asks Marilu Henner. ''I was married at the time, and my now ex-husband's best friend—our best man at the wedding—was Andy Winner,'' who also played one of the doctors.

#76 NINA LOVES ALEX

WRITTEN BY DAVID LLOYD.
DIRECTED BY JOAN DARLING.

Tony, still undecided about what to do with his time now that he's no longer boxing, tells the cabbies that he's joined a neighborhood patrol; Alex, who's exhausted after a hard shift, declines an offer to be his partner. Contrasting Alex's lethargy is the bubbly bounce of a new cabbie who skips into the garage: Nina Chambers (Charlaine Woodard), a young black actress who, depending on her mood, pronounces her first name as either ''Neena'' or ''Nine-a.'' She's immediately attracted to Alex and his dry wit and offers to take him home in her cab. Alex is so tired he agrees. On the way, Nina stops to pick up a young prom couple stranded in the rain—much to the dozing Alex's surprise when he wakes up. Curmudgeonly, Alex doesn't find the irrepressible Nina at all cute. Louie, on the other hand, adores her: She books a fortune each night.

As the days go by, Alex's reactions to Nina get grouchier and grouchier as her overtures get cuter and cuter: For instance, she sends him a bouquet of balloons, with a note asking if he knows how adorable he looks holding them. Elaine can't understand why Alex is being so touchy and says she suspects he really likes her or wouldn't be protesting. Alex replies that he's going to set Nina straight as soon as he sees her. But when she comes bounc-

ing into the garage, she's too rushed to talk: She's got to get to an audition and promises to stop by his place at about seven that evening. When she arrives, she's up, certain she's won the role. But when her agent calls, the news is bad: She was ''too right'' for the part. It was the worst thing she could hear: It's nothing that can be changed or fixed, just ''too right.''

She breaks down, and a sympathetic Alex gives her a list of platitudes even *he* finds saccharine. Listening to his fatherly talk, she realizes Alex isn't interested in her romantically, and Alex tells her that she's looking for magic and that he's just ''a no-magic man.'' They kiss goodnight—softly at first, then strongly. Alex suddenly realizes that he *does* feel something for her after all, but before he can say a word, she tells him that—whaddya know?—he's right. There *is* no magic there! As Alex mumbles something about staying, Nina thanks him for being so together and heads home.

OTHER GUESTS:

John Mengatti and Audrey Berindey (the prom couple)

Poor Alex. He doesn't appreciate what he has until it's too late. Elaine was right when she thought he doth protest too much.

Charlaine Woodard was the costar of *Cindy*, the 1978 TV movie-musical with which the John Charles Walters Co. made its television debut. She later went on to the Broadway hit *Ain't Misbehavin'*, and has since appeared on *Wiseguy* and other TV shows. Joan Darling, who directed this episode, is also an actress and comedienne who costarred as Arthur Hill's secretary on *Owen Marshall: Counselor at Law* and the Danny DeVito short *The Selling of Vince D'Angelo*. As a director, she's helmed several of the MTM shows, as well as *M*A*S*H* and *Mary Hartman, Mary Hartman*.

#77 LOUIE GOES TOO FAR

WRITTEN BY DANNY KALLIS.
DIRECTED BY MICHAEL LESSAC.

Elaine's just finished her shift, and she's in a rush to get to an opening at her gallery. Not only that, but she's just made a date for dinner the next night with her last fare, a rich, adventurous type named Robert. She goes into the restroom to change her clothes and discovers that lecherous Louie has installed an eyehole over the sink and has been peeping at her and other female cabbies. Even the placid Jim and the swinging Vic Ferrari are appalled at Louie's voyeurism.

Elaine is so enraged she seeks the help of the National Organization for Women (NOW). When the group's regional director arrives to investigate Elaine's complaint, Louie brazenly tries to pick her up. This is too much. The two women head upstairs to confront the boss, Mr. Ratledge; the overconfident Louie is fired. On hearing the news, the cabbies are understandably exuberant. Yet at the same time, they know the job was Louie's life. "The reign of terror is over," observes Alex. "So why do I feel so sorry for that broken toilet of a man?"

Louie eventually shows up at Elaine's apartment, groveling for forgiveness. Elaine, who's waiting for Robert to show up at any minute, is frantic about getting Louie out of there. There's a knock on the door: It's Robert, who, in a beautiful bit of irony, sympathizes with the violently ill, hyperventilating ex-dispatcher, and scolds Elaine for being so unfeeling. Robert leaves the two of them alone to work things out. Louie faints, and on waking up keeps apologizing. But Elaine still won't have any of it. She never will, she says, until he feels in his gut just what she felt.

Prodded by her, he talks about a dreaded moment each year when he goes to buy clothes. He has to go to the boys' department, and no matter how carefully he times it, there are always some kids with their parents around. Sometimes the kids make fun of him; always the parents pity him. "Is that the way I made you feel when I peeked?" he marvels from the middle of his hell. She tells him yes.

Finally realizing what he's done, he breaks down and blubbers an apology. They've made a breakthrough, and the two of them hug. Incorrigible Louie runs his hand over to Elaine's rear, and she breaks away from him scoldingly, but from the look on their faces it's become an in-joke between friends.

GUESTS:

Noni White (Andrea Stewart, the NOW representative)

Allen Williams (Robert)

This is a breakthrough episode for Louie: His anger and fear and bitterness and insecurity about his looks and his lot in life finally penetrate his crude and abrasive defense mechanisms. He's always felt the world never cared about him, so why should he care about the world? Elaine, by taking away his job—the only thing besides his mother that has any significance in his life—forces him out of his bubble and into a world of give-and-take and even friendship. And yet ever so realistically, his old habits stay with him. In future episodes, the writers and DeVito brilliantly managed to maintain Louie's caustic humor and hustling excesses while keeping this episode's breakthrough in the back of his mind. None of this is to suggest, by the way, that this isn't one of the funniest of episodes of *Taxi*. The table-turning by Elaine's date alone is priceless!

"The speech," DeVito says quietly, turning it around in his mind. "That speech came out of an improv that I did with Jim and Ed, about how I always hated going with my mother to Robert Hall or Barney's or wherever she'd take me. I hated it 'cause I could never just go in and get something off the rack. Since I was always short and stocky, they'd give me a jacket that'd fit *you*," the roughly five-foot-tall DeVito says, pointing to a 5'9" coauthor, "and then they'd have to cut it down. It was always embarrassing. That's where the speech came out of."

#78 I WANNA BE AROUND

WRITTEN BY GLEN CHARLES AND LES CHARLES. DIRECTED BY JAMES BURROWS.

Jim is singing a ditty to himself as he goes to get a cup of coffee from the vending machine. The machine jams, and Tony goes to get a screwdriver from the tool room. The room is locked, and the cabbies wonder what Louie has up his sleeve. They get their answer when they see him wheeling in huge barrels of food. He says they've discovered his little secret—a bomb shelter. It seems that a discussion on *Donahue* has scared the hell out of Louie, and he's been spending all his time and money stocking his shelter with dehydrated foods, a water purifier, a grain mill, a generator, four cots, and radiation-proof suits. Should the apocalypse threaten, he plans to enter the shelter with a hand-picked team: Tony, for muscle; assistant dispatcher Jeff, "to convince the black hordes I'm cool"; and Elaine, to breed. Elaine, understandably, declines the invitation. But when Lou proposes a weekend drill, Tony goes along enthusiastically, and Jeff reluctantly.

On Friday evening, the intrepid trio ventures forth. Jeff is impressed with Tony's combat gear and wonders how he can get the same. Tony says he had to enlist in the army and spend a year of his life in 'Nam. Jeff's interest turns to just the hat. Louie comes in, but before he can get the drill under way. Alex has him imagine a starving little girl tapping weakly at the door. What will Lou do then? Lou considers that possibility and pronounces the girl "buzzard bait." Lou, Tony, and Jeff enter the shelter and slam the door behind them.

The drill is immediately a huge bore, and for want of anything better to do, they decide to eat. Jeff and Tony refuse to eat their legumes, however, and take a vote on ice cream. Three hands raise: Jeff's, Tony's, and Jim's. It seems Iggy has stowed away, and now, in a test of leadership, Louie orders Tony to throw Jim out. Tony is reluctant, but tells Jim it's only make-believe. Louie insists that they pretend it's real or else the drill will be no good. He describes a nightmare holocaust that Iggy takes all too seriously. Tony says he can't do it: He can't throw Jim out. Louie, however, has no such compunction, but Jim says he'll go voluntarily. All he wants before he goes is a hug. When Louie grudgingly complies, Jim throws himself on his mercy. Louie gives up; he calls the whole thing off after just eleven minutes. (He has a bit of trouble getting out the door, however, since Jim still thinks there's a holocaust out there.)

Back in the real world, Jeff and Tony go out for a beer. Lou says he's too soft: He's doomed like all the rest. "I'm a loser," he tells Alex. "Like you." In a rather sappy speech, Alex tells Lou he shouldn't be ashamed of feeling compassion. Lou

pretends he's not listening, but Alex knows he is. For maybe the first time, Louie goes with Alex to Mario's for a drink.

The humanity Lou finally recognized in the previous episode is further explored in this very funny survivalist tale. It almost all comes crashing down at the end with one of the most maudlin speeches Judd Hirsch—or anybody else, come to think of it—has ever had to deliver. "I Wanna Be Around" also gives J. Alan Thomas his biggest role to date, and he handles it with quirky aplomb.

#79 BOBBY DOESN'T LIVE HERE ANYMORE

WRITTEN BY GLEN CHARLES AND LES CHARLES.
DIRECTED BY JAMES BURROWS.

A banner in the garage welcomes Bobby (Jeff Conaway), who's been in California the last six months trying to break into Hollywood. He's filmed a TV show pilot, and his old friends are excited. Latka has giftwrapped a beach ball, although when the cabbies tell him Bob won't need it if the pilot doesn't sell, he goes to exchange it for earmuffs.

Bobby strolls in, all smiles, and there's a warm reunion—except for Louie, of course, who paraphrases the old song lyric and tells Bobby, "If I'd known you were comin', I'd have baked a *ham*." He tells the cabbies bluntly that of the many TV pilots filmed each year, only a handful make it to series. And since "George C. Scum" here is a loser in Louie's book, this particular pilot is crash landing. A fed-up Alex gets Lou to agree that if the show gets picked up, he has to apologize to Bobby.

The cabbies then troop over to Mario's where Bobby gives them the scoop: It's a prime-time soap called *Boise* (as in Idaho), and he'll earn $3,500 a week! The bar phone rings: It's Bobby agent, Sid, with the fantastic news that *Boise* has been picked up! There's a party at The Plaza. On their way out of Mario's, they run into Latka with the earmuffs—which Bobby won't need now.

At The Plaza, Bobby keeps room service hopping. So does Jim, who complains that the little meatballs all have toothpicks in them. But then—tragedy: Sid calls to tell Bobby he's out. They're going to recast his part because he wasn't "sexy enough." Bobby's ego completely collapses; he catatonically says he's going to wander the streets and ride the subways all night mumbling to himself. His friends gather round to spend the night consoling him and pumping him up—except for Latka, who'd come in with a beach ball again, only to be told Bobby's staying in New York now. As dawn breaks, the tired and sleepy cabbies stretch, and Alex convinces Bobby he can't stay; he *must* go back to California and keep plugging away. Bobby agrees—to the dismay of Latka, who's returned with useless earmuffs and has finally had enough.

The next day, on his way to his noon flight, Bobby stops by the garage to say good-bye. Lou, who knows only that the pilot got picked up, apologizes rather nicely, and congratulates Bob on doing what he himself never will—escaping the garage. Bobby, touched, sits down next to him and confesses he was canned. A seemingly crestfallen Lou buries his face in Bobby's arm and starts crying—except he's actually laughing hysterically and says this is the funniest thing he's ever heard. He skips out of the garage to tell the story to strangers. Now the cabbies all have to bid farewell to Bobby. Alex is the last; he tells Bob candidly that the young actor is going to get busy and make new friends. "Y'know, Bob, if you become a star, there's a good chance we'll never see each other again." He pauses. "Here's hoping we never see each other again." They hug one last time, and Bobby departs.

OTHER GUESTS:

Tony Gaetano (the room-service waiter)
T. J. Castronova (Tommy, the bartender at Mario's; background only this episode)

There is a scene at Mario's where Bobby momentarily gets upset with Tony. His anger has almost a too-real edge to it. The reason was the tension everyone felt at the prodigal son's return. "It really wasn't a very enjoyable experience," Conaway

Hirsch on the set for "Mario's," the cabbies' hangout.

says. "Doing the episode itself was great, but the week of rehearsal—that was rough. I understand now, though at the time I didn't, that I had left the family and people were hurt. But boy, it was a tough week. The producers asked me to come back and do more, but I said no, even though I felt I owed it to them. I just couldn't face that again." (For more on the departure of Bobby and Jeff, see Conaway's biography and chapter 2 "Awake, A Wake.")

This biting, insightful episode was the last of the seventeen scripted by the brothers Glen and Les Charles, who also coproduced *Taxi* for a time. They went on to create *Cheers* with director Jim Burrows.

#80 TONY'S LADY

WRITTEN BY KEN ESTIN.

DIRECTED BY MICHAEL ZINBERG.

Vic Ferarri, Latka's other self, can't understand why Latka leaves the mechanic's area so messy and oily. Tony comes in with the news that he's landed a part-time, two-night-a-week job as a chauffeur. Latka reemerges and Alex passes on Vic's message. Latka, understandably, has one of his own for Vic.

Sometime later, we see Tony on his first night behind the wheel of a limo. He meets Christina Longworth (Rebecca Holden), the flawlessly beautiful daughter of the wealthy family who hired him. She's a nice person, completely unsnobby, and Tony takes to her immediately. Later that night, Tony drives Christina and her rich, arrogant date, Doug Blakely, to Blakely's home at 115 Central Park West. When Blakely starts to get fresh and Christina protests, Tony cleverly gets Doug to "step outside," and then roars off. Tony and Christina become friends, sharing fast food in the front seat and relishing what Tony sees as the fruits of his boxing career: "amusing anecdotes"! He mentions an early fight with a nationally ranked fighter named Manzo, whom Tony beat on a technical knockout, and a forty-three-year-old former great named Ron Thomas, who beat him.

Sure enough, Tony falls for Christina. He can't bring himself to tell her, however, and at the garage, the sympathetic cabbies urge him to ask her out. Elaine talks about the day she fell in love with her ex-husband, who squired her on a spring day with a picnic basket on the Circle Line cruise around Manhattan. Louie contributes a story about a broken heart he suffered at the hands of a ballerina. (Alex adds that Lou suffered another at the hands of a female prison guard.) Tony decides to tell Christina how he feels. The next time he drives her, she's with a handsome businessman named Nick, who's telling Christina professionally how much he liked the fashion designs she'd just showed. There's an unspoken tension between them. When they arrive at Nick's destination, he starts to leave the car, then returns, apologizes for something in a way that shows he's known her well and long, and finally, he proposes. Christina read-

ily accepts. They kiss passionately. Tony lamely asks, "Christina, will you go out with me?"

Tag: In the garage, Elaine bemoans, "Romance never works out." But romance does live: Jim is meeting a date to go and collect aluminum cans from the street.

OTHER GUESTS:

John Calvin (Doug Blakely)
Joel Brooks (Nick Dwyer; last name given only in the end credits)

When you think about it, this amusing episode is one of *Taxi*'s most thematically pure: Most of the cabbies aspire to do something else, and yet most of their dreams will come to nothing. But although Bobby's acting career looks hopeful and Elaine's art dealer career is progressing, Tony's boxing dreams seem dead. Though he had a comeback later (episode #85), it looked by the end of the show's run that family responsibilities were going to force him into a blue-collar prison.

Prior to this, guest star Rebecca Holden had appeared on *Hart to Hart, Magnum, P.I., Private Benjamin,* and other shows, as well as on the unsold ABC pilot, *Hot W.A.C.s.* Afterward, she spent a year as April Curtis on *Knight Rider* and filmed another pilot, *Johnny Blue.* She remains a frequent guest star on episodic television.

This was the first *Taxi* episode directed by Michael Zinberg, a producer and director with a slew of MTM productions and other shows to his credit.

#81 SIMKA RETURNS

WRITTEN BY HOWARD GEWIRTZ AND
IAN PRAISER.

DIRECTED BY MICHAEL ZINBERG.

Latka, his just-shaved face covered with pieces of tissue paper, is nervous about his imminent reunion with Simka Dahblitz (whom he'd met in episode #40). As Latka goes off to apply a styptic pencil, Simka (Carol Kane), the young lady from his old country, comes in. The cabbies are glad to see her, and she confesses to them how's she's suffered one bad relationship after another since she and Latka broke up. Latka nervously emerges from the restroom, and greets her, and invites her to lunch. While he goes off to shave yet again, Alex warns a skeptical Simka about Latka's multiple personalities.

Later, at Latka's apartment, with a native version of "Love Me Tender" playing on the phonograph, Simka arrives for dinner. Latka says he's prepared a special dish from the old country, despite the fact, he explains, that "it's hard to find self-basting warthog in America." He pours two glasses of the native drink, *brefnish,* which resembles green molasses. ("Here is mud in your *byefnik!* Simka heartily toasts.) The romance is progressing swimmingly when Latka, trying hard to tell Simka he loves her, turns into Vic Ferarri. "Where am I?" he wonders. "The Ramada Inn of Romania? Ha, ha, ha." Simka is dubious and starts to leave, but Vic charms her into bed.

The next morning, a singsongy Simka greets . . . Latka? She tries telling him how funny he was last night, pretending to be some guy named Vic, but Latka is furious with her for going to bed with "another man." Alarmed, she splits.

At the garage a few days later, Alex wonders why Latka's so silent. In response, Latka pulls out two plane tickets to Bermuda, along with a note from Simka to Vic saying the trip sounds OK to her. Alex tells Latka to stop pitying himself, to fight Vic for his woman. Latka resolves to. At his apartment later, Simka shows up, expecting to find Vic. But Latka is there instead, and he apologizes for getting mad at her the other day. Again, he starts to tell her he loves her, and again, Vic emerges. This time, Simka throws Vic out and shuts the door behind him. And this time, Latka comes back through the door, shouting at "Vic" in the hallway to never bother him again. Latka finally tells Simka he loves her, and they kiss.

Carol Kane won the first of her two *Taxi* Emmys for this episode, recreating her role as the old-country girl with new-world ideas. Not only did the Emmy judges applaud her performance, but so did the *Taxi* team, who decided to invite her back for another guest shot (episode #87, "The Wedding of Latka and Simka") and, immediately afterward, asked her to join the cast.

Yet Carol says her enchanting performance emerged only after she realized she was trying too hard to be "funny." After the misunderstandings that had dogged her debut, "by now I'm aware of the fact there are such things as quote-unquote jokes. And so naturally, the first run-through was a complete disaster. Jim [Brooks] and Ed ripped me to shreds, and rightly so, because I was trying to be funny rather than trying to be Simka: I was trying to make jokes rather than approach it as an actress. So Jim said to me, 'I don't care if you're funny or not, I don't care about the jokes, I just want you to be honest.' Which is an extraordinary thing for someone in television comedy to say and which, of course, is the first rule of good acting. Because if you're true to your character and something is written funny, then it'll be funny. So it was a devastating experience followed by one of the best lessons I ever learned."

Andy Kaufman, by the way, provided the voice of the old-country Elvis.

#82 JIM AND THE KID

WRITTEN BY DAVID LLOYD.
DIRECTED BY MICHAEL ZINBERG.

Tony comes into the garage with a ten-year-old boy named Terry (Tony La Torre), who ran up a $12 fare but only has $2 on him. Lou, of course, calls the cops (and mistakenly tells them it's $13). Elaine and Alex try to learn who Terry's parents are, but the kid isn't talking. Jim (who's had his own experience breaking away from his folks) sides with the boy. A policeman arrives to take Terry away, but later, when Terry is left alone at the station house, he simply gets up and leaves. The boy shows up at Jim's—"You're the only Ignatowski in the phone book," he explains—and announces he wants to live with his new friend. Okey-doke.

The next day, they play catch in the apartment, and Jim tutors Terry in philosophy and morality. The philosophy lesson: If a tree falls in the forest and there's no one around to hear, is there a sound? Jim: "Of course there is! Don't let anybody fool you. People try to make that complicated. If a tree falls, there's a sound! The bigger the tree, the bigger the sound! OK. So much for philosophy. . . ."

At the garage that day, Jim extols the virtues of fatherhood, telling the cabbies he's adopted Terry. They're aghast: the boy's parents are frantic, they tell him. There's even a puppy—Snowball—who hasn't touched its food since Terry left. Jim finally submits to this "emotional blackmail" and goes home to tell Terry he has to return to his parents; Alex will bring them around and explain things in the best possible light.

At Jim's, Terry rebels at the thought of going home. He runs into another room and locks the door. Alex shows up with the parents. While Jim tries to tell Alex that Terry is adamant about not leaving, the boy and his parents have a tearful reunion. Before Jim knows it, they are out the door; Terry's father thanks Jim sincerely for taking good care of his runaway son.

Jim is stunned. Alex doesn't know what to say to him. He turns to go, but Jim asks for one favor: Could he say good-bye to Alex as he would have said good-bye to his "son"? Alex reluctantly accepts. Jim takes him by the shoulders and tells him, beautifully, "You don't have to call. You don't have to write. All I ask is that you remember me." At this, Alex tries to leave, but can't! "How can you make a simple thing so heart-wrenching?" Consolingly, Jim asks Alex to stay for lunch. Alex accepts and asks what they're having? Jim smacks his lips: "Spaghetti-Os, popcorn, and herring." Alex drops back to cold, hard reality and says good-bye. Jim ruminates on that: "No matter how many leave the nest, it never gets any easier."

OTHER GUESTS:

Rebecca Clemons and Mark Harrison (Mr. and
 Mrs. Booth, Terry's parents)
Wendall W. Wright (the policeman)

Taxi once again explores the joy and pain of fatherhood. Jim sees it as an ideal platonic state of civilized thought and emotion being handed down from generation to generation—and ideally it is.

The writers very wisely had Alex run interference for the good-hearted Jim, who might otherwise have been accused of kidnapping or worse.

Tony La Torre went on to become a regular on *Cagney & Lacey,* playing Mary Beth Cagney's son, Harvey Jr.

#83 TAKE MY EX-WIFE, PLEASE

WRITTEN BY IAN PRAISER AND HOWARD GEWIRTZ.

DIRECTED BY NOAM PITLIK.

Spirits are high at the Sunshine Cab Co. Latka has won the employee-of-the-month award for putting out an engine fire, and Tony has a date with a model named Randi, whose charms grace a suntan-oil ad in a magazine he proudly displays. Randi has a twin sister, Candi, and Tony asks Alex along to double-date. Unfortunately, Jim gets the mistaken impression that *he's* been invited.

Later, at a fancy Greenwich Village restaurant called La Belle Chateau, we see Alex's ex-wife Phyllis (Louise Lasser) humbly getting a table for one. "Where are lonely, desperate woman usually seated in the better restaurants?" she asks. "Table four," the maître d' crisply replies. After she's seated, Tony and Alex show up, soon followed by Randi and Candi, two knockout blondes in red dresses. Then Jim enters, and when introduced to the twins observes, "Egg split in the womb, eh?" Alex notices Phyllis and feels he should go over and say something. She's lost thirty-five pounds, following what she refers to as the three-month, postdivorce grief diet. She's been hurt, and she reaches out to old, familiar Alex, who gently tells her they just aren't part of each other's lives anymore.

The next day, Elaine hard-heartedly tells Alex he did the right thing—now get away from me, you worm. While Alex is out driving, Phyllis shows up at the garage looking for him. Louie decides to strike. Phyllis—vulnerable and genuinely amused by Louie's sense of humor—agrees to go out with him at 8 P.M. that evening. When Alex returns twelve hours later, Louie is still at work. He and a reluctant Jeff read stiffly from prepared scripts.

Alex, appalled and angry when Louie finally tells him what's up, rushes over to Phyllis's room at The Mayflower Hotel (#1112) to try and talk her out of her date. She's insulted and informs Alex she's capable of making her own decisions and doesn't appreciate his intrusion.

There's a knock on the door, and Phyllis dispatches Alex to the bathroom. Lou arrives in a long coat, and while Phyllis is putting on some last-minute touches, he takes it off to reveal pajamas, and jumps into bed. "I already called room service, and they are sending up champagne (*pause*) canapes (*pause*) and oxygen (*mimics heavy breathing*)." Phyllis calls for Alex and has to be convinced this isn't a joke he cooked up to teach his ex a lesson.

Lou doesn't understand what all the fuss is about. Alex tells Lou he *can't* understand "because *you've* never been married. *You've* never been engaged. You've never even been *invited* to a wedding, for that matter. But there's something that happens to people," he continues, his voice rising, "when for six years they go to bed together and they get up together, who have some kind of connection because they were married and because they had a child. And if that's not true, then something's wrong with you or life!"

Alex asks Phyllis to dinner. She appreciates it and wants to assure him she won't be crazy or demanding—but she can't. Louie, nonplussed, says he'll call her next week. As she and Alex leave, Phyllis admits she somehow gets a kick out of Lou.

OTHER GUESTS:

Randi and Candi Brough (Randi and Candi Moratta)

Alex Rodine (maître d'; misspelled "maitre'd" on the end credits)

Note: Gary Quinn is credited as the hotel bellman, but his scene was cut before the episode aired.

If the world were only as Jim Brooks imagines it, even bitter antagonists would respect each other. Here, Alex affirms the lifelong connection of spouses—even ex-spouses—and families. Fortunately for this world, this is more often true than not. Still, just to keep things from getting cloying,

Lou tries to demonstrate that Alex isn't any better than *he* is. Judging from Louie's wildly inappropriate behavior, we'd say in this case, Lou was wrong. (On a lesser scale, so was Alex: Lou *has* been invited to weddings—his mother's and also a cousin's to which he invites Zena on their first date; but Alex is upset, after all.)

Randi and Candi Brough are professional twins whose many TV and movie appearances include playing Teri and Geri Garrison on the final season of *BJ and the Bear* (the cast of which also included *Taxi* guest Carlene Watkins) and twins in Steve Martin's *The Lonely Guy*. Incidentally, The Mayflower is a famous New York hotel.

#84 THE UNKINDEST CUT

STORY BY BARBARA DUNCAN AND HOLLY HOLMBERG BROOKS.

TELEPLAY BY SAM SIMON.

DIRECTED BY NOAM PITLIK.

Elaine bops into the garage, talking about this great guy, Fred Collins, that she's trying to nab. There's a Japanese costume show opening at the Metropolitan Museum that night, and Elaine has not only gotten herself invited, but also arranged to sit next to Collins at the dinner afterward. To primp for the occasion, she's spent $25 on a hairstyle, which the cabbies don't notice. She practically has an anxiety attack and wishes she could go to Vincenzo Senaca, a hot Manhattan stylist who probably charges $100. Just then, Lou unveils the garage's new Pac-Man machine and gives obsessive Iggy the honor of breaking it in. Lou explains the game as Jim hilariously chomps at the bit.

Meanwhile, Elaine gets off the phone and announces there's been a one o'clock cancellation at Vincenzo's, and she's grabbed it. She rushes to his salon at 53rd Street and Lexington Avenue (though we see a shot of Park Avenue), and finds the fee is a whopping $225. Gulping, Elaine plunges in. Vincenzo (Ted Danson) comes prancing out with a well-coiffed woman who is also attending tonight's opening. He sits Elaine down and engages in some repartee while convincing her to "leave it to me."

The result is a nightmare—a permed helmet that

leaves Elaine in tears and prompts a stunned Louie, at the garage, to note, "I haven't seen a mess like that since someone stuck a firecracker up Uncle Emilio's parrot." Lou is genuinely upset. "Is this a twisted cry for help?" he asks her. Elaine is angry at herself for being intimidated, and for denying her identity in that snooty, high-fashion milieu. Louie and Alex stir Elaine up to seek restitution.

Alex accompanies her to Vincenzo's, where the smarmily gorgeous receptionist thinks she's returned to apologize for causing a scene earlier. A wily and witty Vincenzo deflects all criticism. Even the arrival of uncouth Louie doesn't faze him. Elaine tries to stir up Vincenzo's customers, who are all too deep in his personality cult to complain. "Joan of Arc did less whining at the stake," Vincenzo snickers as Elaine grabs a couple of squeeze bottles of glop to squirt him with. Alex rushes to stop her—if she tries to humiliate him that way, she's no better than he is. Elaine agrees, and puts the bottles down. Louie, however, dumps a bowl of the glop over Vincenzo's head. "*She* may be better than you," he announces happily, "but I ain't!" Victorious, he kisses the shocked receptionist full on the mouth, and he and Elaine leave arm in arm.

OTHER GUESTS:

Gela Jacobson (the receptionist)
Sari Price (the woman also going to the art opening)
Karen Anders (tipsy woman waiting for a cancellation when Elaine returns)
Frances Welter, Torill, Marcia Wolf (Vincenzo's clients; mostly background)

Note: Sam Scarber is credited as the video installer, but his scene was cut before the episode aired; the late Al Rosen, the old boxer who was a resident extra on *Cheers*, is an extra in this episode.

Holly Beth Holmberg Brooks, Jim Brooks's wife, and Barbara Duncan, his invaluable right-hand person, provided the basic story here. So did real life, in the form of an actual chichi hair stylist who'd recently murdered their coifs. Barbara smiles. "I won't say his name, but everybody in L.A. knows who it was."

Marilu Henner brought her own hairdresser to the set as a consultant: "They got a lot of lines from him because he's a real character." She laughs. "He rushed over to [the producers] and said, 'You're not going to believe this, but I left some woman with her head in a bowl, and I hope her hair's not green by the time I get back!'" Incidentally, don't fret for the fair Marilu's own hair: A wig got mangled.

As the smarmy Vincenzo, Ted Danson boosted his career by tackling—indeed, sacking—the difficult role of a flamboyant, Little Richard–style gay hairdresser. Anyone who thinks Danson can only play variants of his Sam Malone character from *Cheers* should check out his dazzling act here (and in the film *Body Heat* as well). "Ted really plugged into that role," Jim Brooks recalls, "and I think it helped him get his part on *Cheers*. But it just wasn't working for the first two or three days. I think we were trying to be very dignified and three-dimensional in terms of his character, and then I think on Thursday I said, 'Fly!' and he flew and it was funny and he was great! That's when he impressed all of us, including [*Cheers* cocreators] the Charles brothers."

This supremely funny episode and Danson's big break almost didn't happen, however. ABC, on the strength of only the story outline, had demanded that the episode be scrapped. Brooks and Paramount Television president Gary Nardino had to fight for it—almost, as it turned out, to the last man (see chapter 2 "Awake, A Wake").

#85 TONY'S COMEBACK

WRITTEN BY SAM SIMON.
DIRECTED BY MICHAEL LESSAC.

A very large, gentle black man named Lucius Franklin (Bubba Smith) is sitting at the table in the garage. Tony notices a Super Bowl ring, and Lucius explains he was a third-string player for the champion 1979 Pittsburgh Steelers. He was cut last season, and is driving a cab while he awaits word on some tryouts. Tony tells his fellow athlete he knows how he feels: A year ago, his boxing license was revoked. Lucius suggests he and Tony help each other work out, and that Tony get back in shape and demand a license review. Just then, Louie comes in, anxious to make an example of the new cabbie. When he sees how big Lucius is, he takes a breath and plunges forth anyway, going over the rules of the garage in a loud, theatrical voice. Lucius calmly accepts it and tells the cabbies that if you're there to do a job, you play by the rules. ''And don't you forget it!'' Louie adds, poking Lucius in the back. Wrong move.

Sometime later, at Bobby Gleason's Gym, Tony and Lucius are working out. Lucius puts Tony through his paces until Tony can't take it anymore. Tony finally says he's kidding himself, that he's washed up as a fighter. Lucius says Tony *can't* give up, because the two of them have a symbiotic relationship. ''Uh, I don't know wha'cher gettin' at, Lucius,'' Tony answers nervously, ''but I *swear*— I'm not attracted to you in the least!'' Lucius explains what he means and goes on to tell Tony (hilariously) about a childhood pet—a duck—and a lesson he learned about not giving up. Tony reluctantly gets the point and goes back to his workout.

Later, in the garage, Jim takes a phone call for Lucius. ''Who shall I say is calling?'' he asks. ''The Dolphins? Wow!'' he says incredulously. ''I'm talkin' to a fish! Excuse me—I mean mammal. Boy, I knew you guys were smart—from Miami? They can dial!'' Lucius asks to talk to the ''fish'' and learns the Miami Dolphins are offering him a tryout. Before he goes, he says, he wants to find out if Tony's been recertified. Tony grudgingly calls up the boxing commission and finds out—yes! He's got his license back! The elated Tony drives Lucius to the airport.

Many days later, however, it's apparent Tony is slacking off, despite the fact he's got a fight coming up with a promising middleweight named Eddie Burke. He talks Alex into helping motivate him, but he's just not Lucius. Meanwhile, Louie's Aunt Lucia comes by to tell her nephew that his Uncle Emilio has died, and the family needs money to bury him. Louie demurs, but Aunt Lucia reminds him she's ''the only one in the family who hasn't put a curse on you.'' Lou tells her he's got a sure thing $1,000 bet against Tony and will kick in $300 after the fight. Lucia isn't sure, but when Louie demonstrates Tony's nimble mind and fast reflexes, she thanks him profusely.

The night of the match, the ring announcer gives Tony's record as 8 wins, 24 losses, and his weight as 161. His opponent—nicknamed The Albany Assassin—has never fought professionally before, but has racked up an astonishing 72–1 record as an amateur. He batters Tony pretty good, but just when Tony decides to throw in the towel and give up, Lucius returns. He tells Tony he's made the Dolphins, and not to give up. ''Do it for the duck,'' he says. Lucius even gets up a cheer to that effect. Tony, *Rocky*-like, finds the will to knock out Burke. Lucius climbs into the ring, and exultantly, he and Tony hug amid the crowd.

OTHER GUESTS:

Naomi Stevens (Aunt Lucia)
Jimmy Lennon (the announcer, as himself)
Gene LeBell (the referee)
John Steve (Eddie Burke)

Note: Ed Weinberger and Jim Brooks are visible among the boxing crowd.

What can you say about Bubba Smith? The former football superstar—a college All-American who went on to shine for the Baltimore Colts, Oakland Raiders, and Houston Oilers—is one of the most appealing personalities on television. By playing a less successful version of himself in this episode, he made the most of television's uncanny ability to pick up on and magnify a person's natural persona. A frequent TV guest star (can anyone forget his great early appearance on *The Odd Couple?*), Bubba's been a regular on four series: *Semi Tough, Open All Night, Blue Thunder,* and *Half Nelson.*

James F. ''Jimmy'' Lennon reprises his recurring role as *Taxi*'s resident ring announcer, and Gene LeBell turns in another performance as a referee. LeBell is a well-known stuntman. Lennon, an actual West Coast boxing announcer, is an uncle of the singing trio The Lennon Sisters.

A very funny final-draft scene scrapped at the last minute had the cabbies at ringside just before the fight. Jim climbs into the ring and hands the befuddled referee a camera to take a picture of himself and Tony. The camera has evidently sat unused for a long time: ''I can't wait to see how my Woodstock pictures came out,'' Jim says happily. Elaine thanks Tony for the great ringside seats.

Tony tells her she's in for a treat: You can hear every punch and really feel the action. Oh, by the way, watch out for splattering blood. And earlier in the episode, Louie tells Banta to try practicing something he's good at—like clotting.

#86 ELEGANT IGGY

WRITTEN BY KEN ESTIN.

DIRECTED BY NOAM PITLIK.

Instead of cards, the cabbies are playing Scrabble. Jim, filling in for Alex, comes up with "Blorf." This pricks up Latka's ears. "It was my nickname in the old country," he explains, adding, "Kids can be cruel." Elaine notices a pair of tickets in Jim's shirt pocket. They're for a concert by classical violinist Itzhak Perlman; some fare gave them to Jim as a tip. Jim asks if anyone wants to come along, and when Elaine and Alex both express interest, he has to make a tortured choice between "Elaine, who is a beautiful woman, and Alex . . . who is not a beautiful woman. No contest!" he declares.

Some evenings later, a sharp-looking, cleaned-and-pressed Jim shows up at Elaine's door and cordially presents "flowers, for a beautiful woman," followed by a corsage, a box of chocolates, a pen-and-pencil set, a dozen lamb chops ("or navel oranges, I forget which") and finally, "A Yoda doll, for a beautiful woman." Elaine, flattered, is nonetheless still in her robe—the concert is *tomorrow* night. The next evening, Jim and Elaine are riding the elevator after the concert when Elaine spots Mrs. Weber (Fran Ryan), one of her gallery's most important patrons and a major figure in the art world. Though panicky at the thought of Mrs. Weber seeing her with Jim, Elaine can't manage to avoid her. But the three of them chat pleasantly, much to Elaine's relief—which quickly turns to horror when Mrs. Weber invites Elaine and her "handsome young man" to a formal-dress musicale she's hosting on Sunday.

Sometime later, at work, a distressed Elaine begs Alex for the right way to keep Jim from attending the important affair. Alex's advice, it turns out, is less helpful than Louie's, who makes a pungent observation on self-interest: "I would dump him

[snaps fingers] without a second thought. You would dump him, but only after you torture yerself with guilt. Either way, it's heartbreak hotel for Iggy. So make it easy on yerself. Do what you have to do, but do it gentle and quick." Elaine is impressed: "Well, what do you know?" Her plan goes out the window, however, when Jim shows up in tux and tails, singing "Top Hat." After first telling Jim he can't go, she feels his (brilliantly portrayed) disappointment and changes her mind.

At the musicale, looking very much the smashing couple, Jim goes over his plan to avoid embarrassment with Elaine: "When you talk to these high-brows and they get you confused, the best thing to do is stay calm and make small talk. But if someone says something really baffling to you, simply laugh knowingly and walk away." He demonstrates with Mrs. Weber and the weather. "Wouldn't it be wonderful if it could always be this nice," she comments. Jim laughs knowingly and walks away.

Later, after a perplexed Jim has patiently listened to a poor little rich woman's romantic complaints, a distraught Mrs. Weber confides to Elaine that the pianist has canceled at the last minute. To Elaine's shock, Jim volunteers to provide entertainment. After a grateful Mrs. Weber assembles the guests and singles out a shell-shocked Elaine for her help, Jim proceeds to impersonate a water cooler—quite messily. As a mortified Mrs. Weber looks on, Elaine urges Jim to play the piano where he attempts to plunk out "London Bridge Is Falling Down." He finally decides the heck with it, and almost subconsciously launches into an accelerated version of Chopin's "Fantasy Impromptu." ("I musta had lessons," he tells himself, thoroughly confused.) We fade to the afternoon ending, as the guests gather around the piano, singing "Two Sleepy People."

Tag: Elaine and Jim leave the parlor arm in arm, her head on his shoulder. Jim: "Tell me somethin' Elaine. Did I have a good time?"

OTHER GUESTS:

Nina Van Pallandt (Lindsay, the rich woman Jim listens to; name is given only in end credits, not in episode)

Note: Mrs. Weber's first name, Elizabeth, is given

only in the end credits, not in the episode. Robert Denison, credited as an art lover named Earl, was cut for time.

"Elegant Iggy" is the authors' favorite episode of *Taxi,* and it's almost impossible to find any TV comedy fan for whom this show isn't the equal of *The Mary Tyler Moore Show*'s "Chuckles Bites the Dust" or *I Love Lucy*'s "Lucy Does a TV Commercial" (remember "Vitameatavegamin"?) Ken Estin deservedly won an Emmy for his script, and the episode certainly didn't hurt Chris Lloyd's chances that year as Outstanding Supporting Actor in a Comedy. Iggy's party scene is a TV classic, as is his appearance at Elaine's door.

"My baby," Ken Estin fondly recalls. " 'Elegant Iggy' is one of those experiences I hope to duplicate in my life but don't expect to. That year, [coproducer] Richard Sakai came to me and said, 'We don't have THE show to submit for the Emmys—we have a lot of good shows, but not the standout. Go write an Emmy show.' And, of course, it was kind of a joke. 'Sure, Richard, whatever you say.'

"There had been an episode the second season called 'Elaine's Secret Admirer' [#33], about Jim's feelings toward Elaine. I had always wanted to do a follow-up story, and I told Jim [Brooks] my idea and everyone said fine. So I held on to it, because I wanted to do it at just the right time. And now here it was. So I sat down and wrote it in, I think, a week. It just came to me very easily, an extremely enjoyable experience, and as I wrote it I was having this feeling that, hey, maybe this *could* be an Emmy-winning show. I know that sounds arrogant, but there was suddenly this feeling it was really gonna happen!"

Chris Lloyd sure thinks it did. "That was a great script," he remembers wistfully. "It changed during the week like every other script, but really not very much. That was the kind of script you read and think to yourself how lucky you are to have writers this good."

"The Yoda doll scene was almost cut," Marilu Henner recalls, "but in the end, that script was probably the one that stayed pretty much intact from beginning to end."

On shooting night, the episode filmed out at more than ten minutes too long. The reason? People simply laughed too hard. "We normally incorporate a certain 'laugh spread,' " Ken explains. "After you've been doing this awhile, you know how much time to leave for the actors to hold during the audience reaction. In this show, Chris had to hold so many times that some bits became just too long—the audience wouldn't let him go ahead!"

Two major bits were excised. In the first, Jim approaches an abstract sculpture, and a fancy-Dan by the name of Earl tells Jim how interesting it is . . . notice the angst of the curvature and the psychological message, blah, blah, blah. And Jim answers, "Yeah, and if you squint, it looks like a chicken." Thinking that Jim is an eccentric genius, Earl obligingly tries to discern the chickenness of the piece as Jim walks away. (The sculpture is visible in the actor's end credit, which was retained.)

Another bit came after the water cooler impression (which Sam Simon remembers "as a trick that [*Taxi* writer-producer] Howard Gewirtz actually does at parties"). This was a moment of mime: Man walking dog up windy hill. If you can imagine Iggy being blown back by the wind while pressing forward, you can see why people laughed so hard and so long.

Jim's brilliantly insightful advice to Elaine about how to handle conversation at high-brow affairs originally appeared virtually word for word in the tag of an earlier script, "Louie's Fling" (episode #72). Excised when the ending was reshot, it had Jim demonstrating for Latka (rather than Elaine) when Alex (rather than Mrs. Weber) came by.

Guest star Fran Ryan is one of the most familiar faces on television. A versatile character actress, her roles have included the original Doris Ziffel on *Green Acres,* Miss Kitty's successor on the last season of *Gunsmoke,* and Rosie Carlson on the soap opera *Days of Our Lives.* Among her many TV movies is *Stalk the Wild Child,* with *Taxi* colleague Rhea Perlman. Jet-setter Nina Van Pallandt—consort at the time to author-hoaxster Clifford Irving—played the decadent, sophisticated woman who whispers sweet-somethings into Jim's ear. "I kept saying to myself," Chris Lloyd remembers, "I know this person from somewhere, and she sure the fuck ain't an extra!"

Chopin's "Fantasy Impromptu" is a perfect choice for Jim's last-minute, saving performance—

an impromptu fantasy if ever there was one. Both it and Frank Loesser–Hoagy Carmichael's "Two Sleepy People" were played off-stage by *Taxi*'s ad hoc musical director, Stan Daniels. "Top Hat," of course, is the title song of the perennially magical Fred Astaire–Ginger Rogers movie musical.

#87 THE WEDDING OF LATKA AND SIMKA

WRITTEN BY HOWARD GEWIRTZ AND
IAN PRAISER.

DIRECTED BY JAMES BURROWS.

Latka enters the garage overjoyed that his multiple personality problems are over. He knows his friends will be skeptical, however, so he's brought along his therapist—Dr. Joyce Brothers! The famous columnist and author explains that Latka had called a phone-in talk show she was on, and his case intrigued her (reasonably enough, given the rarity of true multiple personalities). Latka announces that since he's cured, he can now ask Simka (Carol Kane) to marry him. The cabbies are overjoyed, but Latka himself is strangely morose. It seems, he explains, that he and Simka are orthodox members of their religion and must go through a complex series of tests. "In my country, there is a belief, and rightly so, that the only things that separate us from the animals are mindless superstition and pointless rituals."

The first of these involves the choosing of a *Gewirtzal*, the surrogate who must propose for the groom-to-be. Latka explains that though it's generally the village idiot or a leper, Alex will do in a pinch. Later at Latka's, Alex, dressed in traditional garb, goes through a hilarious proposal ritual with Simka. In response, she grabs the nose of the *Gewirtzal* to signify her acceptance.

Sometime later, it is time for the *Mertzig*, the traditional imparting of wisdom from the man's mother to the prospective bride. At Latka's apartment, his visiting mother, Greta (Susan Kellerman), somberly informs Simka: "Men are nothing but lazy lumps of drunken flesh. They crowd you in bed, get you all worked up, and then before you can say, 'Is that all there is?' that's all there is.

Your flaxen hair will become like dead grass, and your once-firm breasts will fall to the floor." Simka replies, deadpan, "Thank you, I will store that away." Despite the *Mertzig,* Simka still wants to marry Latka, and the garage is transformed into a wedding site.

The big day arrives, with Louie inexplicably serving as best man. Elaine and Alex notice some of Latka's countrywomen crying loudly: Mascha, the wedding translator and a weatherman for the BBC, cheerfully explains the ritual, "They're lamenting the bride's future as slave to her husband, and the groom's burden of family responsibility, which will eventually crush him." The Reverend H. L. Gorky, who speaks no English, steps up to the altar alongside Mascha. Latka and Simka come down the stairs, dressed in traditional old-country garb—the man wearing the gown, the woman wearing her husband-to-be's finest suit.

The first part of the wedding involves placing the "Crown of Rue" on the head of the bride—if she can walk without its falling, she will be proven a virgin and the wedding can continue. Simka takes one step, and the crown virtually flies off. She begins explaining, in terms ranging from innocent to hilariously graphic, that this is a mistake, that she "has never felt the hot breath of a *lover*. . . ." The reverend lets this go by and moves on to the "Ritual of Questions"—three riddles. The happy couple get two of them right, but fail the third. The wedding is over. Simka, in a rage, denounces her religion and says she and Latka will get married anyway. The reverend, landing on his feet, says this is exactly what he needed to hear: This loud demand to be married is simply part of the ritual. Right. The marriage is completed, and the garage erupts into the lively Dance of the *Plumas*.

OTHER GUESTS:

Vincent Schiavelli (Reverend
  H. L. Gorky)
Peter Elbling (Mascha)

This episode, another of *Taxi*'s best, is a devastating satire about the realities and the illusions of marriage. Sad to say, but the *Mertzig* and the old-country lamentations are probably more appropriate than happy church bells and wedding cakes in a country with such high divorce rates, spouse beating, infidelity, and single parenthood. Yet despite these harsh realities, Simka—and perhaps the viewers as well—keeps finding what a Bruce Springsteen song calls "reason to believe."

Carol Kane found herself pleasantly surprised with her third guest appearance as Simka. "After the 'Return' episode [#81], Jim Brooks asked me that if it were alright, would I mind doing another episode? So, of course I said yeah, and later on somebody happens to mention that Latka and I are getting married! And I'm saying to myself, 'Ohhhhh, OK.' And I'm wondering what this means. And then Ed [Weinberger] sort of sidles up to me after we shot the wedding episode and he says to me, 'We were wondering [mumble, mumble] arrangement [mumble, mumble] you know, maybe [mumble, mumble] next year?' "

By the time Friday night rolled around, Carol was more than ever a part of the family. Consequently, Danny DeVito didn't hesitate to try and make her break up. "That thing with the 'Crown of Rue' and the long monologue about the hot breath of a lover, I just couldn't get through that thing." She chuckles at the memory. "Every time I looked at Danny, it was over. Over!" She laughs. "His expressions and everything—he's just so funny! I never did get through that monologue in rehearsal, and I was practically crying at the thought that I might not be able to get through this without laughing. But on shoot night," says the true pro, "I just gritted my teeth and got through it."

By the way: The *Gewirtzal* is indeed named for *Taxi* writer Howard Gewirtz.

#88 COOKING FOR TWO

WRITTEN BY KEN ESTIN AND SAM SIMON.
DIRECTED BY JAMES BURROWS.

Jim is sitting around his apartment in his pajamas, eating cereal and watching a soap opera, when a giant wrecking ball crashes through his living room. In more of a daze than usual, he wanders into the garage with an overnight bag and tries to tell his friends what happened. "You put up with a few inconveniences when you live in a condemned building," he explains. He lays down on a bench, but Louie yells at him to get up, that he can't sleep in the garage. Alex gets on Louie's case about it, but Lou says nobody should talk big unless they're willing to put Jim up themselves.

At that, everyone demurs, and Louie presses them to take Iggy in. Jim assures them he's a good houseguest, except that he sometimes leaves the cap off the toothpaste and screams in his sleep. With that out in the open, Lou suggests that Jim stay with his "best buddy." Alex whitens, but Jim picks an unflattered Louie instead. The next day at work, Louie says Jim wasn't so bad: They played pool, went to sleep, Jim screamed, they went to sleep again. Jeff announces that Latka and Simka are inviting the cabbies to dinner with them. Louie, getting sentimental, says Jeff ought to think about marrying and settling down. He did, Jeff answers—eleven years ago. Oh. Meanwhile, Alex, on the pay phone, is speaking to a very distraught Jim. Something terrible has happened, and Alex rushes over to Louie's apartment. When he arrives, the place looks like a doused campfire. Jim explains he'd left something on the stove, and now the place is a cinderbox. Jim gets panicky and begs Alex to tell him everything's going to be alright. But then Lou comes home to find everything quite wrong. The only thing saved was his beloved violin, which the shocked and tearful Louie promptly cracks over Iggy's head. He breaks down, then fires Jim and throws Alex out.

At the garage, days later, an apologetic Jim comes by with a blank check from his wealthy father. Louie's eyes light up—jackpot! The only hitch is that Jim has to call his dad to OK the amount. Alex tells Lou he should write down the real figure—maybe eight or nine thousand. But Lou, calling like a high-wire artist for complete silence, says he has to find a figure high enough to make Jim's dad shiver, "Ee-ewghhhhh," but not so high that he won't shrug, "Ehhh-uhhh." In one of the show's funniest routines, Lou arrives at $29,542. Jim phones his father, who clears it and then hangs up on him. Louie is overjoyed. Dad is relieved, too, says Jim: He thought Lou would ask for $200,000.

Episode #88: "Cooking for Two."

"This was toward the end of the season, and once again," recalls coauthor Sam Simon, "we were just desperate for scripts. So Ken [Estin] and I snagged Jim Brooks and said, 'We have this idea for a show where Iggy moves in with Louie.' And Jim says, 'No, absolutely not, I don't wanna do an *Odd Couple* story.' But we said that wasn't what we had in mind, and we pitched this story and he loved it. In fact, Jim was the one who came up with that last scene. I don't remember how Ken and I originally ended it, but now here we all are in Jim's office trying to come up with a new ending, and Jim not only thinks of this great bit but starts acting it out just like Louie! He was just so immersed in those characters he created, he knew exactly how they would react. He just railed through that routine, sitting at his desk and laughing at the stuff, enjoying the comedy of it. It's just another example of how Jim works, and his genius."

The formidable-looking wrecking ball was made of plastic and actually weighed only about eighty pounds. Water inside it gave it that weighty, swaying motion. Incidentally, the voices on Iggy's soap opera belong to Marilu Henner and, as a couple of people remember, *Taxi* writer-producer Ian Praiser (sounding nothing like he did in "Of Mice and Tony").

Two small inconsistencies pop up in this episode; the first of them is reconcilable: Louie comes home seemingly minutes after he came to work (with the cabbies greeting him as if they hadn't seen him all day). The best explanation is that he'd had an appointment or had come in late, and that the drivers had been given their cab assignments by Jeff. Thus, when they finally do see Louie it's at the end of the shift. The second inconsistency—which appears only in the syndicated version due to questionable editing—also involves Louie's arrival at the garage.

After his night with houseguest Jim, Alex needles Lou by asking, "How's married life, Latka?" In the original network airings, that line really *was* addressed to Latka; when the episode got snipped for syndication, it ended up being directed at Louie.

#89 THE ROAD NOT TAKEN, PART I

WRITTEN BY KEN ESTIN AND SAM SIMON.
DIRECTED BY JAMES BURROWS.

After Jim demonstrates a card trick—with typically Iggy results—Elaine rushes in with news of an important decision she has to make. She's been offered a job as manager of a new art gallery in Seattle. It's small, but has potential, and it's better than being a receptionist/assistant. On the other hand, her family's friends and roots are in New York City. What should she do? Alex doesn't want to give advice on such a large scale, but Tony suggests that maybe if they tell Elaine of crossroads decisions in their own lives, they can help her.

Tony flashes back to one of his first pro fights. He's in the locker room with manager Jack (Eugene Roche) when mobster Frank comes in. Frank tells Tony that his opponent Wilkes is going to win in the third round. "Geesh," Tony says innocently, "no wonder Jack didn't want you to talk to me. You're so discouraging." Frank tries again. "I represent some people who've got a lotta money against you." Tony replies naively, "Oh, no, are they right very often?" Frank finally decides upon the direct approach. Grabbing Tony's face with one big hand, he tells him, "I want you to take a dive. In the third round. In the ring. Tonight." When Tony refuses, Frank shrugs and leaves. Jack comes back in, and when he hears Tony refused to throw the fight, says how proud he is—and that he'll call Tony later from his sister's house in Union City, New Jersey. In the ring during a clinch, Wilkes says that since Tony refused, now *he's* taking the dive, which he comically proceeds to do.

Back in the present, Lou tells Elaine she's wasting her time with "profiles in sewage." He harkens back to the story of how he upgraded himself from lowly cabbie to (lowly) dispatcher. Louie's predecessor is a kindly old gent named Tom (J. Pat O'Malley), who cares so much for the cabbies that he gives away his lunchtime desserts to cheer up low-booking drivers, and promises to assign a sniffling Felipe Rodriguez to cab #512, which has "the best heater in the fleet." Louie comes in—with a full head of hair—and after suggesting strip poker to an offended female cabbie named Lydia, reluctantly takes over the dispatcher's cage for Tom, who's taking his sister to the doctor. A disgruntled Louie gives the virtually unheated cab #222 to Rodriguez and tells him tough luck about the heater. Rodriguez offers Lou five bucks for the cab with a good heater. A celestial light shines on Louie's face as it breaks into a heavenward grin.

In the present, Alex explains that in one week, Louie undermined poor Tom's authority and got him to semiretire as a crossing guard. Jim relates a tale that finds him at Harvard. There, four students—including Jim's roommate Gordon (Tom Hanks) and Jim's girl friend Heather (Wendy Phillips)—are sitting around a dorm room studying, eating marijuana brownies, and staring at a lava lamp. Enter Jim—a real straight drip—who's doing a term paper on Plutarch and wants to go study in the library with Heather. Not only doesn't he want to join them in smoking pot, but he unplugs "the groo-oovy lamp," and pontificates, "It's not just 'doing your own thing,' it's doing the *right* thing!" The two other guys and the other girl leave, with Gordon unsuccessfully trying to take a hot lava lamp in his hands, and returning in a minute for a memorable fall. Heather finally sweet-talks Jim into eating a marijuana brownie. Very hesitantly, just to shut her up, he takes a bite. There, see? Nothing. But then, for a moment, his eyes widen, his features turn rubbery—it's Iggy! But just for a moment. Jim quickly snaps out of it and insists it's time they were running along to the library. He leads Heather out the door—and then stops, considers, and pockets a brownie for later.

OTHER GUESTS:

Charles Cioffi (Frank)
Gene LeBell (the referee)
Jim Echollas (the boxer Wilkes; actor not listed in end credits)
Michael A. Salcido (Felipe Rodriguez; actor not listed in end credits)

Tony Eldridge (the other boy in the dorm room)

Note: The other girl in the dorm room is uncredited.

#90 THE ROAD NOT TAKEN, PART II

WRITTEN BY IAN PRAISER AND HOWARD GEWIRTZ.

DIRECTED BY JAMES BURROWS.

After flashbacks to the previous episode, Elaine's still undecided about moving to Seattle to head a small art gallery. Latka helpfully tells his own crossroads story, about the snowy, windswept night (captioned "Summer, 1977") on which he told his mother he was moving to America. Mama Gravas (Susan Kellerman) can't understand why her son wants to live there. They keep dogs as pets and eat chickens, she explains—it's completely backward. Latka decides to go anyway—mainly for the women, it seems.

Back in the present, Elaine's young children, Jennifer (Melanie Gaffin) and Jason (David Mendenhall), arrive after school. "We're here to see Mommy," Jennifer innocently tells Louie, who answers cheerfully, "Awww, Mommy, how cute! Gimme a buck." Elaine rescues them, however, and after she explains the situation, the kids say they want her to take the job, but that whatever she decides is OK by them. The kids leave to go home, and Elaine turns to Alex's story for help.

His flashback finds him on the ladder of corporate success. One day at 3:15 P.M. his boss, Mr. Ambrose (Max Wright), calls him in for a meeting about a promotion to regional manager. Ambrose notes that Alex is an excellent worker and very ambitious: He even drives a cab at night to better support his wife and daughter. The company is, however, a shining beacon of capitalism: When Alex is invited to sit, Ambrose marks on a psychological form which chair he picked. When Alex makes a small, conversational joke, Ambrose notes efficiently that the company appreciates a sense of humor, and that Alex can stop now.

Ambrose gets to why Alex was called in: Did he or did he not punch a time card for a fellow employee named Mrs. Callan? Alex says yes, he did,

but it was only five minutes for a fellow worker to take her sick child to the hospital. Ambrose replies coldly, "Oh, so you admit stealing from the company?" Alex tells him, no, that's not what he meant, but Ambrose corners him. Everything will be alright, Ambrose tells Alex, if he'll just say, "I was wrong, I'm very sorry, and it will never happen again." At first Alex finds this silly and can't believe Ambrose is serious. Ambrose childishly insists, however, and repeats the exact wording. Alex apologizes in his own, quite reasonable words. Ambrose remarks that Alex really likes to have his own way, doesn't he? That's not the way a team operates, Ambrose tells him. Now repeat after me. . . . Alex demurs, and Ambrose curtly sends him off. Seeing his promotion about to fly off into the wind, Alex turns at the door and repeats what Ambrose wants to hear, adding, "you miserable worm" before bolting out the door.

Elaine mulls over all the stories when her prospective employer, Mr. Thompson, arrives unexpectedly. He's leaving for Seattle sooner than he thought, and he needs an answer right now. Elaine panics and starts to spill her guts out, going over all the "what ifs" and "if thens" jumbled up in her mind—until finally she says, Yes! She wants the job! A disdainful Thompson withdraws the offer. He tells her she's a looney and couldn't possibly run an art gallery or anything else. Elaine, infuriated, punches him in the stomach. She immediately apologizes as the winded Thompson staggers out. Elaine turns to her friends and says that after all the anguish she put herself through, it wasn't so hard to make the right choice—to stay with her friends in New York. She leaves to tell her kids that she's decided to stay, while a bewildered Tony rightly observes, "But she *took* the job . . . !"

OTHER GUESTS:

Jill Jaress (Sally, Ambrose's secretary)
Matthew Faison (Mr. Thompson)

The last of the four "pickup" two-parters gives us fascinating insight into the personal histories of Alex, Louie, and Jim, and two equally funny if less eventful background stories about Tony and Latka. The episodes are a special treat: In real life, after all, don't we sometimes wish we could go back in time to see our friends and family in the days before we knew them?

Some terrific guest stars grace these episodes. Tom Hanks went on to Oscar-winning stardom with *Splash, Big, Philadelphia, Forrest Gump* and other films. At the time of this episode he was costarring with Peter Scolari (*Newhart*) in ABC's *Bosom Buddies*, which, like *Taxi*, was shot on the Paramount lot (and produced for a time by *Taxi*'s Ian Praiser and Howard Gerwirtz). "He was great, man!" Jim Brooks enthuses. "Just 'cause he loved the show and wanted to do it." Hanks didn't come up with the great lava lamp gag, but he did devise "a lot of moments. He came in, and it wasn't a star turn; we were struggling to make it work, and he struggled with it as an *actor*."

David Mendenhall and Melanie Gaffin enter the roles of Elaine's young children, Jason and Jennifer. They both returned in episode #111 ("Arnie Meets the Kids"); Mendenhall was also featured in #105 ("Sugar Ray Nardo"), and Gaffin appeared in the finale, #112 ("A Grand Gesture"). Mendenhall recently made his feature film debut in *Over the Top,* and his TV work includes the eighties' *Twilight Zone* ("Examination Day") and voiceovers for the animated *Berenstain Bears.*

ALF costar Max Wright, who plays Alex's ultra-corporate employer, played a far wimpier boss in *Buffalo Bill.* He also had a nice turn in the three-part closing episodes of the fourth season of *Cheers,* playing a Boston politician whom Diane supports. Secretary Jill Jaress had a small role in the very first episode of *Taxi.*

J(ames) Pat(rick) O'Malley (1901–1985) was one of the best-loved players in the business (though understandably, people *still* get his name confused with those of fellow actors Pat O'Malley and John P. O'Malley). The British-born actor's career stretches back into the mists, and he was an old, familiar face on television since its infancy. Some of his most notable roles were as Bert Beasley, who married *Maude*'s housekeeper, Mrs. Naugatuck; as Tim O'Hara's boss on *My Favorite Martian;* and (along with two other actors) as Rob Petrie's father on *The Dick Van Dyke Show.* He was a costar of the short-lived ABC series *A Touch of Grace* (1973) and of a 1975 sitcom pilot, *Where's the Fire?* His Irish and British brogues have graced the animated Dis-

ney features *101 Dalmatians, Alice in Wonderland,* and *The Jungle Book.* His roles on *Taxi* and on a concurrent episode of *Barney Miller* were among his last.

As with "Jim the Psychic" (episode #65), Chris Lloyd approached his part in this episode warily. "I was resisting the brownie scene a little bit," he says, "because I thought it wasn't going to be believable. I think the change was too quick: I wanted more method, I wanted him to wait until it was ingested." Better ingested than digested. By the way, *Taxi* continuity buffs might have deduced that Iggy's Harvard story takes place in 1970—specifically on Friday, October 16 of that year, according to a calendar in the background. The nearest other year when October 16 is a Friday is 1964, and the clothing, hairstyles, and Indian music rule that year out. Since other episodes tell us Jim only attended college his freshman year, and only studied during his first semester, he must have been about nineteen in the flashback, and thus about thirty-one at the time of *Taxi.*

#91 THE SHLOOGEL SHOW

WRITTEN BY KEN ESTIN AND SAM SIMON.
DIRECTED BY NOAM PITLIK.

Simka and Latka arrive at the garage all lovey-dovey. It's enough to make Louie want to puke, but he changes his tune when the two announce they're throwing a *Shloogel.* It's an old-world tradition, they explain, where newly married couples share their happiness by setting up their friends with perfect mates. Simka, who has searched for the cabbies' counterparts for two months, says, "Like many people in my country, I am born with the gift to match people. Comes to us naturally as eating, sleeping, and disemboweling sheep." Alex wants no part of it: He still believes in old-fashioned chance encounters and "that old black magic." Simka laughs—the date they chose for him said the very same thing. Alex decides to go along.

Sometime later, at Mario's, the cabbies each sit with their respective matches. Simka asks Tony to describe his perfect woman. He says blonde, leggy, feminine—none of which describe the earthy, attractive Vicki DeStefano (Anne De Salvo), who when asked about her perfect man answers, "It

Episode #91: "The Shloogel Show."

tive, well-bred Susan McDaniel (Carlene Watkins), who, as the evening slips on to the strains of *The Love Boat* theme, seems more and more disenchanted with her increasingly smitten date. Everyone else seems to be getting along.

Judy is taken with Louie's lack of pity. "I'll lead you home," he joshes at evening's end. He thanks Simka for a perfect match. "Before you know it, she'll be takin' me home to meet the dog!" Vicki, giving Tony boxing tips, clips him good and earns his respect. (He accidentally clips her, too, but she rebounds, explaining, "I'm lucky yer a bum.") At 1 A.M. the evening's over, and everyone departs happily—except for Susan, who only reluctantly accepts a ride offer from Alex. When they arrive at her place, she gradually gives him her phone number (555-2437).

Back at Mario's, Simka realizes that Alex will never see Susan again. "I think we're all going to die," she somberly tells Latka. "I think love's an illusion. I think we failed with Alex, who laughed at our traditions, and he was right . . . and so we are frauds." "Oh. Too bad," says Latka. "Damn right, too bad," Simka answers with a sad smile, realizing the fragility of our beliefs in life.

OTHER GUESTS:

T. J. Castronova (Tommy, the bartender at Mario's)

The fifth season opener is another classic episode, with Brooks and company on a roll. Cowriter Sam Simon remembers being proud of having such a great show that consisted almost entirely of people sitting around tables and talking.

And what a bounty of guest stars: Anne De Salvo is an Obie Award–winning theater actress whose films include *My Favorite Year, Perfect!* (with Marilu Henner), *Stardust Memories,* and *Compromising Positions.* Wallace Shawn is a well-known New York playwright-actor, and the son of the longtime *New Yorker* editor William Shawn; he first reached mass audiences with his film *My Dinner with Andre* (1981), and has since appeared in *The Princess Bride, The Moderns, Head Office* (with Danny DeVito), and other movies.

Murphy Cross had starred in the short-lived CBS series *Phyl and Mikhy,* and had appeared in the film

ain't *this* meatball." She and Tony start to argue, but Simka assures them intimately, "there will be plenty of time for that later!"

Elaine is introduced to Arnie Ross (Wallace Shawn) a good-humored nebbish and self-styled romantic loser. After a few minutes he tells Elaine it's silly for him to hang around, and he gets up to leave. Elaine insists he sit back down with her. "Oh, good," he says delightedly. "You're gonna prolong my agony!"

Jim meets a star of the seventies' *Bob Newhart Show.* "Why, you're Carol! Played by Marcia Wallace!" he sputters, adding, "Jim Ignatowski, as himself." Louie gets an adorable, curly-haired blonde named Judy Griffith (Murphy Cross), who, unfortunately, is blind from glaucoma. Louie confronts Latka about that. "Oh," says Latka, "you think that Simka picked a blind girl so she could not see you? . . . Well, you may be right." Finally, there's skeptical Alex. He's paired with the attrac-

Annie. Since then, her TV credits have included *Night Court, Knot's Landing, Cheers* (as a younger woman for whom Coach falls), and the miniseries *Scruples* and *Maximum Security.* Carlene Watkins—who became Ed Weinberger's girl friend and is now his wife—was already a prolific TV actress, and has since gone on to guest shots on *Magnum, P.I., Remington Steele, Hotel,* and other shows, and was a cast member of *Mary* and *The Tortellis.*

Finally, there's Marcia Wallace of the classic *Bob Newhart Show.* "I don't remember exactly why we picked her," says Simon, "but it was always her, right from the first draft. She was great about helping out: She came up with Jim's line about the spiked water cooler, and when we asked her if there were anything distinctive Jim could ask her to do, she suggested that laugh she had on *Newhart.* She was a great sport."

#92 ALEX GOES OFF THE WAGON

WRITTEN BY DANNY KALLIS.
DIRECTED BY NOAM PITLIK.

Elaine is using the garage pay phone to call the police about Alex, who's been missing with his cab for fifteen hours. Louie, who'd already sent Tony to check Alex's apartment, is genuinely worried (though not so worried that he doesn't cop a feel when sympathetic Elaine hugs him and blubbers, "Oh, I'll take care of you, Louie"). Alex finally shows up and is greeted by Elaine in typically maternal fashion: First she smothers him with kisses, and then she scolds him for making everyone worry. (Later, Alex even tells her right out, "Don't mother me.")

Alex explains he took a high roller to Atlantic City and was rewarded with a $200 tip. Though he'd sworn off gambling, he tried his luck at dice and won $2,000—and, he's even prouder to say, he got up and walked away a winner. Louie, however, tempts Alex in a crap game held in the back room of a fancy restaurant at 1 West First Street, "not five minutes from here." Over Elaine's protests, off they go.

An hour or two later, we see Alex hit three times in a row, followed by two quick crap outs. Louie warns Alex to quit and tells him straight out his hot streak is over. Alex responds by betting everything he's won—$9,000 by now—on his next pass. He rolls nine, a "point" number: To win, he has to roll nine once more before rolling a seven or an eleven. He fails to, and craps out big. Louie, who'd stopped betting, offers his condolences and then goes home to roll around in his winnings. A disheveled Alex heads to the restroom.

He calls the garage and asks Jim to go to his locker (combination three-fourteen-sixty), take some money out of a box of Ritz Crackers there, and bring it to him. After some initial confusion, Jim does so. Alex bets and loses all but a portion he'd asked Jim to hold on to no matter what. Then he loses even that.

In the restroom again, Alex badgers Jim for some money. Jim agrees to loan it on one condition—that Alex listen to a story about his own past obsession with drugs. As Alex listens impatiently, Jim tells how one night, doing hallucinogenic mushrooms in the New Mexico desert, he learned about wanting to feed an obsession so badly he'd almost betray a friend. That's when he knew, he says, that he'd hit rock bottom. Now, he tells Alex, "Welcome to rock bottom." He puts his money away. Alex, desperate, distracts Jim and picks his pockets. As he greedily counts his booty, he looks up and sees himself in the mirror, he sees what he's become. Alex starts to put the money back into the seemingly out of it Jim's jacket pocket. Jim, well aware of things, smiles and pulls the pocket flap open for him.

GUESTS:

Anthony Charnota (the craps table stickman)
Keone Young (the Japanese gambler)
Carolyn DeMirjian (the lady gambler)

This episode is another *Taxi* classic.

Alex is predisposed to gambling, as evidenced in countless past episodes: He bets on football and boxing with Louie, and he goes to the racetrack to bet on horses. In a nice bit of irony, it is Jim who, in a Carlos Castaneda–inspired moment of philosophy, helps Alex literally see the light; after all, it was Alex who helped curb Jim's own appetite for gambling in "Jim Gets a Pet" (episode #38).

#93 JIM'S INHERITANCE

WRITTEN BY KEN ESTIN.

DIRECTED BY NOAM PITLIK.

Louie gets a tragic phone call from Jim's brother: Jim's father died on Friday and was buried on Sunday. Jim couldn't be reached. Louie decides he's the one who should break the news to Iggy. The cabbies object, but Lou says he has experience in these sorts of things. "Ask Perez over there," he challenges, pointing to a mechanic. "Hey, Perez, didn't I just tell you a couple of days ago your father died?" From the look on Perez's face, no. Regardless, Jim considers Lou his closest friend, and when Jim wanders in, Louie sits him down. "[Your father] is no longer with us," Lou says gently. Jim: "He never was. He lives in Boston." Lou tries again. "No, no, Jim—he's gone on to his final resting place." Jim: "A condo in Palm Beach?" When the news finally sinks in, an anguished Jim asks for a cab so he can work through his grief.

Days later, in the garage, Tony is discussing the George Steinbrenner domino theory: The New York Yankees' controversial owner continues to screw up the beloved team, causing discontent among the service class, which affects the city's movers and shakers, who, in turn, make bad business and political decisions, thus undermining the nation's economy. At that moment Elaine walks in, saying she heard the Russians have just launched "another killer satellite" (sic). Tony nods knowingly: "Steinbrenner . . . !"

Jim's father's attorney, John Bickers, arrives to discuss Jim's inheritance. Louie, with dollar sign eyes, tries to make Bickers comfy. He buys him coffee, and when Jeff gives him a mere cake doughnut, Lou angrily throws it out the door. "This man is an attorney!" he scolds Jeff. "Eight years of school! Here," he says to Bickers, "a maple log!" Then Jim ambles in, showing off a great doughnut he's just found. Bickers wants to speak with Jim privately, but Jim insists on having his friends listen in.

Bickers tells Jim that his father, who'd disinherited him when Jim dropped out of Harvard, reinstated him a few months ago. He left Jim $3.5 million. However, Jim's brother and sister want to have Jim declared incompetent, and the money put

into a conservatorship. Alex tells Jim this means he will get an allowance and be treated like a child. That sounds pretty good to Jim, but the cabbies convince him that this is against his dad's wishes. Jim gets fighting mad. He vows, "I'm gonna get my three-and-a-half-million! Or fail to do so!"

At the hearing, held informally in the judge's chambers, Louie speaks in Jim's behalf, as does Alex, whose impassioned speech about decent human behavior prompts the judge to comment, "It's one of the problems in this court that they tend to rerun *Mr. Deeds Goes to Town* as often as they do." He rules against Jim.

That night at Jim's new apartment—in a brick tenement with the fire escape out front—Elaine finds a large trunk at the door. It's from Jim's father's estate, and Jim, after wrestling with his memories, asks Elaine to leave him to open it alone. She understands and tells him to call if he needs to talk.

In a stunning monologue that swerves astonishingly from pathos to humor, Jim goes through the trunk's contents. He places his father's suit on a reclining chair, which falls back under the ghostly weight. In the jacket, Jim finds an audiocasette. He plays it on a small tape recorder, and listens as Stevie Wonder sings "You Are the Sunshine of My Life." Chillingly, Jim listens and understands, and we fade out on a tour de force.

GUESTS:

Dick Sargent (John Bickers)

F. William Parker (Judge Herring; name is given in end credits, not in episode)

Santos Morales (Perez)

Richard Monahan (Winslow, the siblings' attorney at the hearing; no lines, though referred to by name)

Like the Yankees' Don Mattingly, who recently tied the record for consecutive home runs, *Taxi* kept bashing out one classic episode after another. This one is the TV equivalent of a grand slam. The previous year's Emmy-winning comedy writer, Ken Estin, scored a nomination for this episode, losing by a nose to old *Taxi* hands Glen and Les Charles for a *Cheers* script. And another astonishing performance helped Chris Lloyd clinch another Emmy win.

In typically modest fashion, Chris shyly gives

credit to the writers and to happenstance. The episode was "brilliantly aided," he says, "by an accident. When I was draping my dad's huge clothes over the chair, and the chair fell backward as if his ghost were there—that was accidental. It was perfect timing, and ghostly—like suddenly he were alive. And it sure helped me out. It was one of those moments you just . . ." his voice trails off as he looks for the right word. He doesn't need one. The scene speaks for him.

The familiar Dick Sargent made over three hundred TV appearances and played Darren No. 2 on *Bewitched* before passing away in 1994. Oh, and in case you're wondering, the Russians do *not* have any "killer satellites." Neither does the United States—yet.

#94 SCENSKEES FROM A MARRIAGE, PART I

WRITTEN BY HOWARD GEWIRTZ AND
IAN PRAISER.

DIRECTED BY NOAM PITLIK.

It's brutal winter, and stranded cabbie Cindy Bates (Allyce Beasley) is panicking over the radio. Her cab's crashed, the window's broken, and she's on an unmarked country road off the Roxhill exit of New Jersey's Garden State Parkway. As Louie indelicately puts it just before her radio dies, "She's doomed!" Latka, however, says he knows the road: It's near the farm where he and Simka buy goat knuckles. He braves the storm, but wrecks the tow truck three miles from Bates's cab. He trudges to her, and when it looks as if they're going to freeze to death, Bates says the only way they can generate enough heat to survive is by having sex. Latka is reluctant, but there seems to be no other way.

Later, at the garage, Jeff exultantly takes the news that the state police found the wrecked cab and rescued Latka and Bates. The cabbies cheer the news, with Jim taking their applause in stride as he coincidentally walks in. He's happy, he tells his friends, because he's discovered family—in this case, the "family" of MasterCard holders. Alex tries to explain that "family" in this case is advertising fodder. Jim says strictly, "Don't bad-mouth the family, Alex."

Latka comes in, and the cabbies are overjoyed to see he's OK. But he angrily shoos everyone away and tells Alex privately that he cheated on Simka to stay alive. Alex says Latka can't tell Simka and hurt her to relieve his guilt; Latka understands— the noble thing to do is to deceive her. To make the evening seem perfectly normal, then, Alex must come to dinner tonight with them as planned. But Simka knows her husband too well. She rushes up to him happily on his arrival, stops short, and screeches, "You did it with another woman!" Latka explains his actions, to little avail. Alex tries to leave, but old-world etiquette demands he stay. "The damn guest must come first," Simka loudly explains. She plops some food on his plate. "Here, damn guest!" Simka packs Latka a bag, cursing in her language.

They finally allow Alex to leave and decide that for their marriage to continue, they must seek the guidance of their reverend. At their church, they find Reverend Gorky and begin their confession-like "Unburdening." Mascha, the translator from their wedding, interrupts; he has three older ladies with him who are touring the church. The priest invites them to stay and witness the Unburdening. Latka and Simka explain the situation, and the priest sagely decides that since Latka has sinned with someone he works with, Simka must also sin with someone Latka works with. They leave the two alone with that instruction. Latka asks Simka, "You mean to tell me you're going to sleep with one of my friends?" When she nods yes, he tells her (ironically echoing Ralph Kramden), "Baby, you're the greatest."

OTHER GUESTS:

Vincent Schiavelli (Reverend H. L. Gorky)
Peter Elbling (Mascha)

Note: The three elderly women are uncredited.

#95 SCENSKEES FROM A MARRIAGE, PART II

WRITTEN BY IAN PRAISER AND HOWARD
GEWIRTZ.

DIRECTED BY NOAM PITLIK.

The story picks up at Latka and Simka's apartment, where the two of them try to decide with which of Latka's coworkers Simka must sleep. She says Alex is a stranger to her, Louie turns her stomach, and Tony—the one "with arms of steel"—isn't Latka's first choice. Simka suggests they do as they would in the old country—throw a dinner party and pick the last man to arrive. ("Oh," nods Latka, "you mean the way we elect our president.") Later, in a daze, he invites the male cabbies to dinner. That evening, Louie is first to arrive. Simka's relief is short-lived, however, as he only sticks his head in to say he's double parked and will be right back. Tony arrives, and then Jim, who says he just beat Louie out of a parking space. "I sure love dinner parties," he adds happily. "It's one of the few occasions you get to be formal and ill at ease." Finally, Alex shows up. Simka is a goner—it'll be Lou. But before Alex can enter, Lou arrives, and after some jockeying gets in first. Latka stands up, thanks his guests for coming, and shows them out.

At the garage soon afterward, Simka, upset and afraid about what she has to do, seeks out Elaine. She can't quite say what's on her mind; she asks Elaine if she's religious, and what's Alex like, and have the two of them ever . . . you know. (Elaine avoids answering.) Simka gets more and more upset about what she has to do, but won't say what it is "that contaminates my one life on earth! . . . It's just *girl talk, Elaine.*"

Simka eventually arrives at Alex's and explains what she needs. A sleepy Alex doesn't quite understand, but he's willing to listen if she needs to talk. "Talk is cheap," she answers. "I want your body." Alex starts to laugh nervously. She insists her request is for real. Alex, finally awake, calls her religion barbaric. Angrily, she asks the Jewish Alex, "Do you mock us? Do I mock you because you do not eat animals with cloven hooves unless they chew their cud?" She accuses him of playing hard to get, and (brilliantly) goes through a half-hysterical series of seduction clichés. Alex calms them both down, and remains steadfast in his refusal to violate her. He says he'll take her home and caringly makes sure she's bundled up.

At her apartment, they find Latka and a consoling Jim. Before Alex can say anything, Latka gives him his thanks. "Now get out of here, you swine." But Simka tells her husband, "I have bad news for

you, my darling. I have been faithful to you." Now, they have to circle each other once for their divorce ritual. They are heartbroken. Simka tells Latka that she will miss the children they could have had together. As they slowly circle each other, Jim wonders offhandedly, "Why don't they just get married again?" Alex tells him not to be silly: Would they go through this hell if it were that simple? But Latka and Simka look at each other and kick themselves. They leave immediately to meet the reverend, vowing "to make it work this time." Jim turns to Alex: "Piece o' cake!"

This wonderfully sad and funny two-partner, with a title based on Ingmar Bergman's *Scenes from a Marriage,* explores, among other things, the day-to-day rationalizations we use to get through our lives and relationships with as little pain as possible. It also makes some daring observations on the nature of religious beliefs, and how unnervingly susceptible they are to superstition.

Part I of this classic episode introduced Allyce Beasley to television. She met her future husband, the great character actor Vincent Schiavelli, on the set. When she was called on for *Taxi,* "I had only been in California several months," Allyce told Phil Donahue. "Actually, I came in at the last minute, so it was really a fateful meeting, because I replaced somebody in the role the night before it was shot. When I walked in I was real nervous, and Vincent was sitting in a chair, and I just had to talk to somebody, and I walked over and said, 'Excuse me, do you work on the show?' And he said, 'Yes, I do.' And I said, 'Well, what do you do?' He said, 'I'm an actor.' I said, 'OK,' and then we talked for the rest of the day and we've never stopped talking since." Now well established as the dippy Ms. Dipesto on *Moonlighting,* Allyce went on after *Taxi* to do one of the most exquisite episodes of *Cheers,* playing Coach's lovely, plain daughter.

Vincent Schiavelli and Peter Elbling reprise their roles from "The Wedding of Latka and Simka" (episode #87). Schiavelli, one of the most familiar and distinctive faces on television, has been a regular on two series, *The Corner Bar* and *Fast Times.* He also co-stars with Tim Conway in the popular made-for-video comedy, *Dorf on Golf*. Elbling, who once used the stage name Peter Oblong, has played snooty characters on TV shows such as *Barney Miller* and *Magnum, P.I.* and in such movies as *Baby Boom*.

Incidentally, there is *no* Roxhill exit on New Jersey's Garden State Parkway. There's a Roxburg, New Jersey, and a Rocky Hill, New Jersey—neither of them is near the Parkway—but no Roxhill. She really was lost!

#96 ALEX THE GOFER

WRITTEN BY DAVID LLOYD.
DIRECTED BY MICHAEL LESSAC.

A theatrical producer (Matthew Laurence) and a dirctor (David Paymer) are arguing in the back of Alex's cab about whether or not audiences like to see the orchestra. The director patronizingly asks, "average man" Alex if he's ever been to the theater, and if he has, did he notice where the music was coming from? Theater-lover Alex resentfully gives a very well informed opinion with examples. After he makes his point, the three chat, and the producer says it's too bad Alex isn't twenty years younger, since tomorrow they're interviewing for a "gofer." A hopeful Alex says he likes to think that "a man is never too old to be a flunky," but they tell him to drop it.

At the garage the next night, Simka follows Latka in, saying he has a fever and must go home. Latka says he can't afford to take a day off. Louie says that in America, there is such a thing as sick pay. "You pay me ten bucks, you can go home." Simka does so, with money she says they were saving for cable television. Alex comes in with Elaine, discussing the gofer job, and while Lou is out of the room the cabbies talk him into "going for it." Alex makes them promise not to tell Lou, since he knows Louie will try to humiliate him. Lou catches wind of that last part and gleefully gives himself five minutes to see which cabby will crack first.

Tony leaves to drive Alex to the interview, and Lou decides to "play a game" with Iggy: They'll ask each other a question that has to be answered truthfully. Okeydoke, says Jim, and craftily asks Louie, "Where's Tony taking Alex?" At the gofer interview, Alex falls into the job. He's ecstatic, yet later, at the garage, he complains to Elaine about the indignities he's suffering. Lou keeps prodding until Alex finally tells him he's got a job in the theater. Lou, rather than make fun, congratulates him and wishes him luck: "I always knew that you would be the first guy to dig himself out of this slime." Alex leaves, and Lou tells the cabbies knowingly, "He must have the crummiest job in the world!" He finally convinces Jim—who as a former reverend wants to give Louie a chance to resist the temptation to humiliate—to tell him where Alex is working (the Ambassador Theatre).

On the job, Alex is casually treated like dirt, and his sensible (if somewhat clichéd) solution to a staging problem the producer is having meets with disdain. He's further humiliated when he runs lines with a lovely blonde actress, takes the dialogue seriously, and, to her shock, kisses her. He discovers he's been spied on by Lou, who's so stunned and disillusioned he can't bring himself to insult Reiger. "How long have you been here?" Alex demands. "Too long," says Lou in a daze. Alex: "What have you seen?" Louie: "Too much." Alex: "Who let you in here?" Louie: "Two guys."

Lou says he always considered Alex special. "You knew you were nothin', and you were *great* at it." He urges the bitter Alex to shove an egg-salad sandwich in the director's face. Alex weighs that possibility when the director comes in and apologizes for his brusqueness, and says they're giving Alex's suggestion a try. He tells Alex to come in and watch—and bring coffee. His dignity partially returned, Alex goes off. Louie stays with the sandwich and the lovely actress, who comes by wanting to run through some lines.

OTHER GUESTS:

Caren Kaye (the actress playing "Michelle" in the play)
Brian Robbins, Kerry Noonan (a young actor and a young actress in the producers' waiting room, who comment on Alex's age in a scene cut from the episode)

Note: The end credits name Matthew Laurence's and David Paymer's characters Allen and Ned, respectively; only Ned is named in the episode, however.

How many classics in a row does this make, already? In the episode, we finally get the scoop on Alex.

Alex, the dreamless dreamer, reveals his love—his *passion*—for theater, rattling off places like the La Mama off-Broadway theater as well as a slew of plays. Now, finally, we understand his self-imposed pragmatism, and why he falls for actresses and artists, and hangs out with would-be actors and art mavens rather than other career cabbies. Alex is in his forties, older than his friends, and from a generation where the man worked and the woman had babies and kept house. He never thought to pursue his dreams of working in the theater. Now, he feels his time has gone by—except, maybe, for this one final shot, which, judging from his age and his bitterness toward his menial gofer status, will never be repeated. When Louie stumbles across him, the two fortyish men, whose dreams have gone by, have more in common than Alex and the rest ever will. It's a devastating episode.

Speaking of devastating, the well-regarded comic actress Caren Kaye played the lucious title character of the teen sex farce *My Tutor* (1983). Earnest-looking Matthew Laurence appeared in the movie *Eddie and the Cruisers* (1983) and was a cast member on *Saturday Night Live* in 1980. Most recently, he's been co-starring in the Fox Broadcasting sitcom *Duet*. David Paymer was Oscar-nominated for *Mr. Saturday Night* (1992). And Brian Robbins, who swears he still gets residual checks for his excised scene, is one of the co-stars of *Head of the Class*.

#97 LOUIE'S REVENGE

WRITTEN BY SAM SIMON.
DIRECTED BY STAN DANIELS.

Jim comes into the garage on a cloud, having just seen *E.T.* for the sixty-fourth time. He wants to talk about it with everyone. The down-to-earth Alex, however, has declined to see the movie—he doesn't like science fiction, he says. Jim, in response, gives him $5 for the ticket and insists Alex do himself a favor. Just then, the phone rings in Louie's cage. A slurred voice asks for ''widdle Wouie.'' It's Emily (Andrea Marcovicci), the former friend of Zena's who seduced Lou when she

was drunk and high, and who the next day called him gross and disgusting (episode #72). A flustered Lou hangs up and tells the cabbies about this ''seductress beyond his dreams.'' (Alex: ''You mean that prison guard?'' Louie: ''You love bringin' that up, don't you, Reiger?'')

With the ''help'' of Alex's translations, Louie tells them about Emily and brings the story up to date: The same guy's dumped her again, and now she's blotto and wants to meet him at a nearby piano bar. Lou tells the cabbies this is the only score he's never settled and remembers (incorrectly) that he was holding a drink in his hand when she rebuffed him. Now he's going to go to meet her and ''sluice down the little tart.''

At the bar, Lou commandeers a returned mai-tai with a bug in it and prepares to sluice away. Unexpectedly, however, the out-of-it Emily grovels at him, flatters him, and kisses his hand. Lou, momentarily off-balance, regains control and tells her off. His dignity retained, he turns on his heel. Then Emily craftily serenades him with the old standard ''It Had to Be You.'' Louie is hers once more.

The next morning, when they wake up together, Emily screams. Louie, alone and desperate, brilliantly convinces Emily that he can make her happy. A couple of weeks later, Alex is telling Jim how wonderful *E.T.* was. Louie walks in, burdened by dry-cleaning and other icons of errand-running. He's become Emily's slave and valet, haunting fruit stands for fresh blueberries in the dead of winter. A blubbering Lou admits he's turned into the kind of guy he's always hated—a ''wienie'' over a girl. Alex feels sorry for him; he recognizes the trap.

At Emily's apartment after work, Lou is squeezing fresh orange juice when she trundles in all excited. She's just come from her therapist, she says, and they've made a breakthrough. She says off-handedly that she loves him, sending Lou into paroxysms of joy for a microsecond until she explains what she means. Emily discovered that she's always made herself a victim, and that Lou cares for her so much that she's responded the only way she knows how—by making *him* a victim, resenting and hating him in the process. For her to truly love him, she explains logically, he has to reject her victimization and leave. He tries to reject her by sluicing her down with orange juice, but she quickly manipulates him into apologizing and wiping it off her. Lou tries to understand. "You *will* love me," he says slowly, "if I never see you again." Emily: "Right." Louie: "But if I stay, you won't like me." Emily: "I'll despise you." Louie: "And if I walk out that door?" Emily: "I'm yours forever." Lou, after a pause: "You're a very complicated girl, Emily."

She finally starts to convince him. With every step toward the door, she writhes in pleasure. "I'm loving you more with every step you take toward that door," she says, almost crying tears of happiness. Lou does a little sideways dance step, and she actually moans, "Ohhh, Louie!" Louie asks, "Do we write letters?" She replies, "I write to you, and you never answer me." Lou finally accepts the situation. "I guess I had my first sophisticated relationship," he says to himself. To Emily he says her Mr. Right will come along: "And he's gonna be wearin' a white coat and carryin' a butterfly net! Oh, and another thing—I *knew* where to get blueberries, but it was too far and I figured, the hell with it!" He gets his parting shot, and she's been indeed sluiced. Louie's safe again behind his cynical humor.

OTHER GUESTS:

Charlie Stavola (the bartender)

Note: The actress who plays the barmaid is uncredited.

Obsessive relationships and loneliness: These powerful themes are tackled as eloquently in this episode as in most modern novels and plays. The "gross and disgusting" (and bitter and defensive) Louie faces a life alone, his shot with one-in-a-billion Zena gone (and his eventual relationship with the blind Judy Griffith from "The Shloogel Show" clearly nonexistent at this point). And yet as much as he's a slave to Emily, she is even more a slave to her own neurotic preconceptions. Lou at least escaped with a new perspective and a new grip on himself: After all this emotional torture and cleansing, and the subsequent blow of Zena's wedding (episode #100), Lou will never touch bottom quite so harshly again. He's learned how precious true caring is, and how it's not to be taken for granted. This epiphany must have helped Louie

Episode #97: Jim giving Alex a pre-inflationary five bucks to go see *E.T.* in "Louie's Revenge."

steel his emotions enough to approach Judy and risk rejection, and by episode #109, he and Judy have already been in a long relationship.

Actress and noted cabaret singer, Andrea Marcovicci, reprises her role as Emily, the neurotic of Lou's dreams. Very well known to TV audiences, Andrea's done scores of guest shots and TV movies, and with Jeff Conaway was in the regular cast of the short-lived prime-time soap *Berrenger's*. She's also done a couple of films, most notably *The Front*. Coincidentally, this episode of *Taxi* aired on her thirty-fourth birthday.

A vocalist as well as an actress, Andrea "was singing at the Improv once a week, and since we wanted to bring her back anyway we went to hear her," Sam Simon recalls. "And she is a terrific singer, so we worked that into the second time she appeared." Emily's tune, the torch standard "It Had to Be You," is perfectly integrated into the plot. "It's one of the few times I picked a song and it stayed in," Simon chuckles.

#98 TRAVELS WITH MY DAD

WRITTEN BY BARTON DEAN.
DIRECTED BY MICHAEL ZINBERG.

A surprise is waiting for Tony at the garage—his father, Angie (Donnelly Rhodes), a merchant seaman whom Tony seldom saw while growing up. There is still obvious affection between father and son; even the cabbies, who met Angie six months before when he took them all out for beers, welcome him like an old friend. He's been away at sea for several months, as usual, but this time he's returned with a gift for Tony—a union card that'll allow him to join his old man. Tony is less than enthusiastic. He did want to be a merchant seaman ever since he was five . . . and until he was eleven. But he doesn't want to disappoint his dad, so he decides to ship out on the *Hillary Beane* for Singapore, at least for this one trip.

Aboard ship, Tony doesn't take to the constant motion. He spends most of his time vomiting out a porthole and trying not to think about women. They cross the equator—which Angie thought would be exciting to his son—and talk about giant squid and younger days. Angie, a twenty-five-year sea veteran, says that he never cheated on Tony's late mom, no matter how many months he was away; whenever he was tempted, he thought of his kids. Tony says the family would have understood. Angie gives him a *now*-you-tell-me look. Tony decides he wants to sing sea chanteys, just like real sailors do. Angie doesn't know any. Two other seamen come by; they don't know any, either. One of them, Fergie (Dick Miller), suggests "New York, New York." In a very funny bit, the four men start off well but then realize they don't know more than a couple of lines. Many "dum-da-da-da-dums" later, they belt out the chorus—and then sink right back into "da-da-dums."

In a Singapore bar, Tony and his dad talk about Tony's childhood while simultaneously engaging in a brawl. (It's revealed that Tony's from Brooklyn and that he never finished high school.) They wind up the night in a tattoo parlor, ready to pick out matching father-and-son tattoos. Going *with* their better judgment for a change, they exit uninked.

OTHER GUESTS:

Wendall W. Wright (a black seaman, identified as "Sam" in the end credits; he played a policeman in episode #82, "Jim and the Kid")

Note: Neither the speaking brawler nor the stunt brawlers are identified in the end credits.

Highlighted by a very unrealistic and poorly choreographed fight scene, this may be *Taxi*'s worst

clunker. Not only that, but in the squid scene, you can see Tony's shadow thrown up against the "sky." Still, the "New York, New York" bit is fun, and both Dick Miller and former *Soap* regular Donnelly Rhodes have their moments. Tape the sea chantey scene, and then switch channels.

#99 ELAINE AND THE MONK

WRITTEN BY DAVID LLOYD.
DIRECTED BY DANNY DEVITO.

Tony rushes into the garage with news that the chinchilla he bought eight months ago have multiplied to the point where he can start selling them to fur makers. He started with six, and he asks the cabbies to guess how many he has now. Jim, taking the rhetorical question seriously, groggily mumbles that considering gestation period and average litter size, the answer is 162. "No, smarty," says Tony, it's 165!" Jim, mortified: "What was I *thinking* of? I feel about this big!" Elaine, astonished: "Jim, you were off by three!" Jim: "Well, go ahead, lady, rub it in." A happy Tony says that when those little chinchilla start to shed, he'll make a killing. The cabbies give each other uh-oh looks, and Louie gleefully informs Tony, "They don't shed." Tony asks, "Oh, you have to clip 'em?" Lou acts out just what *is* done to animals for their fur.

As Tony lets that sink in, Latka walks in with a monk (Mark Blankfield). This is Simka's cousin Zifka, he explains, who belongs to an old-country monastic order that allows him to enjoy worldly pleasures for one week every ten years. Otherwise, its members adhere to a vow of noncommunication and work at (among other things, probably) making cheese balls. Zifka's week starts at 8 P.M., and Latka invites the cabbies to a party. There, the curly-haired Zifka looks handsome in a sport jacket and tie, and at his cousin's urging plays a song on the eight-string *grock*. (When he was just twelve, Simka explains proudly, Zifka was second *grockist* in the National Symphony.)

With little effort, a charmed Elaine is talked into showing Zifka the sights. They go club-hopping, and for some reason cap the evening in the unaccountably empty garage. Giddy and light-hearted, Zifka starts singing "Cheek to Cheek" and dancing gracefully by himself. Elaine joins in, and soon they're gliding across the garage like Fred and Ginger, ending in an elegant clinch.

Several days later, the happy romantic couple come by the garage, where Alex is sitting reading the paper. He listens patiently as Elaine says how she and Zifka spent the day visiting the Bronx Zoo and the World Trade Center, kite-flying in Central Park, and roller-skating down Fifth Avenue. Zifka gets up to leave and tells Elaine he'll meet her at her apartment for dinner. Starry-eyed, Elaine tells him to come early—it's his last night in America, after all.

Alex is strangely upset by Elaine's romance, comparing it to a Dr. Pepper commercial. He berates Elaine for forgetting her son Jason's birthday the day before; Alex for the last few years has always dropped over for a family outing to Coney Island or someplace. Elaine apologizes and says they had a birthday party with Zifka and she forgot to call. She also says she's fallen in love with him. Alex, angry, says Elaine is simply toying with Zifka. Elaine, self-righteously: "I don't toy with monks." She storms out over Alex's protests, then comes back, saying she's not really angry at him. She sweetly zings him and hits the nail on the head at the same time: "You're just jealous you have no love in your life."

That night, at Elaine's new apartment (#3A), Zifka arrives late; he'd taken the wrong subway. He has only one minute, forty seconds left. They kiss, and he tries to tell her how he feels, but his watch beeps. The week is over. Somberly, he puts on his robe, while Elaine pours two glasses of champagne and, toasting, sips from both of them. Zifka walks to the door. But before he goes, they share one last, brief turn as the soundtrack reprises a moment of "Cheek to Cheek."

Costar Danny DeVito, who made his *Taxi* directorial debut with this episode, was hardly an inexperienced director even then. A scan through his filmography displays a slew of short films and features, including *Throw Momma from the Train* and *The War of the Roses.*

Carol Kane recalls that as a director, Danny "was a ball, and he's real good. It also helped that he knew everyone on the show so well. It's very difficult on a half-hour series to get new directors every week, because there isn't time for the courtship period: You really want to get in bed, so to speak, and to do that you've got to be comfortable. So it's wonderful to have as a director someone you already love and know well and trust."

Playing Zifka is comedian Mark Blankfield, who was called up from the Low Moan comedy troupe to become a regular on ABC's *Saturday Night Live* knockoff, *Fridays.* He's sweet without being sugary here as the romantic monk. Inexplicably, his subsequent career, which includes the abysmal film *Jeckyll and Hyde . . . Together Again* and the long-form music video *Kiss: Exposed,* hasn't done him justice.

A watchful viewer might wonder, incidentally, about night-shift cabbie Elaine coming to the garage at around 4 P.M. after a long day with Zifka, and having Zifka make plans to see her that night before his 8 P.M. deadline. For the sake of continuity it's clear that Elaine, this particular day, was working the early-morning (12 A.M. to 8 A.M.) shift. Then, after going home and sleeping, it's afternoon already, followed by her dinner date. Either that, or it was her day off, and she just came by the garage to see Alex or maybe to pick up a check.

By the way, does anyone not know that "Cheek to Cheek" is the classic Irving Berlin song from *Top Hat.*

#100 ZENA'S HONEYMOON

WRITTEN BY DAVID LLOYD.
DIRECTED BY RICHARD SAKAI.

Louie's old girl friend Zena (Rhea Perlman) comes by the garage with big news for the cabbies: She's getting married! She wants to meet Louie (who's away checking mousetraps) at a nearby restaurant to break the news to him and invite him to the wedding. Lou returns from checking the traps, happily telling the cabbies, "I caught one back there! He didn't even finish the cheese," he says, taking a bite of it. He sees Zena and accepts her invitation. When she leaves, he starts cackling about her "crawling back." The cabbies try to tell him it's not what he thinks, but he doesn't listen.

Episode #100: Louie making a point with his exgirlfriend's new husband in "Zena's Honeymoon," guest- starring Rhea Perlman and Peter Jurasik.

Worse, he admits he's only carrying on, that he really missed her, too.

On the sound of a mournful flute, we segue to a tony restaurant (street address 9474). Judging from the decor, it may Le Belle Chateau of episode #83 ("Take My Ex-Wife, Please"). There, Louie magnanimously says he'll take Zena back—only that's not what she wants to hear. She breaks the real news. Lou, stunned, downs a full bottle of wine in four and a half big glasses.

Zena explains she met a psychologist named Tom Pelton several months ago, and they fell in love. Lou takes it with his usual aplomb: Would she simply have the human decency to go to bed with him one last time? Zena, angry: "I am going to forget you said that." Louie: "Well, then. I'll repeat it." He starts raising his voice and scares Zena away. He also doesn't want to pay for the fancy dinner, though he *will* eat it. The waiter and a fellow diner are upset by his behavior, and to reciprocate their glares Louie challenges a man to stand up. The man does, and a traumatized Louie begins crying on his shirt.

At the garage on the day of the wedding, Louie is adamant about not accepting Zena's invitation— and about ordering poor Jeff to scrape paint all afternoon. The cabbies return from the wedding, and

Alex tells Lou he should have done the classy thing and seen her off with his blessings; after all, Louie was the one who destroyed the relationship. Now it's too late. "Happiness is hard to come by in this life," Alex scolds, "and she's given you more than your share." That's it! Louie figures. That's the perfect thing to tell Zena. Her honeymoon cruise ship (the *Britannia Star*) won't sail for a little while yet: He can still catch her there.

Just before the ship sets sail, Tom carries Zena over the threshold into their honeymoon cabin. They're happy and in love—and certainly not expecting to see Louie. Zena wants him out immediately, but Tom, who can't believe she really dated this guy, tries to be understanding. He appreciates Louie's anguish and sits on the bed with him to clear things up quickly before the ship sails. Louie, true to form, begins choking the poor psychologist and daring him to explain, "Why am I doin' this?!!!" Zena finally pulls Lou off by his hair, and everything calms down. He's going now, but before he goes, he repeats Alex's line about happiness. Zena's touched. Lou asks her if she remembers how they used to go on boat rides and try to identify scum in the water. She does and, genuinely touched, promises that whenever she sees repulsive things floating around in the water, she'll think of him.

OTHER GUESTS:

Peter Jurasik (Tom Pelton)
Robert Woberly (the waiter)
Jim Pollack (the man at the other table)

Note: Jim "Grampy" Davis is credited as "Gramps," but has no lines; he's visible sitting behind Lou at the restaurant.

This is one of *Taxi*'s most touching episodes. In the restaurant scene, Louie's bravado is quickly stripped away and revealed to be the defensive tactic it really is. Yes, Louie is an obnoxious, sometimes cruel, person, but not for the sake of cruelty, not for sadistic reasons. His self-aggrandizing behavior is his way of building a wall that might obscure from others and himself the fact that he's a pitiable human being. And, as Lou figures, better hated than pitied. Louie is Paddy Chayefsky's

Marty grown bitter and angry rather than introverted and self-pitying, and Danny DeVito brilliantly portrays Lou's desperation at losing what may be, for all he knows, his only chance in life to find someone who cares for him.

That desperation doesn't seem to jibe at first with episode #109, "Louie and the Blind Girl." By that episode, Lou and Judy Griffith—whom he met in episode #91—have been seeing each other for several months. What probably happened is that at the time of Zena's wedding, Lou either wasn't seeing Judy or—given his genuinely fragile ego—he may have been seeing her but couldn't believe anything was really going to come of it.

This was the first episode directed by coproducer Richard Sakai, who had worked his way up from a John Charles Walters gofer. "I was fortunate because it was a show spotlighting Danny and Rhea, and Danny's like the sweetest guy in the world and Rhea's one of the sweetest women. I knew they were gonna be supportive. It was *very* scary," he confirms, "because you have to learn so much stuff in order to be even just a *competent* director, but I felt protected: When you have a spectacular cast, as we did, by the fifth year everyone knows their characters and knows pretty much how to stage themselves and deal with the multiple-camera format. Now that I think about it, it was really kind of a dream job!" Richard is characteristically humble about his direction: "I think there are too many zooms in that episode." He's right. Even so, he gave the characters appropriate room and exquisite emphasis.

Like Taurean Blacque, Jeffrey Tambor, and Barbara Babcock, Peter Jurasik was yet another *Hill Street Blues* denizen to appear on *Taxi*. As Sid the Snitch, he went on with Dennis Franz to star in the *Hill Street* spin-off, *Beverly Hills Buntz*. "When we rehearsed," Jurasik remembers cheerfully, "Danny would stand on the bed and gently fake strangle me. And then on the *taping* he turned from an actor into this hummingbird all around my neck! Maybe he was mad that I was kissing Rhea," Jurasik jokes. "We'll never know!"

Incidentally, if Rhea Perlman looks a little fuller than usual in this episode, it's because she was five months pregnant with her and Danny's first child.

#101 LOUIE MOVES UPTOWN

WRITTEN BY DAVID LLOYD.
DIRECTED BY MICHAEL ZINBERG.

Now that Louie's mom has remarried and Louie's got a little extra money thanks to Jim's restitution after burning his place down, Louie decides to buy a co-op apartment in a fancy building. He tries to scam Jim for an ultra-low-interest loan of $48,000, and through spacey Iggy comes up with the dough, he's aware enough to cement the loan at 12½. But now, it seems Louie has to face the snooty co-op board. He talks Alex into accompanying him as his accountant and to help him from saying anything stupid. Alex agrees, but it doesn't look good once they get there: The actress Penny Marshall is getting rejected for another apartment (#16B) despite her huge salary because, as the board's president explains haughtily, "We wouldn't allow an actor to live here even if he were English." Penny doesn't let that indignity go unanswered.

Now it's Louie's turn. The board starts digging in, and one question—regarding Louie's being Italian—rightly angers Alex, who's been getting more and more steamed as the board's discriminatory process (which is actually *legal* in New York State) has gone on. Desperate, Louie deftly plays on the board's prejudices implying that they're *his* kind of people, and the board accepts him almost to spite Alex. In fact, the president asks Alex what he's going to do about it? Alex, feeling that if they want Louie they can have him, answers, "Cartwheels! All the way home." The board's female president gets an inkling of what she's accepted, however, when Louie's hand wanders over to her rear.

OTHER GUESTS:

Gayle Hunicutt, (realtor Ms. Bascombe)
Nelson Welch (board-member Mr. Parker)
Lois DeBanzie (board-member Mrs. Gwinn)
Paul Napier (board-member Mr. Blount)
Peter Frechette (Scott)
Colleen Riley (Muffie)

New York has an interesting law regarding co-operative apartments, which are similar to condominiums, except you own shares in a corporation that owns a building rather than actual real estate, as with a condo. As a result, corporation law comes into effect; therefore, anyone can be excluded from a co-op building on any grounds except, ostensibly, those of race, religion, etc. In practice, however, race, religion, etc., *are* real-life factors used to exclude, and discrimination is exceedingly difficult to prove—a fact New York law prefers to ignore.

Jim Brooks wasn't permitted to ignore it, however. "I think it really happened to him," Danny DeVito says. "I think where that story came from is Jim Brooks going to buy an apartment in New York City, and when he went in front of the board, he found out that they don't take Jews. So he used that in the show."

So why did the snooty board accept Louie? "I think the lady on the board had the hots for him."

Penny Marshall, incidentally, mentions an ironic coincidence: "The apartment number in that show turned out to be the same as the real apartment I have in New York now!"

TAXI

■■■■■■

216

#102 CRIME AND PUNISHMENT

WRITTEN BY KATHERINE GREEN.
DIRECTED BY STAN DANIELS.

The cab company's owner, Ben Ratledge (Allen Goorwitz), is yelling for Lou over the phone. There's a major problem and Lou rushes upstairs to see what's wrong. A few moments later, we hear an incensed Ratledge telling Louie to "take care of that guy!" Louie hustles assistant dispatcher Jeff into the tool room with some bad news: Those "used parts" he had Jeff take to the junkyard and sell for scrap were new, and Lou skimmed the money, but Ratledge thinks the thief is Jeff. Jeff explodes and says he's going straight to the boss. Louie convinces him however, that Ratledge will never believe Jeff wasn't involved. He tells him to lay low and trust him, and he'll straighten everything out. Jeff has no better plan, so he reluctantly agrees. In a show for Ratledge, Lou throws Jeff out and tells the cabbies Jeff was stealing. Not surprisingly, no one believes this. Lou swears he's more hurt than they are—how can he ever replace Jeff? he says before immediately doing so with the first

cabbie he sees who speaks English. Then Ratledge announces that he's thought it over and firing Jeff isn't enough: He's turning him over to the police.

At the police station (18th Street Division), Lou, posing as a lawyer, finds Jeff in an interrogation cell. He asks Jeff to continue to trust him, that no one's going to jail, and even if "someone" does, he would get a bed, meals, and a toilet: "That's pretty much life as we know it!" A guard comes in and tells Jeff that Alex Reiger has posted his bail. Alex comes in, and Jeff spills the beans.

They go back to the garage, where Louie begs an angry Jeff to let him tell Ratledge in his own way. Jeff and Alex give him fifteen minutes. In the boss's office, Louie pleads for "the misguided" Jeff. Ratledge is adamant—steal from the company, pay the piper. Lou finally breaks down and says *he* did it, *he's* the thief. Ratledge wonders why, if that's so, Jeff didn't speak up? "Because he likes me," Louie blubbers. This Ratledge *really* doesn't buy, and no matter what Lou says, he can't convince the increasingly amused boss that he is, in fact, the thief.

Teary-eyed with laughter, Ratledge tells Lou that if Jeff is so special he'd lie for him like that, he can keep him. Louie, half-laughing himself now, repeats his claim: "I'm the thief!" Craftily, he brings in Alex, whose recitations along the same lines bring only more laughter. Hysterically, Ratledge sends them out; Louie, now part of the joke, pretends he's stealing an adding machine. Ratledge roars even louder. He's in such high spirits, he even asks if Louie plays golf. "Why, yes sir, I do," Louie answers and adds assuredly, "But I cheat on my score!" Lou and a very confused Alex leave Ratledge in tears.

Later on, in the empty garage, Lou sits with a bottle of liquor and a cigar, trying to sort things out with Alex: "I mean, I stole. I lied. I betrayed a friend. And now I got extra money in the bank, and a nine o'clock tee-off time on Saturday. . . . Let's face it, Reiger, crime pays." Alex says Lou's penalty is that he'll never know the warm feeling of being honest. Lou laughs at that homily. He takes his cigar and his liquor up a ladder to a locked air duct where he keeps such treasures. Alex tells Lou he lives a crummy little life, having to sneak around like that, thinking everyone else is a thief like him. Lou dismisses that thought as well. Alex

Episode #102: "Crime and Punishment," a showcase for longtime *Taxi* bit-player J. Alan Thomas (right).

vengefully takes the ladder away, leaving Lou stuck on a ledge. But what the hell: Lou pulls out a bottle and a portable TV set, and settles there for the night.

OTHER GUESTS:

Martin Garner (Cabbie who speaks English)
Thom Koutsoukos (policeman)

This very funny episode demonstrates that even though Lou has been through hell and has grown and is partially redeemed, he still has a way to go. "Everybody in the garage talked about wanting to be something else," says DeVito, "except for Reiger, who [despite his dashed theatrical ambitions; see episode #96] wanted just to be a cab driver. But Louie, he just wanted to make a lot of money. And it didn't matter how. He just wanted to keep things on an even keel and to get into Nardo's pants. Those were all the things that Louie wanted. And, ah, he accomplished *all* of them." Wait a minute. When did Louie and Nardo ever go to bed together? "At the end of that date episode," DeVito says devilishly. C'mon. He put the food by the door and walked away. "What? You don't think he comes back? Of course he did!" We'll leave this discussion to future historians.

"Crime and Punishment" is another fine showcase for Jeff Thomas. It's a little less so for guest

star Allen Goorwitz, a.k.a. Allen Garfield, who's developed a well-deserved strong reputation as a movie character actor, but whose laughter here isn't convincing. That's OK. The viewers' laughter is.

#103 GET ME THROUGH THE HOLIDAYS

WRITTEN BY KEN ESTIN AND SAM SIMON.
DIRECTED BY MICHAEL ZINBERG.

As a white Christmas begins to huddle around New York City, Alex and Tony are watching an awful football game. "It isn't a bowl game," Tony gripes, "it's a tapestry." Alex: "It's not a tapestry; it's a travesty." Tony: "Yeah, well, I admit, there was some pretty good action in the first quarter." Then Alex gets an unexpected visitor—his ex-wife, Phyllis (Louise Lasser). As Tony (who's in a Santa suit) leaves to go distribute presents at a center for wayward kids, Phyllis starts singing the blues. Now that she's divorced and has moved back to the United States, she has no close family around. She spent last Christmas alone, she tells Alex, and is terrified of doing so again.

Alex doesn't want to put up with her, but after she pleads that for dignity's sake she wants to stay out at least long enough to impress her doorman, he relents and invites her to stay while he works. She's surprised that he plans to work on Christmas, but she'll make the best of it, despite the fact that Alex has no cable television.

At the garage, a tearful Elaine is wondering why she let her kids spend the holiday with their dad, who has a ski chalet in Aspen. But rich Jim has sent a singing telegram to her to help cheer her up. Alex ends up getting one himself. Simka and Latka invite all the cabbies to their apartment later for a small celebration. Louie isn't exactly invited, but he controls who gets cabs when and how long Latka has to work, and so Simka sweetly sing-songs that "if we *have* to" invite him, she will.

Partway through his shift, Alex, out of pity, decides to go and ask Phyllis to join them. Jim, Louie, and Elaine are already at the Gravas' apartment. Simka is decorating the Christmas tree, making Jim remember the family holidays of his youth, when his family would all gather and watch the servants

Episode #103: Party animals Latka and Simka in "Get Me Through the Holidays."

decorate the tree. As Simka is about to place an ornament, Jim asks, "May I, for old times' sake?" She says sure. Jim, pompously: "Not there, you fool! Higher. And to the left!"

Alex and Phyllis arrive, soon followed by Tony, still dressed as Santa and accompanied by three street kids from the community center. Simka says that according to tradition, the time has arrived for the oldest woman to offer a prayer. Phyllis asks Elaine when she was born—February, 1952. Which day in February? The fourth.

Phyllis immediately begins praying. Simka stops her to gather everyone around, and Phyllis begins again: "Dear Lord: No offense, but could you spend less time with people who don't need it? I mean, like the women from the Ice Capades and ballplayers. I mean, Lord, what do you care if a guy's stranded on second base? You got better things to do." Alex whispers. "Phyllis, you're noodging God!" She goes on to plead for longer skirts and, to Jim's nodding approval, more refills on Valium prescriptions. And as an added thought, peace on earth and goodwill toward men. Phyllis's depression starts to get everyone down, but there's a knock at the door that well-to-do Jim figures will cure everything—and in come the dancing costumed snowmen, reindeer, toy soldiers, and elves that he hired. Later, in cab ZQ45, Alex is taking Phyllis back to her apartment house. She tells him not to worry about New Year's Eve, that she'll be leaving the country: That's her Christmas present to him. He loves it.

OTHER GUESTS:

Joseph Brennan, Hillary Carlip (telegram messengers)
Gary Quinn (toy soldier)

Note: The actors playing the kids are uncredited. Hal Smith is credited as "The Announcer," but his part was cut before the episode aired.

For this *Taxi* Christmas, "pragmatic" Alex gives in to the frivolous holiday spirit, Latka and Simka force themselves to invite lonely Louie (whose mother has remarried and is probably off somewhere with her new husband), and Jim finds the true meaning of an American Christmas: spending money.

Cowriter/coproducer Ken Estin remembers what fun it was to choose the costumes for the big finale. "I think at some point we had just wanted to do a conclusion like that, where we would simply fill the set with all these weirdly dressed people. We just needed an acceptable, believable reason. I remember the bunch of us sitting in a room, and the costume people sending over guys dressed up as trees or as snowmen or whatever, and asking us, 'Do you want this? How about this?' and we'd be rolling laughing, going, 'Yeah, yeah, great, yeah!'"

#104 ALEX'S OLD BUDDY

WRITTEN BY KEN ESTIN AND SAM SIMON.
DIRECTED BY RICHARD SAKAI.

Jim has gotten a rejection letter from the Kenderson Literary Agency, to which he'd sent a *M*A*S*H* script: Hawkeye has to operate on Col. Potter amid shelling by the North Koreans and a Zaxalonian starship. While the cabbies are digesting that, Jeff comes in with a fluffy, gray-and white, shaggy dog named Buddy that he'd just picked up at the airport for Alex. When Alex comes in, he tells them that for the last few years, the nineteen-year-old dog has been living with his sister and her kids. But now that he's gotten so old and ill, Alex wants to spend as much time as he can with him.

Everyone loves the little mutt; Simka even drops by Alex's apartment to offer an old-country blessing. It's quite short ("*Kepz!*"), and Alex asks if there's more. Simka: "You wanna bigger blessing, you shoulda gotta elephant." Alex offers to show her a trick Buddy's done for years—playing dead when Alex "shoots" him. Buddy doesn't perform, however, and a concerned Alex takes him to see a veterinarian. The vet says that the old dog has advanced diabetes and other maladies and should be put to sleep. Alex refuses. He turns his apartment into a veritable dog playground.

One evening, the attractive Shawn drops by for their date; judging by their easy give-and-take, she and Alex have been seeing each other for some time. Alex suggests they stay at home tonight so he can watch over Buddy; he's even started taking Buddy with him in his cab. Shawn, not wild about the idea, nonetheless agrees. While Alex is preoccupied, she samples what he has cooking on the stove. Alex, too late, rushes to tell her it's dog food he was warming up for Buddy. She's nauseated, but tries to be a good sport. Later, when she nibbles on some doggie treats that look like candy, Alex doesn't have the heart to tell her the truth.

He has to face some truth himself, however, when he shows up at the garage with the obviously ill dog, and Louie and the cabbies gently suggest it may be time to put Buddy out of his pain. Alex refuses, and Jim comes up with the idea that maybe Buddy should do the trick that Alex keeps talking about. If he's still playful and alert enough to do it, he suggests, then maybe they're wrong. Alex says OK, and does his routine. He points his finger at Buddy, squeezes the trigger, and fires. It works! Buddy drops over, playing dead. Alex is greatly relieved. Now get up, Buddy. C'mon, Buddy, get up. Long moments pass, and Buddy does pick himself up at last. Later, however, Alex comes back to the garage without the dog. Buddy just looked too sick, he'd decided, so he took him to the vet for the last time. Louie understands, and he orders everyone out of the garage so Alex can be alone in his grief. Seeing he can't help, Louie leaves as well.

GUESTS:

Judith-Marie Bergan (Shawn)
John Hancock (Dr. Brandon, the veterinarian; name given in end credits, not in episode)
Tucker (Buddy)

"We hadn't planned to end this episode as we did," Ken Estin remembers. "Originally, it was going to end with that false, misleading death where the dog was playing dead, and it would be a touching, funny moment to end the show on. But somehow, we got more personal with this dog we had. This dog was really an old dog himself, something like fifteen years old. And he was the sweetest old show dog, and still so able to do tricks that he just won everybody over. I mean, we just loved that dog. And when I wrote this episode, I had a dying dog myself, so this was all very close to me; maybe a little too close. Anyway, we became so attached to this dog that its false death seemed like a cheat, and we wanted not to cheat. So we suggested having the dog die, and seeing how a person deals with it. You can't feel as bad about it as you would about a human being. And yet, you loved it, it was a part of you. And we thought it'd be interesting that the pragmatic Alex—who would say it's just an animal, and while there's some affection, it's not like a person—would cry in spite of himself."

Guest Judith-Marie Bergan went on to become a cast member, along with Carol Kane, on the well-liked yet short-lived *All Is Forgiven*.

#105 SUGAR RAY NARDO

WRITTEN BY KATHERINE GREEN.
DIRECTED BY DANNY DEVITO.

Much to Jeff's anger, Louie's girlie calendar is covering up Jeff's picture of his mother, whose looks Lou indelicately compares to Swamp Thing. Tony comes in with Alex, who's dressed in a referee outfit and compliments him on his skills as a ref for the kids' boxing classes Tony is coaching. Elaine comes in and proudly announces that her son, Jason, had his first oboe recital and is coming by with a tape she wants everyone to hear. Jim admires her for having Jason take oboe lessons: Everyone should learn how to hop a freight car, he says. Tony, who doesn't confuse "oboe" with "hobo," thinks it's sissy, and when Jason (David Mendenhall) arrives, kicking his oboe case across the garage floor, Tony suggests Elaine let him teach her son boxing. Jason wonders if the kids Tony coaches "get beat up as bad as you used to?"

With Tony's prodding, Elaine reluctantly agrees to take Jason to the gym and let him watch. The day they go, Tony is coaching two kids named Mattie and Carl; when they finish their bout, a chubby kid named Gregory is left without a sparring partner, and Tony talks Elaine into letting Jason box. Jason knocks Gregory down and discovers a taste for blood. This scares Elaine, and she tells him no more. Jason cunningly wishes his dad were with him. "*He'd* let me box."

Three days later, in the garage, Elaine tells the cabbies that Jason's miserable, and maybe she needs a man around to help her handle this situation. Jim tries. "The ability of two men to put on gloves," he days dazedly, "stand toe-to-toe in a spirit of sportsmanship and pummel each other into insensibility is what separates us from the animals." That doesn't help much, and Elaine turns to Alex, who thinks Jason should box. So be it.

At parents' day, Louie shows up and sits next to Elaine at ringside. He's got some wagers going. A woman says disdainfully, "How could you bet on little kids?" Louie: "I made little bets." Referee Alex introduces a special guest, the champion of last year's 68-pound division, Johnny DeCeo. Now it's time for Jason's match; at 65 pounds, in blue trunks, he's up against the disdainful woman's son, Benny Jamison (66 pounds, red trunks). One ill-choreographed punch later, Jason is down with a broken nose. Tony and Alex rush out with an extremely upset Elaine.

Later, Alex drives everyone home from the emergency room. Elaine won't speak, and Alex tells Tony she's in "one of her moods." She finally accepts Tony's apology, but not Alex's. *His* opinion she respects, she tells him, and she feels he let her down. Alex apologizes again, and Elaine says, boy, if you thought I was overprotective before, watch me now. But Alex gives her a pep talk—which soon turns into pablum talk—and says Jason probably is all set to get back in the ring. A sleepy Jason tells him he's gotta be kidding.

OTHER GUESTS:

Elizabeth Hill (Benny Jamison's mother; listed as Hillary in the end credits)

Brad Kesten (Gregory)

Michael Saucedo (Johnny DeCeo; listed as "The Kid" in the end credits)

Note: Michael Alldredge is listed as "Todd," but there's no character by that name.

Danny DeVito directed his second episode of *Taxi*, and again turned in a terrific job. It's not always easy, of course, to act in and direct the same episode. "There's a scene in that show where I'm sitting at ringside without my jacket on. What happened was, I was supposed to have it on, but I was in another scene, and then I'm settin' up the cameras, getting ready for the boxing scene, right? And I forget I'm supposed to make an entrance. So I run like a son of a bitch around the corner and just made my entrance. And I forgot my jacket, I was so caught up in the directing."

This was story editor Katherine Green's final *Taxi* script; she went on to produce the Fox series *Married . . . With Children.*

#106 ALEX GETS BURNED BY AN OLD FLAME

WRITTEN BY BARTON DEAN.
DIRECTED BY HARVEY MILLER.

Tony wins the garage arm-wrestling championship, although, the cabbies kid, he hasn't challenged Elaine yet. Tony, going along, wants to be the champ fair and square, and he tells Elaine she can use both hands, compete standing up, and start with Tony's arm low. Tony's pride goeth before his fall, and Elaine, to the cabbies' great amusement, is now the garage champ. Even Alex finds it funny. Just then a beautiful, classy-looking brunette walks in, looking for Jim. Her name is Diane McKenna (Cathie Shirriff), an old commune mate of Jim's in the sixties; she'd gone on to Stanford Law School and graduated third in her class. When Jim arrives, the two hug and, with a little prodding from Diane, reminisce.

The next day, a smitten Alex asks Jim to set up a date with Diane for him. Jim, misinterpreting, sets up a date for *himself* and Diane, and all three wind up at dinner. The date doesn't go too smoothly, with Jim playing a handheld video game and Alex unable to get a witty anecdote started. Finally, when Diane goes to the ladies' room, Alex asks if Jim would do him a favor and leave ''gracefully'' to allow him and Diane a little room. To Alex's mortification, Jim agreeably erupts in a loud ''deathly illness'' (in order, he figures, for Alex to have witnesses so that Diane will believe why Jim left).

Alone at last with Diane, Alex tells her how everyone in the garage really likes Jim, although, he adds, ''his porch light has been flickering for years.'' Alex tries his best to kindle a romance, but Diane tells him she's already ''emotionally and physically involved''—with Mr. Flickering Porch Light. That morning at 3 A.M., an angry Jim storms into Alex's apartment: How dare he call him flaky? They argue, and Alex points out that Jim lived in a condemned building for four years, kept a horse in his apartment, cut up his van (to make a castle sculpture for Elaine), accidentally burnt down Louie's apartment, and hung around for days in a radiation suit in Louie's fallout shelter. Jim is impressed that Alex remembers all those incidents in his life. So is Alex, who realizes that he and Jim really do love each other.

OTHER GUESTS:

Martin Azarow (Leon, an arm-wrestling cabbie)
Robert Woberly (a waiter)

Virtually all the women involved with *Taxi* whom the authors interviewed commented on what one woman called Chris Lloyd's ''sweet sexuality.'' When you think about it, Jim did OK with women. Besides Diane, there was Tony's sister Monica (episode #52); the rich woman coming on to him in ''Elegant Iggy'' (episode #86), and even Elaine, who went out with him on what looked like a great date in the same episode: They ended the evening arm in arm, with her head on his shoulder; he had just made her an art-world heroine—and probably later, just made her.

Barton Dean, who wrote this episode and ''Travels with My Dad'' (#98), became a producer on *Newhart* and created an unsold CBS pilot, *Kingpins*.

#107 TONY'S BABY

WRITTEN BY DARI DANIELS.
DIRECTED BY RICHARD SAKAI.

Tony jogs into the garage after having run eight miles in preparation for his Tuesday night fight with Dean ''Big Bang'' Gentry, a 15-0, WBC-ranked contender; it's the biggest fight of Tony's career. As the cabbies all get their car assignments, Tony's girl friend Vicki (Anne DeSalvo) comes by to tell him she can't make their date tonight; she's nervous because she's missed her period and is going now to the doctor for a pregnancy test. A stunned Tony offers to go along, but she'd rather he didn't. She leaves, and he sits swirling in confusion. Louie, sensing Tony's plight, advises he get out on the street and drive through whatever's bothering him. Tony, perking up, says that's a good idea and asks for a cab. Lou smiles, ''Sorry, all out.''

Later at Mario's, Tony joins the cabbies at a table but says he wants to be alone. After some kidding around, they leave and pass Vicki on her way in. She haltingly tells Tony she tested positive—she's pregnant. Tony, who'd been suspecting the worst, tells her not to worry, that he'll do the honorable thing and marry her. He despondently starts making plans. Vicki is understandably taken aback by his martyrdom; she says very loudly she doesn't ''gotta'' marry him and storms out.

The night of the Gentry fight, Alex is in Tony's locker room at Madison Square Garden, trying to pump his friend up and find out what's bothering him. Jim shows up with Elaine, who assures Tony ''even though I don't like boxing, I really do hope it goes as well as can be expected, and that it's not too terrible, and that you manage to do whatever you need to do to that poor man before he does it to you.'' Jim, about as helpfully, says he loves Tony's apartment here—''elegant without being pretentious.'' Elaine offers to show Jim the rest of the place.

Louie walks in to see how Tony's doing and whether or not there's anything he or anyone else can do to lift him out of his depression. No? In that case he'll double his bet against him. Tony's new manager, Leo Goodman (Keenan Wynn), enters. Alex takes the dotty but very savvy old guy aside

TAXI
▪▪▪▪▪▪
221

and expresses his concerns about Tony. Leo says from the look on Tony's face, it's either a pregnant girl friend, or piles—and if it were piles, Tony would have said something. His problem out in the open, Tony heads for the ring. The announcer introduces Gentry as a 165-pound, former Golden Gloves champ, and tenth-ranked middleweight with 11 knockouts in 15 straight wins. "And over here, Tony Banta." (Leo explains he likes short introductions, since he's the one who has to write them.)

The fight's not going too well, but just before the fifth round, the canny Leo says he "forgot about" an important phone call from Vicki. Tony gets so angry he finally comes back to life in the ring. At the end of the 10-round fight, both boxers are standing, and they have to wait for the judges' decision. Vicki, whom Tony thought hadn't shown up, comes over to his corner. She's upset with him and (unadmittedly) proud of him at the same time. Tony, on the ropes, repeats his demand she marry him. She wants to hear a proper proposal. He does his best. She'll think about it.

As the announcer recites the split decision, Tony keeps asking Vicki to please marry him. The first judge scores it 97–95, Gentry; the second judge, 95–93, Banta. As the final score is announced—94–92 in favor of Gentry, giving him the win—Vicki says yes, and Tony jumps up and down exultantly.

Tag: Tony, showered and dressed in his locker room, tells Alex he's not sure if Vicki loves him—or whether he loves her. He wants to know how you can tell when you've found the right person. Alex says philosophically, "That's a question for a wiser man than I." "You're right," Tony answers. "I'll go see if I can catch up with Leo."

OTHER GUESTS:

James F. "Jimmy" Lennon (the announcer, as himself)
Gene LeBell (the referee)
T. J. Castronova (Tommy, the bartender at Mario's; no lines)

Note: The actor who plays Dean Gentry, who has no lines, is uncredited.

This gutsy episode was written by the daughter of *Taxi* cocreator Stan Daniels. Without being the least bit heavy-handed or preachy, "Tony's Baby" illustrates a timeless dilemma that's been explored in literature. Tony does like Vicki, but that doesn't mean he loves her or wants to have a child with her. Yet his upbringing has trapped him in a situation for which he sees no solution except a marriage that he's clearly not ready for and that he's forcing upon himself. Vicki is more level-headed about her options, including terminating the pregnancy. Yet her conscious decision not to use birth control signals that the pregnancy and marriage may have been what she wanted all along. It's a tragic episode, despite its many laughs.

So was the shoot. Tony Danza sadly recalls that at 7:30 A.M. on the day it was filmed, his father passed away. Danza valiantly plunged ahead. "There's a line in the show, " he says, "right before the fight, where Louie tells me, 'I know something's botherin' you. Is there anything I or anybody can do to make you feel better?' And I say, 'No, Louie, thanks.' And I was thinkin' about my father at that moment, and Danny knew it, too."

The episode marked one of the last appearances of veteran character actor Keenan Wynn (1916–1986), one of Hollywood's all-time best. The son of vaunted vaudevillian comic and TV dramatic actor Ed Wynn, and the father of screenwriter Tracy Keenan Wynn, Wynn performed in more than 220 films, 250 TV shows, and 100 plays. Toward the end of his life, he was one of the two actors to play Digger Barnes on *Dallas,* and was a semiregular on *Call to Glory.* Ironically and strangely appropriate, given this episode, one of Wynn's most famous roles was the amoral yet compelling fight manager in the original live TV production of Rod Serling's *Requiem for a Heavyweight.*

#108 JIM'S MARIO'S

WRITTEN BY KEN ESTIN AND SAM SIMON.
DIRECTED BY DANNY DEVITO.

An overly madeup Simka has taken up selling door-to-door cosmetics—her native Sheeshkaflu brand. She pitches Elaine, who buys a jar (sic) of perfume. Jim comes in, proudly announcing that he's using his inheritance to make wise investments—such as buying a 1916 "Standing Liberty" quarter worth $5,000. Unfortunately, he goes to the coffee machine and inadvertently winds up with the most expensive cup of coffee on earth. Plunging ahead, he makes his next investment—buying Mario's, which he renames, none too euphoniously Jim's Mario's.

Jim's brother, Tom (Walter Olkewicz), who evidently controls a trust fund for Jim, is less than taken with the little Italian joint. Even worse, an inspector Donovan from the New York State Liquor Authority tells the new owner that he's observed three liquor violations in the last two hours. With that, a fed-up Tom threatens not to let Jim have any more large sums of cash at all. Jim (who later tells the cabbies that his brother has discouraged his ambitions since they were kids) asks Tom to return in a week and see how the place is doing before making any decisions. Tom agrees.

Jim's management is unsuccessful, however, and as the week goes by, it looks as if Tom were right. Even Jim starts to believe that. But Louie, seeing a source of sponge money about to dry up, devises a plan: He orders the cabbies to shanghai tourists to Mario's. Soon the place is packed with customers to whom the cabbies have promised variously, an "in" spot, a celebrity hangout, a quiet piano bar, etc. For the latter, Jim presses Alex into service. He's reluctant, until a pretty blonde asks if he knows "Ebb Tide." By evening's end, the place is a big communal cocktail party, with customers around the piano all singing "Lazy River."

Come closing time, the place empties out save for Jim and Tom, who'd dropped by expecting the worst. Tom graciously apologizes for thinking his brother was a failure. They hug and he offers to drive Jim home. Just then, a man comes in pleading soberly for a bottle of brandy to take home to a mother sick with arthritis—all the liquor stores are closed. Jim says he can't give him one, that it's illegal for him to sell bottles of liquor, and that one more violation may close the place down. But the guy begs, and a sympathetic Jim wraps up a bottle in a bag and gives it to the man. Straightening, the man says he's an undercover agent for the Liquor Authority, and that this is the final violation. Tom, who'd apologized to Jim, quickly recants, hurt and upset. "You're gonna stay a failure your entire life!" he yells. But Jim calmly pulls a seltzer bottle

out of the bag he gave the agent and throws the man out. Tom apologizes again, and the brothers go off together.

OTHER GUESTS:

Peter Iacangelo (Donovan)
William Hootkins (the undercover Liquor Authority agent)
T. J. Castronova (Tommy, the bartender at Mario's)
Thomas Murphy (customer #1)
Charles Bouvier (customer #2)
Sharon Madden (the nun)
Ro Kendall (the pretty blonde)

Although this episode does have its funny spots, it nonetheless feels contrived. The incredible number of business details that a restaurant owner has to deal with—insurance, health inspections, taxes and garbage collection, to name just a few—are obviously beyond Jim's capabilities. And the plot to fill Mario's with customers is just too hokey and unbelievable. The incredible cast of *Taxi* can only partially save a late-in-the-season desperation script that commits a cardinal sin: being sitcomy.

The song that the young woman asks Alex to play, "Ebb Tide" by Carl Sigman and Robert Maxwell, was a popular tune for Vic Damone and others in the fifties. From her apparent age, she probably was thinking of the sixties' cover version by blue-eyed soul singers The Righteous Brothers. "Lazy River," by Hoagy Carmichael and Sidney Arodin, dates to 1931; Carmichael himself performed it in the classic film *The Best Years of Our Lives*. It, too, was repopularized in the sixties, in an orchestral arrangement by Si Zentner. Ken Estin, though, just remembers it being an old banjo tune he used to play in a stage act.

#109 LOUIE AND THE BLIND GIRL
STORY BY LARRY SCOTT ANDERSON.
TELEPLAY BY KEN ESTIN, SAM SIMON,
AND AL AIDEKMAN.
DIRECTED BY NOAM PITLIK.

Louie's in an exultant mood: He's just come back from a class with girl friend Judy Griffith (Murphy

Cross), the blind girl he was paired with in the *Sho-loogel* (episode #91). The class, at a school for the blind, was designed to help teach sighted people to better understand blindness. Lou demonstrates by putting on a blindfold and offering to pick out who's standing near him, using only his other senses. He does well, and then reveals he's using a trick blindfold he got at a magic shop. He defends deceiving Judy that way by saying how proud she was of him in class. That's very important to him, he says, because tonight he's giving her a half-carat diamond engagement ring. Alex is "appalled at the prospect of you breeding," but Lou turns serious, and first Tony and then the other cabbies realize it and say they believe him.

That evening, Judy is preparing dinner in her high-rise apartment. Lou lets himself in and comes up behind her, playing "guess who?" with humorous irony. She's enchanted by it and gives him a deep kiss. Lou, breaking open an uncooperative bottle of champagne, tells her he's got big news, but so does she, and she can't wait to tell him. Her doctor says there's been improvements in surgical techniques, and he wants to operate on her tomorrow. She may be able to see again! She asks about his news. A stunned Louie mumbles something abut buying foot deodorizer for the first time. She giggles and says he can always make her laugh, as he quietly puts the ring back into his pocket.

The next day, at the garage, Jim offers to officiate at Lou's wedding. Lou tells him he'd rather have a baboon do it. "I don't blame you, " Jim answers reasonably. "I've seen that. It's lovely." Elaine asks the somber Lou what happened, but Lou merely snaps and gets them on the road—all except Alex, who impatiently says cold feet and refusals aren't unique, and that he'll talk to Lou after the shift. Lou acquiescently gives him a cab and mentions the operation. That stops Alex. Lou goes on to say he can't ask Judy to marry him now. Somewhat dimly, Alex asks, "What is it, Louie? You afraid she's not gonna like yer looks?" Louie: "No, Reiger, my tie! I'm afraid she's not gonna like the way I knot it!"

He tells Alex about "that look"—the one he got on blind dates when he used to go on them. He can't stand to see that look again from someone he cares about. Louie buries his head in his hands.

Alex offers to go with him to the hospital. There, the tall, handsome Dr. Gordon tells Lou it's time for the bandages over Judy's eyes to come off. An anxious Lou steadies himself and enters her room. He tells her, half-despite himself, that he hopes the operation's worked. And then he warns her gently, "I'm not the best-lookin' guy in the world."

The final bandages are lifted. She can see—and she thinks he's beautiful, just as she pictured. Lou leaves the room jumping for joy. "It's a brave new world, Reiger!" And one more thing he adds, throwing the ring away, "I'm gonna have to buy her a real diamond."

OTHER GUESTS:

David Young (Dr. Gordon)

The most dramatic episode of the series is an updated twist on the "Beauty and the Beast" fable. *Taxi* fans who grew up reading Marvel Comics will also recognize Louie's dilemma as the same one faced by the Fantastic Four's monstrous Ben Grimm, a.k.a. The Thing, who was constantly both afraid of and hopeful of his blind girl friend Alicia regaining her sight.

"A very touching episode," remembers DeVito. "That was so nice at the end where she touched Louie's face. She was in that other episode [#91] where I say she's gonna 'take me home to meet the dog', " He chuckles. "So many lines that Louie says, you can use in real life, 'cause there're so many 'losers' around and it's good to joke around in this crazy life."

Unfortunately for the episode, needless compression hurts its believability. Judy's doctor wants to try a relatively new eye surgery procedure, and he wants to do it tomorrow with no advance warning or preparation—without even admitting Judy into the hospital a day in advance to prep her for anesthesia, etc. And then the bandages are supposed to come off the same day! By merely tweaking a line or two of dialogue, the writers could have indicated a realistic passage of time. As it is, the one-day-to-the-next compression is distracting and points out the inherent artificiality of the medium. Ironically, early script drafts do show a realistic time passage, but one of the producers insisted it be tightened, figuring that nobody follows that kind of thing. Actually, it's pretty hard *not* to notice it.

#110 SIMKA'S MONTHLIES

WRITTEN BY HOLLY HOLMBERG BROOKS.
DIRECTED BY HARVEY MILLER.

A dressed-up Latka tells his friends in the garage that he's off to meet Simka at the Department of Immigration; they're scheduled to have an interview so that Simka can obtain her resident-alien "green card" and stay in the United States. He tells the cabbies to come by their place later for a party, but the barbecued yak lips from his last affair prompts their offer to handle all the preparations.

At Latka and Simka's apartment later, Jim has the place done up in patriotic bunting; it all came, he says, from the 1968 Democratic Convention, where he was arrested for stealing decorations (and John Chancellor's tie). Simka and Latka enter crying and arguing, and she vanishes into the bedroom. Latka explains that Simka never made it into the building due to the strange, debilitating, almost psychotic moods she suffers every month about this time. All the cabbies nod knowingly except Jim, who wonders, "Are we supposed to have realized something?" Alex delicately explains that Simka "is having her monthly problem." Jim says he understands: "Bills, bills, bills,"

Another interview is arranged—the last before Simka will be deported. Latka isn't counting on her showing up—her *krimkapoosh* is ruining everything. Elaine thinks *krimkapoosh* means "monthly period," but Jim rightly figures it's PMS—pre-menstrual syndrome, a chemical imbalance that drastically affects many women. As Jim goes to answer the phone, Alex suggests that if Latka tells Simka what her malady may be, she might be able to contain it long enough to get through the interview. Latka rushes off to meet her.

As soon as he leaves, Jim announces that it was Simka on the phone, and that despite his entreaties, she's not going to the interview. Louie, who'd been riding Alex about his "Mary Worthiness," wonders aloud who shall save the fair damsel. Alex gets going. He finds Simka looking like a madwoman and convinced that she is one. In a memorably

funny scene, she and Alex go back and forth until he convinces her to go to the interview.

At the Department of Immigration, the officer is a little suspicious about Simka's repeated absences and her lateness today. He tells Latka that many aliens get involved with false, "paper" marriages to stay in the country. But at the last moment, Simka appears. The harried officer asks what was the last movie the two of them saw together—part of a real technique used by immigration officials whereby answers to day-to-day questions may reveal whether or not "married" couples really are. Simka says it was *Gandhi;* Latka, who'd earlier answered *An Officer and a Gentleman,* says oh, yes, she's right, I'm sorry. Simka explodes: Now she's going to be deported because Latka "can't tell the difference between Richard Gere and a bald Hindu!" They begin bickering loudly in their native language, until the immigration officer finally calls a halt to it. Simka's passed the exam: These two have got to be married!

GUESTS:

Howard Witt (immigration officer)

This episode's a marvel; it not only gets laughs out of a serious subject without being the least bit offensive but also uses television's powerful reach to educate viewers about the existence of PMS, which was, at the time, even less understood than it is today. Brooks's wife, Holly Holmberg, was formerly an airline stewardess, yet no matter how many rewrites her script—like every other *Taxi* script—may have gone through, the central notion shows a true scriptwriter with brains and muscle.

#111 ARNIE MEETS THE KIDS

WRITTEN BY JOHN MARKUS.
DIRECTED BY RICHARD SAKAI.

Simka rushes into the garage with wonderful news for Latka—their homeland wants her to be ambassador to France. It's a great honor and pays $2.75 an hour besides. Latka, however, refuses to uproot himself. Simka, sulking, begins speaking nothing but French until he relents. As they leave, Elaine walks in with the nebbishy but sweet and funny

Arnie Ross (Wallace Shawn). The two have had a great time attending the opening of a new art gallery in Soho. They kiss good-bye, and while Elaine goes to change her clothes, Louie shakes the hand of the man who "climbed Everest." Arnie has to admit he's pretty proud of himself for dating an intelligent knockout like Elaine.

After Arnie leaves, Louie hypothesizes that the attraction is "his boyish insecurity. It's gotta be—there's nothin' else!" He tries out his theory on a good-looking female cabbie, bashfully inviting her out for a soda. She thinks that's sweet and accepts. Louie goes on to shyly ask if afterward they can "do it till we pass out," whereupon she slaps him. Elaine asks Alex for a favor: Arnie is coming to dinner the next evening, and her ex-husband is out of town (indicating that he probably still lives in New York). Can Alex watch her kids, Jason and Jennifer? She explains that although she and Arnie have been seeing each other for five months, she hasn't introduced him to her kids. Elaine says she doesn't yet know how she feels toward Arnie and doesn't want her kids to develop an attachment in case the romance doesn't work out. Alex finally convinces her to let Arnie meet the kids.

The next day, Latka and Simka come by the garage, still arguing over Simka's ambassadorship. Latka finally gives in, and Simka tells him that's all she wanted to hear from him, the offer has been withdrawn because their country just broke off diplomatic relations with France. Arnie comes in, panicking and pleading for help in winning over Elaine's kids. Alex tells him to just be himself. Arnie is incredulous: "Oh, really? Was Buffalo Bob himself? Was Bozo the Clown himself? Tony: "I hear Mr. Rogers is really like that." Lou makes Arnie even more nervous by telling him about this guy Peterson that Elaine liked, but that her kids didn't. She dropped him cold—prompting Arnie to come prepared.

When Arnie arrrives at her latest apartment (#6A in a high-rise), he's armed with facts (Jason's favorite sport is soccer; Jennifer is in third grade), puppets, balloon animals, and cold cash. The kids are overjoyed at getting twenty bucks apiece, but Elaine is shocked at his well-intentioned bribery. A commotion erupts, and Elaine sends the kids to their room. She tells Arnie he can't keep this up.

"The hell I can't!" he proclaims joyously. "As long as there's ice cream to scoop or a riddle to tell or a toy on the shelf, those kids're *mine!*" But Elaine insists the kids return the money, and there's another scene.

Arnie finally gets the picture, and he apologizes and starts to leave. But the kids don't want him to go, and neither, really, does Elaine. Arnie tells the children that what Mom says goes, and he can't give them any more money. "You still like me?" he asks. "Yeah, sure," says Jason, to which Jennifer adds, "just not as much." After a successful dinner, Elaine is pensive and a little nervous. The kids love "Uncle Arnie" and kiss him goodnight; tomorrow, he's taking them to the zoo. After they're gone, Elaine says she's delighted, but. . . . She tells Arnie she doesn't know how she feels about him, and the fact the kids like him complicates matters. It dawns on Arnie what a terrible spot he's put her in. "I think," he begins helpfully, "this might call for some champagne!" Elaine wears a strange half-smile and gets misty-eyed. "You're such a dear man," she says softly. "I'm glad you think so," Arnie says tentatively, "because now you know you may be stuck with me." Elaine nods. "I guess I am." Her half-smile becomes a full one. "You know what?" she says, discovering her feelings. "I love it." The knockout and the nebbish hug.

OTHER GUESTS:

David Mendenhall (Jason Nardo)
Melanie Gaffin (Jennifer Nardo)

It is a tribute to the writers and producers of *Taxi* that an episode about a witty, nebbishy, neurotic New Yorker having a love affair with a beautiful, energetic, slightly less-neurotic New Yorker isn't anything at all like a Woody Allen movie. The story of Arnie and Elaine has its own flavor, one that's less cerebral and more emotional then Allen's contemporary work. The look on Elaine's face toward the end, as she realizes she's falling in love with someone who doesn't look at all like the man of her dreams, is almost incredibly honest—nervous and excited all at once. It's as if she suddenly sees her future, and gets that strange, awful, exhilarating feeling we get when we first realize that the person sitting beside us may be the one that we'll marry. In real life, the people we fall in love with often don't look anything like what we'd expect, and it says something quietly horrible about television that until *L.A. Law* the only time such a visual mismatch ever took hold on a network show was, perhaps, in this episode of *Taxi*.

Wallace Shawn, recreating his role from "The Shloogel Show" (episode #91), never lets Arnie get whiny or wimpy. Even at his most openly insecure, Arnie's a fighter with a great sense of humor about himself, and that quality attracts Elaine, as well as his love of fine art. Arnie is the antithesis of Elaine's roguish first husband, another plus for her after having been burned so often by handsome Romeos. Finally, the instinctively maternal Elaine has found a boyfriend she can mother, as she's always tried to mother Alex and the other cabbies.

Shawn almost didn't get got, however. As Marilu Henner remembers, she was attending the Cannes Film Festival when Jim Brooks called her to say that the canceled *Taxi* had been picked up by NBC, "and that Wally Shawn was somewhere at Cannes and could I find him, because they had a great idea for an opening episode pairing off the two of us. I tried, but I couldn't, and then I left for Paris and then Italy. So I'm all over, right? And afterward, I go to this obscure location in Bangkok to visit [then-husband Frederic Forrest], who was shooting [the aborted CBS miniseries] *Saigon*. And I'm in this tiny dressing room, and Freddie is introducing me to people in the cast, E. G. Marshall was there, and suddenly here's Wally Shawn! And I go, oh my God, I can't believe this! I mean, I hadn't even told Freddie I was looking for Wally Shawn, and here I find him in Bangkok!" It was literally a case, it seems, of searching the world over for the right actor.

#112 A GRAND GESTURE

WRITTEN BY KEN ESTIN AND SAM SIMON.
DIRECTED BY NOAM PITLIK.

A panhandler wanders into the garage, begging for loose change, gum, or traveler's checks. Louie throws him out, but not before nouveau riche Jim gives the grateful man $1,000. Alex finds this irresponsible, no matter how much money Jim has inherited. He threatens to phone the administrator of the estate immediately and have Jim cut off for his own good. Jim says Alex wouldn't behave that way if he knew how good it felt to give money to downtrodden people. In fact, he adds, he's going to give each of his friends $1,000 for them to give away, so that they can experience the same joy of giving. The cabbies all agree, though Latka at first turns down the cash. "The tradition of my country forces me to protest . . . I'll *take* the money, but first I must protest. 'No, no, no! I won't take it! This is an insult!' [taking the money] Tenk you veddy much." Even Louie gets $1,000 to give away, though Alex says Louie will only pocket the dough and lie about it. "Will you do that?" Iggy asks him. Louie replies, "Of course." But he says he wants to play, too, and that he'll give the money to Jeff so that they can check. So there.

In a back-alley church, Latka and Simka give the money to their Reverend Gorky (who now speaks some English). He protests loudly and then takes it. Simka looks disappointed, however, and when he asks, she tells him she was hoping to use the money to help start a family. Reverend Gorky generously hands her the $1,000; she protests, and then jumps for joy into the tall priest's arms.

Tony stops by the top floor of an old apartment building to find his friend Walt (Scatman Crothers), an old black man whose life revolves around TV shows. Tony unveils a 21-inch, high-end, remote-control color TV set. The gruff Walt silently cries at his friend's generosity, and then shoos him out.

Elaine, at home, wakes her daughter, Jennifer. Jim had said it was OK for Elaine to give the money to her kids. But, she tells Jennifer, since Jason's not here right now, I'll give the money all to you. Elaine leaves the choice to Jennifer about sharing with her brother, and drops a few not-so-subtle hints about the right thing to do. Jennifer agrees to share. She also wants to buy her mother a present with the money—a ColecoVision video game console and eleven cartridges.

Back at the garage, Louie presents the money to Jeff, without explanation, and tells him to take it. Jeff refuses. Louie doesn't understand why. "It could be dirty money," Jeff says harshly. "I'm not

TAXI
227

Guest star Scatman Crothers with Tony Danza in the final episode: "A Grand Gesture."

askin' you to eat off it!'' Louie replies. Jeff tells him that knowing Lou, it could be counterfeit or stolen or irradiated by the Russians for some warped experiment.

Meanwhile, Alex thinks he's finally got a customer. It's a broke young political cartoonist, on his way to the Port Authority Bus Terminal to start his trip back home to Oregon. Alex readies his cash while the cartoonist displays his portfolio. His work stinks. "So—what're you gonna do in Oregon?" Reiger asks. Back at the garage at the end of his shift, Alex says he ran across an old lady with seven kids who surely needed that $1,100—Jim's thousand, plus a little extra of his own. He feels great, as do all the cabbies and even Simka.

They all go off to Mario's together. Jeff enters the now-empty garage from the tool room, closely followed by Louie. Jeff is still refusing. Louie finally tells him about Jim's plan and practically forces the money on him. Exasperated by Jeff's insinuations, he has a fit. "Iggy said I'd feel great!" he sputters. "I said I wouldn't feel anything. I never *imagined that I would feel like a sack of dirt!* . . . You couldn't believe that I was capable of doin' one decent thing. You couldn't believe that I thought of you as a friend." Louie storms into his cage and shuts out the light. Jeff, ashamed, apologizes and holds out his hand to shake. Louie finally takes it, and they hug—while Jim pokes his head in and waves to them.

OTHER GUESTS:

Vincent Schiavelli (Reverend H. L. Gorky)
Melanie Gaffin (Jennifer Nardo)
Tracey Walter (the panhandler)
Tom Villard (the cartoonist, identified as Jeremy in end credits, not in episode)

The final episode of *Taxi*.

The cast members and the creators say today that they didn't get to write a wrap-up show, and that's true in the sense of what was done for *The Mary Tyler Moore Show* and *M*A*S*H*. Yet this *is* a wrap-up episode in a way, for it allows each of the characters to exit on a gracious note. This wasn't a "Louie" episode or a "Jim" episode or an "Alex" episode—this was an ensemble episode. What better way to say farewell to an ensemble show? There is, indeed, a classically structured epiphany, as Louie, in a blackened cage like a ring of hell, is rescued by Jeff, who in this episode has seen his own dark side, as well as that of Lou. If *Taxi* was the microcosm everyone intended it to be, then Louie and Jeff managed no less than to save each other's souls. Considering what set all that in motion, a case can be made for Jim as the series's powerful, benign, wise *but*—and this is key—not infallible Christ figure.

Vincent Schiavelli returns one last time as Reverend Gorky, and Melanie Gaffin reprises her role as Elaine's daughter, Jennifer. Tracey Walter, an actor-friend of Danny DeVito's, costarred in Earl Pomerantz's series *Best of the West*. Tom Villard, who died in 1994 at age 40, costarred on the sitcom *We Got It Made*, and pitched in "heartwarming" commercials for a chemical company. And then there was the late, great Benjamin Sherman "Scatman" Crothers, who died in 1986 at the age of seventy-six after adding an air of distinction to even the most abysmal TV show or movie. Imagine what he adds to this exceptional episode.

"All I can say about that last episode," muses DeVito, "is that everybody was very emotional due to the fact we were all splittin' up and we knew it and we didn't want to."

The grand gesture ended production on February 18, 1983.

#113 RETROSPECTIVE, PART I
#114 RETROSPECTIVE, PART II
(A.K.A. A *TAXI* CELEBRATION)

This two-part compilation of great *Taxi* bits was originally broadcast as a one-hour special on March 23, 1983. Part I opens with a newly taped Danny DeVito introduction, followed by Elaine's arrival, from episode #1, "Like Father, Like Daughter" (erroneously but helpfully subtitled "The First Show"); Jim's reintroduction and his driver's test, from episode #27, "Reverend Jim: A Space Odyssey"; Alex meeting Angela Matusa, talking with Elaine, and later confronting Angela, from episode #2, "Blind Date"; a snippet of the marriage announcement from episode #87, "The Wedding of Latka and Simka"; followed by Latka's "seduction," Simka's arrival at Alex's apartment, and the finale (slightly trimmed) from "Scenskees from a Marriage" Parts I and II; and Kirk's private talk with Tony, Tony's talk with Alex, and Alex's talk with Kirk, from episode #50, "Elaine's Strange Triangle."

Part II features the Tom Selleck sequence from episode #22, "Memories of Cab 804, Part II"; Zena's introduction to Lou, their private talks with Alex, and Zena's conquest of Lou, from episode #25, "Louie and the Nice Girl"; Jim's prediction and its outcome from episode #65, "Jim the Psychic"; and the big musical number from episode #44, "Fantasy Borough, Part II" (erroneously but helpfully subtitled "Elaine's Fantasy"). Cut from the original one-hour broadcast for the two-part syndicated version of the retrospective is a scene from episode #86, "Elegant Iggy."

CREDITS FOR OPENING SEGMENT:

Videotape Editor: Bill Petty
Postproduction Facilities: Vidtronics

Note: Rita Taggart is among the actors thanked in the end credits, but no scenes from her episode (#8, "Paper Marriage") appear.

FINAL-DRAFT SCRIPT

"JIM'S INHERITANCE"

![checkered pattern]

The final-draft script for episode #93 was turned in on Wednesday, August 18, 1982. It was shot on Friday, August 20, and aired on Thursday, October 7, 1982. Note that even in this "final" form, there are differences between what's on the page and what was shot. Note also that this particular script spells Alex's last name "Rieger," not the more accepted "Reiger." Christopher Lloyd talks about one impromptu addition to the ending in the background story for this episode (pages 206–7).

TAXI

"Jim's Inheritance"

#60275-093

Written by

Ken Estin

Created and Developed by

James L. Brooks

Stan Daniels

David Davis

Ed Weinberger

THE WRITING CREDITS MAY NOT BE FINAL AND SHOULD NOT
BE USED FOR PUBLICITY OR ADVERTISING PURPOSES WITHOUT
FIRST CHECKING WITH THE TELEVISION LEGAL DEPARTMENT.

This script is not for publication or reproduction.
No one is authorized to dispose of same. If lost,
or destroyed, please notify script department.

Return to Script Department
PARAMOUNT PICTURES CORPORATION
5555 Melrose
Hollywood, California 90038

FINAL DRAFT

August 18, 1982

TAXI
"Jim's Inheritance"
#60275-093

CAST

ALEX RIEGER .... JUDD HIRSCH

LOUIE DE PALMA .... DANNY DE VITO

ELAINE NARDO .... MARILU HENNER

TONY BANTA .... TONY DANZA

JIM IGNATOWSKI .... CHRISTOPHER LLOYD

JOHN BICKERS .... DICK SARGENT

JUDGE .... F. WILLIAM PARKER

PEREZ ....

DAVID WINSLOW ....

SETS

INT. GARAGE

INT. JUDGE'S CHAMBERS

INT. HOVEL

T A X I
234

TAXI
"Jim's Inheritance"
#60275-093
ACT ONE

<u>A</u>

FADE IN:

<u>INT. GARAGE - NIGHT</u>

VARIOUS NIGHT SHIFT PERSONNEL
ARE PRESENT. TONY, ALEX AND ELAINE
ARE TALKING AT THE TABLE. LOUIE
IS TALKING ON THE TELEPHONE
IN THE CAGE.

                    LOUIE

          (INTO PHONE) No, no, I understand . . .
          Goodbye.

LOUIE HANGS UP THE PHONE AND
HURRIES TO THE TABLE.

                    LOUIE

          Rieger, Nardo, Banta. I just talked
          to Jim's brother. There's some bad
          news. Maybe I shouldn't say bad
          news. That's a scary way to put
          it.

                    ELAINE

          What is it?

                    LOUIE

          His dad croaked.

THEY REACT.

                    LOUIE

          I guess I'm going to have to break
          it to him.

                    TONY

          You?

                    LOUIE

          (DEFENSIVELY) Yeah, me. I've done
          this before. Ask Perez over there.
          (TO A CABBIE ACROSS THE GARAGE)
          Perez, didn't I tell you just a few
          days ago that your father died?

                    PEREZ

          (GRIEF STRICKEN) What?

                    LOUIE

          Oh, Perez, I meant to. I'm so
          sorry. Take the rest of the day
          off.

PEREZ GOES OUT OF THE GARAGE.
LOUIE CALLS AFTER HIM.

                    LOUIE

          I'll make it up to you. (EXPLAINING
          TO THE OTHERS) I've been very busy.

                    ELAINE

          Louie, you better let one of us
          tell Jim.

                    LOUIE

          I can't. It has to come from me.
          Iggy and I have a special relationship.

                    ALEX

          Actually, crazy as it sounds, Jim
          does consider Louie his closest
          friend.

JIM ENTERS, HUMMING.

                    ALEX

          Louie, do this right.

                    LOUIE

          You're insulting me. Look, Jim,
          I have some bad news for you and
          I think the best thing is to come
          right out and say it.

                    JIM

          Okey-doke. Shoot.

LOUIE LOOKS AT ALEX, TONY AND
ELAINE, THEN ADDRESSES JIM.

LOUIE

It's about your dad. (BEAT) He
is no longer with us.

JIM

He never was. He lives in Boston.

LOUIE

No, Jim. He has gone on to a better place.

JIM

Aw, no. I loved that house.

LOUIE

He has passed over Jordan.

JIM STILL DOESN'T UNDERSTAND.
ALEX PUTS HIS ARM AROUND JIM.

ALEX

Jim, your father is dead.

JIM

(STUNNED) What? (NOT KNOWING
WHERE TO TURN) Alex, couldn't
you have been a little more delicate?

T A X I
▪▪▪▪▪▪▪
237

DISSOLVE TO:

B

INT. GARAGE - NIGHT

VARIOUS NIGHT SHIFT PERSONNEL ARE
PRESENT. ALEX IS BUYING COFFEE.
LOUIE AND JEFF ARE WORKING IN
THE CAGE. TONY IS READING A
SECTION OF THE NEWSPAPER AT THE
TABLE.

TONY

Damn it. What's this world coming
to? It's not a decent place to raise
kids anymore. I'm appalled.

TONY THROWS THE PAPER DOWN.

ALEX

The Yankees lost another one?

TONY

Hey, would I be this upset just
because the Yankees lost a game?

ALEX

A double-header?

TONY

To Seattle. But it's more than that.
Steinbrenner is doing it again. He's
undermining his team and breaking
a proud New York tradition.

ALEX

Tony . . .

TONY

Am I the only one who thinks that
Steinbrenner's changing the world?

ALEX

How can he be changing the world?

TONY

The domino theory. He ruins the
spirit of the Yankees. They lose.
Their fans become depressed and
irritable. Bus drivers, cops,
waitresses, go to work and do a bad
job and that affects everybody in the
city including the politicians and the
bankers, who make bad decisions that
hurt the economy and that affects the
world. And the next thing you know,
OPEC is raising its prices and another
war is breaking out in South America.

ELAINE HAS ENTERED AND OVERHEARD
THE LAST SENTENCE.

ELAINE

I just heard on the news that the
Russians launched another killer satellite.

TONY

Steinbrenner.

HE WALKS AWAY FROM THE TABLE.
<u>JOHN BICKERS, AN ATTORNEY,</u>
<u>ENTERS</u> WEARING AN EXPENSIVE
BUSINESS SUIT. LOUIE AND JEFF
ARE IN THE CAGE. A MECHANIC
IS TALKING TO A FEMALE CABBY.

> LOUIE
>
> (YELLING TO THE MECHANIC) Hey, no
> flirting in the garage. You've got
> work to do. If you don't have that
> cab fixed and out of here in two
> minutes, I'll have you fixed and
> thrown out of here in three.

> BICKERS
>
> (TO ALEX) Excuse me. Who's in
> charge here?

> ALEX
>
> That's him in the cage.

> BICKERS
>
> (HOPEFULLY) The quiet Black
> gentleman?

> ALEX
>
> No, the pit bull.

BICKERS GOES TO THE CAGE.

> BICKERS
>
> (TO LOUIE) Excuse me. I'm looking
> for James Caldwell. I believe he
> changed his name. You may know
> him as Jim Ignatowski. I'm an
> attorney for his father's estate.

> LOUIE
>
> (SOMBERLY) Oh, I bet it's about the
> will. Jim isn't in right now. Why
> don't you have a cup of coffee and
> wait for him?

> BICKERS
>
> Thank you. Do you have a donut?

> LOUIE
>
> Jeff, find the man a donut.

                    TONY

              Hey, what's going on?

                    LOUIE

              (TO BICKERS) Excuse me.

LOUIE WALKS TO THE TABLE.

                    LOUIE

              This is the attorney for Iggy's
              father, who was loaded. I bet my
              buddy Iggy's going to be rich!

LOUIE CROSSES BACK TO BICKERS
WHO NOW HAS A CUP OF COFFEE AND
A DONUT.

                    LOUIE

              (TO BICKERS) How's the coffee?

                    BICKERS

              Fine. The donut's a little boring.

                    LOUIE

              A cake donut? Jeff, this man is an
              attorney. Get him a jelly donut.
              (TO BICKERS) How much did you say
              Jim is inheriting?

                    BICKERS

              I didn't say. Jeff, do you have a
              maple log?

                    LOUIE

              (TO JEFF) Give him the box. Let
              him pick.

JIM ENTERS.

                    TONY

              Jim . . .

LOUIE RUNS TO JIM AND HUGS HIM.

                    LOUIE

              Iggy, Iggy, Iggy, Iggy, Iggy.

                    JIM

              (DELIGHTED) Boss, Boss, Boss, Boss,
              Boss.

BICKERS APPROACHES JIM.

                    BICKERS

          Hello, James. It's good to see you
          again. It's been a long time.

                       JIM

                Who are you?

                    BICKERS

          I'm John Bickers. (BEAT) Your
          father's attorney. I used to come
          to your family picnics every year.
          You and I used to have long
          political talks by the tennis
          court. Do you remember that?

                       JIM

          Yeah, sure. The cement thing with
          the net in the middle.

                    BICKERS

          Uh . . . yes. (BEAT) I'm sorry about
          your father. I want you to know he
          went peacefully. I was at his
          bedside in the hospital when he died.

                       JIM

          He should have taken off weight.
          410 pounds was simply too heavy for
          his frame. (BEAT) Do you remember
          what his last words were?

                    BICKERS

          Well . . . his last words were . . . "Watch,
          when I press this button it raises my
          feet."

JIM MANAGES A SMILE.

                       JIM

                I like that.

                    BICKERS

          James, it's time for us to talk about
          your father's will.

LOUIE CLIMBS UP TO THE SCREENS
OF THE CAGE AND HANGS ON AS HE
EAVESDROPS.

TAXI

241

                    JIM

          I know. He left me out of the will
          when I dropped out of Harvard.

                  BICKERS

        Jim, he reinstated you in his will
        a few months before he died. I don't
        want your friends to know this, but
        your father did leave you . . .

BICKERS WRITES SOMETHING ON A
PIECE OF PAPER AND SHOWS IT TO
JIM.

                    JIM

          Three hundred and fifty dollars!
          Dad didn't hate me!

BICKERS POINTS TO THE PAPER.

                    JIM

          Thirty five hundred dollars! Dad
          really did like me.

BICKERS POINTS AGAIN.

                    JIM

          Three and a half million dollars!
          Dad wasn't in his right mind.

ALL THE SCREENS OF THE CAGE
SUDDENLY COLLAPSE FROM LOUIE'S
WEIGHT AND FALL TO THE FLOOR.

                  LOUIE

          Excuse me. I couldn't help
          overhearing.

                  BICKERS

          James, there is a problem. But I
          don't think this is the time and
          place to go into it.

                    JIM

        There's nothing you can tell me you
        can't say in front of my friends.

                  BICKERS

        Your brother and sister have
        petitioned the court to establish
        a conservatorship of your inheritance.

JIM

Bless them.

BICKERS

James, you don't understand. They're
going to take you to court and try to
prove that you're incompetent. If
they do, your brother will be appointed
permanent conservator. Your assets
will be held in trust indefinitely.
He will determine how that money is
invested and disbursed. He'll give
you an allowance, determine how and
where you live and assume complete
responsibility for your well-being.
In other words, the inheritance will
be yours, but you will be treated
like a child.

JIM

Sounds pretty good.

BICKERS

You will lose the rights and
privileges of an adult.

JIM

(DISAPPOINTED) Oh. (THEN) Well,
you tell my brother and sister they're
in for more than they bargained for.
I haven't had many fights in my life
but what I've had I've won. I got
my drivers license. Got my throat
examined without a tongue depresser.
Got my frisbee back from the Secret
Service. Now I'm going to get my
three and a half million dollars.
Or fail to do so!

FADE OUT.

END OF ACT ONE

C

INT. JUDGE'S CHAMBERS - DAY

EXCEPT FOR CASES OF LAW BOOKS,
NOTHING ABOUT THE ROOM DESIGNATES
IT AS A JUDGE'S OFFICE. IT COULD
JUST AS WELL BE THAT OF A
SUCCESSFUL ACCOUNTANT OR INSURANCE
BROKER. THERE IS A LARGE DESK
BEHIND WHICH IS AN EXECUTIVE
CHAIR. THERE ARE SEVERAL SMALL,
COMFORTABLE CHAIRS LOCATED IN
FRONT OF THE DESK, BY THE WINDOW
AND IN THE CORNERS BY THE DOORWAY.
ALEX, ELAINE, TONY, LOUIE, JOHN
BICKERS, ANOTHER ATTORNEY (DAVID
WINSLOW), A COURT REPORTER, AND
A BAILIFF ARE IN THE CHAMBERS.

TONY

Maybe I shouldn't be here. I didn't
know they were going to swear us in.
Oh, man, what if they ask me if I
think he's an air head?

BICKERS

Let's hope they don't ask.

ELAINE LOOKS AT HER WATCH.

ELAINE

We should have brought Jim with us.
We should have insisted.

ALEX

He wanted to handle this himself.
We went over the directions, the
time, what he should wear.

LOUIE

He'll be late and show up looking
like a rat's behind.

JIM ENTERS DRESSED IN A CONSERVATIVE
BUT TASTEFUL MANNER. HE COULD PASS
FOR AN ATTORNEY.

JIM

Excuse me, is this where the
Ignatowski hearing is being held?

ALEX

Yes, Jim.

BICKERS

James, sit over here with me. And
say as little as possible.

JIM

Can do. I want to thank all of you
for coming to help me.

THE JUDGE ENTERS.

JUDGE

Don't bother to rise. I prefer that
hearings in my chambers be informal.

JIM WINKS TO THE OTHERS, A
CONFIDENT, COMPETENT MAN.
THE JUDGE SITS AT THE DESK
AND LOOKS AT PAPERWORK.

T A X I

245

JUDGE

(TO THE ATTORNEYS) Gentlemen, do you
have anything to add to your papers?

WINSLOW

No, Your Honor.

BICKERS

No, Your Honor.

JUDGE

Fine. We'll try to make this as easy
as possible on everyone. (TO JIM)
Are you James Ignatowski?

JIM LOOKS AT BICKERS.

BICKERS

Yes, he is, Your Honor.

JUDGE

I prefer to talk directly to Mr.
Ignatowski. (TO JIM) How are you
feeling today, Mr. Ignatowski?

JIM

Competent, and you?

JUDGE

Fine, thank you. You're listed in
the affidavits as James Caldwell.
Why did you change your name to
Ignatowski?

JIM

Your Honor, Caldwell is my father's
name. I changed it to Ignatowski
for a very good reason. I was under
the mistaken impression that Ignatowski
was Starchild spelled backwards.

JUDGE

Mr. Ignatowski, I have affidavits
from your employer and your friends
here, swearing that you have held
a job continuously for three years.

LOUIE

May I elaborate on that, Your Honor?

JIM

Attaboy, Boss. Jump right in there.

JUDGE

You are . . . ?

LOUIE

Louie De Palma.

JUDGE

Go ahead. But let me remind you
that you're governed by the law
of perjury while you're here.

LOUIE

Your Honor, I consider myself governed
by the law of perjury at all times.

JUDGE

You're Mr. Ignatowski's superior,
are you not?

LOUIE

Only in terms of the cab company,
Your Honor. In all other areas I
consider him my superior.

JUDGE

Do you believe him to be competent?

LOUIE

Do I believe him competent? Was
Copernicus competent? Was Mahatma
Ghandi competent? Was Moses competent?

JIM STOPS LOUIE WITH A GESTURE.

JIM

(TO JUDGE) Yes, they were.

JIM GESTURES FOR LOUIE TO CONTINUE.

LOUIE

Jim is the wisest man I've ever met
and I come from a bright crowd. It's
a privilege to know him, to put my feet
up after a hard day and listen to his
wisdom. He's so far ahead of the rest
of us that people often mistake his
wisdom for burned out brain cells.
Take it from me. This guy over here
is one smart cookie.

JIM

Boss. If you feel like that about
me, who cares about the money?

LOUIE

(WHISPERING) Shut up, Idiot!

JUDGE

I'd like to be frank with you. At
this point the paperwork submitted by
your brother's attorney and the court
investigator presents an extremely
strong case for conservatorship.

BICKERS

I'd like to address some of that
evidence, Your Honor.

JUDGE

You already have in your papers filed
with the court. At this point I'd
like to talk to Mr. Ignatowski.

JIM

Well, if Your Honor doesn't mind, I'd
like to trot out my big gun. Could
Alex Rieger say something about how
competent I am?

JUDGE

Certainly. I'd like to hear any arguments
on your behalf.

ALEX

Your Honor, I know in those papers on
your desk there are going to be a lot of
unusual things Jim has done. But I'm sure
there are acceptable reasons for all of them.

JUDGE

The court has to wonder why he lived
in a condemned building for five years.

ALEX

There was a time he couldn't afford
anything else. He found a shelter
for himself and made it livable.

JIM

(INVOLVED) Why didn't I move out
after I started making money?

JUDGE

That's what I was about to ask.

JIM

Looks like I beat you to it.

JUDGE

I have a check here that his father
wrote to Mr. Louie De Palma to
compensate him $29,452 for burning
down his apartment.

LOUIE

This isn't a trial. It's a witch
hunt! He fell asleep while bar-b-queing.
It could happen to anyone.

JUDGE

He was also cited for driving a van
with the windows, doors, sides, and roof
missing. Can you explain that?

JIM

May I remind the court that incompetency
should not be confused with style.

ALEX

When you look through your papers, Your
Honor, the biggest argument against
Jim's competency are that he's so
decent he invariably puts other people's
welfare above his own. He tends to care
nothing about materialistic things
and no matter what happens to him, he
usually ends every day happy. I'm
scared that maybe we have all reached
a point where that means a person is
incompetent. And if we have I feel
sorry, not only for Jim, but for the
whole damn bunch of us.

JUDGE

You know it's one of the problems of
this court that they rerun ''Mr. Deeds
Goes To Town'' as much as they do. I
understand the fervor and appreciate the
sentiment, however, this hearing wasn't
about sentiment, Mr. Ignatowski—

LOUIE

Before you do that, one more thing.

JUDGE

What is it?

LOUIE

What about Howard Hughes? A man
who had billions of dollars and
four-foot toenails.

TONY

Forget Howard Hughes. What about
George Steinbrenner? Is a man competent
who lets Reggie Jackson go to the Angels?
Who goes through four pitching coaches in
one year?

                    JUDGE

        Mr. Steinbrenner isn't the subject of
        this hearing . . . unfortunately.

                     JIM

           Can I say something?

                    JUDGE

              If you wish.

                     JIM

          Do you want me to stand?

                    JUDGE

        However you're most comfortable?

JIM TRIES SEVERAL POSITIONS
ENDING UP IN A COMFORTABLE
BUT SOMEWHAT BIZARRE POSITION.

                     JIM

          This is as comfortable as I can
          get. I don't feel like lying down
          in court.

                    JUDGE

           What did you want to say?

                     JIM

          Nothing. Except I'd like to invite
          everybody here to my victory party
          at the Pierre Hotel. We're going
          to have plenty of those big shrimp.

                    JUDGE

        Mr. Ignatowski, I must rule in favor
        of the conservatorship. I'm appointing
        your brother, Thomas Caldwell, the
        conservator. He will be required to
        obtain a bond in the amount of
        three-point-seven million dollars.

                     JIM

        I have something to say that might
        change your mind. Please, pretty please.
        And I don't mean that in any childlike
        way. I mean it as one man to another.
        My inheritance is a matter between me
        and my dad, no one else. Please don't
        take it away from me. No kidding
        around. Please.

T A X I
▪▪▪▪▪▪▪
250

                    JUDGE

                  I'm sorry.

                     JIM

                   I lost?

                   BICKERS

      Your Honor, we want to go on record
      as intending to appeal this decision.

                    JUDGE

                  So noted.

                     JIM

                   I lost.

                                              DISSOLVE TO:

                      <u>D</u>

INT. HOVEL - NIGHT

JIM IS SITTING ON HIS COUCH.   T A X I
THERE'S <u>A KNOCK AT THE DOOR</u>.   ✖✖✖✖✖✖
JIM CROSSES AND OPENS THE DOOR.   251

                   ELAINE

                  Hi, Jim.

                     JIM

                 Hi, Elaine.

                   ELAINE

           Do you want to be alone?

                     JIM

            Hell, no. Come on in.

<u>ELAINE ENTERS</u>, STEPPING OVER A
TRUNK.

                   ELAINE

      You know, you have a trunk out there.

                     JIM

         Yes. It's my dad's trunk—some
         of his belongings. A couple of guys
         delivered it yesterday. Make

yourself comfortable. Let me get
you something to drink.

JIM CLOSES THE DOOR.

                    ELAINE
          What about that trunk?

JIM CROSSES TO THE REFRIGERATOR AND
OPENS IT.

                     JIM
          Forget about it. (LOOKS INTO
          REFRIGERATOR) Looks like all I've
          got is a club soda and a Rob Roy.
          What'll it be?

                    ELAINE
          Nothing, thank you. Jim, you should
          bring the trunk inside.

                     JIM
          I don't think so.

                    ELAINE
          You've got to bring it in.

                     JIM
          I don't.

                    ELAINE
          Well, I'm going to bring it in.

                     JIM
          I wish you wouldn't.

ELAINE OPENS THE DOOR AND STARTS
TO DRAG THE HEAVY TRUNK IN WITH
DIFFICULTY.

                     JIM
          Please don't.

ELAINE CONTINUES TO STRUGGLE WITH
THE TRUNK.

                     JIM
          Well, if you insist upon it, why
          don't you put it there by the
          couch?

JIM POINTS TO A SPOT FAR ACROSS
THE ROOM. ELAINE STOPS DRAGGING
THE TRUNK.

                    JIM (CONT'D)
            Or, right there is fine. So what
            do you think of my place?

                    ELAINE
            I like it. Did you pick everything
            out yourself?

                    JIM
            No, a decorator friend helped me.
            (THEN) You know what really makes
            me feel bad?

                    ELAINE
            What, Jim?

                    JIM
            Leaving me that money was Dad's way
            of saying to me, "You're okay after
            all, Jim." And I never got a chance
            to say back to him, "You're not so
            bad yourself." Elaine, I've changed
            my mind. I think I would like to be
            alone.

                    ELAINE
            Are you sure?

                    JIM
            Yeah.

                    ELAINE
            Okay. But I want you to know the
            reason I came is to tell you why I
            didn't say anything at the hearing.
            It was because, in that situation,
            it seemed impossible to make anyone
            understand you. But, God, you know
            you're not incompetent.

                    JIM
            Sure. If I was incompetent, would
            I feel this bad?

                                    ELAINE
                        No. You wouldn't. Call me if you
                        want to talk.

                                     JIM
                          Would you like a trunk?

                                    ELAINE
                           No. Goodbye, Jim.

SHE EXITS.

                                     JIM
                          (CALLING AFTER HER) Maybe for your
                          kids?

THERE IS NO RESPONSE. JIM SITS
OPPOSITE THE TRUNK AND STARES AT
IT FOR A MOMENT.

                                 JIM (CONT'D)
                          Why did Dad want me to have this
                          stuff?

HE TAKES A KEY OUT OF AN ENVELOPE
AND OPENS THE TRUNK. HE LOOKS
INSIDE, REACHES IN, AND TAKES OUT
A PHOTOGRAPH OF HIMSELF.

                                 JIM (CONT'D)
                          My graduation picture. Gee, I didn't
                          know Dad kept that.

HE TAKES OUT A SHEET OF PAPER.

                                 JIM (CONT'D)
                          My freshman transcript. A B +
                          "Physics for Poets." Sounds like
                          a tough class. I could have used
                          this in court.

JIM LOOKS INTO THE TRUNK AGAIN, AND
IS MOVED BY WHAT HE SEES. HE TAKES
OUT AN ENORMOUS WELL-TAILORED SUIT.

                                     JIM
                          Dad's best suit. (TENDERLY UNFOLDING
                          THE SUIT) He was married in this.
                          He was so proud that twenty-five
                          years later he could still fit into it.

HE DRAPES THE SUIT OVER A CHAIR
AND SITS OPPOSITE IT.

TAXI
254

                    JIM (CONT'D)

        Dad, I'm sorry I haven't cried. I
        don't know why I haven't cried.
        (CRYING) I feel awful that I haven't
        cried. Wait, I'm crying. (STOPS
        CRYING) But am I crying because I
        lost you or because I didn't cry?
        Wait, I stopped. (CRYING) But I
        was crying. I didn't want to stop.
        (STOPS CRYING) I'm crying again.
        No, I stopped.

HE SITS QUIETLY A MOMENT AND DRIES
HIS TEARS.

                    JIM (CONT'D)

        I wish we could have said goodbye, Dad.
        I don't remember if I told you that I
        love you. I do. Did you know that? I
        wish you could give me an answer. I
        wish I could hear you say you love me.

JIM STARTS TO PUT THE JACKET AWAY,
THEN FINDS A CASSETTE TAPE IN THE
POCKET.   T A X I
                                                          ▟▚▟▚▟▚▟
                        JIM   255

               Dad left me a tape.

JIM PUTS THE TAPE INTO A PLAYER.
WE HEAR AN UP-TEMPO MOTOWN RECORDING.

                        JIM

        (REALIZING, DELIGHTED) Dad was into
        the Supremes! I told him they were
        hot, and he listened to me!

AND AS JIM LISTENS TO THE MUSIC, WE . . .

                                              FADE OUT.

                    END OF ACT TWO
                       THE END

UNUSED
STORY
OUTLINE

"WHO WILL BE MISS TAXI?"

▩▩▩▩▩

This funny and incredibly detailed story outline—practically a script—was eventually brought to life as the "Who Will Be Miss Boston Barmaid?" episode of *Cheers*.

TAXI "Who Will Be Miss Taxi?" Story Outline—David Lloyd 12/14/79

ACT ONE

T A X I
▩▩▩▩
256

GARAGE

Bobby and Tony are talking. Bobby is in a jam; he has a bit part in an off-Broadway show and has been consistently upstaging the lead actor, who has finally gotten fed up and threatened to punch his face off. Bobby is scared.

Tony sympathizes but says maybe he could teach Bobby a bit about self-defense so he could handle the other guy. Bobby resists—is a lover not a fighter and doesn't want any part of it. Before Tony can persuade him, Alex enters with the paper (a tabloid that could be either the *News* or the *Post*) and asks if they've seen it?

Reverend Jim joins them and Alex directs their attention to Page 36 and the article on the "Miss Taxi" contest. They all gape, and we gather from their comments that there are pictures of the five finalists and one of them is Elaine!

As they're murmuring about that, Elaine enters and Alex, concealing the paper, asks her how she feels about the "Miss Taxi" contest. She is very scornful on the subject; it's nothing but a beauty contest—a bunch of women cab drivers send in their pictures and the paper's readers vote on the prettiest and name her "Miss Taxi." She finds it demeaning and can't imagine what kind of woman would allow herself to be party to such a thing.

Alex nods . . . he thought that was her opinion. In that case, she won't want to look at the paper . . .

Which of course prompts a scuffle which Elaine wins; she grabs the paper, takes one look and flips. It's not only her picture, but in a bathing suit! She rushes to the phone to call the paper—Louie suggests she not make the call, but she does and demands to know how they dare run such a picture without her permission. It turns out they got a signed released from her with the picture and was immediately declared one of the finalists. Already votes are pouring in for her.

Off the phone she ponders how it could have happened—and then the light dawns. Louie! He admits it cheerfully; he thought it would be good publicity for the Sunshine Cab Co. if one of its drivers were named Miss Taxi—it would impress the new owner. Where did he get the picture? Her kid gave it to him; Louie told him it was for her license renewal. In a bathing suit? In case you ever had to drive a water-taxi. And you forged my signature on the release form? Not at all, says Louie—you signed it yourself; you sign dozens of things for me in the course of a week. Yeah, she says—but I read every one of them first. There is such a thing as carbon paper, Nardo . . !

Elaine is furious; the guys don't see why. How would you like to see your picture in the paper—in a bathing suit? she asks. They discuss how they would react. The point is, they say—she's very pretty. That's all very well, she says, but the idea of having all the news-paper readers drooling over her, fantasizing about her, and eventually wrapping their gar-bage in her is too much! Then withdraw says Alex. Too late, she says—and besides she has a better idea; she'll wait until the vote is announced and the winner crowned at the Union Hall, and then refuse the title! Much more publicity that way.

She looks at the pictures again, hers and the other finalists. You know, she says—there's only one thing that would be worse than being in this contest with those women. What, they ask? Losing!

DISSOLVE TO:

THE UNION HALL

Where the vote is to be announced. It's days later. Elaine and the guys come in. Elaine concedes that things have been a bit different since her picture appeared; she's enjoyed the status of a minor celebrity. Guy got in her cab and called her by name. (Alex hates to break it to her, but does; they all have their names on the ID plaque; people get in his cab and call him by name, too.)

Bobby comes in late and nervous; the other actor is really mad now (maybe some further bit of upstaging took place) and has threatened to beat him up if he shows up at the theater the following day. Tony now insists; at the garage later he will give Bobby a boxing lesson and show him all he needs to know to take care of the guy.

Tony also tells Elaine confidently that he's just scouted the competition and she can't lose tonight—it's oink city. Elaine bridles; that's exactly the attitude that makes her despise this kind of thing. They're like cattle with everybody feeling he has a right to criticize their looks. When she gets up there she's gonna let them have it! If she gets up there, says Alex. That's what I meant, she says.

A guy from the paper gets up, announces the tabulation, talks about the heavy response, then announces the winner: it's Elaine. Our guys cheer and go wild.

She gets up, goes to the stage with great determination. The guy hands her a kind of cheesy-looking award and says "I give you the crown of Miss Taxi," she says "I have something to say," he says "And with the crown this year, Miss Nardo, comes an invitation to appear on the TV show, 'Wake Up New York,' tomorrow morning. Congratulations!" and Elaine says "Yeah, well, I just want to say one thing: Thanks to everyone who voted for me!"

ACT BREAK

ACT TWO

THE GARAGE—THAT NIGHT

Alex is giving her a lot of grief of the "your majesty" variety; Louie is baiting her for not taking the stand she said she was going to. Elaine, however, has an explanation; if she had done it at the Union Hall it would have reached a handful of people at best. But when she appears on "Wake Up New York" she'll be able to make a statement that will reach a large audience.

So, says Alex, you're really going to renounce your crown on television tomorrow morning? Absolutely, she says—and tell them a few things about how demeaning beauty contests are while I'm at it. And that was why you didn't say anything at the coronation? Why else? she asks. I thought maybe it was the thrill of victory, says Alex. Get out of here, she says. He gets out of there.

Tony now gives Bobby a boxing lesson to get him ready for the guy at the theater. He explains that most amateurs start out by throwing a roundhouse punch which is easily blocked. Try it, he urges. Bobby, after some hesitation, does . . . and Tony blocks it easily. See? he says. It's the short punches, the jabs, that do the damage. He demonstrates. Bobby tries one . . . and knocks Tony cold.

While he's kneeling on the floor, holding Tony's head in his hand while Tony blinks and clears his head, he gets a phone call from the other actor, apologizing for his loss of temper. Bobby accepts, saying it's better this way, no one gets hurt, no harm done, etc. The guy invites him for a drink and Bobby eagerly accepts, sets Tony's head down, and exits, thanking Tony over his shoulder. My pleasure, says Tony uncertainly. We either go out on that or on a comment from Louie.

DISSOLVE TO:

THE TV STUDIO

Where the host of "Wake Up New York" is introducing Elaine—something on the lines of "If you think that all New York cabbies are fat, bald-headed men who smoke cigars and talk out of the corner of his mouth, my next guest will be an eye-opener, in every sense of the word . . ."

We intercut the guys in the garage watching on a TV set A) to hear her renounce the crown and B) to see if she mentions their names. Elaine appears ready to make a statement, but the host starts right out asking questions which require answers: When did you decide you wanted to drive a cab for a living? She explains not a full-time job, art gallery, just supplement her income for the moment, etc. How do the guys at the garage treat you? Fine, she says. Anybody give you any trouble? No, she says—well, except our dispatcher and he gives everybody trouble; he's a pretty nasty guy. Louie explodes—"Names, Nardo," he complains aloud; "would it kill you to mention names? My mother could be watching." Any romances in the garage, the host persists. No, she says. No one come on to you? No, she says. What about you—do you like any of the guys? Well . . . she thinks; one of them is pretty cute . . . (uproar of speculation in the garage) . . . but he knows who he is. (Worse uproar.)

Now Nardo clears her throat and tells the host she has something she wants to say. Fine, he says, but before you do I want to say something myself: I think you're remarkable. At a time when so many people are climbing up on soapboxes to shoot their mouths off or complain about this and that, you've done something much more effective; quietly taken a job in a traditional male field and done it so well you've been recognized with this award . . . I think that's sensational. She blushes (verbally) and says thanks. Now, he says—what's your statement? Oh, she says . . . just that I . . . hope everyone watching will buy Easter Seals . . . (OR SOMETHING FUNNIER)

DISSOLVE TO:

THE GARAGE

Where even Elaine is now mad at herself, feels she was coopted, and used. She comes in saying, "I know, I know. I know!" However, rationalization still reigns; one of the staff people on the show told her that guests they discover often go on to The Tonight Show, and if that happened Elaine would <u>really</u> have a forum to denounce beauty contests. Millions of viewers, etc. Right, right, says Alex. Yeah, I know, she says—down again; I blew my chance, didn't I? At which point a guy from the tabloid that sponsored the contest arrives to say they were very upset by the TV appearance. It was clearly stipulated from the beginning that the contest was for "working, full-time cab drivers;" it even said so right on the application form. Elaine says she didn't submit the form, never saw the form, etc. The guy says he's sorry, but they feel they were made to look foolish and the paper's editorial board voted to rescind the victory, strip her of her crown, and crown the runner-up instead.

You can't do that, Elaine protests, but he's already on his way out. She calls after him that she was going to refuse it anyway, never wanted it, etc. (the "you can't fire me—I quit" bit) but he won't even stand still long enough for her to make her renunciation speech to his departing back.

Distraught, Elaine says now she's really blown it; waited so long she never got the chance to tell the world what she thinks of the award. At which point Louie steps out of his cage and offers her his microphone to make her statement. Elaine can't believe it. I've never been in your cage, she says—you never let anyone use your microphone. Yes, says Louie, but you're not yourself, you're out of control, there's no telling what you might do, therefore— and again he gestures for her to step inside.

Elaine does so, pulling down the microphone and asking everyone in the garage if she can have their attention. Louie, meanwhile, sidles up to her and "welcomes" her to "his turf, his hunting ground, his lair." She pays no attention.

Instead, having got everyone in the garage listening, Elaine proceeds to make the speech she wanted to make right along. "I don't know how many of you know what happened to me the last couple of days," she says, "but I won this award. Which I didn't want. And I'd like to explain why. I think so-called beauty contests are undignified and stupid. It's nice to be nice-looking, sure, but nobody wants to be a sex object—we're all people, with minds and feelings and personalities and a lot more than just our physical appearance." Etc. Etc.

And while she is saying all this, behind her Louie does the following: locks the door, pulls down the shades along the side, takes out a bottle of wine, takes out a candelabra (which he lights!), loosens his tie, sprays binaca in his mouth, unscrews the overhead light, and finally pulls the shades in the front as well—immediately after which we hear the music of "Bolero" coming over the PA system.

There follows the sounds of a brief tussle, a squeal from Elaine, then a groan from Louie, after which the door is unlocked and Elaine storms out. After a beat Louie appears at the doorway, on his hands and knees, still groaning, to call after her: "Can I assume from this that I'm not the guy in the garage you think is cute?"

And we can go out on that, or on Louie making an offer: Back in this cage for half an hour and you get a twenty per cent raise and the best cab every night for a year!" to which Jim says "I can't pass that up" and goes in the cage.

END OF ACT TWO

TAG: (Not shot in front of audience)

Shows Elaine in her cab, trying to make her statement individually to passengers as they get in and out. But of course they don't listen.

EARLY
CASTING
SHEETS
"ALEX GOES OFF THE WAGON"

▪▫▪▫▪▫

An original and a revised guideline prepared for the casting director to follow. The numbers and letters in the descriptions refer to page numbers of the script. Note how dramatically different the script being described from the final product (episode #92). At this early stage, most of the action takes place in Atlantic City, and the use of many more characters than in the final version may have diluted the core interplay between Alex and Jim.

PARAMOUNT
TAXI
"ALEX GOES OFF THE WAGON"
EPISODIC/NBC
FIRST DRAFT: 6/2/82

Exec. Producers: James L. Brooks
                   Stan Daniels
                   Ed. Weinberger
Producers: Ken Estin
          Sam Simon
          Richard Sakai
Director: Noam Pitlik
Casting Director: Vicki Rosenberg
Casting Coordinator: Carole Ingber
Start Date: August 2, 1982 Tapes: Aug. 6

VICKI ROSENBERG AT PARAMOUNT
ROOM 113, Building E

T A X I
▪▫▪▫▪▫
261

<u>WRITTEN SUBMISSIONS ONLY TO:</u>

<u>NO PHONE CALLS, PLEASE.</u>

Submissions for all roles will be considered regardless of ethnic group, sex, etc.—unless a specific requirement is indicated within the breakdown.

STICKMAN: This stickman oversees the crap games in Atlantic City. He is fast-talking and business-like. Even when Alex starts getting upset, this fellow keeps cool . . . 12 speeches & 16 lines, 2 scenes (16B)

POLICEMAN: This New York cop answers a call at the garage. He is a patient type who seems to have seen it all. When Louis claims that one of his cabs has been stolen, this cop calmly tries to get a report from him . . . 14 lines, 1 SEVEN PAGE SCENE

DOMINIQUE: A beautiful, "tall, winsome hooker", Dominique is a classy woman who appears on the arm of Louie at the Atlantic City gambling establishment . . . 2 lines, 1 scene (15B)

....

FOUR WAITRESSES: These waitresses work at the Golden Nugget in Atlantic City where Alex goes gambling. They are friendly sorts who continually offer him free drinks . . . 1 line, 1 scene (13B); 1 line, 1 scene (19B); 1 line, 1 scene (24B) and 2 lines, 1 scene (31D) respectively

MAN: This fellow thanks Jim for saving his life with some good advice . . . 1 speech, 1 scene (46)

TEXAN: This lanky Texan expresses his delight at playing craps . . . 2 lines, 1 scene (34)

DRUNK: This drunk at the Golden Nugget tells Alex that he feels miserable . . . 1 line, 1 scene (35D)

STORY LINE: Alex goes off the wagon and goes on an intense gambling binge in Atlantic City. Though he doesn't want to admit that he's addicted, the truth of the matter is that it's running him ragged . . .

REVISED CASTING SHEET

TO: ALL AGENTS AND MANAGERS

RE: Paramount
    TAXI
    "ALEX GOES OFF THE WAGON"
    EPISODIC/NBC

Exec. Producers: James L. Brooks
                    Stan Daniels
                    Ed. Weinberger
Producers: Ken Estin
           Sam Simon
           Richard Sakai
Director: Noam Pitlik
Casting Director: Vicki Rosenberg
Casting Coordinator: Carole Ingber
Start Date: August 2, 1982
Tapes: Aug. 6, 1982

T A X I

▪▪▪▪▪▪▪

262

WRITTEN SUBMISSIONS ONLY TO: VICKI ROSENBERG AT PARAMOUNT
                                    ROOM 113, Building E

NO PHONE CALLS, PLEASE.

ORIGINAL BREAKDOWN RELEASED JULY 23, 1982.

NOTE: PLEASE DISREGARD THE ORIGINAL BREAKDOWN AND NOTE THE FOLLOWING ADDITIONAL CHARACTERS AND CHANGES, AND SUBMIT ACCORDINGLY.

STICKMAN: This stickman oversees the crap games in Atlantic City. He is fast-talking and business-like. Even when Alex starts getting upset, this fellow keeps cool . . . 12 speeches & 16 lines, 2 scenes (16B)

POLICEMAN: This Irish, New York cop answers a call at the garage. He is a patient type who seems to have seen it all. When Louie claims that one of his cabs has been stolen, this cop calmly tries to get a report from him . . . 20 lines, 5 page scene

....

WAITRESS: This waitress works at the Golden Nugget in Atlantic City where Alex goes gambling. She is a friendly sort who offers him a drink . . . 1 line, 1 scene

ARAB: This fellow is placing heavy bets in the casino. He is dressed in a business suit and wears a head dress . . . 2 lines, 1 scene

BOUNCER: He is a bouncer at the casino . . . 2 speeches, 1 scene

LARGE WOMAN: She is a large and somewhat pushy woman in the casino . . . 4 lines, 1 scene

STORY LINE: Alex goes off the wagon and goes on an intense gambling binge in Atlantic City. Though he doesn't want to admit that he's addicted, the truth of the matter is that it's running him ragged . . .

RESEARCH
SHEET
"ALEX'S AFFAIR" (A.K.A. "ALEX'S ROMANCE")

▨▨▨▨▨▨

Before a script can be filmed, it has to be gone over for legal and technical fine points, errors in the logic, and typographical mistakes. Note that names, titles, and copyrighted materials such as song lyrics come under special scrutiny.

Sometime between October 15, 1979, and shoot day, the title of this episode (#34) changed from "Alex's Affair" to the less harsh-sounding "Alex's Romance."

de Forest Research
October 15, 1979
For: TAXI

RESEARCH ON: "ALEX'S AFFAIR" by Ian Praiser and Howard Gerwitz, 10/10/79

T A X I
▨▨▨▨▨▨
264

CAST	COMMENT
Joyce Rogers	We find no prominent person with this name; three possible listings in the N.Y. area. There is no member of the American Federation of Television and Radio Artists with this name. Do not consider usage to conflict.

PAGE	COMMENT
1	KLEENEX—Indicated commercial identification as prop.
2	Nine-nine percent of the actors in this city aren't working—According to our sources, this figure is exaggerated, but there are no accurate figures readily available.
4	Karen—First name usage only. No conflict.
4	"For Better of (sic) Worse"—Established in previous script.
7	"My squadron's pulling out in the morning"—V-J Day—Presume this reference and allusion to WWII is intentionally 10–15 years too far back (Alex is not supposed to be in his mid-50's, is he?)
7	Blanche Bain—We find no prominent person with this name: no conflict for the N.Y. area. There is no prominent character on daytime drama series television with this exact name.
7	voted the most despised woman on daytime TV—Non-specific reference.
10	SHELVES OF BOOKS—Advise avoid emphasizing copyrighted publications.

11	Fifty-Ninth and Central Park West—Reference to actual streets in N.Y., which factually do not intersect.
11	A BOTTLE OF WINE—Advise avoid commercial identification. Note: there are additional references in direction to such generalized prop-usages of alcoholic beverage containers.
12	"Notorious" with Ingrid Bergman—Reference to 1946 motion picture, and its living star.
12	"The Lady's Vulnerable" . . . "The Man Understands" We find no prominent motion picture properties with either of these exact names.
13	Staten Island Ferry—Reference to actual N.Y. transportation.
26	I'll you something else—Word missing? "I'll *tell* you something"?
28	THE SCRIPT—Advise avoid prop-usage of copyrighted material.
28	about a divorced mother of two children who goes to San Francisco to start a new life—We find no former or current television series with this exact premise.
35/36	STRUMMING HIS GUITAR . . . "THE HAWAIIAN WEDDING SONG" . . . "This is the moment. . . ."—Music clearance.
38	CANDY BAR—Advise avoid commercial identification.
46	Simka—First name usage only. No conflict.
49	(SINGING) "This is the moment. . . ."—See Page 35–36.

IV

THE *TAXI* TRIVIA QUIZ

QUESTIONS

WARMUP

1. What's the name of the taxi company the cabbies work for?
2. What's the nickname for Louie's office?
3. Where do the cabbies hang out after work?
4. Who's the regular bartender there (played by T. J. Castronova)?
5. What country does Latka come from?

ALEX

6. Match the women in Alex's life:
   A) Cathy Consuelos   1) sister
   B) Charlotte Reiger   2) ex-wife
   C) Phyllis Bornstein   3) a girlfriend
   D) Joyce Rogers   4) daughter
   E) Elaine Nardo   5) friend
7. Alex's apartment number is:
   A) A2   B) 5B
   C) 4A   D) 11D
8. What was the name of Alex's dog?
9. What was the name of his childhood cat?
10. Which of the following is *not* one of Alex's hobbies:
    A) Skiing   B) Hunting
    C) Fishing   D) Piano Playing
11. What's the name of Alex's step-brother?
12. What was Alex's youthful dream?
13. Why did Alex become a *Gerwirtzal*?
14. What's the name of Alex's dad (played by Jack Gilford)?
15. Why did Alex's parents separate?

PHONE NUMBERS

16. Match the phone numbers with the person or place to which they belong:
    A) 555-4276   1) Elaine Nardo
    B) 555-6382   2) Sunshine Cab Co.
    C) 555-2437   3) Susan McDaniel (Alex's date at the *Shloogel*)

BOBBY

17. What was the name of the historical one-man play in which Bobby starred?
18. Which TV personality uses the same answering service as Bobby?
19. Which of the following is the soap opera on which Bobby appeared?
    A) *All Is Forgiven*   B) *The Days of the Week*
    C) *Another World*   D) *For Better For Worse*
20. What was the name of Bobby's TV pilot?
21. Who or what once threw up in the back of Bobby's cab?
22. What baseball team does Bobby root for?
23. What play did he rehearse with the young actor (played by Michael Horton) who breezed into New York and immediately landed an off-Broadway role?
24. Which of the following plays did Bobby *not* perform in?
    A) *Under the Yum-Yum Tree*   B) *Stalled*
    C) *Death of a Salesman*   D) *Charles Darwin Tonight*

25. True or False: Bobby was once married.
26. Which of the following was *not* a girl Bobby dated:
A) Janet
B) Dominique
C) Nora

A FAMILY AFFAIR

27. Name the following relatives:
A) Louie's younger brother   _____
B) Elaine's ex-husband   _____
C) Louie's mother   _____
D) Latka's mother   _____
E) Jim's brother   _____
F) Jim's sister   _____

LATKA AND SIMKA

28. Which of the following is *not* one of Latka's split personalities?
  A) Vic Ferrari   B) Alex Reiger
  C) Sir Geoffrey   D) Tony Clifton
     Hypen-Hill
29. What native delicacy did Latka prepare for dinner the night he proposed to Simka?
30. What is *brefnish*?
31. What was the name of Latka and Simka's priest (played by Vincent Schiavelli)?
32. What occupation did Latka's father have, and what happened to him?
33. Name three rituals from the old country.
34. Was Simka a virgin at marriage?
35. What type of visa did Latka have with which to enter this country?
36. What rank does Latka hold in the army of his old country?
37. Who were Zifka (played by Mark Blankfield) and Baschi (played by Lenny Baker)?

ROOTS

38. Where do the following come from?
A) Jim's family   _____
B) Bobby   _____
C) Tony   _____
D) Elaine's aunt and grandparents _____
E) Tony's sister   _____

JIM

39. What is Jim's original family name?
40. How much money did Jim inherit?
41. Where did Jim go to college?
42. How long did he attend college?
43. Which of the following was *not* Jim's girl friend:
  A) Suzanne   B) Monica Banta
     Caruthers
  C) Diane McKenna   D) Heather
44. In which borough was Jim's first apartment?
45. In which church is Jim an ordained minister?
46. Which TV series rejected Jim's script?
47. Who is Jim's favorite composer?
48. What is Jim's favorite musical instrument?

GUEST STARS

49. Fill in the names of *Taxi* guest stars associated with the following shows:
A) *Baretta*   _____
B) *Falcon Crest*   _____
C) *Max Headroom*   _____
D) *Magnum, P. I.*   _____
E) *Bosom Buddies*   _____
F) *The Associates*   _____
G) *The Duck Factory*   _____
H) *Evita*   _____

ELAINE

50. What are the names of her two children?
51. Where does her son go to school?
52. At what art gallery does Elaine work?
53. Which two of the following are *not* one of Elaine's apartments?
A) A   B) 5B   C) A2   D) 682
54. What is Elaine's maiden name?
55. What was the name of her high school?
56. What brand of vodka does Elaine serve at her first art crowd cocktail party?
57. Where in Europe do her kids sometimes go for the holidays?
58. In which city was she offered an art gallery management job?
  A) Spokane,   B) Boston
     Washington
  C) Seattle,   D) Washington,
     Washington   D.C.

59. Who was Arnie Ross (played by Wallace Shawn)?

DOCTORS

60. Match the doctor with the cabbie:

   A) Dr. Bernard Collins   1) Latka
   B) Dr. Joyce Brothers   2) Tony
   C) Dr. Webster   3) Elaine
   D) Dr. Jeffries
   E) Dr. Frazier

LOUIE AND ZENA

61. With whom does Louie live throughout most of the series?
62. What's Louie's favorite "classy" nightspot?
63. What's the house drink there?
64. What does Zena do for a living? What does her father do?
65. What guy did Zena cheat on Lou with? What woman did Louie cheat on Zena with?
66. Why doesn't Louie like his mother's fiancé?
67. Which of the following professions was *not* one that belonged to a woman Louie dated?

   A) prison guard   C) graphic
                            designer
   B) ballerina   D) rich housewife

68. How much was Louie's record-high tips for a night of cabbing?
69. What TV panel-discussion show does Louie like to watch?
70. What instrument does Louie play?

   A) piano   B) violin   C) flute   D) oboe

SHIPS

71. What was the name of the ship on which Tony sailed with his father?
72. What was the name of the cruise ship Zena and her husband took on their honeymoon?

TONY

73. In what weight category did Tony box?
74. In what branch of the armed forces did Tony serve during the Vietnam War?

75. Who were George and Wanda?
76. Who was Kid Rodriguez?
77. True or False: Tony never graduated from high school.
78. To what South Sea port did Tony journey with his merchant seaman father Angelo (played by Donnelly Rhodes)?
79. What does the tattoo on Tony's upper arm say?
80. What's the name of Tony's fiancée?

   A) Judy Griffith   B) Anne De Salvo
   C) Vicki DeStefano   D) Marcia Wallace

81. What is the significance of "Do it for the duck"?

OTHER SHOWS

82. Match the other shows in which the *Taxi* actors were regular cast members:

   A) *Wizards and*   1) Carol Kane
      Warriors
   B) *All Is Forgiven*   2) Judd Hirsch
   C) *Six O'Clock*   3) Randall Carver
      Follies
   D) *Detective in the*   4) Tony Danza
      House
   E) *Berrenger's*   5) Jeff Conaway
   F) *Who's the Boss?*
   G) *Forever Fernwood*
   H) *The Law*
   I) *Delvecchio*

JOHN BURNS

83. Where did John hail from?
84. What was his favorite recreation?
85. Where did he meet his wife (played by Ellen Regan)?
86. What was he majoring in at night school?
87. True or False: John was a good booker.

IN THE GARAGE

88. What was "Mrs. McKenzie's Revenge"?
89. What were the names of the garage's two successive owners/managers?
90. What make of taxi did the cabbies drive?

91. Which is *not* a TV show that Jim was asked to evaluate during his brief time consulting for a network executive (played by Martin Short)?

A) *Hometown Girl*   B) *Stunt Wife*   C) *Old Friends*

92. When and where was the coca harvested that Latka used in his homemade cookies?

93. What was the name of the movie shot in Latka's native village?

94. Where was the reception held for the wedding of Alex's daughter?

95. What's the original name of the horse Jim adopts? What does Jim rename him?

96. Match the vacations with the vacationer:

A) Sugarloaf   1) Alex
B) Lake Placid   2) Alex and Elaine
C) Europe   3) Latka

97. Which two real-life boxers and which two real-life football players guested on *Taxi*?

98. Which two real-life actresses and real-life actor played themselves?

99. Match the actor/producer with the real-life relative who guested or otherwise was connected with the show:

A) Tony Danza   1) Holly Holmberg
B) Danny DeVito   2) Michele
C) Marilu Henner   3) Suzanne Carney
D) Jeff Conaway   4) Marc Anthony
E) Jim Brooks   5) Julia

100. Why did ABC cancel *Taxi?*

1. The Sunshine Cab Co.
2. The Cage
3. Mario's
4. Tommy
5. It was never revealed.
6. A-4, B-1, C-2, D-3, E-5
7. A-A2; 5B was one of Elaine Nardo's apartments; 4A was Lucy and Ricky's first apartment on *I Love Lucy;* 11D is Oscar (*The Odd Couple*) Madison's shoe size.
8. Buddy
9. Scheherazade, after the Sultan's storyteller-bride in *The Arabian Nights.* The name was his sister's idea; Alex wanted to name it Taffy.
10. B-Hunting
11. Mel
12. To work in theater
13. According to the traditions of Latka's country, a surrogate called a *Gewirtzal* had to propose marriage for a man. As Latka explained, the job usually fell to a leper or the village idiot, but Alex had to do in a pinch.
14. Joe Reiger
15. Because his father fooled around with other women
16. A-1, B-2, C-3
17. *Charles Darwin Tonight*
18. Gene Shalit
19. D-*For Better For Worse;* A was the name of the titular soap opera on the short-lived *All Is Forgiven,* created by ex-*Taxi* hands Jim Burrows and Glen and Les Charles; B is the soap opera satire that ran on *SCTV;* C is the real-life soap on which *Taxi* guest Susan Sullivan appeared from 1971 to 1976.
20. *Boise*
21. The Qantas Airlines koala bear
22. The New York Mets (judging from the pennant he prominently displays in his apartment)
23. *Romeo and Juliet*
24. A-*Under the Yum-Yum Tree;* he *rehearsed* it, but then got thrown out of the bus-tour company before the play opened.
25. False
26. C-Nora, his (temporary) personal manager; he did go to bed with her, though.

27. A-Nick; B-Vince; C-Gabriella; D-Greta; E-Tom; F-Lila
28. D-Tony Clifton; he was one of *Andy Kaufman's* split personalities!
29. Roast warthog
30. A syrupy, green alcoholic drink of Latka's country.
31. The Reverend H. L. Gorky
32. He was a policeman killed by freedom fighters.
33. Among them: The *Mertzig,* or the imparting of wisdom from a groom's mother to the bride-to-be; the Unburdening, similar to Catholic confession; the Ritual of Questions, the Crown of Rue, and the Dance of the *Plumas,* seen at weddings; the Blessing of the Beasts; and the *Shloogel,* a sort of inspired matchmaking
34. Apparently not. That Crown of Rue flew right off her head, and her explanation didn't help matters.
35. A student visa
36. General
37. Zifka was Simka's cousin, the monk; Baschi was the friend with whom Latka immigrated to the United States.
38. A-Boston; B-The Bronx; C-Brooklyn; D-Buffalo, New York; E-Spokane, Washington
39. Caldwell
40. $3.5 million
41. Harvard
42. One year
43. A-Suzanne Caruthers, who was John Burns's wife.
    B was Tony's sister (episode #52);
    C was an old hippie friend turned lawyer;
    D was his college girlfriend.
44. Brooklyn
45. The Church of the Peaceful
46. *M*A*S*H*
47. Vivaldi
48. The gong
49. A-Tom Ewell; B-Susan Sullivan; C-Jeffrey Tambor; D-Tom Selleck; E-Tom Hanks; F-Martin Short; G-Jack Gilford; H-Mandy Patinkin
50. Jason (played by Michael Hershewe and David

Mendenhall) and Jennifer (played by Melanie Gaffin)
51. P.S. 33 in Manhattan
52. The Hazeltine
53. C-A2 (Alex's apartment) and D-682 (the room number of the hospital where Alex's father was admitted in episode #23)
54. O'Connor
55. East Side High School
56. Betty's Vodka; she also served champagne in cans
57. To her ex-husband's ski chalet in Switzerland
58. C-Seattle, Washington. A-Spokane is where Tony's sister lived for five years; B-Boston is where Jim's family lives; D-Washington, D.C., was added just to throw you off.
59. Elaine's boyfriend at the end of the series—and from the looks of things, Mr. Right
60. A-3, B-1, C-2, D-1, E-2
61. His mother
62. The Tidepool, a Polynesian joint
63. Monsoons
64. She delivers candy; her father is a minister.
65. Dwight; Emily
66. Superficially because he's Japanese, but actually because he's "taking" Louie's mother away from him
67. C-graphic designer; that was the profession of Karen (Barbara Babcock), a woman Alex (and his father) dated. A and C are alluded to as past acquaintances, and D is the "profession" of Alex's ex-wife, Phyllis (Louise Lasser), whose date with Lou was short-lived.
68. 80 cents
69. *Donahue*
70. B-violin. Alex and Jim played A, Tony's sister Monica played C, and Elaine's son was taking lessons playing D.
71. The *Hillary Beane*
72. The *Britannia Star*
73. Middleweight
74. The army
75. Tony's two goldfish, inadvertently killed by Bobby's neglect
76. A boxer whose license Tony bought and whose identity he assumed in order to keep boxing after his own license was revoked

77. True
78. Singapore
79. "Keep on Truckin' "
80. C-Vicki DeStefano.   A was Louie's date at the *Shloogel,* and D was Jim's.   B was the actress who played Vicki.
81. It was the motivational phrase Tony's football player friend Lucius (Bubba Smith) used to pump up Tony and himself. It's not exactly "eye of the tiger," but that was the point.
82. A-5, B-1, C-3, D-2, E-5, F-4, G-3, H-2, I-2
83. Like Latka's native country, John's hometown was never revealed.
84. Bowling
85. At Mario's
86. Forestry
87. False
88. A mysterious disappearance visited upon the unlucky cabbie whom the boss's wife, Mrs. McKenzie, picked to fool around with, and then squealed about to her husband to make him murderously jealous
89. Ed McKenzie and Ben Ratledge
90. Checker
91. C-*Old Friends* was the name of a post-*Taxi* pilot in which Christopher Lloyd starred.
92. As Jim put it: "Southern Peru. 1974. Before the rain."
93. *Here Come the Huns*
94. The Waldorf-Astoria
95. On Dasher; Gary
96. A-3 (as Vic Ferrari), B-1, C-2
97. Boxers Carlos Palomino and Armando Muniz, and football players Bubba Smith and Dick Butkus
98. Penny Marshall, Marcia Wallace, and Herve Villechaize
99. A-4 (his son); B-5 (his mother); C-3 (her niece); D-2 (his sister); E-1 (his wife, who scripted)
100. To this day, no one knows.

AWARDS
AND
NOMINATIONS

EMMY AWARDS

Awarded by The National Academy of Television Arts and Sciences, each award covers part of two consecutive years.

OUTSTANDING COMEDY SERIES

Award:	1978–79
Award:	1979–80
Award:	1980–81
Nomination:	1981–82
Nomination:	1982–83

OUTSTANDING WRITING IN A COMEDY SERIES

Nomination:	1978–79	(Michael Leeson, "Blind Date")
Nomination:	1979–80	(Glen and Les Charles, "Honor Thy Father")
Nomination:	1980–81	(Glen and Les Charles, "Going Home")
Nomination:	1980–81	(David Lloyd, "Elaine's Strange Triangle")
Award:	1980–81	(Michael Leeson, "Tony's Sister and Jim")
Nomination:	1981–82	(Barry Kemp [teleplay] and Holly Holmberg Brooks [story], "Jim the Psychic")
Award:	1981–82	(Ken Estin, "Elegant Iggy")

Nomination:	1982–83	(Ken Estin, "Jim's Inheritance")

OUTSTANDING DIRECTING IN A COMEDY SERIES

Award:	1979–80	(James Burrows, "Louie and the Nice Girl")
Award:	1980–81	(James Burrows, "Elaine's Strange Triangle")
Nomination:	1981–82	(James Burrows, "Jim the Psychic")

OUTSTANDING FILM EDITING IN A COMEDY SERIES

Award:	1978–79	(M. Pam Blumenthal, "Paper Marriage")
Award:	1979–80	(M. Pam Blumenthal, "Louie and the Nice Girl")
Award:	1980–81	(M. Pam Blumenthal and Jack Michon, "Elaine's Strange Triangle")

PERFORMERS

JUDD HIRSCH

OUTSTANDING LEAD ACTOR FOR A SINGLE APPEARANCE IN A DRAMA OR COMEDY SERIES

Nomination:	1977–78	(*Rhoda,* "Rhoda Likes Mike")

OUTSTANDING LEAD ACTOR IN A COMEDY SERIES

Nomination:	1978–79
Nomination:	1979–80
Award:	1980–81
Nomination:	1981–82
Award:	1982–83

DANNY DEVITO

OUTSTANDING SUPPORTING ACTOR IN A COMEDY SERIES

Nomination:	1978–79
Award:	1980–81
Nomination:	1981–82
Nomination:	1982–83

CHRISTOPHER LLOYD

OUTSTANDING SUPPORTING ACTOR IN A COMEDY SERIES

Award:	1981–82
Award:	1982–83

OUTSTANDING LEAD ACTOR IN A DRAMA

Award:	1991–92	(series *Avonlea*)

CAROL KANE

OUTSTANDING LEAD ACTRESS IN A COMEDY SERIES

Award:	1981–82	("Simka Returns")

OUTSTANDING SUPPORTING ACTRESS IN A COMEDY SERIES

Award:	1982–83

GUEST STARS
(*TAXI* AWARDS/NOMINATIONS ONLY)

RUTH GORDON

OUTSTANDING LEAD ACTRESS IN A COMEDY SERIES

Award:	1978–79	("Sugar Mama")

EILEEN BRENNAN*

OUTSTANDING LEAD ACTRESS IN A COMEDY SERIES

Nomination:	1980–81	("Thy Boss' Wife")

* Brennan won the same year for Outstanding Supporting Actress in a Comedy Series (*Private Benjamin.*)

GOLDEN GLOBE AWARDS

Awarded by The Hollywood Foreign Press Association

BEST COMEDY OR MUSICAL SERIES

Award:	1979	
Award:	1980	(tie with *Alice*)
Award:	1981	
Nomination:	1982	
Nomination:	1983	

JUDD HIRSCH

BEST ACTOR, COMEDY OR MUSICAL SERIES

Nomination:	1979
Nomination:	1980
Nomination:	1981
Nomination:	1982
Nomination:	1983

JEFF CONAWAY

BEST SUPPORTING ACTOR, COMEDY OR MUSICAL SERIES

Nomination:	1979
Nomination:	1980

DANNY DEVITO

BEST SUPPORTING ACTOR, COMEDY OR MUSICAL SERIES

Nomination:	1979	
Award:	1980	(tie with Vic Tayback of *Alice*)
Nomination:	1981	
Nomination:	1982	

BEST ACTOR, COMEDY OR MUSICAL (FILM)

Nomination:	1987	(*Ruthless People*)
Nomination:	1988	(*Throw Momma From the Train*)

MARILU HENNER

BEST SUPPORTING ACTRESS, COMEDY OR MUSICAL SERIES

Nomination:	1979
Nomination:	1980
Nomination:	1981

Nomination: 1982
Nomination: 1983

TONY DANZA

BEST SUPPORTING ACTOR, COMEDY OR MUSICAL SERIES
Nomination   1980

ANDY KAUFMAN

BEST SUPPORTING ACTOR, COMEDY OR MUSICAL SERIES
NOMINATION: 1979
NOMINATION: 1981

CAROL KANE

BEST SUPPORTING ACTRESS
Nomination: 1983

JAMES L. BROOKS

BEST MOTION PICTURE, MUSICAL OR COMEDY
Award: 1984   (*Terms of Endearment*)
Nomination: 1988   (*Broadcast News*)
BEST DIRECTOR
Nomination: 1984   (*Terms of Endearment*)
Nomination: 1988   (*Broadcast News*)
BEST MOTION PICTURE SCREENPLAY
Award: 1984   (*Terms of Endearment*)
Nomination: 1988   (*Broadcast News*)

ACADEMY AWARDS

The "Oscar" is awarded by the Academy of Motion Picture Arts and Sciences. The following are awards or nominations for *Taxi* cast and crew members.

JAMES L. BROOKS

BEST PICTURE
Award: 1984   (*Terms of Endearment;*
                            James L. Brooks,
                            producer)
Nomination: 1988   (*Broadcast News;* James
                            L. Brooks and
                            Penney Finkelman
                            Cox, producers)

BEST DIRECTOR
Award: 1984   (*Terms of Endearment*)
BEST SCREENPLAY ADAPTATION
Award: 1984   (*Terms of Endearment*)
BEST SCREENPLAY WRITTEN DIRECTLY FOR THE SCREEN
Nomination: 1988   (*Broadcast News*)

JUDD HIRSCH

BEST SUPPORTING ACTOR
Nomination: 1980   (*Ordinary People*)

CAROL KANE

BEST ACTRESS
Nomination: 1975   (*Hester Street*)

GRAMMY AWARDS

Awarded by The National Academy of Recording Arts and Sciences

BOB JAMES*

BEST INSTRUMENTAL COMPOSITION
Nomination: 1979   ("Angela" [Theme
                            from *Taxi*])

*James had earned Best Instrumental Arrangement Nominations for 1973, 1974, 1976, and 1977, and won (with Earl Klugh) for Best Pop Instrumental in 1980.

AWARDS TO NBC's "SAME TIME, BETTER NETWORK" *TAXI* PROMOTIONAL CAMPAIGN

International Film and TV Festival of New York
    Silver Award, Program Promotion Category
American Advertising Federation "Addy" Award
    First Place, Entertainment, Television Network
Chicago International Film Festival, Television
Commercial Competition
    Certificate of Merit, Promotional Category

Note: Tony, Obie, and Drama Desk awards to *Taxi* cast members are listed under "Selected Theater Credits."

TAXI FILMOGRAPHY

This filmography for each *Taxi* cast member includes: theatrical and direct-to-video movies; TV-movies; other series or series pilots in which he or she starred as a regular cast member; and television guest appearances and specials. Appearances on talk, game, and tribute/awards shows are not included. Information on *Taxi*-related reunion specials follows.

JUDD HIRSCH

FILMS

Serpico (1973)
King of the Gypsies (1978)
Ordinary People (1980)
Without a Trace (1983)
In Our Hands (1984 documentary)
Teachers (1984)
The Goodbye People (1984)
Running on Empty (1988)
Independence Day (scheduled 1996)

TV MOVIES AND MINISERIES

Tha Law (NBC 1974)
Fear on Trial (CBS 1975)
The Legend of Valentino (ABC 1975)
The Keegans (CBS 1976)
Sooner or Later (NBC 1979)
Marriage Is Alive and Well (NBC 1980)
First Steps (CBS 1985)
Brotherly Love (CBS 1985)
The Great Escape II: The Untold Story (NBC 1988 miniseries)

She Said No (NBC 1990)
Betrayal of Trust (NBC 1994; working title *Under the Influence*)

TV SERIES AND PILOTS

Starred as Sergeant Dominick Delvecchio in police drama *Delvecchio* (CBS 9/9/76–7/17/77); as Press Wyman in private-eye drama *Detective in the House* (CBS 3/15–4/19/85); and as John Lacey in *Dear John...* (NBC 10/6/88–7/22/92 [last first-run episode]).

TV guest appearances include:

Medical Story ("Wasteland"; NBC 11/13/75)
Visions ("Two Brothers"; PBS 10/21/76)
Rhoda ("Rhoda Likes Mike"; CBS 11/7/76)
Rhoda ("The Weekend"; CBS 11/14/76)
Rhoda ("Fringe Benefit"; CBS 11/6/77)
The Halloween That Almost Wasn't a.k.a. *The Night Dracula Saved the World* (ABC special 10/28/79)
The Robert Klein Show (NBC 5/30/81 special)
I Love Liberty (ABC 3/21/82 special)
Loretta Lynn in the Big Apple (NBC 11/8/82 special)
The Comedy Zone (CBS; at least one appearance on 8/17–9/7/84 five-episode series of New York City playwright sketches)
An American Portrait ("Joshua Albook"; CBS interstitial spot 12/21/84)
American Masters: Isaac in America—A Journey With Isaac Bashevis Singer (PBS 7/6/87; public debut of 1985 Documentary Academy Award nominee, previously screened at film festivals; Hirsch narrates)
Little Miracles (syndicated 1987 documentary; host)

The Magical World of Disney (NBC 10/9/88 special)
Super Bloopers & New Practical Jokes (NBC 3/24/89 special)
Super Bloopers & New Practical Jokes (NBC 2/25/90 special; *Dear John...* outtakes)
Going, Going, Almost Gone! Animals in Danger (HBO special 11/13/94; voiceover)

Also on video:
Maia: A Dinosaur Grows Up (1988; narrator)

JEFF CONAWAY

FILMS

Jennifer on My Mind (1971)
The Eagle Has Landed (UK 1977)
I Never Promised You a Rose Garden (1977)
Pete's Dragon (1977)
Grease (1978)
Covergirl a.k.a. *Dreamworld* (Canada 1981; released U.S. 1984)
The Patriot (1986)
Elvira, Mistress of the Dark (1988)
Tale of Two Sisters (1989)
The Banker (1989)
The Sleeping Car a.k.a. *Sleeping Car* (1990)
Total Exposure (1991)
A Time to Die (1991)
Mirror Images (1992)
Sunset Strip (1992; also associate producer)
Almost Pregnant (1992)
Bikini Summer 2 (1992; also director, associate producer)
L.A. Goddess (1992)
In a Moment of Passion (1993)
Alien Intruder (1993)
The Rape of Eden 2002 a.k.a. *Bounty Hunter: 2002* (produced 1992, released direct-to-video 1994)

TV MOVIES AND MINISERIES

Delta County U.S.A. (ABC 1977 TV-movie/pilot)
Breaking Up Is Hard to Do (ABC 1979)
For the Love of It (ABC 1980)
Nashville Grab (NBC 1981)

Making of a Male Model (ABC 1983)
Bay Coven (NBC 1987)
The Dirty Dozen: The Fatal Mission (NBC 1988)
Ghost Writer a.k.a. *Ghostwriter* (syndicated 1990)

TV SERIES AND PILOTS

Costarred as Terry Nichols in TV-movie/pilot *Delta Country, USA* (ABC 5/20/77); starred as Prince Erik Greystone in fantasy-comedy *Wizards and Warriors* (CBS 2/26–5/14/83); as John Higgins in primetime serial *Berrenger's* (NBC 1/5–3/9/85); and as Mick Savage on daytime serial *The Bold and the Beautiful* (CBS) for a time beginning 5/19/89.

TV guest appearances include:

From Sea to Shining Sea (syndicated special 12/19/74)
Movin' On ("Landslide"; NBC 1/16/75)
Happy Days ("Richie Fights Back"; ABC Oct. 1975)
Movin' On ("The Long Haul"; NBC 12/2/75)
Joe Forrester ("The Best Laid Schemes"; NBC 12/9/75)
The Mary Tyler Moore Show ("Menage a Lou"; CBS 1/24/76)
Barnaby Jones ("Wipeout"; CBS 3/4/76)
Barnaby Jones ("Killer on Campus"; CBS 3/24/77)
Kojak ("May the Horse Be With You"; CBS 2/25/78)
Having Babies ("Sterile Wife"; ABC 3/28/78)
The Jimmy McNichol Special (CBS 4/30/80 special)
Cheryl Ladd... Looking Back—Souvenirs a.k.a. *Cheryl Ladd Souvenirs* (ABC 5/19/80 special)
Battle of the Network Stars X (ABC special 5/8/81)
Mickey Spillane's Mike Hammer ("Shots in the Dark"; CBS 3/8/84)
Murder, She Wrote ("Birds of a Feather"; CBS 10/14/84)
Who's the Boss? (episode data N.A.)
The Love Boat ("Heartbreaker"; ABC 12/7/85)
New Love American Style ("Love and the Stranger"; ABC 1/30/86)
New Love American Style ("Love and the Private Eye"; ABC 2/27/86)
Matlock ("The Affair"; NBC 10/7/86)

Murder, She Wrote ("Corned Beef and Carnage"; CBS 11/2/86)

The New Mike Hammer ("Little Miss Murder"; CBS 1/7/87)

Hotel ("Class of '87"; ABC 3/4/87)

Stingray ("Cry Wolf"; 4/3/87)

Tales from the Darkside ("My Ghostwriter—The Vampire"; syndicated 7/11/87)

Monsters ("Fool's Gold"; syndicated, 1988–89 season)

Freddy's Nightmares ("Identity Crisis"; syndicated 1989)

Good Grief ("Bury Me a Little"; Fox 10/14/90)

Murder, She Wrote ("For Whom the Ball Tolls"; CBS 9/26/93)

Matlock ("Matlock's Bad, Bad, Bad Dream"; ABC 12/2/93)

Murder, She Wrote ("Murder of the Month Club"; 12/4/94)

Burke's Law ("Who Killed the Hollywood Head-shrinker?"; CBS 7/20/95)

DANNY DeVITO

SHORTS AND STUDENT FILMS

Hot Dogs for Gaugin (1971; actor; student film directed by Martin Brest at New York University)

The Sound Sleeper (1973; director; co-writer/producer with Rhea Perlman; 16mm black-and-white

Minestrone (1976; actor, director; co-writer/producer with Rhea Perlman; 35mm color)

Vinyl Visits an FM Station (year N.A.; actor)

A Lovely Way to Spend an Evening (1983; with Tony Danza; writer, director; cameo appearance as extra standing by cigarette machine)

The Selling of Vince D'Angelo (1983; actor, director; telecast as half-hour Showtime special 10/4/92 after debuting on video mid-1980s)

FILMS (as actor)

Dreams of Glass (1969)

Lady Liberty a.k.a. *La Mortadella* (Italy-France 1972)

Hurry Up, or I'll Be 30 (1973)

Scalawag (Yugoslavia 1973)

One Flew Over the Cuckoo's Nest (1975; with Christopher Lloyd)

The Van a.k.a. *Chevy Van* (1977)

The World's Greatest Lover (1977; with Carol Kane)

Goin' South (1978; with Christopher Lloyd)

Going Ape! (1981; with Tony Danza; working title *Love, Max*)

Terms of Endearment (1983)

Romancing the Stone (1984)

Johnny Dangerously (1984; with Marilu Henner)

The Jewel of the Nile (1985; also in the film's Billy Ocean video, "The Tough Get Going")

Head Office (1986)

Wise Guys (1986)

My Little Pony: The Movie (1986; voiceover; with Rhea Perlman)

Ruthless People (1986)

Throw Momma from the Train (1987; also director)

Twins (1988; working title *Brothers*)

The War of the Roses (1989; also director)

Other People's Money (1991)

Hoffa (1992; also director, producer)

Batman Returns (1992)

Look Who's Talking Now (1993; voiceover)

Last Action Hero (1993; uncredited voiceover)

Jack the Bear (1993)

Renaissance Man (1994)

Junior (1994)

Get Shorty (1995; also producer)

Other non-actor film credits:
Reality Bites (1994; producer)
8 Seconds (1994; executive producer)
Pulp Fiction (1994; executive producer)

TV MOVIES AND MINISERIES

Valentine (ABC 1979)

The Ratings Game (The Movie Channel 1984; also director; with Rhea Perlman)

TV guest appearances include:

Delvecchio (episode data N.A.)
Starsky and Hutch ("The Collector"; ABC 12/3/77)
Police Woman ("Death Game"; NBC 12/21/77)

Saturday Night Live (NBC 1982 and 1983)

The CBS Schoolbreak Special: All the Kids Do It (CBS 4/24/84)

WonderWorks: Happily Ever After (PBS 10/21/85; voiceover; with Rhea Perlman)

The Joe Piscopo New Jersey Special (ABC special 5/13/86)

Amazing Stories ("The Wedding Ring"; NBC 9/22/86; also director; with Rhea Perlman)

Our Kids and the Best of Everything (ABC 6/21/87 special)

Saturday, Night Live (host; NBC 12/5/87)

Sesame Street Special (PBS special 3/14/88; with Rhea Perlman)

A Very Special Christmas Party (ABC 12/22/88; working title *Special Olympics Christmas Party*)

WonderWorks: Two Daddies? (PBS 5/6/89; voiceover; with Rhea Perlman)

Time Warner Presents the Earth Day Special (ABC 4/22/90 special; with Rhea Perlman and Christopher Lloyd)

The Simpsons ("Oh Brother, Where Art Thou?" a.k.a. "Brother Can You Spare a Dime?"; Fox 2/21/91)

First Person With Maria Shriver (NBC 6/29/91 special)

The Simpsons ("Brother Can You Spare Two Dimes?"; Fox 8/27/92)

The Larry Sanders Show (HBO; 1992 episode as himself)

Sesame Street's All-Star 25th Birthday: Stars and Street Forever! (ABC 5/18/94 special; with Rhea Perlman)

Also on video:

Likely Stories, Vol. 2 (includes *The Selling of Vince D'Angelo*)

Likely Stories, Vol. 4 (includes *A Lovely Way to Spend an Evening*)

TONY DANZA

SHORTS

A Lovely Way to Spend an Evening (1983; writer-director Danny DeVito)

The Joke (1992)

Mamma Mia (1994; director only)

FILMS

The Hollywood Knights (1980)

Going Ape! (1981; with Danny DeVito; working title *Love, Max*)

Cannonball Run II (1984; with Marilu Henner)

She's Out of Control (1989; working title *Daddy's Little Girl*)

Angels in the Outfield (1994; with Christopher Lloyd)

TV MOVIES AND MINISERIES

Murder Can Hurt You! (ABC 1980)

Single Bars, Single Women (ABC 1984)

Doing Life a.k.a. *Truth or Die* (NBC 1986; also co-executive producer)

Freedom Fighter (NBC 1987; also co-executive producer; working title *Wall Of Tyranny*)

The Whereabouts of Jenny (ABC 1991; cameo; also executive producer)

Dead and Alive—The Race For Gus Farace a.k.a. *Mob Justice* (ABC 1991; Katie Face Productions)

Deadly Whispers (CBS 1995)

TV SERIES AND PILOTS

Stars as Tony Canetti in police-detective sitcom *Hudson Street* (ABC 9/19/95–present; also executive producer). Starred in unaired ABC comedy pilot *Fast Lane Blues;* starred as Tony Micelli in domestic sitcom *Who's the Boss?* (ABC 9/20/84–4/25/92 [last first-run episode]); also directed or co-directed some episodes); provided voiceover for infant Mickey Campbell in domestic sitcom *Baby Talk* (ABC 3/8/91–5/8/92 [last first-run episode]); provided voiceover for Vinnie the Alligator in comedy fantasy *The Mighty Jungle* (Family Channel, produced 1994).

TV guest appearances include:

The Love Boat ("When Worlds Collide"; ABC 11/5/83)

The Love Boat Fall Preview Party (ABC special 9/15/84)

Battle of the Network Stars (ABC specials 12/20/84 and 5/23/85)

99 Ways to Attract the Right Man (host; ABC special 5/7/85)

The Real Trivial Pursuit (ABC special 5/9/85)

ABC Saturday Sneak Peak and Fun Fitness Test (ABC special 9/6/85)

An American Portrait ("Albert James Myer"; CBS interstitial spot 2/6/86)

Comic Relief (HBO 3/29/86 special)

Saturday Night Live (NBC 1986)

Mr. Belvedere ("Separation"; ABC 5/1/87; as himself)

Happy Birthday, Hollywood (ABC special 5/18/87)

Hanna-Barbera's 50th: A Yabba Dabba Doo Celebration (TNT 7/17/89 special; co-host)

Living Dolls ("It's My Party"; ABC 9/30/89) and ("Martha Means Well"; ABC 10/7/89). As Tony Micelli from *Who's the Boss?*

The Wonderful Wizard of Oz: 50 Years of Magic (CBS 2/20/90 special)

Baby Talk ("The Big 'One'"; ABC 4/23/91; on-screen guest role)

Studio 59 a.k.a. *Into the Night* (ABC talk show; guest host 9/30–10/4/91)

Gettin' Over (ABC; series of reality-based specials on struggles of urban youth; host and executive producer) 9/2/92; 8/8/93 (two editions back-to-back, later subtitled "A Tale of Two Schools"); 9/5/93 (two editions back-to-back); 6/25/95; 7/6/95 (two editions back-to-back)

Kathie Lee Gifford's Celebration of Motherhood (ABC 5/5/93 special)

Road to Hollywood (NBC 5/21/93 special; also executive producer)

The Opening Ceremonies of the 1995 Special Olympics World Games (NBC special, 7/5/95)

Other non-actor film and TV credits:

Living Dolls (ABC 9/26–12/30/89; executive script consultant)

George (ABC series 11/5/93–1/19/94; executive producer)

Before They Were Stars (ABC 5/15/94 special; executive producer)

An All-New Before They Were Stars (ABC 11/27/94 special; executive producer)

The Jerky Boys (1995 film; executive producer)

A Special Half-Hour Edition of Before They Were Stars ABC 4/30/95 special; executive producer)

Before They Were Stars III (ABC 5/11/95 special; executive producer)

Before They Were Stars (ABC 11/4/95 special; executive producer)

Also on video:

Likely Stories, Vol. 2 (includes *The Selling of Vince D'Angelo*)

I'm From Hollywood (1992) (documentary on Andy Kaufman; with Marilu Henner)

MARILU HENNER

FILMS

Between the Lines (1977)

Bloodbrothers a.k.a. *A Father's Love* (1978)

The Man Who Loved Women (1983)

Hammett (1983)

Cannonball Run II (1984; with Tony Danza)

Johnny Dangerously (1984; with Danny DeVito)

Rustlers' Rhapsody (1985)

Perfect (1986)

L.A. Story (1991)

Noises Off (1992)

Chains of Gold (1992)

Batman: Mask of the Phantasm (1993, voiceover)

Chasers (1994)

TV MOVIES AND MINISERIES

Seventh Avenue (1977 miniseries; uncredited bit part)

Dream House (CBS 1981; working title: *Dream House on West 71st Street*

NBC Live Theater; Mr. Roberts (NBC 1984)

Stark (CBS 1985)

Broadway on Showtime: Grown Ups (Showtime 1985)

Harlequin Romance: Love With a Perfect Stranger (Showtime 1986)

Grand Larceny (Lifetime 1988; made for European TV 1987)

Ladykillers (ABC 1988)

TV SERIES AND PILOTS

Host and executive producer of daytime talk show *Marilu* (syndicated, premiering 9/12/94). Starred as Ava Evans Newton in sitcom *Evening Shade* (CBS 9/21/90–5/23/94 [last first-run episode]). Starred as Susan McDowell in sitcom pilot, *Channel 99* (NBC 8/4/88); co-starred as Janet in college sitcom pilot *Off Campus* (CBS 6/8/77) and as barmaid Susu in law school comedy-drama pilot *The Paper Chase* (CBS 9/9/78); also appeared in unaired pilot *Leonard*, starring Leonard Frey. Provides voiceovers for *Batman: The Animated Series* (Fox 1992–present); provided voiceover for *The Legend of Prince Valiant* (Family Channel, produced 1991).

TV guest appearances include:

The Paper Chase ("Great Expectations"; CBS 9/12/78)

The Celebrity Football Classic (NBC 11/16/79 special 1979)

Fridays (ABC 3/19/82)

Alfred Hitchcock Presents ("Method Actor"; NBC 11/10/85)

Who's the Boss? ("Seductive Neighbor"; ABC 3/25/86)

The Tracey Ullman Show (Fox 10/22/89)

Stop the Madness (CBS public-service announcement 11/17/91)

Designated Driver (CBS public-service announcement 12/11/91; rerun 2/28/92, 7/19/92)

AIDS/Facts for Life (CBS public-service announcement 3/29/92; rerun 4/22/92, 6/12/92)

Cybill ("Since I Lost My Baby"; CBS 10/01/95)

Comic Relief VII (HBO 11/11/95 special)

Also on video:
I'm From Hollywood (1992)(documentary on Andy Kaufman; with Tony Danza)

Dancerobics (1993)

Non-actor credits include:

Abandoned and Deceived (ABC 1995 TV movie; executive producer; working titles *ACES: The Gerri Jensen Story* and *A.C.E.S.*)

Medicine Ball (Fox 3/13–5/15/95 [last first-run episode]; executive producer

CHRISTOPHER LLOYD

FILMS

One Flew Over the Cuckoo's Nest (1975; with Danny DeVito)

Another Man, Another Chance (France–U.S. 1977)

Three Warriors (1978)

Goin' South (1978; with Danny DeVito)

Butch and Sundance: The Early Days (1978)

The Lady in Red a.k.a *Guns, Sin and Bathtub Gin* (1979)

The Onion Field (1979)

The Black Marble (1980)

Schizoid a.k.a. *Murder By Mail* (1980)

Pilgrim, Farewell (1980)

National Lampoon Goes to the Movies a.k.a. *National Lampoon's Movie Madness* (1981; unreleased theatrically)

The Postman Always Rings Twice (1981)

The Legend of the Lone Ranger (1981)

Mr. Mom (1983)

To Be or Not to Be (1983)

The Joy of Sex (1984)

The Adventures of Buckaroo Banzai Across the Eighth Dimension (1984)

Star Trek III: The Search for Spock (1984)

Miracles (U.S.–Mexico 1985; unreleased theatrically)

Back to the Future (1985)

Clue (1985)

Walk Like a Man a,.k.a. *Bobo* (1987; working title *Bobo the Dog Boy*)

Track 29 (UK 1988)

Who Framed Roger Rabbit (1988)

Eight Men Out (1988)

The Dream Team (1989)

Back to the Future Part II (1989)

Back to the Future Part III (1990)

Why Me? (1990)

DuckTales: The Movie: Treasure of the Lost Lamp (1990; voiceover)

Legend of the White Horse (made 1985; released 1991)

Suburban Commando (1991)

The Addams Family (1991)

Twenty Bucks (1993)

Dennis the Menace (1993)

Addams Family Values (1993; with Carol Kane)

Radioland Murders (1994)

Angels in the Outfield (1994; with Tony Danza)

Camp Nowhere (1994)

The Pagemaster (1994)

Rent-A-Kid (produced 1995)

Things to Do in Denver When You're Dead (produced 1995)

TV-MOVIES AND MINISERIES

Lacy and the Mississippi Oueen (NBC 1978; TV movie/pilot; Lloyd in guest cast)

The Word (CBS 1978 miniseries)

Stunt Seven (CBS 1979; TV movie/pilot)

American Playhouse: Pilgrim, Farewell (PBS 3/23/82; released theatrically 1980)

Money on the Side (CBS 1982)

September Gun (CBS 1983)

The Cowboy and the Ballerina (CBS 1984)

Dead Ahead: The Exxon Valdez Disaster (HBO 1992)

T Bone N Weasel (TNT 1992)

The Right to Remain Silent (Showtime 1996)

TAXI

284

TV SERIES AND PILOTS

Co-stars as Sebastian Jackal in fantasy-adventure series *Deadly Games* (UPN, premiered 9/5/95). Appeared as Czar Alexander I in *The Adams Chronicles* (PBS series 1/20–4/13/76); host of, and Doc Brown voiceover for, Saturday-morning series *Back to the Future* (CBS, premiered 9/14/91). Co-starred as Skip Hartman in action-adventure TV movie/pilot *Stunt Seven* (CBS 5/30/79); starred as Jerry Forbes in sitcom pilot *Old Friends* (ABC 7/12/84), and as President for Life Joseph Domino in sitcom *The Dictator* (CBS), scheduled to begin 3/15/88 but postponed due to the Writers Guild strike and eventually canceled without airing though at least two episodes were shot. *Note:* The producer Christopher Lloyd (*Fraiser, Wings,* other shows) is a different person.

TV guest appearances include:

Barney Miller ("The Vandal"; ABC 11/9/78)

Visions ("It's the Wilderness"; PBS 11/9/80)

Semi Tough (ABC 6/19/80)

Freebie and the Bean ("The Seduction of the Bean"; CBS 12/20/80)

Best of the West ("The Calico Kid"; ABC 9/10/81)

Best of the West ("The Calico Kid Returns"; ABC 10/1/81)

Best of the West ("The Calico Kid Goes to School"; ABC 1/14/82)

Cheers ("I'll Be Seeing You" [parts 1 and 2]; NBC 5/3–5/10/84)

Street Hawk (ABC 1/4/85; guest cast of TV movie-length debut episode)

Shortstories ("The Penny Elf"; A&E 3/13/86)

Amazing Stories ("Go to the Head of the Class"; NBC 11/21/86; preempted from 10/27/86)

Great Performances: Tales from the Hollywood Hills ("Pat Hobby Teamed with Genius"; PBS 11/20/87)

Avonlea (Disney Channel 4/92)

Mrs. Piggle-Wiggle ("The Not Truthful Cure"; Showtime children's 6/14/94)

In Search of Dr. Seuss (TNT 1994 special)

RANDALL CARVER

FILMS

Midnight Cowboy (1969)

Time To Run (produced 1974)

Murphy's Law (1986)

TV-MOVIES AND MINISERIES

The Daughters of Joshua Cabe Return (ABC 1975)

The New Daughters of Joshua Cabe (ABC 1976)

Once an Eagle (NBC 1976-77 miniseries)

Detour to Terror (NBC 1980)

Flag (completed 1986)

TV SERIES AND PILOTS

Co-starred as Jeffrey DiVito in soap-opera satire *Forever Fernwood* (syndicated 1977–78; 30 episodes); co-starred as Lt. Vaughn Beuhler in Vietnam War sitcom *Six O'Clock Follies* (NBC 4/24–4/26 and 8/2–9/13/80).

TV guest appearances include:

America, You're On (ABC 11/24/75 special), *Emergency, The FBI, Flo, The Mod Squad, The Rookies, Room 222, The Six Million Dollar Man, Too Close for Comfort, The Waltons, Babes.*

CAROL KANE

FILMS

Is This Trip Really Necessary? a.k.a. *Trip to Terror* (1970)
Carnal Knowledge (1971)
Desperate Characters (1971)
Wedding in White (Canada 1972)
The Last Detail (1973)
Hester Street (1975)
Dog Day Afternoon (1975)
Harry and Walter Go to New York (1976)
Annie Hall (1977)
The World's Greatest Lover (1977; with Danny DeVito)
Valentino (UK 1977)
The Mafu Cage a.k.a. *My Sister, My Love* (1978; working title *Clouds*)
When a Stranger Calls (1979)
The Muppet Movie (UK 1979)
La Sabina a.k.a. *The Sabina* (Spain–Sweden 1979)
Keeping On (1981)
Les Jeux de la Comtesse Dolingen de Gratz (France 1981; unreleased in US)
Norman Loves Rose (Australia 1982)
Pandemonium a.k.a. *Thursday the 12th* (produced 1981; test-screened 1982; released to video 1987)
Can She Bake a Cherry Pie? (1983; very brief cameo)
Over the Brooklyn Bridge (1984)
The Secret Diary of Sigmund Freud (1984)
Racing With the Moon (1984)
Transylvania 6-5000 (1985)
Jumpin' Jack Flash (1986)
Heaven (1987 documentary; credited for "assistance" only)
Ishtar (1987)
The Princess Bride (1987)
Sticky Fingers (1988)
License to Drive (1988)
Scrooged (1988)

The Lemon Sisters (1989)
Flashback (1990)
My Blue Heaven (1990)
Joe Versus the Volcano (1990; uncredited role as Hairdresser)
Ted & Venus (1991)
In the Soup (1992)
Baby on Board (Canada 1993)
Addams Family Values (1993; with Christopher Lloyd)
Even Cowgirls Get the Blues (1994)
The Crazysitter (1995)

Announced upcoming films include: *Edie & Pen; The Pallbearer, If Lucy Fell, Sunset Park* (produced by Danny DeVito); *Trees Lounge*

TV-MOVIES AND MINISERIES

American Playhouse: Keeping On (PBS 2/8/83; released theatrically 1981)
An Invasion of Privacy (CBS 1/12/83)
Burning Rage (CBS 1984)
Drop-Out Mother (CBS 1988)
When a Stranger Calls Back (Showtime 1993)
Dad, the Angel & Me (Family Channel 1995)
Freaky Friday (ABC 1995)

TV SERIES AND PILOTS

Co-starred as Nicolette Bingham in sitcom *All Is Forgiven* (NBC 3/20–6/12/86); co-starred as Lillian Abernathy in sitcom *American Dreamer* (NBC 9/13/90–6/22/91). Starred in unaired sitcom pilot *Let's Get Mom* (Fox, produced 1989).

TV guest appearances include:

The Felony Squad ("Epitaph for a Cop"; ABC 2/26/68)
American Parade: We the Women (CBS 3/17/74 special)
Great Performances: Out of Our Father's House (PBS 8/7/78)
Visions ("Fans of the Kosko Show"; PBS 10/23/78)
The American Short Story ("The Greatest Man in the World"; PBS 2/18/80)
Laverne and Shirley ("Jinxed"; ABC 11/30/82)

Shelley Duvall's Faerie Tale Theatre ("Sleeping Beauty"; Show-time 7/7/83)

Cheers ("A Ditch in Time"; NBC 12/20/84)

Tales from the Darkside ("Snip, Snip"; syndicated 2/9/85)

Crazy Like a Fox ("Bum Tip"; CBS 2/24/85)

Shelley Duvall's Tall Tales and Legends ("Casey at the Bat"; Showtime 3/21/86)

Cinemax Comedy Experiment ("Bob Goldthwait—Don't Watch This Show"; Cinemax 5/24/86)

On Location: Paul Reiser: Out On a Whim (HBO special 12/5/87)

Tales From the Crypt ("Judy, You're Not Yourself Today"; HBO 06/12/90)

Why Bother Voting? (PBS special 9/9/92)

Rap Master Ronnie—A Report Card (Cinemax special 2/14/88)

The Ray Bradbury Theater ("Tomorrow's Child"; HBO/USA; date n.a.)

Brooklyn Bridge ("Sylvia's Condition"; CBS 10/18/91)

Brooklyn Bridge ("Boys and Girls Apart"; CBS 1/22/92)

Brooklyn Bridge ("Boys and Girls Together Again"; CBS 1/29/92)

Brooklyn Bridge ("On the Road"; 2/5/92)

Brooklyn Bridge ("Great Expectations"; CBS 3/4/92)

Seinfeld ("The Marine Biologist"; NBC 2/10/94)

Empty Nest ("The Courtship of Carol's Father"; NBC 12/3/94)

Aladdin a.k.a. *Disney's Aladdin* (CBS/syndicated 9/5/94–present; at least one episode voiceover as Brawnhilda)

A.J.'s Time Travelers (Fox/syndicated children's show 12/3/94 present; at least one appearance as Emily Roebling)

ANDY KAUFMAN

FILMS

God Told Me To a.k.a. *Demon* (1976)

In God We Tru$t (1980)

Heartbeeps (1981)

My Breakfast with Blassie (1983; also director, editor, co-producer, under psuedonym "Johnny Legend")

TV SERIES AND PILOTS

Ensemble member of variety show *Van Dyke and Company* (NBC 9/20–12/30/76). Guested on variety-show pilot *The Lisa Hartman Show: Hot Stuff* (ABC 6/30/76). Starred as robot Andy on science-fiction sitcom pilot *Stick Around* (ABC 5/30/77).

TV guest appearances include:

Performances on *The Tonight Show Starring Johnny Carson, The Mike Douglas Show, Dinah!, The Midnight Special, Saturday Night Live* (19 appearances), *Fridays,* and *The Redd Foxx Show.* Also:

Cher and Other Fantasies (NBC 4/3/79 special)

A Johnny Cash Christmas (CBS 12/6/79 special)

The Fantastic Miss Piggy Show (ABC 9/17/82 special)

The Rodney Dangerfield Show: I Can't Take It No More (ABC 11/29/83 special)

Also on video:

Saturday Night Live: George Carlin (1975)

Comedy Tonight (1977)

Andy's Fun House (ABC; scheduled to air 8/28/79; released on video as *The Andy Kaufman Show*)

Catch a Rising Star's 10th Anniversary (1983)

Soundstage: Andy Kaufman (1985)

I'm From Hollywood (1992 documentary; with Tony Danza and Marilu Henner)

A 1982 NBC *Taxi* press release notes that Kaufman's next movie project at the time was *The Tony Clifton Story,* "based on the life of the fictional Las Vegas singer Kaufman has created in his night club routine."

TAXI-RELATED TV SPECIALS

Best of Taxi
CBS 12/19/94; 90 minutes; working title: *Hey Taxi*

Episode highlights and clips, plus reminiscences by Marilu Henner (host), Jeff Conaway, Tony Danza, Danny DeVito, Judd Hirsh, Carol Kane, Christopher Lloyd, Rhea Perlman, and Bill Zehme (the late Andy Kaufman's manager).

Writer-Director: David Jackson
ZM (Zaloom-Mayfield) Productions; Gracie
Films; Paramount Network Television; John
Charles Walters Productions

A Comedy Salute to Andy Kaufman
NBC 3/29/95; 60 minutes

Reminiscences by friends and colleagues, who
introduce Kaufman performance clips. With:
Marilu Henner and Bob Saget (co-hosts), Richard
Belzer, Jim Carrey, Rodney Dangerfield, Bobcat
Goldthwait, "Super Dave Osborne" (Bob Ein-
stein), Judd Hirsch, Carol Kane, Alan King,
Robert Klein, Jay Leno, David Letterman,
Richard Lewis, Lorne Michaels, Mary Tyler
Moore, Carl Reiner, Michael Richards, Rita
Rudner, Garry Shandling, Sinbad, Lily Tomlin,
Dick Van Dyke, Robin Williams.

Writers: John Davies, Bob Zmuda
Director: Ellen Brown
Comic Relief: Shapiro/West Productions

SELECTED THEATER CREDITS
AND AWARDS

Note: Dates given are those of a play's **entire** run, not of the performer's association with it. The same is true of the number of performances; the number of unofficial "preview" performances is given separately.

JUDD HIRSCH

REGIONAL THEATER

The Line of Least Existence
1969–70 season; Theatre of the Living Arts, Philadelphia; with Danny DeVito

NATIONAL TOURING COMPANIES

Harvey (revival)
July 31 to November 20, 1971; Hirsch succeeded original actor in role of Duane Wilson
I'm Not Rappaport
Autumn, 1986 to Summer, 1987

OFF-BROADWAY

On the Necessity of Being Polygamous
December 8, 1964 to January 3, 1965; 32 performances
Scuba Duba
October 10, 1967 to June 8, 1969; 704 performances; succeeded by Jim Friedlander as The Thief when Hirsch replaced Jerry Orbach as Harold Wonder
Mystery Play
January 3–7, 1973; 7 performances
The Hot l Baltimore
Opened February 4, 1973, at Circle Theatre Company; moved March 22, 1973, to Circle in the Square; 1,166 performances; succeeded by David Groh
Prodigal
December 16, 1973 to January 6, 1974; 19 performances
Knock Knock
January 18 to February 22, 1976; moved to Broadway
Talley's Folly
April 18 to June 3, 1979; 50 performances; moved to Broadway
Life and/or Death
May 15 to June 1, 1979; 11 performances; three one-acts; appeared in "How I Crossed the Street for the First Time All By Myself" and "I'm With Ya, Duke."
The Seagull
November 17 to December 17, 1983; 21 performances, 26 previews

BROADWAY

Barefoot in the Park
October 23, 1963 to June 25, 1967; 1,532 performances; Hirsch entered role of Telephone Man in 1966–67 season
Knock Knock
February 24 to May 23, 1976; 104 performances
Chapter Two
December 4, 1977 to December 8, 1979; 857 performances; as George Schneider; succeeded by David Groh
Talley's Folly
February 20, 1980 to October 19, 1980; 279 performances; succeeded by Jordan Charney
I'm Not Rappaport
June 6, 1985 to January 17, 1988; as Nat; succeeded by Hal Linden and Jack Klugman before returning to role in October 1987.
Conversations With My Father

DANNY DEVITO

REGIONAL THEATER

The Line of Least Existence
1969–70 season; Theatre of the Living Arts, Philadelphia; with Judd Hirsch

OFF-BROADWAY

Shoot Anything with Hair That Moves
February 2–16, 1969; 17 performances

The Man with the Flower in His Mouth
April 22 to June 29, 1969; 80 performances; three one-acts; appeared in ''The License'' and ''The Jar''

The Shrinking Bride
January 17, 1971; 1 performance

One Flew Over the Cuckoo's Nest
March 23, 1971 to September 16, 1973; 1,025 performances; DeVito, as Anthony Martini, left before the end of the 1971–72 season

Du Barry Was a Lady
Limited run: May 4–21, 1972

A Phantasmagoria Historia of D. Johann Fausten Magister, Ph.D., MD, DD, DL, Etc.
April 24, 1973; 1 performance

Where Do We Go From Here?
October 27 to November 3, 1974; 8 performances, 27 previews

The Merry Wives of Windsor
Limited Central Park run: July 25 to August 24, 1974; New York Shakespeare Festival; as Rugby

The Comedy of Errors
Limited Central Park run: August 6–24, 1975; New York Shakespeare Festival; as Balthazar; modern-dress version

Three by Pirandello
Three one-act plays; August 27 to September 12, 1981

CHRISTOPHER LLOYD

REGIONAL THEATER

What Every Woman Knows
Production of October 1975 to June 1976 season; The Long Wharf, New Haven, Connecticut

PROFESSIONAL RESIDENT COMPANY

The Hot l Baltimore
First production of the June 1973 to May 1974 season; The Center Theatre Group, Los Angeles, California

Happy End [and] *A Midsummer Night's Dream*
Two productions of the October 1974 to May 1975 season; The Yale Repertory Theatre; New Haven, Connecticut

OFF-BROADWAY

Kaspar
February 26 to March 18, 1973; 48 performances; as Kaspar

The Harlot and the Hunted
Playwrights Horizon showcase; limited run: November 6–11, 1973

The Seagull
December 18, 1973 to March 17, 1974; 105 performances

Total Eclipse
February 20 to March 10, 1974; 31 performances

Macbeth
April 13 to June 23, 1974; 82 previews; New York Shakespeare Festival; as Banquo in production also starring Carol Kane, Christopher Walken, Stephen Collins, John Heard, and Peter Weller

In the Boom Boom Room
December 4–15, 1974; 32 performances

Cracks
February 10, 1976; 1 performance

Happy End
March 3 to April 3, April 12 to April 30, 1977; 56 performances; moved to Broadway

BROADWAY

Red, White and Maddox
January 26 to May 1, 1969; 41 performances, 15 previews; original cast album on MGM Records

Happy End
May 7 to July 10, 1977; 75 performances; Lloyd as Bill Cracker in production that also starred Meryl Streep

TAXI

MARILU HENNER

REGIONAL THEATER

They're Playing Our Song
    March 24 to July 2, 1983; Burt Reynolds Dinner Theatre, Jupiter, Florida; first four weeks of the show's run.
Super Sunday
    Limited run: July 21–23, 1988; Williamstown Theater, Williamstown, Massachusetts
Carnal Knowledge

NATIONAL TOURING COMPANIES

Grease
    Tour began December 20, 1972; Henner with tour through December 16, 1973

BROADWAY

Over Here!
    March 6, 1974 to January 4, 1975; 341 performances
Grease
    June 7, 1972 to April 16, 1980; 3,388 performances; as Marty; succeeded original actress and left and returned to role several times; original cast album on MGM Records
Pal Joey (revival)
    June 27 to August 29, 1976; 73 performances, 33 previews
Social Security
    April 17, 1986 to March 22, 1987; 385 performances, 26 previews; succeeded Marlo Thomas

JEFF CONAWAY

REGIONAL THEATER

The News
    1985; Burt Reynolds Dinner Theatre, Jupiter, Florida

NATIONAL TOURING COMPANIES

Grease
    Tour began December 20, 1972

BROADWAY

All the Way Home
    November 30, 1960 to September 16, 1961; 334 performances
Grease
    June 7, 1972 to April 16, 1980; 3,388 performances; as Danny Zuko; succeeded Barry Bostwick and left and returned to role several times; original cast album on MGM Records
The News
    November 7–9, 1985; 4 performances, 20 previews

CAROL KANE

REGIONAL THEATER

The Resistible Rise of Arturo Ui
    Charles Street Playhouse, Boston; with Al Pacino
Miss Lulu Bell
    1985
The Lucky Spot
    1986
A Woman of Mystery
    1987; Los Angeles

PROFESSIONAL RESIDENT COMPANIES

Benefit of a Doubt
    Third production of the October 11, 1978 to July 15, 1979 season of The Folger Theatre Group, Washington, D.C.
Tales from the Vienna Woods
    First production of the September 29, 1978 to May 21, 1979 season of the Yale Repertory Company, New Haven, Connecticut

NATIONAL TOURING COMPANIES

The Prime of Miss Jean Brodie
    1966; with Tammy Grimes

OFF-BROADWAY

The Tempest
    February 10 to April 7, 1974; 81 performances;

New York Shakespeare Festival; as Miranda, daughter of Prospero

Macbeth
April 13 to June 23, 1974; 82 previews; New York Shakespeare Festival; as one of the three witches in production also starring Christopher Lloyd, Christopher Walken, Stephen Collins, John Heard, and Peter Weller

Sunday Runners in the Rain
May 3–4, 1980; 4 performances, 17 previews

Linda Her [and] The Fairy Garden
June 19 to July 1, 1984; 30 performances; two one-acts; appeared in ''The Fairy Garden''

Frankie and Johnny in the Claire de Lune
October 27, 1987– ; Kane succeeded Kathy Bates in the role of Frankie

BROADWAY

Ring Around the Bathtub
April 29, 1972; 1 performance, 3 previews

The Effect of Gamma Rays on Man-in-the-Moon Marigolds
Broadway revival of off-Broadway show from a previous season; March 14–26, 1978; 16 performances, 5 previews

ANDY KAUFMAN

BROADWAY

Teaneck Tanzi: The Venus Flytrap
April 20, 1983; 2 performances, 13 previews; with Deborah Harry

SPECIAL EVENTS

V.I.P. Night on Broadway
Sunday, April 22, 1979; multistar production to benefit the New York City Police Department; Andy Kaufman, Sarah Jessica Parker, and Alfred Toigo performed ''Tomorrow'' from *Annie*

Night of 100 Stars
Sunday, February 14, 1982; multistar centennial celebration to benefit the Actors' Fund of America; Danny DeVito and Judd Hirsch also participated

TONY AWARDS

The American Theatre Wing's Antoinette Perry (Tony) Award is presented by the League of American Theaters and Producers

JUDD HIRSCH

Best Actor in a Dramatic Play
Nomination: 1980 (*Talley's Folly*)
Award: 1985 (*I'm Not Rappaport*)

OBIE AWARDS

Awarded by *The Village Voice* for Off and Off-Off-Broadway Distinguished Performer (awarded to several actors and actresses each year, either for specific works or for general excellence)

JUDD HIRSCH

Award: 1979 (*Talley's Folly*)

CHRISTOPHER LLOYD

Award: 1973

DRAMA DESK AWARDS

Awarded by The Drama Desk, an organization of New York theater journalists, editors, and critics

JUDD HIRSCH

Supporting Actor in a Play
Award: 1976 (Broadway's *Knock Knock*)

CHRISTOPHER LLOYD

Outstanding Performance
Award: 1973 (off-Broadway's *Kaspar*)

CODA

Ken Estin drove onto the Paramount lot, excited. Today they would shoot a new framing sequence that would introduce the *Taxi* best-of retrospective and connect all the various clips. He and his writing partner, Sam Simon, had come up with a great idea, and Brooks and Weinberger both liked it and were ready to go with it. It appealed to their love of the absurd.

The idea was to open with the ending; that is, the "signature tag" at the end of each show, where a harried producer (played by Weinberger himself) leaves the office, his back to the camera, and a female voice (supplied by real-life secretary Ellen Halprin) chirps, "Goodnight, Mr. Walters!" The imaginary Mr. Walters grunts tiredly and then the Paramount logo comes on with a boom.

The retrospective episode was to *start* with the tag. Mr. Walters would leave the office, the secretary would wish him goodnight, and then, all of a sudden—Pirandello!

From out of nowhere, we hear the secretary calling out "Oh no! Wait, Mr. Walters! You're supposed to look at a screening!" Mr. Walters never bothers to turn around, and so for the first time we see the secretary (played by Molly Cheek, now of Showtime's *It's Garry Shandling's Show*) as she rushes up to him. With both their backs to us now, we hear Mr. Walters say he doesn't want to, and the secretary gently insists he has to. "If you don't do it, who's going to look at the footage?"

We cut to a viewing room where we see the two of them from behind, watching clips to put together the retrospective. All through it, the secretary is in awe of her highly creative boss, asking him how he comes up with these things, telling him what a great writer he is. The grumpy Mr. Walters doesn't pay her much mind. Finally, at the end of the show, the credits run as usual. We see Mr. Walters leaving and hear the secretary saying goodnight, as usual. And then Mr. Walters stops at the end of the hall. He says to the secretary, "You wanna go out for a drink?" The flattered secretary gushes, "Oh, Mr. Walters!" and hand in hand, they leave together.

That sequence was scripted, cast, and even rehearsed, but except for a test shooting, was never filmed. "It was a matter of economics, primarily," Estin sighs. He was as disappointed as anybody not to see it done. "I thought that when fans of *Taxi* were watching that final logo and feeling sad because *Taxi* didn't exist anymore, and then Mr. Walters turns around and asks her out for a drink, it was a way of saying, everything's going to be OK. Like we're kind of going out for a drink with him." Perhaps, even, to Mario's.

Goodnight, Mr. Walters, wherever you are.

The last-season cast of *Taxi*, signing off.

AUTHORS' BIOGRAPHIES

Frank Lovece has written four other books about television: *The X-Files Encyclopedia* (upcoming from Citadel); *The Brady Bunch Book* (with Andrew J. Edelstein); *The Television Yearbook 1990–91*; and *Thirty Years of Television*. A contributing editor of *Entertainment Weekly*, and a former nationally syndicated columnist for United Feature/NEA, he writes for *Newsday, Parenting, Audio/Video Interiors*, the online service *Baseline*, and others. He's also scripted the Marvel Comics series *Atomic Age, Hokum & Hex, Nightstalkers*, and more. He is the father of two sons, Vincent Thomas Lovece (to whom *The Brady Bunch Book* was dedicated) and Erik Morgan Lovece.

Jules Franco is a screenwriter, journalist and film/TV extra who's appeared in *Miami Rhapsody, Fair Game, Bad Boys*, and the TV series *Grapevine* and *South Beach*. A former DJ and record-industry publicist, he's written for the *New York Daily News, New York Nightlife, Video Review* and other periodicals.

INDEX